ALL THINGS CLEAR

By Linda L. Allison

All Things Clear

ISBN-10: 0615584780
EAN-13: 9780615584782

ALL THINGS CLEAR

By Linda L. Allison

"TIME MAKE ALL THINGS CLEAR"

Steve's journal, 1950

DEDICATION

This book is dedicated to my husband,
whose love changed my life and made it complete,
and to my sons who've given me joy and
happiness beyond measure. Without them
I couldn't have told this story.

It's also dedicated to the memory
of my great-grandmother, Georgoula Krouskos.
Without her, there would be no story to tell.

ACKNOWLEDGEMENTS

For the soul of this book, I sincerely thank:

Shirley – for writing things
John – for saving things
Steve – for writing and saving things

*For the body (the printed page, via computer)
of this book, I sincerely thank:*

My husband Ken
My sons Christopher and Jay and daughter-in-law Melissa.

CONTENTS

SECTION

- I -

LEAVING THE FARM

CHAPTER 1

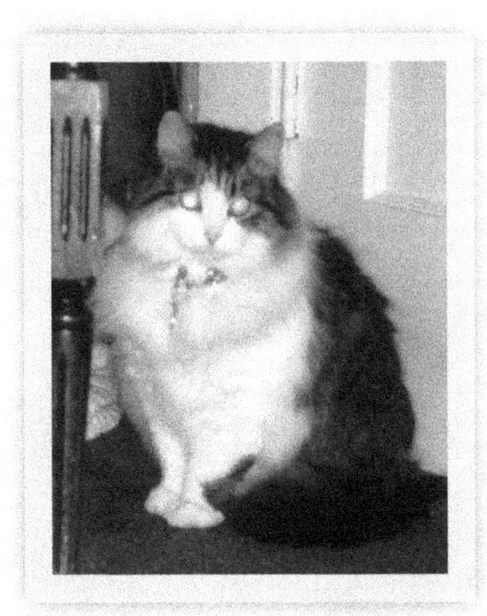

"Molly died a week ago."

Molly was only six years old, and completely healthy - we thought. We loved her very much and her death last week came as a shock! But this book is her legacy. The sad and unforeseen ending of her life has prompted me to begin this story.

She was a farm cat, a young farm kitten really, when I first met her. She and her extended family were living at my dad's farm when he died in 1988. He died on the summer solstice of his seventy-seventh year. By the time the property was sold a year and a half later, of the cats, only Molly remained. The others had either been killed (raccoons and foxes lived in the neighborhood also), or moved on. Because of her survival skills, we named her The Unsinkable Molly Brown.

Figure 1.1 Ken at the Farm (1988).

Molly watched from the periphery as my husband Ken and I sorted through, and made decisions about, the thousands and thousands of items we found at the farm. She sat silently in the background as we discussed final destinations for possessions accumulated by my father, and his father, over the past hundred years. She followed us through the house, barn, garages, chicken coops and numerous other outbuildings that were filled with things they had saved.

The stuff in the main part of the house was mostly my father's; and was pretty neatly organized and clean. The conditions we encountered in the attic and outbuildings were another story. Some of these structures were filled to the ceiling! They were also filled with over one hundred years of dust and dirt! It was very much like an archeological dig. The personal and cultural history to be gleaned was comparable to a "dig", as was the amount of dust and dirt. We wore some very large coveralls of my father's that we'd found, covered our hair with hats and bandannas and wore surgical masks during our digs. (And *still* we coughed up dust for months afterwards.)

Figure 1.2 Linda at the Farm (1988).

And Molly watched us as we readied the farm for sale.

Of course "the farm", was no longer exactly a farm in 1988. When my relatives purchased it in 1916, it *had* been - a good-sized farm. But over the years my father had sold off all but five acres. Now town houses and tract homes surrounded all that was left - the farmhouse and outbuildings. I could never stop referring to it as the farm though. It had been called that (or "the ranch") for way too long.

At the time of his death, I knew very little about my father or about his father. I knew even less about their hopes and dreams or disappointments and heartaches. As we encountered the things they had used, cared about, and even cherished, we came to know something of their emotional and physical lives. We also glimpsed something of the history of their times. A century of household appliances and furniture were jumbled together with treasured keepsakes. Personal belongings were "stored" with furnishings and implements that had been used in three family businesses - a pool hall, a candy store and, of course, the farm.

Seventy-year-old embroidered baby gowns shared space in a building that also housed two regulation size billiard tables (unassembled). The chicken coop held sea shells and pre-World War I candy tins, as well as "window bills" advertising such coming attractions as a performance by the dancer Isadora Duncan, or a boxing match between Boston's Red Chapman and Denver's Joe "King" Leopold. Straight edge razors, wicker porch furniture, business ledgers, government pamphlets, hundreds of photographs, cigar boxes, keys, books, and tools were found betwixt and between letters, dog racing programs and a century of eating utensils and bedding.

And that wasn't the half of it!

We could have spent at least a year, full time, excavating, cataloging, researching, cross-referencing and documenting everything. Of course, we didn't. We had about four months. Since Ken had a full time job, and I had a full time job for two of the four months, we worked a lot of evenings and weekends.

During the summer, when I wasn't teaching, I'd work all day at the farm. Sometimes our sons, Chris and Jay, college students at the time, would join me. And always, on weekends Ken worked with me, side by side. Day after day, we'd find ourselves in incredibly hot buildings, wearing giant coveralls, our heads covered as best we could, and our teeth blackened from the dust - as we opened yet another box or trunk from another era and time. We overlooked, neglected and trashed many things that we should have saved, I'm certain. But we salvaged what we could afford to store, and did the best we could with the rest. We brought home all the photos, letters, documents, mementos and keepsakes.

And I promised myself that sometime, in the future, I'd organize and study these things and write down what I learned from them.

All this time, we'd been feeding Molly. She wouldn't come to the food till after we'd driven away. We'd watch her through a slit in the wooden fence after we'd closed the gate. About a month before the farm was sold, I asked the vet what he thought I should do about her. I was afraid she'd never make it on her own, even through the buyer, the city of Westminster, was going to leave the property as part of a greenbelt. He told me to leave her there, since she was still completely feral. I didn't follow his advice. Perhaps I should have. In the end, I put her through a lot of physical suffering and emotional trauma.

Figure 1.3 Linda in front of one of the barns at the Farm (1988).

My friend helped me trap her. She cut herself, in many places, while trying to escape from the trap. I took her immediately to the vet's office, so he could check her out before I brought her home to our other two cats and two dogs. This was a mistake. When the vet opened her cage, she ran up the wall and halfway across the ceiling (the truth!) before she fell to the floor and took off. Next she ran along the shelves - sending medicines and supplies flying in all directions. Shattered glass was everywhere. The vet was cursing her *and* me. Finally, I smothered her under a blanket, stuffed her back in the cage, drove home (crying) and locked her in the downstairs bathroom. The next day, Jay, who was visiting from college, unsuspectingly tried to touch her. She scratched him up pretty badly. I felt bad for him - and for her.

Two weeks later, with the help of another vet, we trapped her again. This vet came to the house, tranquilized Molly and then took her to be spayed and immunized. When she returned home, we had to quarantine her in the bathroom again for another two weeks. When she got to come out, everyone - people and animals included - gave her a very wide berth.

Figure 1.4 Backside of the main house at the Farm (1988).

Over the next six months, she slowly came out of hiding. Ken's father made her a window seat that looked out over the garden, and she often sat there. Always looking out at the world from which I'd snatched her. Finally, I began to relax and hope that maybe I'd made the right decision about her.

It was two years later that she first allowed a human to touch her. My life had changed drastically after the disposition of my father's estate. I could actually choose not to work. Which I did! Besides time, there was also money for travel. When Ken and I made our first visit to Africa in 1991, Chris stayed at our house to take care of the animals. While we were gone, *Molly let him pet her!*

After that, she became a fairly contented house cat. She'd crawl up on my lap and let me pet her for as long as I liked. She and Boston, another of our three cats, would actually play together sometimes. Things were good with her for the next two years.

And then she died. Just like that. I wrote in my diary, earlier today:

Friday February 04, 1994

Molly died a week ago.

I found her lying on her side, still warm. I kept thinking that perhaps she was just unconscious. But Ken came and said that she was, indeed, dead. And he gently closed her eyes. I looked and looked to see if I could figure out what had gone wrong. There was no blood. There were no visible injuries. There was nothing in her mouth or throat. There was nothing around her neck. Nothing.

It took a long time to say good-bye to her. I said good-bye to all of her - the soft pads of her feet, the little tufts of fur between her toes and on top of each ear, her nice round belly, her fat, pattable thighs, the beginnings of another spot of matted fur in the usual place on her hip.

Ken wrapped her in a blanket, laid her in a box and put her in the garage. The next day we took her body to the vet for an autopsy. Her heart had hemorrhaged. The vet said that her heart was about one-third normal size. He said that often farm cats have such congenital problems because they are so inbred. He was surprised she had lived for six years with such a deformed heart. She was unsinkable for a long time.

Ken buried her in the garden, just outside the window where she'd always sat looking out at the world. It was very cold, and I thought the ground would be frozen, but it wasn't. Putting her into the ground, she felt about the size of a baby. We buried her just after sundown. It snowed all that night, completely covering her grave.

As I've thought about her these last few days, I've relived those days when she first came into our lives. She was a part of the legacy left by my father and grandfather. She was with us when we closed and walked away from the farm - their home and her home. And her death has reminded me that tomorrow isn't a guarantee. If I'm sincere in wanting to learn more about and then write about, the two men who also called the farm "home" - then now is the time.

And so, as she lays so tenderly and freshly buried under the winter's snow, I'll begin to sort through and organize the many boxes filled with books, personal and business letters, legal documents, diaries, journals and photographs. All the things that we brought home - along with Molly - from the farm.

First I'll separate my dad's stuff from my grandfather's stuff - no easy task. Then I'll organize each set chronologically. And then, I hope, the story will tell itself - as I write about what I find.

We'll see.

"Molly died a week ago."

Linda's diary – February 04, 1994

CHAPTER 2

"Love, Mom"

But...

Before I even begin, I'm realizing that my grandfather's story and especially my father's story can't be told without telling, at least in part, some of my story. Two recent events brought this fact home to me - I had lunch and I had a dream.

First, I had lunch with my mom.

A few weeks ago, in preparation for a visit to my brother Travis, in Texas, I took Shirley to have her hair done. We arranged to have lunch together after the hair appointment.

Let me explain, by way of a little family history, why I was apprehensive about this meeting.

Eighteen year old Shirley had married thirty-one year old Steve in 1942. Two years later, I was born - their first and only child. They separated when I was eight months old and divorced a year later. I stayed with Steve and Shirley moved on.

Although I'd always wondered about the short time we'd spent together *as a family* - because of the delicate nature of our relationship, I'd never asked my father about it.

I'd next "met" my mother when I was twenty-two years old. In the years since that meeting I'd tried a few times to ask her about her marriage to my father, my birth and their divorce. But I'd never learned much.

She'd say something like "He divorced me because I had three jars of mayonnaise, opened, in the refrigerator at one time."

"Meaning?" I'd ask.

"Meaning that I was just a child emotionally, and not capable of being much of a wife." she'd respond - or something along those lines.

She always told me she couldn't remember much from those years. "It's all kind of a blank." she'd say.

I never pushed for more detailed facts - or feelings.

When Ken was cleaning the garage at the farm after my dad's death, he found a metal box labeled "For L L" (hereafter referred to as "The Box"). In it, my father had placed letters, documents and journals that were meant, I think, to tell me about our lives together when I was a very young child. It's a story told from *his* perspective of course, but it gave me, *finally*, some inkling about those years.

And now, if I wanted to write truthfully about my father's life, the time had come to ask my mother for her interpretation of the contents of the box. Lunch, after the hair appointment seemed a quiet, calm place to do so - but my apprehension had been warranted. It ended up being hard for both of us. This is part of the day's entry in my diary:

Monday February 14, 1994

Ran at Sloans. 28 degrees. Almost balmy.

Now this was a really weird day. Picked up my mom to take her to get her hair done and to talk, over lunch, about 'the early years'.

I ask her to please tell me how she and Steve decided to divorce - and why. Like the logistics of it. Was it decided over many months and in serious discussions? Was it after a big fight? Was it because of anything in particular? I get the 'mayonnaise jar' explanation.

Taking a deep breath, I tell her what I've concluded from reading Steve's journals - from his version of the events that lead to their separation and divorce - that she had just kind of walked out. Sincerely trying to be helpful and honest, she says that although she was an immature wife and mother - she was never a bad mother or wife. And that she doesn't remember the circumstances of her leaving.

Later, after we'd returned to her house, she read some pages from Steve's journals. When she read of the family that had briefly cared for her baby after her departure, I asked her, "Who actually took me there? Was it you?

She was genuinely perplexed. She doesn't remember. With some anger, and perhaps to hurt her, I ask if her arms ached for her baby after this parting. She doesn't remember. I ask if she cried or wanted her baby back.

Then, she too, became somewhat irritated. But, in a matter of fact manner, she told me that, no - she couldn't remember missing me, that she had blocked out that whole period of her life. And no, she'd never cried for any of her children. She hadn't cried about me, or about Travis, once she'd made decisions regarding our futures. *She knew at the time that she'd done what was best for us, and if she had allowed herself to feel, she would not have been able to carry on.* She said that later, when our brother Paulie was hospitalized for a year after his birth, she hadn't allowed herself to cry then either. *She'd just had to carry on.*

She said that she had endured a hard childhood herself and that I should, in effect - stop pushing.

Since I'd been far from a perfect mother and wife myself, and wasn't in *any* position to be judgmental, I agreed. Bringing the conversation to an end, I told her I'd wanted only to understand the circumstances and chronology of my early life with her and my father. *But of course I'd wanted more. I'd wanted her to be sorry - sorry for leaving me.*

But she wouldn't talk much after that, so I went home.

A few days later my mom *did* reach out with an apology.

I received a letter in which she not only said she was sorry, but also offered some explanations from her heart. It reads:

Linda:

I have spent many sleepless nights since our conversation and reading of diary.

Do not know what to say that won't sound like I'm being phony, but I do say I am truly sorry, I'm positive now that I shut out all bad memories not because of your Dad's treatment of me, but because of my own treatment of you and him too. It's not too easy to know yourself to be a terrible person, so denying it must have been my criteria (shutting it out of mind). He was a very wise man to leave you the diaries. I am so glad to know he cared for you (I thought he didn't have too much to do with you) and saw you through your bad times, and I suppose he didn't want to have a baby because he knew in his heart I wouldn't be a good mother, and in my warped mind I thought he was being mean: as for loving you I think I did in a crazy kind of way. I know I always included you in my prayers and had my dear practitioner Mr. Jones pray for you and always tried to keep track of your life (what was going on in it) and I think if I hadn't been so sure you would find me, I would have come to you, not when you were little but later like I did Travis. one more thing. I do remember when I went to the hospital to the psychologist and they gave me the truth serum, I was coming out of it I remember hearing myself screaming that I wanted my babies, not one baby but two!

As to the why I was like I was I can't tell you because I do not know. I'm not going to correct spelling etc in this as I'll try to make it sound better etc.

Love,

Mom

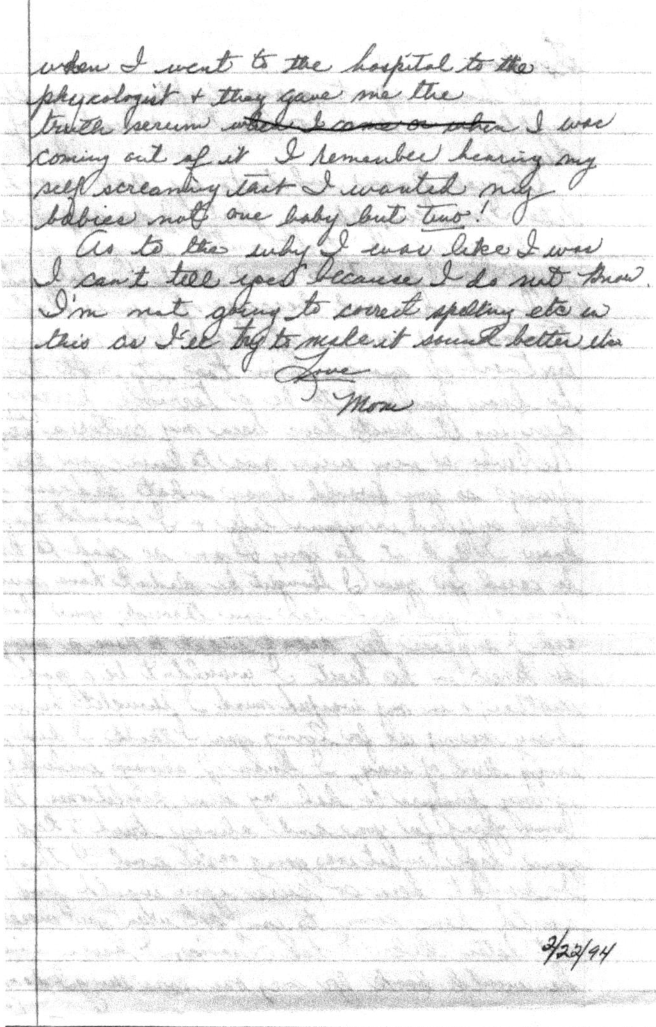

when I went to the hospital to the
phycologist + they gave me the
truth serum ~~when I came or~~ when I was
coming out of it I remember hearing my
self screaming that I wanted my
babies not one baby but two!
As to the why I was like I was
I can't tell you because I do not know.
I'm not going to correct spelling etc in
this as I'll try to make it sound better than

Love
Mom

3/22/94

Figure 2.1 Letter from Shirley to Linda (1994).

There are so many things about my mother that I love and *cherish* - her eternal optimism, her ability to live and enjoy each and every day to the fullest, her generous and giving nature, her intelligence and love of learning and her complete lack of self-pity, jealousy or bitterness. Plus, she has been a good and loving mother to me for all of my adult life. The image at the beginning of this Chapter, taken at her 75th birthday party celebration, is a reminder to me of many of these positive characteristics.

I was grateful that she'd been able to look back honestly at our early times together. And it was easy to accept her apology. I was reminded of a quote I'd come across recently:

We are very much a continuation of our parents and our ancestors.
To be angry at our parents is to be angry at ourselves.
To be reconciled with our parents is to make peace with ourselves.

Thich Nhat Hanh

I've had two *other* mothers in my lifetime. One was a blessing and the other - if not a curse, certainly a hardship to endure. After Shirley, came my foster mother Betty - she who nurtured me, loved me and saved me. And then there was Steppy (what I called my stepmother - behind her back of course).

As I contemplated writing about my father's life, I had a dream about Steppy. I think my subconscious mind must have gone roaming on ahead, in the anticipated chronology, to the time when Steve brought me to live with them. And that's why I think I dreamed this:

> *Chris, my oldest son, is about six years old. For some reason, he has to go to live with STEPPY! True horror fills me! I'm panic-stricken and powerless. He's so sad, it's breaking my heart. I keep hugging and kissing him and telling him not to worry, that I'll figure out some way to get him away.*
>
> *All my desperate plans fail, in typical nightmare fashion. Feelings of pure dread and helplessness overcome me. I come to the conclusion that the only way to get Chris away is to kill Steppy. I must shoot her many times - to make sure she's dead.*

Before I can do this though, I wake up.

I think Chris represented me in this dream - and the two years I lived with my father and stepmother. When I recall this time of my childhood, it's almost like it happened to another person. I feel sorry for the child, but she's not exactly "me". I feel for her a love more like what I would feel for my child - much as I did for Chris in the dream.

After these encounters with two mothers, I'm ready *and looking forward to,* spending some time with my grandfather.

"Love, Mom"

Shirley's letter - February 22, 1994

SECTION
- II -

JOHN STEPHEN ALLISON

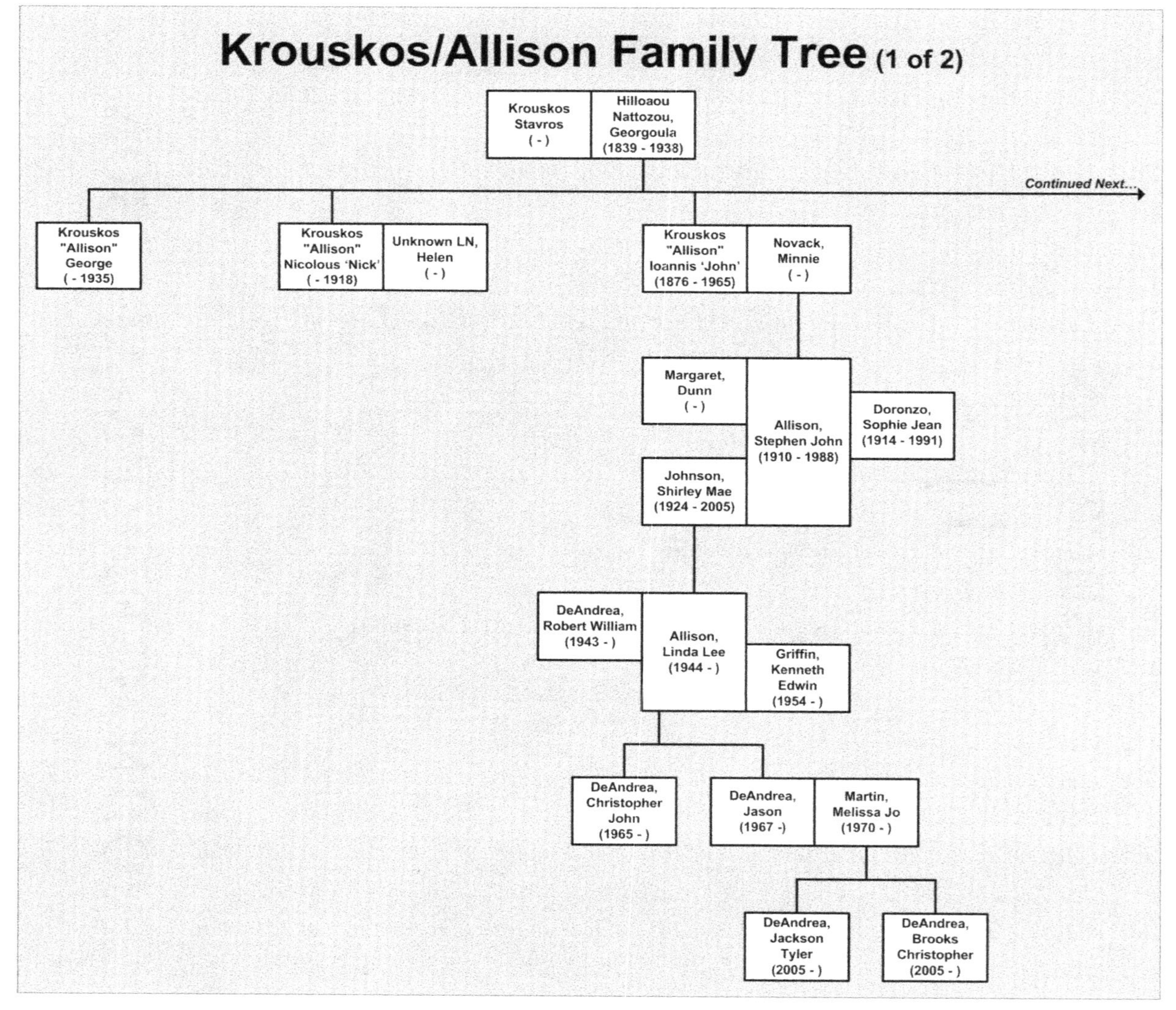
Krouskos/Allison Family Tree (1 of 2)
Krouskos Stavros (-)
Hilloaou Nattozou, Georgoula (1839 - 1938)
Continued Next...
Krouskos "Allison" George (- 1935)
Krouskos "Allison" Nicolous 'Nick' (- 1918)
Unknown LN, Helen (-)
Krouskos "Allison" Ioannis 'John' (1876 - 1965)
Novack, Minnie (-)
Margaret, Dunn (-)
Allison, Stephen John (1910 - 1988)
Doronzo, Sophie Jean (1914 - 1991)
Johnson, Shirley Mae (1924 - 2005)
DeAndrea, Robert William (1943 -)
Allison, Linda Lee (1944 -)
Griffin, Kenneth Edwin (1954 -)
DeAndrea, Christopher John (1965 -)
DeAndrea, Jason (1967 -)
Martin, Melissa Jo (1970 -)
DeAndrea, Jackson Tyler (2005 -)
DeAndrea, Brooks Christopher (2005 -)

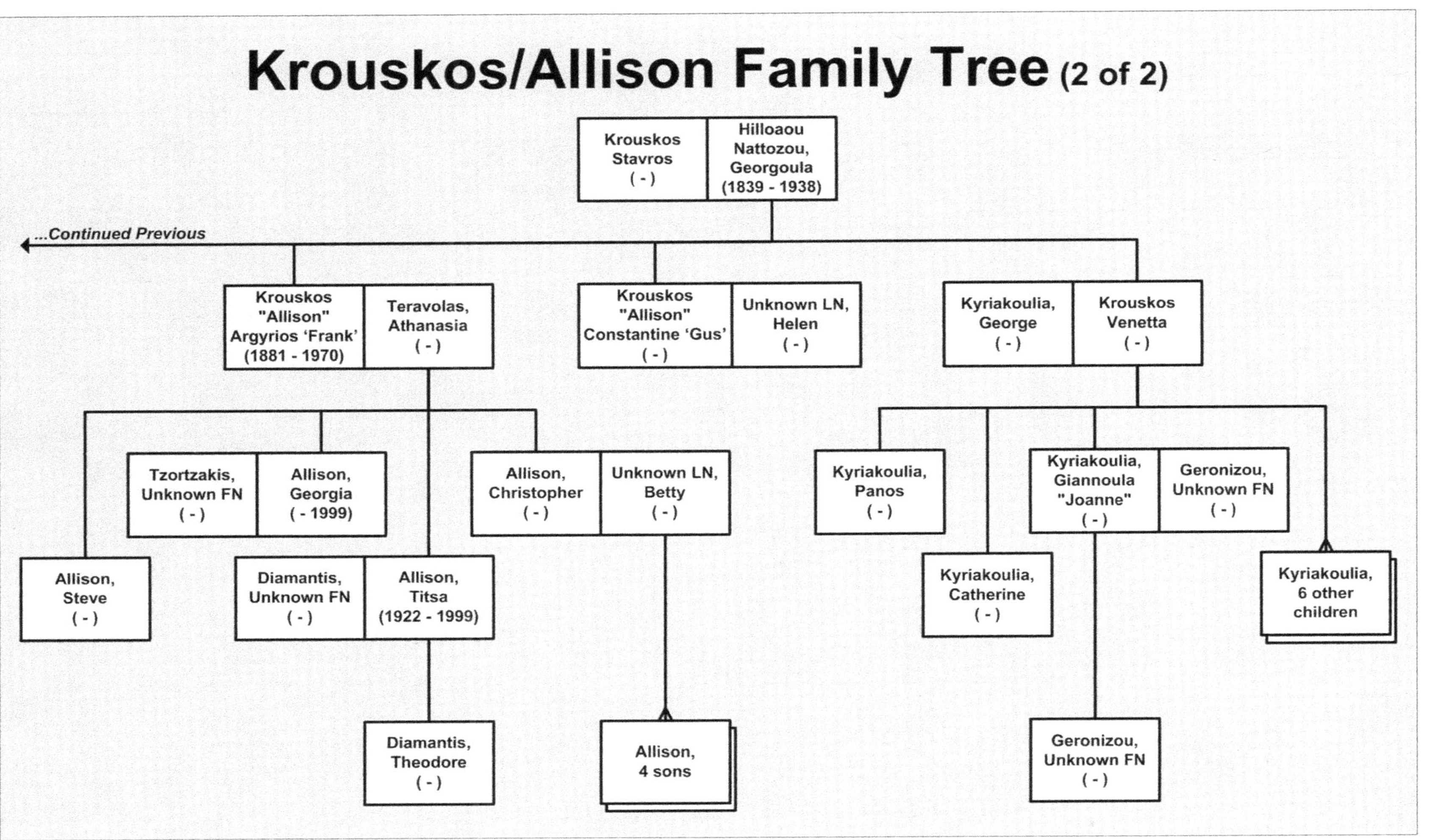
Krouskos/Allison Family Tree (2 of 2)
Krouskos Stavros (-)
Hilloaou Nattozou, Georgoula (1839 - 1938)
...Continued Previous
Krouskos "Allison" Argyrios 'Frank' (1881 - 1970)
Teravolas, Athanasia (-)
Krouskos "Allison" Constantine 'Gus' (-)
Unknown LN, Helen (-)
Kyriakoulia, George (-)
Krouskos Venetta (-)
Tzortzakis, Unknown FN (-)
Allison, Georgia (- 1999)
Allison, Christopher (-)
Unknown LN, Betty (-)
Kyriakoulia, Panos (-)
Kyriakoulia, Giannoula "Joanne" (-)
Geronizou, Unknown FN (-)
Allison, Steve (-)
Diamantis, Unknown FN (-)
Allison, Titsa (1922 - 1999)
Kyriakoulia, Catherine (-)
Kyriakoulia, 6 other children
Diamantis, Theodore (-)
Allison, 4 sons
Geronizou, Unknown FN (-)

CHAPTER 3

"Service honest and Faithful."

This is all I know about my paternal grandfather, John Stephen Allison:

He was born John Krouskos in Greece in the latter part of the nineteenth century. He followed his older brother, George, to the United States before the turn of the century. Thinking his Greek name a handicap in his new country, George had chosen a nice Anglo name, Allison, from the New York City phone book. (Did they have phones then?) Later, in the same city, my grandfather sold chewing gum, as he called it, on the street corner and at night slept under newspapers in the gutters. He saved every penny he made in order to come to Denver, where George had settled. In Denver, after serving in the Spanish American War, he owned and operated a candy store and a pool hall for many years. He married, had a son, my father, and his wife left him shortly thereafter. He purchased the farm and lived there until a few years before his death in his eighties. His younger brothers, Frank and Gus, eventually came to Denver from Greece also.

At my father's funeral, I met his cousins, Georgia and Titsa, whom I had last seen in 1950, when I was the flower girl at Titsa's wedding. They had visited Greece in the 1970's with their father, Frank, the youngest and last surviving Allison brother. They were able to tell me a little about the part of our family that was left behind. They told me that they lived in a small village in the mountains, tended olive trees for a living and were very, very poor (at least by our American standards).

And that's all I know.

Unfortunately, six years ago, when clearing out the farm, I didn't feel I was able to save all the legal and business documents belonging to John. I should have. With them, perhaps I could have figured out how he came to be a millionaire after starting out penniless in the streets of New York. There were many invoices, from several candy stores, for purchases and payments. There were bills of sale for properties (including the farm) and for goods (including produce from the farm). They would have given me an idea of the original size of the land and how it was utilized throughout the years. But I threw much of it away! There was just so much stuff!

But I did save many things that related to his personal life - things that will help me learn more about him.

I've just returned from retrieving those letters and other personal documents belonging to my grandfather, having wiped yet another layer of dirt and dust from the boxes containing them. Besides regular boxes and trunks, there must be at least a hundred cigar boxes and many very large, very heavy, wooden crates. They're reinforced with metal bands and are from "Ghirardelli Chocolates" in San Francisco. He used some high quality ingredients at his candy store, I'd say.

At one point, I found some horsehair in amongst some of the stuff. That makes sense I guess, since we did find many of the boxes in the barn. How strange that a horse who lived sixty or seventy years ago, received my passing attention today. And speaking of hair, I also came across an envelope containing a large lock of beautiful, chestnut colored human hair. It's long and wavy. The envelope is marked "Millie". Who was Millie? Maybe she was John's wife?

It'll probably take days to sort through this stuff. I've put it off for many years. But now it's time to try and understand more about my grandfather's life, and hopefully in so doing, also pay him my respects…

Well, it took more than days - it's now months later (Monday, April 25, 1994). Let me tell you about some of the things I found, and found out, about my grandfather. Since the very first "artifact" (other than hair) that I encountered was a description of John as a young soldier, I've decided to join him first, at that time of his life.

In the pages that follow I've listed some of the items I found, followed by a description of and/or a discussion of the facts gleaned from that item.

➢ **PLAIN ENVELOPE**

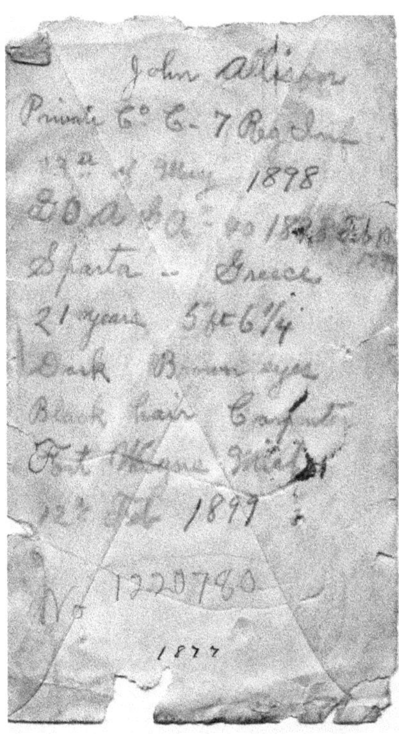

Figure 3.1 Plain envelope.

Handwritten on the back, it reads:

> *John Allison, 1877, Private C, C - 7 Reg Inf., 13th of May 1898, Feb 10, 1891, Sparta Greece, 21 years, 5 ft 6 1/4, Dark Brown eyes, Black hair, Carpenter, Fort Wayne Mich., 12th Feb 1899.*

So, he was born in 1877, and it looks like he emigrated to the U.S. from Sparta Greece in 1891 - he was only fourteen years old when he was living such a hard life on the streets of New York City! People grew up a lot quicker in those days I guess. This is the first I've heard of him being a carpenter or, for that matter, living in Fort Wayne Michigan before settling in Denver.

He was twenty-one years old when he joined the army. He was always very proud of his days as a soldier. He had several framed photos of himself, in uniform, hanging in his kitchen - the room where he kept all the things he treasured most.

- **WALLET**

In a very dilapidated wallet I found a Certificate of Recognition as a Veteran of the War with Spain. It says that John Allison was born on March 22.

- **DISCHARGE PAPERS**

My grandfather's (framed) discharge papers had also always hung in his kitchen. After several applications of Windex, I learned that this young private with the "dark complexion" was 5 foot 6 inches tall, single and of good health and character. And he was, indeed, a carpenter by trade. His Seventh Regiment, Infantry, saw action against General Santiago in the summer of 1898 and he was discharged on February 12, 1899, less than a year after he enlisted.

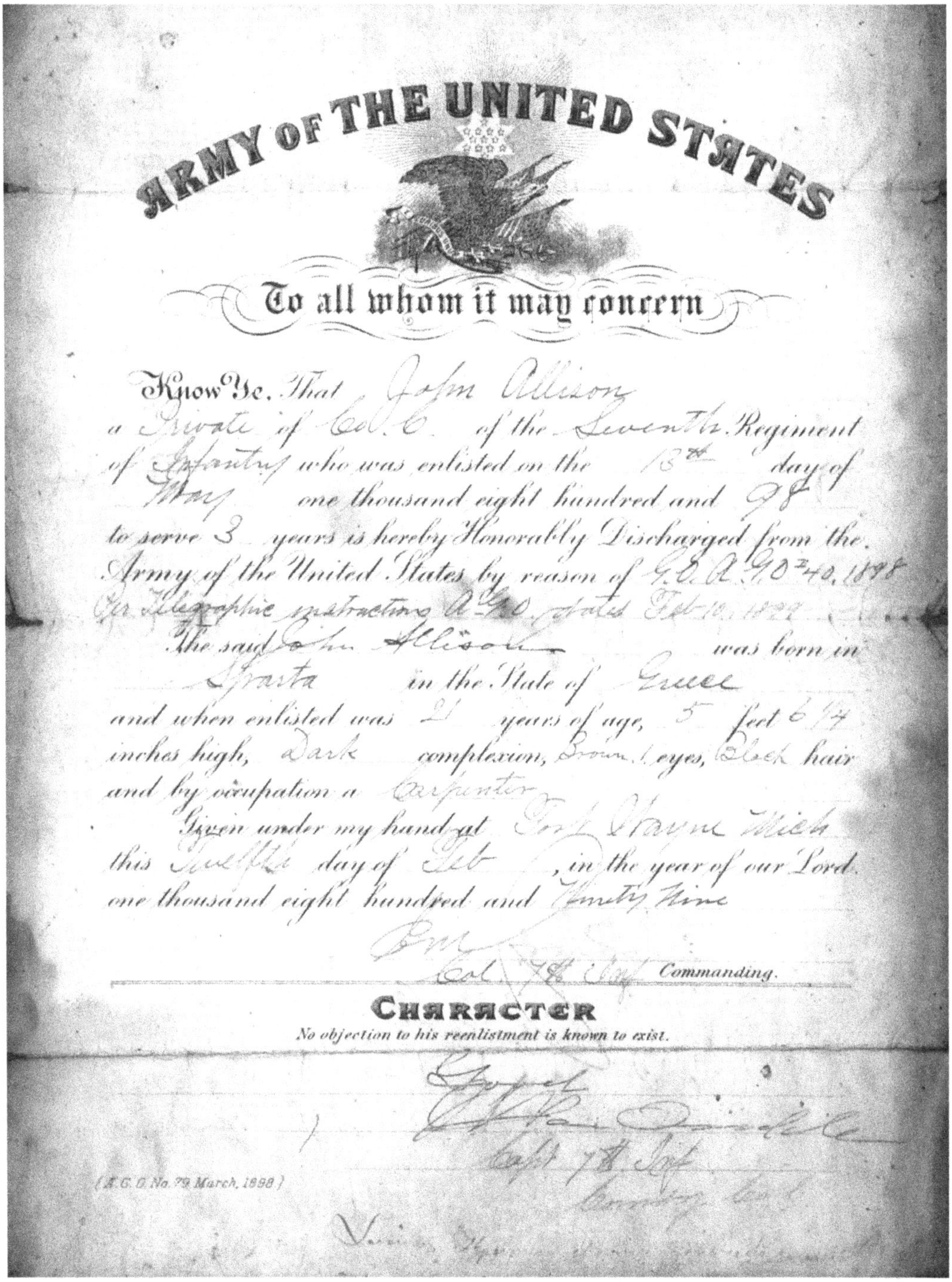

ARMY OF THE UNITED STATES

To all whom it may concern

Know Ye, That John Allison a Private of Co. C of the Seventh Regiment of Infantry who was enlisted on the 13th day of May one thousand eight hundred and 98 to serve 3 years is hereby Honorably Discharged from the Army of the United States by reason of G.O.A.G.O. 40, 1898 Per Telegraphic instructions A.G.O. dated Feb 10, 1899.

The said John Allison was born in Sparta in the State of Greece and when enlisted was 21 years of age, 5 feet 6 1/4 inches high, Dark complexion, Brown eyes, Black hair and by occupation a Carpenter.

Given under my hand at Fort Wayne Mich this Twelfth day of Feb, in the year of our Lord one thousand eight hundred and Ninety Nine

Col 7th Inf Commanding.

CHARACTER

No objection to his reenlistment is known to exist.

Capt 7th Inf
Comdg Co.

(A.G.O. No. 79 March, 1898.)

Figure 3.2 John's discharge papers.

This document reads, in part:

ARMY OF THE UNITED STATES

To all whom it may concern;

Know Ye, that John Allison a Private of Co. C. of the Seventh Regiment of Infantry who was enlisted on the 13th day of May one thousand eight hundred and 98 to serve 3 years is hereby Honorably Discharged from the Army of the United States.

The said John Allison was born in Sparta in the State of Greece and when enlisted was 21 years of age, 5 feet 6 1/4 inches high, Dark complexion, Brown eyes, Black hair and by occupation a Carpenter.

CHARACTER

No objection to his reenlistment is known to exist.

MILITARY RECORD

Previous Service: None

Battles, engagements, skirmishes, expeditions: War with Spain Battle of El Caney, July 1st 1898 and all subsequent operations against Santiago until formal surrender July 17, 1898.

Wounds received in service: None
Physical condition when discharged: Good
Married or single: Single
Remarks: Service honest and Faithful

- **PHOTO**

Figure 3.3 Photo of John and the Seventh Regiment.

Next to the discharge papers in the kitchen had always hung a framed photograph of John (second from left) and three soldiers from his Seventh Regiment. All are in uniform and hold rifles equipped with bayonets. John looks very thin and very young. The photo tugs at my heart because of the man who lies on a bed behind the four serious soldiers. He is obviously very sick and/or wounded. He holds a photo in his hand of a large group of uniformed men.

➢ REGIMENT LIST

Buried in a dusty box, I found a complete list of the members of the seventh regiment - Company Officers, Sergeants, Corporals, Musicians, an Artificer, a Wagoneer and Privates. It makes special note of those that died (or were wounded) in battle. I won't reproduce the list here, but I did read each and every name. For them, and for the parents and spouses who lost them, I wanted to at least acknowledge their sacrifice. So many years ago they gave their young lives, to a cause I hope they believed in sincerely.

➢ MEDAL

John was presented a medal at his discharge. It's pretty elaborate, with a ribbon that looks like a U.S. flag. There's a large eagle and a cross with the words PHILLIPPINE ISLANDS, CUBA, PORTORICO AND U.S.A. It also says Spanish War Veteran 1898-99 (see image at the beginning of this chapter).

➢ PHOTO

In his kitchen gallery was a framed, but blurry and faded photo, of John and many fellow soldiers standing at attention. They look to be about ten years older than in the previous photo. They wear heavy winter overcoats, hats, and fur mittens and still carry the rifles with the bayonets. I think they'll be marching in a Veteran's Day parade, or perhaps are at a reunion of their regiment.

➢ PHOTO

Figure 3.4 Photo of John and the members of General Henry Lawton Camp in Denver (1925).

Beside the photo of John and the veterans hung one showing <u>many</u> middle aged men standing on, or beside, a <u>very large</u> gun. I'm almost sure that the rather rotund man near the top of the photo is John. He sure was proud of being a veteran. At the bottom of the picture someone has written:

Members of Gen Henry W. Lawton Camp #1 of U.S. W. V. of Denver Colo. on largest of W.S. Ry guns at Denver, Armistice day Nov. 11, 1925.

➢ LETTER

A few years later John sent a letter to his congressman, requesting his help in getting an increase in his military pension. Evidently he hadn't been as healthy as they'd thought at his discharge, because he mentions his "disabilities". He kept a copy:

April 27, 1929

Hon. William R. Eaton,
Congressman,
Washington, D.C.

Dear Sir:

I am a veteran of the Spanish American War. Have lived in Denver for thirty years. I always voted the Republican ticket, including yourself last election. You perhaps do not remember me, but I have known you a long time, and am now asking you to assist me in trying to get a raise in pension.

Am drawing $20.00 pension now. Was examined for increase on the 18th. Am now 53 years of age. On account of my age and disabilities I think that I am entitled to some raise.

I hope that you will give me whatever assistance that lies in your power. My pension claim No. is 1,220,780, and I served in C. Company 7th U. S. Infantry during the war period.

Thank you in advance for what you may do for me, I am

Most sincerely yours,

John S. Allison
1011 15th Street
Denver, Colorado

He tells the congressman that he's lived in Denver for thirty years, which means that he must have lived for several years in New York City and/or Fort Wayne before coming to Denver when he was discharged in 1899.

- **NEWSLETTER**

John saved the several newsletters that he received from the 7th U.S. Infantry Association - the "Grand Old 7th". The last one is dated 1945, but an earlier one announces the upcoming "First Annual Re-Union in Philadelphia, Penna.", to be held on August 18, 1930.

- **LETTER**

John didn't attend this 1930 reunion in Philadelphia, but he received shortly thereafter the following letter from a man who did:

N.Y. City N.Y. Sept 6/ 1930
#116 W. 36 St.
Mr John Allison

Denver/ Colo.

Dear Comrade: - Just a word to you. I attended the convention at Phila. Pa., And I see that comrade who runs the elevator Henry I think you call him, Well Phila., Pa., was rotten. I had a bum time. this is not the East I left 32 yrs ago. And I'll say they will not get me in Phila again. Well John I run on to some boys I soldiered with in the Island and I'll say some change. - Anderson was not here. Anyway I did not see him. - I was working most of the time. Society Army of Philippines, and 6th U.S. Inf Assoc. Shure done good Business. The bamboo is a pretty good scout. Yes he is with you he'll pay But he is no lover of a pen pushing Job, - Well Jno in the Parade I had on my left a colonel. I being #1 in the front Rank. and a Geral was in the rear Rank. Boy! some difference from 30 years ago.

Well at our banquet. we fell in as at mess in the Army. all a like, reveivied the past and I did get a kick out of that. New Orleans 1931. Milwaukee 1932. Well John if I take in these 2. that will be no more. there is getting to be two much politics and a form I do not like. - Underhand. and if you cant except a mans word. and he does not made good a promise. What would you call him?

It was said in Denver last yr, Phila. Pa., 1930 And the best conventin Ever. Well John its my contention it will be a long time before the East gets it again there was many who left went home discusted on the 2d day. And if I could of got read of my duties that is got releived I shure would of pulled out too.

Well I have been in N.Y. City 10 days looking it over attended one camp meeting And will say they dont do things here the way we do in the West. - One thing there is more money here common labor $8.00 per day. and it dosent cost much more to live here. You have more amusement. More to see. But when winter comes its cold. - But I hope to be in New Orleans then.

Say John those shoes I bought in Denver crippeled me and I sent them back to the factory in Boston Mass A wk ago no work sense. the lining broke in the toe round holes the size of a dime. God I now have 2 corns out of it Never till now have I had a blemish on my foot. This is the fault of the material in the shoe. havent heard a word from them as yet. - Well I can hardly walk. in misery all the time. going to Vetrans Bureau tomorrow and see what they can do for my feet.

Well you can tell the fellow with the big hat, the Bamboo and Candy Kid he lost nothing by (not) comeing East. - I'll see him in New Orleans this winter Am going as soon as I can get a ship. and Monday I'll start looking up Standard oil and the fruit boats.

Well John give all the boys my best wishes.

same to your self.

dont take any wooden money for its going to be a bad winter.

Hoover Prosperity. Lots of bunk.

Yours in F.P.V.H.

J.H. Caloon

I'll address this Lawton comp dont know your St. address.

I loved this letter! Mr. Caloon must have been quite a guy. He certainly knew what he liked and didn't like, and how to turn a phrase. Poor guy though. He was pretty disappointed with the reunion and besides that, his feet hurt! The nicknames he uses are interesting - Bamboo, the fellow with the big hat, and I think Grampa must have been the Candy Kid. Reread the letter, it's great!

➢ PHOTO

In the same box as this letter, I found a photo of a man standing in front of a sign that says:

NEBRASKA SOLDIERS HOME, visitors welcome.

It's dated November 30,1930. Could this be Mr. Caloon?

➢ NEWS ARTICLES

I don't know if John was granted his original request for a pension increase, but in 1933 he submits another claim - again citing injuries and ailments suffered as a result of his military service. He must have written after reading news articles (which he saved) about changes in the program. One reads:

> With ninety days to complete their task, the first federal boards will be set up next week to review the claims of 150,000 veterans for pension payments on ailments presumed to have originated in service.
> President Roosevelt, announcing his approval Saturday of regulations creating the boards, sanctioned an order authorizing $50 monthly to Spanish-American War veterans 50 years or older who are 50 per cent disabled and in need.

The articles are lengthy and list all types of disability possibilities and their pension amounts. Another article advises that:

> The remainder of this bill will be published in two or more installments. We suggest that those persons interested keep these issues of The National Tribute.

My grampa certainly was (interested), and did (keep the articles).

- **DEPOSITION**

This is a deposition John sent to the Veterans Department at that time (May 1933). It read:

RE:
1220780
John S. Allison

870 11th St., Denver, Colorado

John S. Allison, of lawful age, being first duly sworn upon oath, deposes and says:

That he enlisted in the army of the United States May 13, 1898 at Denver Colorado to serve three years; that he was a Private in company C of the Seventh Regiment, U.S. Infantry; that he was honorably discharged from the army of the United States at Fort Wayne, Michigan, February 12, 1899.

That his military records are as follows:

That he was active in the battle engagements, skirmishes, and expeditions as follows: War with Spain; Battles of Elcaney July 1, 1898, and all subsequent operation against Santiago until formal surrender, July 17, 1898; that his service was honest and faithful; that his certificate No. is 1229780; that he is receiving compensation from the government, for disability, of $50.00 per month; that he is permanently and totally disabled and absolutely unable to work or engage in remunerative employment, because he is suffering from bad eyesight, poor hearing, and is unable to work where the use of the eyes is necessary; that he is suffering from Rheumatism in both legs and arms, which make it very difficult, and almost impossible, to walk, and that he cannot use his arms; that he cannot raise his arms above the level of his shoulders; that he has a very weak heart and has been informed by reputable physicians that he may die from heart failure at any time; that he has very serious indigestion and very bad teeth; that he received treatment at Fitzsimmons Hospital, about two years ago, and was in said hospital for a period of six months, receiving treatment for his general bad condition and for his eyes, and was informed, after six month's confinement in said hospital, that it was impossible for his condition to be improved, and that he received no relief at said hospital from his various ailments, although he was afforded the greatest consideration and care while confined; that he is subject to fainting spells upon numerous occasions; that he is over-weight; that his height is five feet-six inches, and he weighs 250 pounds; that he is fifty-six years of age; that his general health, in addition to the above mentioned ailments, is extremely poor; that he is permanently and totally disabled, as aforesaid, and such disability was directly caused while in active service in the army of the United States as aforesaid, and is the result of unsanitary and filthy living conditions, and insufficient food while in active service; that while stationed in Cuba he went for long periods of time without any food at all and one time was three days without food of any kind, while engaged in active service at an outpost; that he was supplied with decayed beef for food; that he had to sleep on the ground without tent or cover of any kind, and many times he had to sleep on the ground without tent or cover during severe rain storms; that many times while sleeping on the ground without tent or covers, he was partly submerged in water; that he suffered from fever as a result of these living conditions; that he had a severe sun-stroke while in Cuba, as aforesaid, the effects of which are still prevalent; that he incurred a severe injury to the skull causing a fracture of the skull, and at the present time an indentation still remains in the skull, as a result thereof; that said injury was received by contact with some blunt instrument, while engaged in battle; that at no time during said service in Cuba did he receive medical attention, although desperately in need of it; that said fever, sun-stroke, skull injury, rotten food, and filthy living conditions have all directly combined to cause the ailments above set forth; that when he left Cuba he was unconscious, and did not regain consciousness until some time later, and when consciousness was regained he found himself in a hospital in Brooklyn, New York; the period of said unconsciousness is unknown; that upon enlistment in the army on May 13, 1898 he weighted 170 pounds and was in perfect condition; that when he was discharged, he weighed 111 pounds, and that ever since said discharge he has been in continual bad health; that he is entirely dependant on the pension which he receives from the United States, for his support, and that he has no other means of support whatsoever.

I can't tell if he received an increase in his pension. As we've noted, his discharge papers don't mention any injuries or disabilities at all. Since my memories of him are limited, it's hard to know if he was truly as disabled as he said in the deposition. He was overweight and didn't move about much, I remember that. But he was in his seventies and eighties by then, so it's hard to know. He lived 33 years after giving this deposition -hopefully he wasn't in great pain and discomfort during all of these years.

In the years to come, he came to own a great deal of property and received a sizeable income from it. So, for sure, he didn't remain "entirely dependant on the pension which he receives from the United States, for his support."

He remained as patriotic in old age as he had been when he enlisted in 1898. He loved his adopted country. He was always so proud of his military service.

Not long ago, I read an article in the Smithsonian magazine about author Stephen Crane, who spent time with the foot soldiers at Guantanamo, Las Fuasimas, Cusco and San Juan Hill. His words probably describe what John, also, experienced in this war. Here are a few portions of that article:

> Cuba was a grungy war, a torture of insufferable heat, malaria and yellow fever. After only four weeks, three-quarters of Teddy Roosevelt's RoughRiders were too sick to fight.
>
> 'As ... the Army push[ed] toward Santiago, ... There wasn't a high heroic face among them; they were all men intent on business. That was all.
>
> ... the victorious landing at Daiquiri, [was], ... for the average soldier, ... an itch on his skin, a pain in his hand, hunger, thirst, a lack of sleep; the influence of his memory of past firesides, glasses of beer, girls, theaters, ideals, religions, parents, faces, hurts, joys.
>
> [I acted] as jaunty as a real soldier, while all the time my heart was in my boots. ... I was frightened almost to convulsions. ... all that night I was afraid. Bitterly afraid.
>
> [A soldier was] dying near me. He was dying hard. Hard. It took him a long time to die.
>
> I felt that things were often sublime. ...But ... they were not of our shallow and preposterous fictions ... It was the behavior of men on the street.'
>
> [If] real war was horrible, it was ... superb as well - or men were, at least. Courageous men were.

One hundred years later, I recognize my grandfather's experience in these descriptions, respect his sufferings and salute his courage.

"Service honest and Faithful"

John's army discharge papers - 1899.

CHAPTER 4

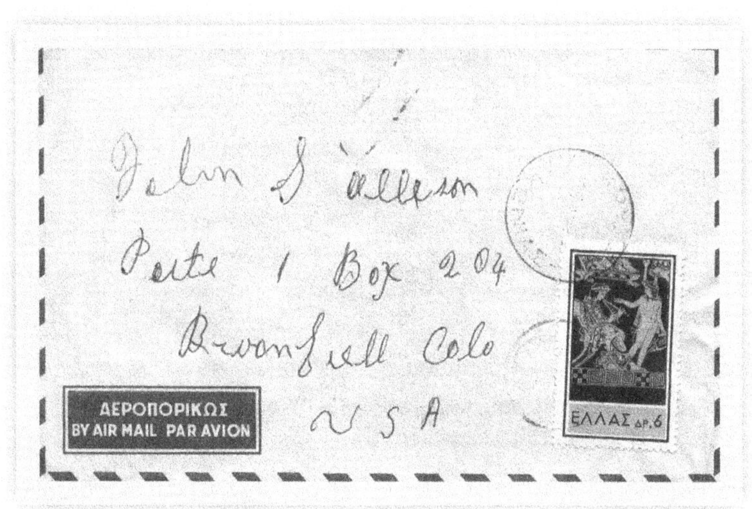

"I kiss your golden hand"

Before becoming Private John Allison of the United States Army, my grandfather was Ioannis Krouskos, son and brother, from the village of Agrianon, municipality of Thorapnoe, Sparta, in the Republic of Greece.

I know this, and other details about his family in Greece, from studying the many personal letters and legal documents he saved and from my recent visit with his niece, Titsa.

First the letters.

From February 11, 1959 through November 10, 1964, John received 43 letters from two of his nieces in Greece. Since he was in his eighties by this time, his son Steve dealt with these letters. All are written in Greek, but some have complete English translations or short English summaries that are attached. Here's a sampling:

May 6,1959

Dear Uncle John,
Happy Easter.

I write you with great sorrow, so please forgive me for writing you because I don't know to whom to turn to now.

Since Grandmother passed away I have been living with the four walls in Hrisafa. Nobody asks if I am alive or dead.

The house you bought, Giannoula was living in it, and paying them rent, until she could buy her own. She couldn't buy anything because her child fell and broke his leg and he is 3 years in the hospital in Athens.

Today I learned that they threw Giannoula out of the house so I went there and felt so sorry for her as did the rest of the people. So I ask them why they did it, so they told me to get out of the house in Hrisafa. My mother has given her son a power-of attorney for your things. My father since Panos was 8 years old he has given him a bill-of-sale for his things. Me they don't think anything of me. Because I told them not to throw Giannoula, they throw me out in Hrisafa.

I write it to you because it is yours and if you wish for your soul you let me stay since I have been so many years in Hrisafa.

If I had known that my mother and father would make a power-of-attorney for him for yours and they would throw me out, I would not of spoken.

I beg you dear uncle to please let me stay in the house in Hrisafa, because I have no place to go. I am awaiting your answer, to stay or to leave. To live here as I have before.

Best regards to Uncle Gus and Uncle Frank and to my cousins. I kiss your hands and your feet, Uncle John.

Your niece,
Catherine

Seems John still owns houses in Greece. Until recently his nieces have lived in these houses. Catherine has lived in one, with her grandmother (John's mother), until her passing, and now lives there alone. Giannoula (Joanne) and her badly injured son have lived in the other. Their brother, Panos, first evicts Joanne for non-payment of rent, and when Catherine protests, he evicts her also.

Four days later, the other niece, Joanne, writes to her uncle:

May 10, 1959

Dear Uncle John,

Many times I have written you before, but this time I write to tell you of my bad luck.

Since I got married I have been living in your house. For 3 years I have had my child in Athens at the hospital.

I have received no help from my parents. My father gave me 4 acres-field as a dowry, but now I find he has given Pano a deed of sale in his name, and my mother has given Pano a power-of-attorney for your things. Pano threatens and bosses our mother. She is afraid of him.

The other day my father notified me to get out of your house that it belongs to Pano. And I asked them why they didn't give me the $300 my uncles sent me instead they bought a radio to enjoy themselves, and I could of bought a house.

So they threw my things outside of the house and the police came and I told them the house belongs to my uncle. So please write if even to the president of the community if I can stay or if I must get out. The police put my things back in the house and gave me a month until I hear from you what I should do.

So please Uncle please let me stay for awhile. Maybe later I can find something else.

My sister Catherine heard of all of this and came from Hrisafa and told them weren't they ashamed of themselves, that all the people knew what they were doing and weren't they afraid of God, they have a home of their own. so they cursed Catherine and told her to mind her own business and to get out of the house from Hrisafa. And that too is in your own power to decide. So please save us.

Kourlos passed away and left his home to the church and it sold for $700, so they will pray for the salvation of his soul.

So please write even if it is to the president of the community, because when you were here you wanted to buy homes so that we would be praying for your good health and to be left so that people would pray for forgiveness for your soul. This isn't about money to be stolen, so please forgive me for all my letter but I am so worried that I had to write to you.

Write me how your Steve is, how is everyone.

I kiss your right hand,

Your niece,

Giannoula Gerouze

Brother Panos, with the backing of his parents (John's sister and brother-in-law), is indeed trying to evict both his sisters. The police and the president of the community have given Joanne and her invalid son a month's reprieve until they hear from John.

At the bottom of this letter my father wrote, "Wants her to stay in house, when John wants the house, then turn it over to him and my heirs."

This is pretty interesting. Do we still own these houses in Greece?

She does get to stay - and rent free, because he then sent an affidavit to the officials in Greece, which reads in part:

I, Stephen John Allison, of 3100 West 38th Avenue, Denver, Colorado, am the son of John Stephen Allison, of Denver, Colorado, and the only child and only heir.

Therefore I am the owner of the house in the community of Agrionoe, Sparta, Lakonias, Greece now occupied by Gianoula Geronizou. Gianoula Geronizou has a right to live in that house at no cost to her except upkeep, on my father's permission and now my permission.

And did Catherine get to stay in her house also? I think so. It's implied in this letter that she wrote exactly one year later:

At Hrisafa the 13th of May 1960

My respected Uncle John, Good Day!

I have not received a letter from your golden hands for a long time. I write to you and you do not answer, and today I write to you with hope and joy.

You had written a year ago to Luke that you were going to perform your heartfelt deed, to me, of course, you had so written. Luke told that you had also written it to him.

Today, a bridegroom came and we discussed the future, and I told him that my uncle would give me the money and had written that he would give it to me.

My Golden uncle if you wish to fulfill your heartfelt desire, send me whatever you have set aside for this purpose. Please answer me "yes" or "no". If you do send something your heartfelt wish will be done, but if you do not, I have no hope from anyone; neither from my mother or father, because you know that I live alone in the house like an owl in a haunted house.

Because you know, Uncle, my condition, do this deed so that your hands and soul might be blessed. If you do this thing it will be like erecting a great church; you will not be giving it to me, you are building a church and you will be memorialized forever.

Forgive me for my writing; you are not obligated to give it to me. It is only your desire for the good of your soul.

I do not have much more to write. Regards to my cousin Steve. I remain with love and respect and I kiss your golden hand no matter how distant you are.

Your niece,
Catherine

I write and wait.

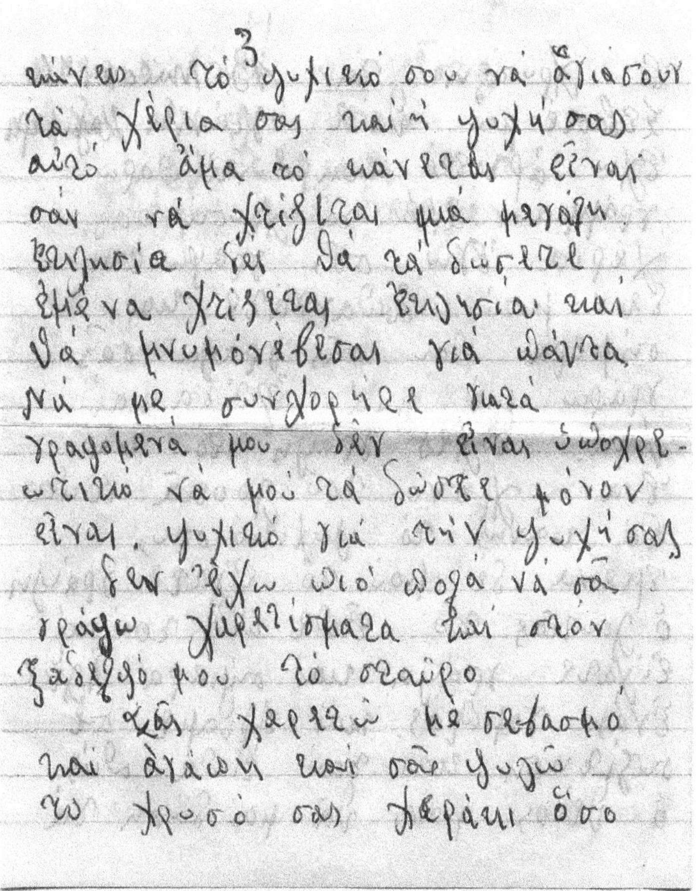

3

κάνεις τό ψυχικό σου νά ἁγιάσουν
τά χέρια σας καί ἡ ψυχή σας
αὐτό ἅμα τό κάνετε εἶναι
σάν νά χτίζεται μιά μεγάλη
ἐκκλησία δεν θά τά δώσετε
ἐμένα χτίζεται ἐκκλησία καί
θά μνημονέβεσαι γιά πάντα
νά με συγχωρήτε γιά τά
γραφόμενά μου δέν εἶναι ὑποχρε-
ωτικό νά μοί τά δώσετε μόνον
εἶναι ψυχικό γιά τήν ψυχή σας
δεν έχω πιό πολά νά σας
γράψω χαιρετίσματα καί στόν
ξάδελφό μου τό Σταύρο
σάς χαιρετώ μέ σεβασμό
καί ἀγάπη καί σας φιλώ
τό χρυσό σας χεράκι ὅσο

Figure 4.1 Letter from Catherine (1960).

Poor Catherine, the aging spinster who lives alone, "like an owl in a haunted house". And she'll most likely continue to do so. A year later, it's obvious from her final (translated) letter, that my grandfather (my father really), didn't come through with the promised dowry:

May 18, 1961

My respected Uncle John

Good Day!

I have written you so many letters and not an answer to any of them. In so many letters you did not reply to a single one and I worry if maybe they are falling in the ocean and are lost, or you do not wish to write to me and therefore they are going to waste.

If I tire you be having to read them forgive me; I'll not write anymore.

Uncle, Luke called mother and I to the Monastery and told us that you wished to do something for me for the good of your soul. You wished to help me, and with that knowledge I take the liberty of writing. I don't know whether it is true or false. You did not answer to me directly; Luke told me. He called for me and suggested I write to you to send the money to his hands.

I told him my uncle cannot send the money to you. He will send it to me to fulfill the pledge for his soul. And he said, 'I will receive the money into my hands, or it will not come.' And later when I asked him again he said your uncle will not send it; he just said so as a joke.

Uncle, you did not write this to me; he told me, and forgive me for writing it to you. He told me that you would send the money so that I might get married. The opportunity presented itself and arrangements were made and we were waiting for the money, but none arrived and nothing happened.

I had no one from my mother's or father's side; not a single hope for help because they had nothing.

Because I was staying with Grandma, and she died, and now I'm living alone, and my folks had nothing having given everything to the other girls.

I was waiting for you to make your offering for your soul, and I had hope, Now I've stopped hoping; I have not further expectation.

You had come here Uncle and I asked you to buy me a home, and you bought it for me. They all wanted it and would not let you put it in my name, so you bought it in your name. Now you wished to make a contribution for the good of your soul and they would not let you. Of course, you were not obliged to, but your soul would be sanctified.

Forgive me for my writings; I'll tire you. Since you do not write, you do not care to, and since you do not care to, this also will be my last letter.

I kiss your right hand Uncle, and wish you good health no matter how far away you may be.

Your niece,
Catherine

Catherine is a very expressive and poignant writer. Her words paint a melancholy picture of her dashed hopes and fading dreams. When her uncle fails to respond to her letters, she writes that she fears they "are falling in the ocean". That sentence broke my heart.

She speaks often of "Luke". I'm assuming that he is a family member, and that he is a monastic priest. "Luke" wrote to my grandfather many times from The Brier of the Holy Monastery, The Virgin Mary Elena, in Leinidien-Kyneurias, Greece. He included several photographs of this monastery, which sits at the base of a mountain and looks to be very old. With these photos was one of a priest - a priest with a long white beard, wearing a large crucifix and standing before an altar. I think it's a photo of Luke.

Do you think Luke pocketed the money sent by my grandfather for Catherine? Or do you think it was never sent? I'm afraid that might have been the case. In response to Catherine's letter, Steve makes it pretty clear that he's not too enthused about sending money to Greece:

7-26-61

Dear Cousin Katherine,

I hope that my letter finds you well. Please be informed that your uncle has been receiving all of your letters, but because of his advanced age is not able to answer them.

I do not know Greek at all, and am unable to read your letters or answer them. It is difficult to find the proper person to interpret and answer for me without obligation, and in order that our personal business does not become known to everyone.

Your uncle has recently been very ill, but is much better at this time.

I would appreciate it if you know English, to write to me in english. If not, find someone who can write in English for you in order that I might understand exactly what you wish and what exactly is the situation there. I do not know if you have made any legal agreements with Father.

Like I mentioned before, because of his advanced age, your uncle has left up to me the business and management of his property and affairs. Therefore, if it is not possible for me to know exactly what the situation is there, how can you expect our help?

In America agreements, contracts, etc. are usually drawn up by lawyers and according to law. That is why I need information and facts in order to decide the proper steps to take.

I await an answer in English. You have love and warmest felicitations from your uncle.

Respectfully,
Your cousin,
Steve

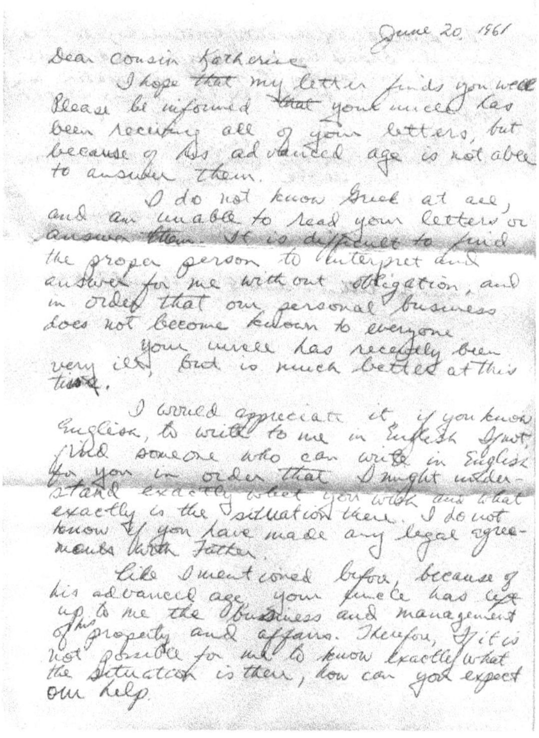

June 20, 1961

Dear cousin Katherine

I hope my letter finds you well. Please be informed your uncle has been receiving all of your letters, but because of his advanced age is not able to answer them.

I do not know Greek at all, and am unable to read your letters or answer them. It is difficult to find the proper person to interpret and answer for me without obligation, and in order that our personal business does not become known to everyone.

Your uncle has recently been very ill, but is much better at this time.

I would appreciate it if you know English, to write to me in English. If not, find someone who can write in English for you in order that I might understand exactly what you wish and what exactly is the situation there. I do not know if you have made any legal agreements with Father.

Like I mentioned before, because of his advanced age your uncle has left up to me the business and management of his property and affairs. Therefore, if it is not possible for me to know exactly what the situation is there, how can you expect our help.

Figure 4.2 Letter from Steve (1961).

In the midst of sorting through all the correspondences from my relatives in Greece, Ken and I decided that we would visit Greece on our next vacation, and perhaps try to visit the Krouskos family at that time. With that in mind, I called my father's cousin, Titsa (i=long e). At my father's funeral she had told me that she and her sister had visited the family in Greece in the seventies, and I was hoping she could tell me how to find them.

She told me that she could direct me to the town they had visited, but beyond that could be of little help. It seems that the cousins who had written the above letters were both dead and that she and Georgia had lost contact with the rest of the family in Greece.

Although she wasn't able to help us much in planning our trip, she did tell me many intriguing bits and pieces of family history. I've attempted to clarify some of what she told me with data gleaned from John's papers and letters. All in all, it makes for quite a story. Using many of Titsa's own words and phrases, this is what she told me:

My great-grandmother, John's mother, Georgoula Hioolaou Natiozou, married my great-grandfather, Stavros Krouskos sometime in the 1860's or 1870's. Six of their children survived to adulthood - five sons and a daughter.

First born was George. In all the papers and letters I've gone through, I've not come across the Greek translation for his name. It must be something like Georgou though, since his mother's name translates to Georgia in English. The next brother, Nicolous or Nick, I'd never heard of - his existence was a complete surprise to me. Then Ioannis or John joined the family. Of the children, for some reason, only John was taught to read and write. He was, Titsa said, the only one who was "literate". Argyrios or Frank and Constantine or Gus were the two youngest brothers. One by one the boys came to America. Eventually George, John, Frank and Gus settled in Denver, Colorado. Nick lived in Detroit, Michigan.

I'm not sure of the birth order of their sister, Venetta, but she remained in Greece - very much against her will. She too, had wanted to come to America, but her father, the original Steve or Stavros, wouldn't let her leave, since she was "the apple of his eye." When a "suitor" asked to marry Venetta, Stavros abruptly refused him the priviledge. A few days later, "while she was out", the suitor "kidnapped" Venetta so they could be married. When Stavros learned of this, "he was out of his mind with anger and fear." He ran to try and intercept the couple before the wedding, or at least before the marriage was consummated - since even at that point it could have been annulled.

Arriving at the man's village after the wedding, but before the wedding night, he headed for the home of the groom. The groom's family and friends intercepted him and tied him to an olive tree until the marriage had been consummated. In struggling to free himself, he actually "pulled up the tree", but to no avail. He "killed himself trying to get free."

On his deathbed, he cried and called for his "favorite son, Frank, who was in America" by this time. Hoping to calm him, his friends and relatives found a young blond boy of about Frank's age, and "presented" him to the dying father. Stavros believed this was Frank and "was appeased". Then "he died of a broken heart - because of his lost daughter."

Venetta and her husband, George Kyriakoulia, had eight daughters and one son. Titsa remembered seven of their names. We've met two of them already - unmarried Catherine, who lived alone and lonely in the village of Hrisafa, and Joanne/Ginnaoula Geronizou (whose young son had spent three years in an Athens hospital) who lived in the "community of Agrionoe". Both resided in houses purchased for them by their Uncle John. Stauroula, Panagiota, Irene and Stamtas were four of the other daughters, one of whom was raped and killed during World War II.

According to the letters of Joan and Catherine, their parents favored their only son, Panos, and gave him an unfair share of the family resources. Their father "arrange*[d]* things so that Panos gains title to all the properties." Their mother, Venetta, is too frightened of her husband to interfere on behalf of her daughters.

What a different life Venetta might have had, had she been permitted, like her brothers, to emigrate.

Our relatives in Greece are very poor, according to Titsa. She told me, "Your father thought he owned a huge mansion there, but it's only a small house. And besides, there's a law that if the owner isn't in the country and doesn't visit it for so many years, it becomes the property of the inhabitants."

(So. I guess I can probably forget about looking into whether I own a house - or two - in Greece, huh?)

At the end of our telephone conversation, Titsa asked if we had, by any chance, come across a very large portrait "of a famous Greek politician" among my grampa's stuff. And if we had, and if it had no great meaning to us, could she and her family have it. Seems it had hung in her family's home for many years, but at some point her father had given it to John. Later, when Titsa married a man (who was born in America, but raised in Greece) who was very interested in Greek history, she knew that her husband would love to have this particular portrait. So she asked Grampa to return it - but he couldn't find it. We had indeed carted home a very large photograph, elaborately framed, of a Greek gentleman, and I assumed that it was the desired "portrait". She said she'd come to get it within the next few weeks.

And she did. I thought she'd just pick up the photo, and then be on her way. But she came intending to visit - which was great. She brought a box of candy, which was such a lovely, old-fashioned gesture. I felt bad though, because I hadn't planned lunch, or even refreshments. She didn't seem to mind though, and proceeded to tell me more about the Krouskos family in Greece.

They've always lived part of the year in one village and part of the year in another. That seemed strange to me, but Titsa explained that in the summer they take the goats "up the mountain" to Agrianous (where Joanne lived with her son). The name means wild, and "commemorates" the beautiful wild flowers of the region. And in the winter they live down the valley, in Chrisaga, which I think she said means olive. Is this a variation of Hrisafa, where Cousin Catherine lived? Both villages are close to the large city of Sparti.

Titsa first visited the family in the 1960's. She, her sister Georgia, her father Frank and her son Ted made the trip. Well, since it was summer, Panos (remember him?) met them at the base of the mountain and drove them, in their rented car, up to Agrianous. She said that it was one of the scariest things she'd ever done - traveling on the steep and winding narrow dirt roads, always a few feet from sheer and deep drop-offs.

When they reached the village, they found that our family there lives "very simply". They had prepared many wonderful food dishes "in anticipation" of their American relatives' visit. The tables were set up outside and were full of beautifully prepared food. She couldn't bring herself to eat much though, because many flies also feasted on the lovingly prepared feast. Her father, who was in his 70's, didn't want to hurt his family's feelings, however, and so he ate all the foods they offered him. He got very sick "with a rash and diarrhea"- whether from the flies or not, she doesn't know. Titsa said that every person she met on this, and a subsequent trip, was friendly, loving and unfailingly generous.

We visited for several hours. She went on to tell me many stories about the Krouskos/Allison brothers in America - but that's for later.

When it came time for her to leave, I asked if she'd look at some of the photographs I'd found at the farm and perhaps identify some of the people in them. She was happy to do so, and was able to tell me specifically about three of them.

One is of Venetta and her husband at their wedding. The husband looks very young and innocent. He doesn't look much like a kidnapper. With them in the photo is the best man, the person responsible for tying Venetta's father to the tree.

In another, Venetta looks very much like her brother John.

The large woman in the third photo is Georgoula - the mother of the brood (see next chapter title page). My great-grandmother looks like a sincere, serious, robust peasant woman. Her head is covered with a scarf and she wears a long skirt and plain black jacket. She looks to be about fifty years old. If that were the case, she'd live almost another half century after sitting for this photograph. The glass and frame of this large photo are encrusted with smoke, dirt and grime - from all those years it hung in Grampa's kitchen.

I liked Titsa very much and very much enjoyed our visit. In return for all her time, graciousness and helpful information, I was happily anticipating giving her the portrait of the "famous Greek politician". When it was time for her to leave, I went to get it - and - it wasn't the guy! We were both so disappointed. It's a picture of Brother George! He's a confident and prosperous looking young man of about 35 years of age. He's well groomed, well dressed and physically fit. I said she could have it if she wanted it, but she said to keep it with the other things from the farm. So that was that.

Unfortunately, because of time constraints, we weren't able to find the Krouskos family when we visited Greece early the next year.

Later that day I found a photograph of a frail looking child of about six years old. Perhaps it's of Joanne's son (see image at beginning of Chapter 22). He's dressed in traditional Greek clothing and stands by a table, holding a book. It's been very handsomely framed by "The Zigmond Frame and Picture Co. of Denver, Colorado". This young boy in Greece was, I think, very dear to the heart of someone in America.

To me, he represents the family that Grampa and his brothers left behind.

"I kiss your golden hand"

Catherine's letter - 1960

CHAPTER 5

"her sons, who are in America"

Meanwhile, George, Nick, John, Gus and Frank went on about their lives in America.

Below, I've listed some of the materials I've come across and the resultant information I've learned from them about the Allison brothers in America. I've tried to include items that reflect their characters and personalities - and also show the direction their lives were taking.

- **GEORGE'S IMMIGRATION INFORMATION**

Titsa gave me the cerificate from Ellis Island's Wall of Honor. It records that he came to America in 1892.

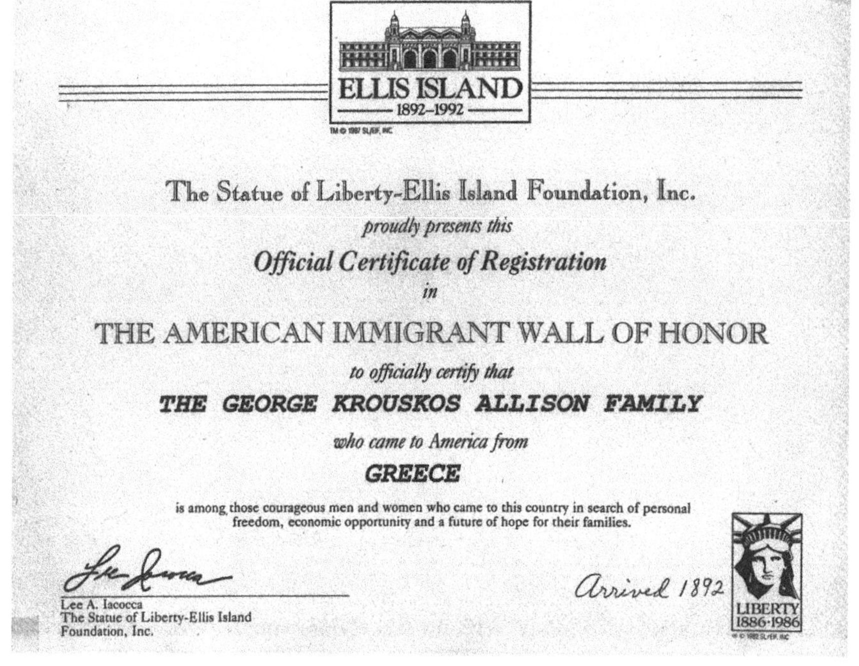

ELLIS ISLAND
1892–1992

The Statue of Liberty-Ellis Island Foundation, Inc.
proudly presents this
Official Certificate of Registration
in
THE AMERICAN IMMIGRANT WALL OF HONOR
to officially certify that
THE GEORGE KROUSKOS ALLISON FAMILY
who came to America from
GREECE
is among those courageous men and women who came to this country in search of personal freedom, economic opportunity and a future of hope for their families.

Lee A. Iacocca
The Statue of Liberty-Ellis Island Foundation, Inc.

Arrived 1892

LIBERTY
1886·1986

Figure 5.1 George's Immigration Information (1892).

But how can that be? One of the few "facts" I've always known about the family is that George came to America first, then John. But John's military papers say that he immigrated to the United States in 1891.

- **TAX INVOICE**

I don't know where George lived, or what he did for a living, but in 1902 he saved tax invoices and receipts for land he owned in Salt Lake City, Utah. These properties were owned jointly with a Wm. J. Wagner.

Remember the name. In a few years, a Mrs. Wagner will have some interesting dealings with George and his brother John.

➢ LETTER

By 1910 George was living in Denver, Colorado. He received this letter at his confectionery business:

JMJ

Mount Carmel
Dubuque, Ia.
May 31, 1910

Mr. George Allison
1011 15th St.
Denver, Colo.

Dear Friend:

I had thought by this time that all my old friends had entirely forgotten me, but on receipt of the box of "sweets" you so kindly sent me I changed my mind. I appreciate your kindness and enjoyed the candy the same as of old.

I am very happy in my new home, in fact, much more so than I told you I would be. I really never knew there was such contentment to be found in this world. I want for nothing in the material way except time and that passes so quickly. I find myself wishing the days were again as long as while at home. There, I did just the opposite.

I trust you are enjoying good health and happiness and that God will continue His blessings upon you. Again thanking you for your thoughtfulness as well as for all the kindness shown me in the past.

I am,

Sincerely yours,
Sister Mary Philomene

I doubt if I'll ever know why George was sending candy to a nun in Iowa, but it sounds like they were long time acquaintances.

➢ WALLET

Sister Philomene writes to George at 1011 15th Street in Denver. In an old, falling apart wallet belonging to my grandfather, I found a business card for a candy store at that address.

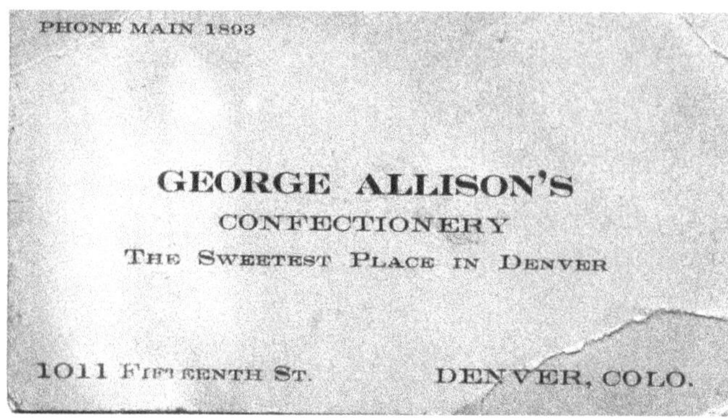

Figure 5.2 Candy Store Business Card.

This property will stay in the Allison family for the next sixty years. I think it's at the heart of much of our prosperity. Brook's Towers, condominium "lofts", currently occupy the site.

- **LETTER**

A letter from the J.C.R.S. Aid Association of the Ex-Patients, 1578 Irving Street, to George is dated July 20,1911.

We beg to thank you in grateful acknowledgment of your kind contribution which helped make our affair a success.

Respectfully yours,
S. Korengold
Secretary

J.C.R.S. was the Jewish Consumptives' Relief Society. Today, the J.C.R.S. retail center is still located near this area of West Colfax Ave.

- **STOCK CERTIFICATE**

A certificate for 5 shares of Apple Association Stock, purchased by George in 1911.

- **RENT RECEIPT**

Rent paid to the Adolph Coors company in 1913 was probably for the building housing George Allison's Confectionery. The receipt reads:

Rent	*4/1 to 5/1/13*	*200.00*
Heating	*4/1 to 5/1/13*	*7.25*

➢ PHOTO

Figure 5.3 Portrait of Brother George.

Brother George must have been very successful by now, at least financially. His large framed photograph (the one that wasn't the famous Greek politician) surely cost a lot. It's about two feet by three feet, and is surrounded by an ornate, gold colored, wooden frame. The portrait is meant to convey success and prominence, and it does.

I would guess he was about 35 years old when he sat for it. He resembles his younger brother Frank, in that his facial features are finer and his complexion fairer than their brothers John and Gus. And, like all his brothers and I'd guess 90% of the men of the time, he has a mustache. It's a nicely trimmed, yet full, dark mustache that complements his finely cut head of dark hair.

He wears a beautiful three piece suit. The buttons on the vest are covered, the shirt collar is very high and very starched and the perfectly knotted tie appears to be made of silk.

➢ CHINA SET

We also unearthed the remnants of a set of china with his name embossed on them. They also, must have cost quite a bit.

- **WARRANTY DEED**

And then, in 1916, Brother George and Brother John purchased "the farm".

I'd always wondered how and when my family came to own this land. I found out when I came upon an inventory for a safety deposit box that had been rented by John Allison in 1962. (I'm sure my dad rented it in Grampa's name, since John was 86 years old at the time.) This inventory contains many items that figure into later parts of the brothers' story, but one listing told me what I'd always wanted to know about the farm:

"Warranty Deed, dated 7-19-16, to farm, John and George".

The property is described as "farming land in Semper, Colorado that occupies the northwest quarter of section twenty-four, township two south, range sixty-nine west of the sixth principal meridian, Jefferson County, Colorado."

I feel that the seller of this "farming land" deserves a few paragraphs at this point in the story.

- **CHARLES SEMPER'S TRUNK**

In the most remote corner of the most remote building at the farm, we found a large trunk that had belonged to Charles Semper. Why had he left it there - filled with his possessions - when he'd sold the farm in 1916? He died less than a year later, so perhaps in his aged state, he hadn't realized he'd left it - or didn't care that he'd left it.

Thinking that the contents of this trunk were of some interest historically, I offered them to the Western History Department of the Denver Public Library. The librarian who accepted them pulled up this short summary of his life as found in library references:

Charles A. Semper died September 16, 1917 at the age of 87. Semper was a typesetter on "The Rocky Mountain News" and sole surviving charter member of the Denver Typographical Union N. 49. Native of England, came to Colorado in 1859, fought in Confederate army.

Figure 5.4 Charles Semper.

He'd arrived in Colorado from England - via Georgia. Thus his service in the Confederate Army.

The library's receipt for the trunk's contents reads:

1 wrapped item, one folio, material includes printed and published material (list attached)

Prints used in The Denver Weekly Post, early 1900's

Miscellaneous prints

Supplement the Denver Post (sheet music), 1902 and 1903

Ledger Book and writing samples, 1880-1910

The Mutual Life Insurance Company of New York, Picture

Calendars, 1900 and 1901

Three Wolfe Londoner broadsides, 1912

Map - Bird's Eye View of the Mountain and Plains from Lookout Mountain

Map of Mexico, 1901

Map of Cities of Sault Ste. Marie, 1888

The Jones Political Chart Company showing electoral votes (McKinley and Bryan)

Writing about two other items from Mr. Semper's trunk, the librarian said in part:

Dear Linda:

It was good to see you again and have a chance to see new 'old' items you have found among the Semper collection materials.

Buffalo Bill pamphlet, pre - 1900, in the shape of a buffalo head sketch prints used in Denver Post, Gibson Girl sketches.

I would say the Gibson Girl sketches are also in the category of prints used in the Denver Post during the time he worked at the Post setting type. Charles Semper was a pioneer with a skill - that of a typographer. It certainly served him well. Those persons who came here as tradesmen were often greater successes and more able to have an influence on their community than those seeking gold.

She's right about Charles Semper being successful. And he was evidently quite an influential person in his neck of the woods. According to the Warranty Deed for the farm, he lived in a town named after himself. Although there's no town called Semper today, there is a water treatment plant and an elementary school named after him. This article appeared in the Denver Rocky Mountain News in September of 1996:

New school knows roots

WESTMINSTER - Charles Semper was a heavy-metal dude.

He sought his fortune by panning gold. But he made his living in lead – setting type for the Rocky Mountain News.

Now, he has a monument – Semper Elementary School, one of the five new schools in Jefferson County. The others are Conifer and Dakota Ridge high schools and Mount Carbon and West Woods elementary schools.

Semper first-graders Catie Bell and Vincent Colson, both 7, talked to a stranger about whom their school was named after.

They are bright-eyed and quick to smile and even quicker to answer questions.

'Semper was a pioneer', Catie said.

'That means they go to places where they don't know what it looked like and they stop,' she explained.

Vincent also clued in a visitor.

'He came out here in a Conestota wagon, a covered wagon,' Vincent said. 'He was a little bit of a farmer. He liked to grow stuff, like corn.'

Catie knew that Semper worked as a typesetter on the first edition of the News.

'There was a race between his writing area and another,' Catie said.

Added Vincent, 'They were in competitioning. His won.'

The Jefferson County public school system has a committee that researches and then suggests school names to the board of education.

Semper's name was a logical choice, the committee said, because he was interested in education, having served on the school board in 1880. In addition, he and his wife, Julia, settled at what is now West 93rd Avenue and Teller Street, close to Semper School, at 7575 W. 96th Ave.

A mural in the lunchroom depicts memorable moments in the Sempers' lives: the Conestoga wagon that brought them to Colorado a rolled-up newspaper, a railroad that dropped off mail in the former town of Semper, also named after Charles, where Julia was postmistress.

About 700 parents, students and teachers attended the dedication Thursday night.

The school's nickname is fitting. It's the Pioneers.

An elegant world atlas from the 1840s was also in Charles Semper's trunk. Unfortunately, I've "stored" it somewhere so safe - that I can't find it. I'd like to complete his library collection with it. Since he was very meticulous about saving these things, I think he'd be pleased to know that they're now preserved in our fine public library.

➢ LETTERS TO JOHN

Two letters received by John at about this time, indicate that he and George not only bought the farm together, but also worked together (co-owned?) in the confectionery business:

The letter writer mentions a young person named "Wilburn". What a name! For years, I tried to figure out who this was - thinking that perhaps it was another, unknown son of John's. It was a real puzzle to me. It wasn't until Titsa's recent visit that I found out who this was. You'll see - later...

Undated
Mr. John Allison,

Dear Friend,

I have been trying to see you but always get to the Store the day after you have been there.

John I want to ask a favor of you and I will not take No for an answer. Would you be so kind as to let little Wilburn come to visit Josephine? we want him Christmas Eve. I will meet him at the Store. I will give him the very best care. this is going to be a very lonely Christmas for Josephine. the only thing she has asked for was a good turkey dinner and to have you and Wilburn help her eat it. so please don't disappoint her. you can come in Christmas day after you have attended the Store. we will arrange the dinner for anytime that will suit you. then leave Wilburn with us the rest of the week. I have bought Wilburn a Sandy Andy. I am sure he will enjoy it for my big Joe as old as he is would play with it if I would let him.

Now John we have set our hearts on having you both in for Christmas. Josephine feels bad enough on account of the way your brother George treats her so please don't disapoint her in this. I am sending the little shirts to you. I hope they will fit him all right. they are the first boy shirts I ever made. I think I will do better on the next ones.

Don't try to tell me that it's too much trouble to have Wilburn for it will only be a pleasure and the little dear is entitled to it for the way he took care of the place when you were gone. Call me up as soon as you can.

Very Respectfully
Mrs. Wagner
3040 West 45 Ave

So, did John and Wilburn go to Christmas dinner with the Wagners? Did Wilburn like his Sandy Andy? What place did Wilburn take care of while John was away? And where had John gone? I can tell you (from hindsight), that Wilburn was only nine years old at the time.

Although it's written to John (at the candy store address), this next letter is primarily *about* George. Ella Wagner (related to the man who owned property with George in Salt Lake City back in 1902?) paints an interesting picture of the then forty-something businessman, George Allison:

John Allison
1011 15th St.

January 11, 1919

Mr. Allison,

Dear Sir;

I was down to see you at the store but you re not there. I hope you found the school bag and pie I left for little Wilburn.

The name of the butcher I spoke of is Chas. Maynard 2610 Federal Blvd or at Fay's Market. he will butcher and smoke you two Hogs for five dollars. we got out meat home today and it is smoked fine.

John, your brother has tried to heap insult upon injury. he told Harry to tell me he did not want me to come down for the meat. he said Harry you are boss down there. tell her to keep out, for Gods sake what have I done that he should insult me so? what is the matter with the Man? I hope God will forgive him as I do. I sat out in my Machine in the cold after he insinuated to George that Josephine was taking his Money, George London told me to come right on in the store as if nothing had happened and not to talk to Mr. Allison but in time he would see his mistake and be a better friend of ours than ever. George London knew I was in debt to Mr. Allison and wanted to pay him back. it was with the consent of George that I undertook to pack boxes trying in that way to save him extra help. I made Josephine wait on his customers during rush hours and on Saturday. not to be rude but thinking I was doing him a good turn. I was told several times by some of his help that he did not appreciate any thing one did for him unless he paid for it. I consider he had paid us well for what we were doing for him.

Every time Harry would talk to me he would say why don't you talk to the boss. I was advised by George to leave him alone till he would talk to me so I told Harry I was going to let him do the first talking. just today Harry told me to ask him what I had done, I called him up spent my five cents for the call and he hung up before I could say a word. just as soon as he found out who was talking. I hope he will never have a friend that will condemn him without a hearing as he has done me. I don't care for myself but I hate to be misjudged. we never took a piece of candy that George London did not say we could have. if George was not there we went to Maria she would insist on Josephine taking plenty, when I would tell Josephine to take no more. maria would say (Go to it kid help yourself he will only give it to his chickens and he told me you should have what you want) so you see he could not be angry on that score. George told us one of the girls were jealous of Josephine.

we asked if it was Ina. George said no its the one that talks to the Boss every night. we asked the girls which one talked to Mr. Allison. they all said Maria was the only one he talked to, as when Maria asked me why I had quit talking to her I told her what I had heard. she has not spoken to me since. she make no denial of what I said, only Mrs. Wagner I hope you don't believe it, I told her I hated to think after all my kindness to her she would be so deceitful but when she will talk about Mr. Allison to Mrs. Keiser as she did saying he was Bug house she will not hesitate to talk about me. I am willing to face any one who ever claimed I tried to harm him in any way. if he was angry at me Joe and Josephine have done nothing to him, the one who has caused us this trouble will suffer for it.

John it would only make it unpleasant for Mr. Allison if we went out to help you with the Hogs. he might go out and not like to see us there. we would enjoy going so much but would not like to make it unpleasant for him. I hope everything will be O.K.

Very Respectfully,
Ella Wagner

I love how Ella Wagner talks! She'd be a good match for J.H. Caloon. Remember him - writing to John about the veteran's convention? She says that Mr. Maynard will "butcher and smoke you two Hogs for five dollars." That has such a twang to it. And she had to sit "out in her Machine in the cold". Her car? That's great! And how about George being "Bug house"? Brother George doesn't sound like a very pleasant person - at least not from her point of view.

I wonder why my grandfather saved these letters?

➢ NICHOLAS KROUSKOS DOCUMENTS

In a large dusty envelope I discovered documents that concerned the death, in 1918, of one Nicholas Krouskos, son of Georgoula.

Although the documents didn't tell how he died, I guessed that perhaps he was a victim of the influenza epidemic of that year. During her visit, Titsa confirmed that such was the case - kind of. She revealed to me this very sad story of Brother Nick:

He lived, with his wife Helen, in Detroit Michigan. "He owned a candy store. He got the flu." On Armistice Day, November 11, 1918, "he was out of his head with fever and sickness, and went out into the street to try to get to a hospital." Since he was crying and unable to make himself understood in English, some people thought he was a "Kraut sympathizer" - upset because of the German defeat. No one would help him; in fact, "they beat him badly and left him near death. He died a few hours later."

➢ PHOTO

I found a photo that I'm assuming is of Nick. The gentleman in the photo resembles the other Krouskos brothers, but isn't one that I recognize. He's standing behind the counter, next to an ornate gold cash register, in a candy store. He's wearing a suit with a white shirt and a cap that resembles a pancake. Offered for sale are Eskimo Pies, Oh Henry candy bars, something called a Big Bobbie for $.05 and many trays and jars filled with candies made on the premises. (You can see the photograper in the mirror.)

Figure 5.5 Nick? In the Candy Store.

➢ LETTERS WRITTEN IN GREEK

I'm further assuming that Brother Nick owned the Mack Avenue Candy Company in Detroit, Michigan. John saved several letters written, in Greek, on letterhead paper from that confectionery. (In going through Nick's estate papers, I see that he banked at the People's State Bank - on Mack Avenue.)

➢ POWER OF ATTORNEY DOCUMENT

Nick's wife didn't automatically inherit his estate. Instead, for some reason, his mother, Georgoula, did. She, in turn, signed power-of-attorney over to Brothers George and John, as recorded in the following document. (John saved this official English translation along with the original document, handwritten in Greek.) It states, in part:

POWER - OF - ATTORNEY

At Sparta and in my Notarial Office, to-day, the twenty fifth of the month of January of the year of one thousand nine hundred nineteen,

before me, the Notary Public of Sparta, George El. Karellas, and in the presence of the following two witnesses, who are Greek subjects, of lawful age and not prohibited, George Psyhogios, a land owner, a resident of Mazoulas, and Panag. Ar. Karellas, an attorney at law, and resident of Sparta,

appeared before us Georgoula, the widow of Stavros Krouskos who is personally known to me and to the witnesses, and who is not prohibbited, and being occupied by her own household, and resident of Agrianon, of the late County of Therapion, of the province of Laconia of Greece, and declared that, for herself and as heir at law of her deceased son, Nicholas St. Krouskos, also known as Nicholas Allison, who died in America,

she appoints as her attorney-in-fact, plenipotentiaries and representatives, her sons, who are in America, George St. Krouskos, and John St. Krouskos. who are also known as Allison and engaged there in business, to whom she gives the special authority, in order that, either together, or each one separately, to appear before all the authorities having jurisdiction in America, and to perform all the acts pertaining to the personal and real property of the said deceased Nicholas St. Krouskos,

and to receive moneys, chattels, and every other personal property and to give discharges; to receive rents which may be due' to negotiate and assign claims; to discharge claims which may be due against him and to collect the claims which are due to him and to give releases;

She hereby promises, acting under her above mentioned capacity, to accept and acknowledge the acts of all as true and irrevocable.

IN WITNESS WHEREOF, this document was executed, which was read in a clear voice for the hearing of all of the above, and having been verified, it was signed by all and by me, except the appointer, who declared ignorance of letters.

So, did George and John, the "sons, who are in America", make sure their brother's estate was fairly distributed? I hope so.

Dear Georgoula, declaring her "ignorance of letters", doesn't even sign the document. In the 1935 she'll again lose a son and again relinquish her rights.

➢ ESTATE LIST

Here's a partial listing of the "Estate of Nicholas Allison":

Personal Property	
Bank balance Nov. 11, 1918	
Chas A. Gild, Special Admr. Account	$1324.96
Bank Balance as per Peoples State Bank, Mack Ave.	$1575.46
Bank Balance as per Dime Savings Bank	$316.00
Uncertified checks	$117.50
Cash on hand	$104.42
Liberty Bonds	$50.00
	$50.00
	$50.00
	$100.00
	$100.00
Bills Receivable (Total)	$938.10
Real Estate	
1/2 interest in land contract on lot 110	$175.00
Lot #389 in name of Nick Allison and Helen Allison	$165.00
Invoice - Fixtures	
1 Cash Register	$40.00
1 Cash register	$60.00
2 Toledo scales	$60.00
Soda Fountain back bar	$150.00
1 Cream beater	$100.00
3 marble slabs	$20.00
800 lbs. milk chocolate	$240.00
Raw peanuts	$140.00
2 cases Cracker jack	$14.00
8 barrells gluccose	$240.00
2 Tons coal	$21.00
1 Ford Touring car	$375.00
1 Ford Delivery body	$10.00

The list of fixtures and personal possessions runs to over 70 items.

I think it's ironic and sad that Brother Nick had purchased Liberty Bonds - and was later severely beaten by those who thought him unpatriotic. Uncle Nick, I'm glad I got to meet you - even though it was posthumously and by eighty years.

The Krouskos brothers weren't very prolific. Like his brothers George and Gus, Nick had no children - at least I found no record of any. Only Frank, the youngest, created and sustained a family that included a wife and children.

➢ BUSINESS CONTRACTS

George Allison continued to do well financially. Several contracts, dated 1923-1926, name him as partial or complete owner of numerous shares of mining stock in Colorado and Utah.

➢ CHATTEL MORTGAGE

In 1926 he purchased, for $7500.00, "all the contents and fixtures from the Alpine Rose Cafe in Denver." The seller was John Christie, as recorded on the chattel mortgage. It lists hundreds of items - from a twelve-foot back bar to twelve ashtrays - that were included in the purchase. Here's some examples:

92 Chairs	Combination Coffee Urns
23 Tables	1 Buffet, solid Oak with mirror
20 Table Cloths	1 - 18 ft. Steam Table, complete
50 Doz. Napkins	1 Cigar Case, 6 ft., Plate Glass
1 New Meat Block	3 Oven New Home Comfort Range
1 Dish Washer Machine	1/2 Dozen Solid Silver Covers for Steaks
25 Doz. Pie Plates	15 Doz. Dinner Plates
Salt shakers	30 Doz. Vegetable Dishes
finger bowls	2 Dozen Silver Tea Pots
1 Battery	electric sign (valued at $800.00)
3 Ice boxes	Pans, Pots and all Kitchen Ware

➢ ROCKY MOUNTAIN NEW ARTICLE

In 1991, Frances Melrose writes a column, about historic Denver, in *The Denver Rocky Mountain News*. A few years ago, she interviewed my father's cousins, Georgia and Titsa, about The Allison Candy Store. They supplied her with a photo of the store's interior, which she included in the published article.

The photo was the same as the one on the many postcards I'd found advertising "Allison's Confectionery - The leading Confectionery in the West".

LEADING CONFECTIONERY IN THE WEST.
GEO. ALLISON. 1011-15TH ST., DENVER, COLO.

Figure 5.6 Allison Confectionery.

A few weeks after the article was published, a letter appeared in the same column from a very adamant man. He said that the photo couldn't possibly show the interior of the Allison Candy Store, since it obviously showed the interior of the Alpine Rose Cafe! For weeks, the controversy continued, as people wrote in voicing opinions on which establishment was represented in the photo.

After finding the above bill of sale, I now understand that everyone was correct. The picture shows the fixtures from the Alpine Rose Cafe, as they appeared in the Allison Candy Store.

A building at the farm was filled to the rafters with many of these furnishings. Through good luck, I met the owner of the K P Cafe (it's in the very old Knights of Pythias building) in Silver Plume, Colorado. To the satisfaction of us both, he paid me about $800.00 and took what he wanted of the lot.

➢ PROMISSORY NOTES

In 1927, Brother George signed five promissory notes, payable to the First National Bank of Denver, for $1500.00, $2000.00, $1500.00 $2000.00 and $5500.00; totalling $12,500 (millions of drachmas). He must have used this money for a trip home. I found a "Sailing Schedule" to Greece, for the Cunard and Anchor Lines, dated April 6, 1927. The notes are maked paid in August 1927 and October 1927.

➢ SAILING SCHEDULE

Figure 5.7 Sailing Schedule.

Listed under the fare schedule is the category of "servant". Did such a thing exist - as recently as 1927? They sailed first class, with their employer, for $165.00.

➢ LETTER TO GEORGE

Now here's a great letter George received, dated August 2, 1930. I call it "the junk pile" letter:

Mr. Geo. Allison
1011 15th St.
Denver Colo

My Dear Mr. Allison

Well I see you are still paying taxes on your junk pile on Grant Ave with no income. And I'm still paying taxes on my lots in Denver where I can't look after them. Nor can you look after your property here. Why can't we get together on a deal and each have property where we live and can look after it? If you do not wish to keep the lots you could easily sell them on payment plan or trade for a home. Let me hear from you.

Respy Yours
H.W. Wistner
2585 Quincy Ave
Ogden, Utah

I'm still wondering how Brother George got involved with real estate and mining in Utah. None of our family has ever lived there, as far as I know. He did end up trading properties with Mr. Wistner - noting on the envelope, "answered - I will take in trade his lots East of Clayton College and $5000.00 cash or payments." (The buildings that housed Clayton College still stand at the corner of Martin Luther King Jr. Blvd. and Colorado Boulevard.) Titsa told me that, of the brothers, only John was literate. But I'm assuming that all the brothers eventually learned to read and write. The notation on this letter seems to indicate that George could write.

Mr. Wistner certainly could write. His handwriting is beautiful. It resembles Chinese writing - more drawn that written. And what phrasing - "your junk pile on Grant Ave"!

➢ LETTERS TO GEORGE FROM PRISONERS

In 1932, Chris Merkuri, a prisoner at the state prison in Canon City, Colorado, sent three letters to Brother George, care of The Royal Delicatessen in Denver. They were dictated to a third party and signed very painstakingly by "Chris". Each is prefaced by a page of printed rules and regulations from the prison, part of which states:

NOTICE No Food Packages received except for the holidays mentioned below.

TO THE PERSON RECEIVING THIS LETTER:

Do not come to visit prisoners on Sunday, Easter, Decoration Day, Fourth of July, Thanksgiving Day or Christmas. YOU WILL NOT BE ADMITTED

Parties corresponding with prisoners must observe carefully the following directions. Write plainly with pen and ink; confine yourself strictly to family and business matters. In directing letters put prisoner's name and register number plainly on envelope. ... All letters and papers are closely examined. Prisoners can write but once in two weeks, and can see friends not oftener than once each month. ...

TO PRISONER: Don't Interline. Put But One Line of Writing on Each Ruled Line.

The first letter from Chris is dated February 24, 1932:

Chris Mercuri		*To: George Allison*
Register No.	*16344*	*Royal Delicatessen*
		Denver, Colo.

Dear Friend George:

I have been down here over six months and have not heard from you yet. I am wondering if you are sick or what.

George, if you have time, I would like for you to come down for I want to talk to you on different matters.

Now if you come, there is no need of bringing anything, for we are furnished with all we need here. If you do come I wish you would come alone for I want to see you on confidential matters.

Give my best regards to your brothers and family.

Your friend,

C.K. Merkuri

p.s. I wish you would drop me a line and let me know if you are coming down and when? When you do come just ask for N. 16344.

Things don't seem to improve much for Chris after a visit by George. He's sounding sad and desperate in the special delivery letters he sends to George on September 27 and October 3, 1932.

Condensed, they convey the following:

As you know I have been bothering you all my life but please George you are the only one I can depend upon while here. It is very important that you come and see me one more time. You have gone thru a lot of expenses on my account, but I know you can come down before it is too late.

I have not been feeling good for the last three weeks for I have been spitting a little color. You must understand this will be my last letter to you. Please George, you must not fail me.

My best regards to John Allison and Earnest.

These letters left me feeling very bad for Chris. I hope things got better for him, but I have grave doubts that they did. And why did George, and then John, save his letters?

We can ask the same about another letter received by George, from another prisoner at Canon City. Louis Charos writes confidently in his own hand:

Name	Louis Charos	Name Mr. George Allison
Register No.	*11673*	*Street Royal Delicatessen*
		Denver, Colo.

June 23, 1933

Dear Friend Mr. Allison:

Thought I would drop you a few lines to let you know that I am enjoying the best of health and sincerely hope this finds you the same.

I also wish to advise you at this writing, that you may look forward to an early call from my attorney Mr. David and Mr. Gurmatakis of Walsenburg, Colo who have some plans to inform you of that I sincerely believe will greatly aid me in securing executive clemency from Gov. Johnson. And I would greatly appreciate it, if you could find it convenient to accompany them when they call on Father Isaias Paskopolus.

I have had an interview with the Warden Mr. Roy Best and he has very considerately informed me that he would gladly recommend me to Gov. Johnson for clemency. And I feel sure that he will act favorably in my behalf, and that you and the above mentioned gentlemen could greatly aid me, by assisting my attorney in bringing this matter before Gov. Johnson in the proper manner.

I really think that my long stay here should be considered enough punishment and quite sufficient to compensate for the crime I did commit in a moment of angry passion.

Thanking you in advance for this favor, and all past favors and assuring you that you will never regret any efforts you may take in my behalf. I remain wishing you the best of health and prosperity.

Yours Sincerely,
Louis Charos
Reg No 11673

I'm more optimistic about this prisoner's future. I think that he probably was granted executive clemency for the crime he committed "in a moment of angry passion".

I'm wondering why these men were writing to George. Perhaps he was something of an "elder" in the Greek community; and because of his business successes, was able to assist less fortunate Greek Americans. If so, his good works ended on May 1, 1935.

- **LETTER FROM GEORGOULA**

The widow Georgoula receives word once again that one of her sons has died. There's lots of documentation about Brother George's estate, but nothing explaining how he died. He was in his 60's by now, so perhaps he'd been in ill health.

But maybe not. In a sweet and sad and touching letter to her surviving sons, Georgoula speaks about some puzzling goings on. It's written in Greek, after being dictated by Georgoula "who can neither read nor write, and then translated into English. Therefore, it's a bit hard to follow:

7-6-35
Chrisafe

My loving boys I greet you we are well and wish the same for you

My Boys a few days ago I received the news of your Brother George's death and I have been delayed (slow) in writing you, therefore, we are endeavoring to make (draw up) the power of attorney but we haven't done so as yet

I am going to put (appoint) all three of you and you must be carefull not to quarrel and for John not to worry he will receive his, for he realy worked much for the house (meaning family) and paid off the debt therefore secase John. You must try with love the three of you (for us to receive them) meaning to receive the assetts of the estate. You have my blessings. Send me the letter they send George which grieved him. And if the Doctor Eorassimos sends you a letter do not accept it at all only Mazarakos has helped me. Write me why George worried and died The week I will send you the Power of Attorney and three of you must read the letter why doesn't my daughter in law write me when you receive the letter write to me at once.

Further I haven't anything to write I greet you your mother

Georgoula Krouskos

The English version is written on the back of what looks to be either an order or an inventory for the candy store. It lists, for example, "Chuckle - Orange Slices. 130 Count, Cassia Imperials - Red Hots. 5 lb Boxes, Family Size Nut Rolls - Johnson". I can picture the scene - the three brothers bending over the candy counter, pushing aside the Chuckles and Red Hots and struggling to translate the Greek they (or only John?) learned so many years ago.

Be carefull not to quarrel. ... You must try with love the three of you to receive the assetts. ... Send me the letter they send George which grieved him. ... Write me why George worried and died. ... why doesn't my daughter in law write me ... Further I haven't anything to write I greet you your mother

What were the contents of the letter that so upset George? And which daughter-in-law doesn't write? George never married, Nick died years ago and John was long since divorced, so it must be either the wife of Gus or Frank.

John was the executor of the estate. He saved all the legal documents concerning the settlement, which I'll detail further in the context of John's story. Suffice it to say, at this point, that he seems to have worked it out peaceably - at least to the satisfaction of his two remaining brothers. God knows what the women in Greece received. Probably not much - although it's at this time that John purchases the houses that the nieces write so poignantly about in the 1950's and 1960's.

George is buried at Fairmount Cemetery in Denver. His tombstone is large and quite impressive; and he shares it with John, who was buried there thirty years later. Two of Georgoula's "sons who are in America" lie side by side - in the soil of their adopted country.

Until last month, I knew very little about Argyros, or Frank, Krouskos. But during her recent visit (Oct-'94), Cousin Titsa told me many stories about her father - and their family. Once again, while paraphrasing her thoughts and memories as she related them to me, I've attempted to retain the flavor of her words:

Although John and Gus married American women, Brother Frank married a very beautiful and sophisticated woman from the city of Sparti (or perhaps it was Athens) in Greece. I'm not sure how this came about, except that he journeyed to his homeland sometime in his early thirties, married Anthenia, and returned to the U.S. soon thereafter. They settled for a short time in New York City, where the young bride had her first encounter with snow and freezing temperatures. Anthenia hung her laundry out the window to dry, and several hours later brought it in, stiff and frozen. She was very puzzled when she couldn't fold the clothes, and even more confused later, when she found puddles of water under the table where she'd left them. They weren't in New York long - they moved to Denver after a few months.

- **LETTER FROM CONGRESSMAN**

  A letter dated March 26, 1919 suggests that Brother Frank encountered some difficulties in obtaining his United States citizenship. It's written to my grandfather:

721 Equitable Building
Denver, Colo.
Frank Allison
Deportation

Mr. John Allison
Semper, Colo.

Dear Mr. Allen: -

The next time you are in town, please call and see me with regard to your brother's case. There are some suggestions I desire to make.

Representative William N. Vaile
Washington, D.C.

It seems like he would have been a settled, married, family man, by 1919. Why would he be having problems that might result in deportation at this late date? I found nothing to give me a clue, much less an answer.

Frank and Anthenia had four children - Georgia, Titsa, Stephen and Christopher. By custom the first boy and girl in each family were named after their grandparent, which was the case with Georgia and Steve (known in the family as Little Steve, to differentiate him from my father, Big Steve). Likewise, by custom, the next children were named after their aunts and uncles - but such was not the case with Titsa and her brother Chris.

No one wanted to be Titsa's godmother, because of the great expense and obligation involved. A very charismatic Greek holy woman was a guest at the Greek Orthodox Church in Denver at this time, and Anthenia asked her to be Titsa's godmother. She agreed, and that's how Titsa got her rather unusual name. It's the last word in the holy woman's title, which was something like "servant of the holy mother". I had a hard time following the story of how Chris got his name, but it involved a shrine for a child who had died earlier and it was a sad story.

All the children, except Titsa, learned to read and write Greek. By the time she, the baby, was ready to learn, the priest who taught the others was gone. (Therefore she wasn't able to help me much with all the letters and documents written in Greek.)

In public school, she and her siblings were teased and harassed because of their nationality and therefore their Uncle George sent them to parochial school.

My stepmother always told me that "the nuns practically raised" my father; and at the farm I'd came across his report cards from Loyola and Sacred Heart Catholic Schools. I'd wondered why, since neither he nor my grandfather were Catholic, he'd gone to these schools. Titsa has, I think, provided me with an answer. I'm assuming that, for the reasons mentioned above, George paid for my father to attend parochial schools also.

Brother George loved his Brother Frank's children very, very much, and when he died he "left everything to us". Steve, Titsa's brother, was to receive extra because he was the oldest, and the "heir". (He should have been called Big Steve then, right? But he wasn't.) The will, dictating such a distribution, mysteriously disappeared after George's death - and John and Gus forced Frank to split the inheritance equally.

Then, to make matters worse, John took a large diamond ring that had belonged to George and gave it to his daughter-in-law (the first of my dad's four wives?). Titsa was very sad to tell me about these happenings. She said that they were the beginning of hard feelings between the brothers, but that the information had never been passed on to her child, or to her brother's children.

I'm not quite sure what to make of the facts, as Titsa knows them. I could tell that she still felt some resentment, and that probably her family still did too. And I could tell that these feelings (at least hers) were heartfelt.

She went on to tell me of her skepticism about my father's sincerity at *his* father's funeral. She said that he had done very little for my grandfather while he was dying, but at his funeral was crying and moaning that he had "lost my right arm", etc. I don't remember this, so it must not have been too noticeable, but it shows her exasperation with her cousin Steve.

Anthenia's health was beginning to fail by the time her youngest daughter reached her twenties. At about this time, John's son was trying to find someone to care for his infant daughter. He asked Frank and Anthenia if they could take her in, if only for a while. But they had to decline, because of Anthenia's poor health. Perhaps the "hard feelings" from the previous decade also had something to do with this decision.

Once again, I'm so grateful to Titsa for taking the time to talk to me about our families. I also appreciate that she and her siblings didn't pass down to their children their resentments. After she left, I went to search for the papers that described the disposition of George's estate - to see if they would shed any light on these matters.

- **OFFICIAL AGREEMENT**

  I found an official agreement signed by the three remaining brothers, one paragraph of which reads:

Argyros is to receive $350.00, which is a debt to him from George before his death, and

FURTHER THEY AGREE AND ACCEPT that the candy store which is now located at the corner of 15th and Curtis St. in the City and County of Denver, State of Colorado, belongs to the brother Argyros (Frank) Krouskos, alias Allison, the valuation of which was paid to the brother George before his death.

Titsa was right about one thing - her father and his family received very little from George's estate. Whether they were denied their fair share or not, I can't know.

Although they're few - I have warm memories of Uncle Frank. He owned and operated the candy store, described above, until the 1960's. It was a scaled down version of George's "finest confectionery shop in the west", which had been founded there. He also owned and operated an adjoining parking lot. In "it's a small world" happening, it so happens that my first father-in-law worked there, parking cars, in the 1940's. He remembers Frank as being "a fine gentleman." I, too, remember him fondly. I loved to visit his store when I was a teenager. He was a soft-spoken, slightly built man, with fine, almost delicate features. In appearance, he didn't much resemble his brothers John and Gus. He was always gracious and generous with his time and his candy - the peanut brittle being the best I've ever tasted.

Figure 5.8 Gus, Chris and Frank Allison, 1947.

➢ FRANK'S OBITUARY

After my conversations with Titsa, I came across a copy of her father's obituary - which *I'd* put away in August of 1970. It clarifies somewhat my interpretations (I thought Titsa said her mother's name was Anthenia, for example) and contributes some additional facts about Frank and his life. It reads, in part:

> Allison, a Denver candy maker for 60 years, died Saturday at Davis Nursing Home after a brief illness.
>
> Allison was born in Sparta, Greece, on Aug. 8, 1881, and came to Denver in 1901. He joined his brother in operating a candy store at 1001 15th St. and their store was one of the city's largest during the 1920's. Allison retired and closed his store in 1963.
>
> He married Athanasia Teravolas on March 22, 1914, in Sparta.
>
> Allison was one of the founders of the Greek Orthodox Church in Denver.
>
> Survivors include two sons, Steve and Chris; two daughters, Mrs. Georgia Tzortzakis and Mrs. Titsa Diamantis; a brother, Gus, all of Denver; a sister, Mrs. Beneta Keriakoulia, Sparta, and five grandchildren.

At the farm, in a trunk filled with many photos, were studio photos of Chris, Georgia and Titsa, as young adults. There wasn't one of their brother, Steve.

- **PHOTO OF GEORGIA**

Figure 5.9 Georgia.

Georgia's shows a strong, healthy looking young woman who resembles her female relatives in Greece. Her beauty is clean and wholesome. It's signed,

Feb, 1938
To my loving cousin Steve
Love Georgia.

Georgia was married briefly, but has spent most of her life unmarried, as far as I know.

➢ PHOTO OF TITSA

Figure 5.10 Titsa.

A very lovely young woman looks out from Titsa's photo - sparkling eyes, perfect teeth, a charming smile and a head of thick dark hair.

Titsa married in 1950. She and her husband, he who wanted the photo of "the famous Greek politician", have enjoyed a long and lasting marriage. They have one son, Ted.

➢ PHOTO OF CHRIS

Figure 5.11 Chris.

From my parent's journals, I've learned that both brothers, Chris and Steve, served in The Second World War.

In his photo, Chris wears what I think is an air force uniform, because it has wings on it. It's unsigned.

He was a prisoner of war for some months in 1944 and received a citation upon his release.

During the two years that I lived with my father and Steppy in the 1950's, Chris, his wife Betty, and their four sons lived a few blocks from us. They were a loving, happy family. At the time, I often wished I could live with them.

➢ PHOTO OF STEVE

Figure 5.12 Little Steve and Friends.

I don't think their brother Steve ever married. He was sickly for some years, as I seem to remember. I never found an official photograph of him, but did find this snapshot. "Little Steve" is the man on the left.

And what about the youngest Krouskos brother, Gus? There were very few items at the farm that pertained directly to him - no photos, no legal papers, and no letters. He's not even mentioned in George's estate papers. His name appears occasionally in my father's journals, though. They were pretty close.

Uncle Gus was a large man with a shock of thick white hair. He was always smoking a cigar (see Figure 5.8). He was a very outgoing man - much more sociable than either John or Frank. But I think that maybe he was always struggling to be as "successful" as his older brothers were. Perhaps that's what led to some eventual problems he had with gambling and with the IRS. He was married to Micki - a dainty, red headed, kind hearted, Irishwoman. They didn't have any children. They were both always very good to me.

According to Frank's obituary, Uncle Gus was still alive in 1970. I don't know when he died, but I do know that gentle Micki lived as a widow, in Texas, for many years.

George, Nick, John, Frank and Gus left their mother Georgoula, their sister Venetta and their native land. They came to America hoping to improve their lives. And, they did.

"her sons, who are in America"

Nicholas' estate document - 1919.

CHAPTER 6

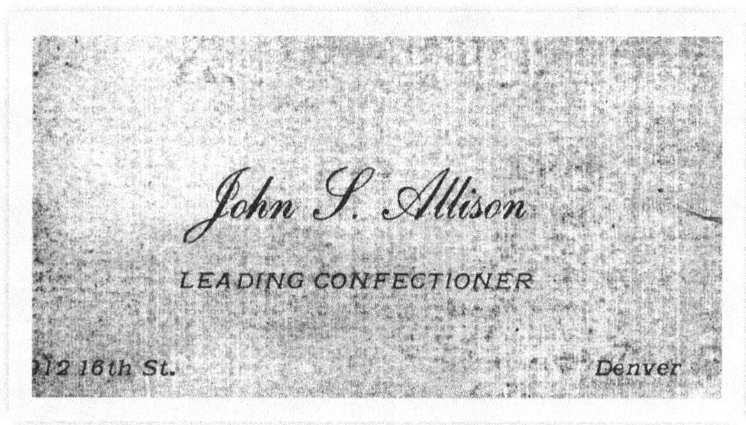

"John S. Allison, Prop'r"

After returning from his military service in Puerto Rico, my grandfather lived another 67 years.

Ninety years after his return, as I sorted through his boxes, trunks, suitcases and drawers of dusty memories, I found that I often had to revise what I thought I "knew" about his life. What follows is the revised story - compiled from the new information that emerged and from my memories of him in the winter years of his life.

- **CITIZENSHIP PAPERS**

Twenty-two year old John Allison was a war veteran in 1898, but he wasn't a citizen. Odd, but true. It wasn't until five years after his military duty that he received his citizenship. The papers read, in part:

> *Be it remembered, that on the seventh day of October in the year of our Lord One Thousand Nine Hundred and three personally appeared before the Hon. Ben B Lindsey Judge of the County Court of the City and county of Denver ... John Allison an alien of lawful age ... and to renounce and abjure all allegiance and fidelity to every foreign Sovereignty whatever, and particularly all allegiance which he may in anywise owe to George I, King of Greece ... IT IS THEREUPON .... ORDERED BY THE COURT, That the said John Allison be admitted to all and singular rights, privileges and immunities of a naturalized Citizen of the United States of America.*

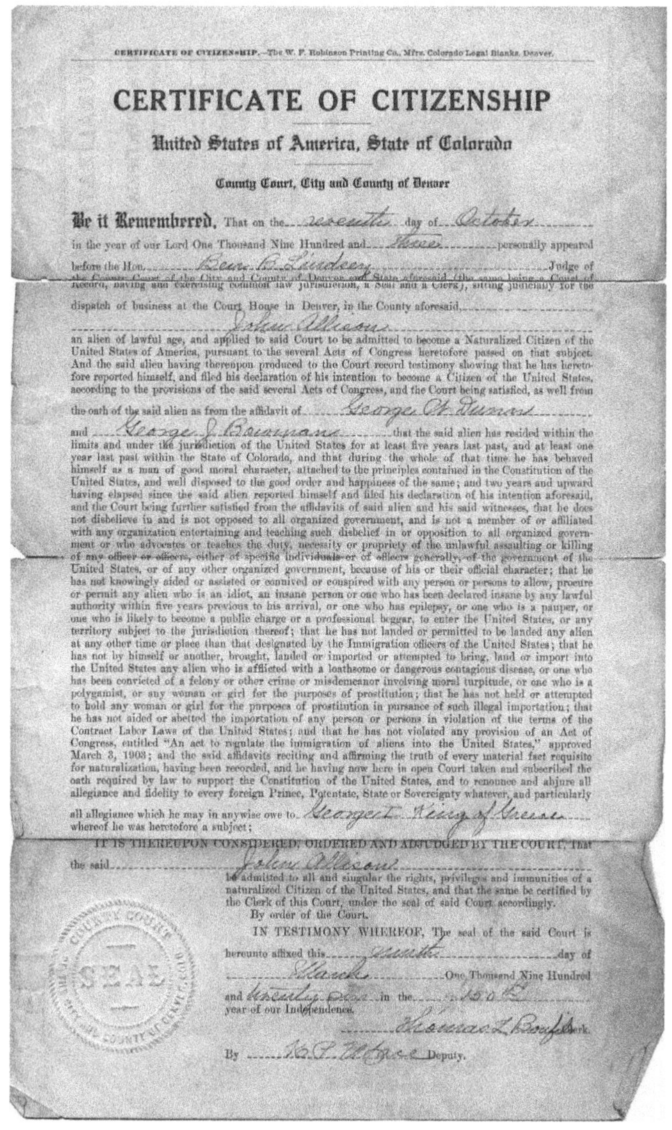

CERTIFICATE OF CITIZENSHIP.—The W. F. Robinson Printing Co., Mfrs. Colorado Legal Blanks, Denver.

CERTIFICATE OF CITIZENSHIP

United States of America, State of Colorado

County Court, City and County of Denver

Be it Remembered, That on the *seventh* day of *October* in the year of our Lord One Thousand Nine Hundred and *three* personally appeared before the Hon. *Ben B. Lindsey* Judge of the County Court of the City and County of Denver and State aforesaid (the same being a Court of Record, having and exercising common law jurisdiction, a Seal and a Clerk), sitting judicially for the dispatch of business at the Court House in Denver, in the County aforesaid, *John Allison* an alien of lawful age, and applied to said Court to be admitted to become a Naturalized Citizen of the United States of America, pursuant to the several Acts of Congress heretofore passed on that subject. And the said alien having thereupon produced to the Court record testimony showing that he has heretofore reported himself, and filed his declaration of his intention to become a Citizen of the United States, according to the provisions of the said several Acts of Congress, and the Court being satisfied, as well from the oath of the said alien as from the affidavit of *George A. Dumas* and *George J. Baumann* that the said alien has resided within the limits and under the jurisdiction of the United States for at least five years last past, and at least one year last past within the State of Colorado, and that during the whole of that time he has behaved himself as a man of good moral character, attached to the principles contained in the Constitution of the United States, and well disposed to the good order and happiness of the same; and two years and upward having elapsed since the said alien reported himself and filed his declaration of his intention aforesaid, and the Court being further satisfied from the affidavits of said alien and his said witnesses, that he does not disbelieve in and is not opposed to all organized government, and is not a member of or affiliated with any organization entertaining and teaching such disbelief in or opposition to all organized government or who advocates or teaches the duty, necessity or propriety of the unlawful assaulting or killing of any officer or officers, either of specific individuals or of officers generally, of the government of the United States, or of any other organized government, because of his or their official character; that he has not knowingly aided or assisted or connived or conspired with any person or persons to allow, procure or permit any alien who is an idiot, an insane person or one who has been declared insane by any lawful authority within five years previous to his arrival, or one who has epilepsy, or one who is a pauper, or one who is likely to become a public charge or a professional beggar, to enter the United States, or any territory subject to the jurisdiction thereof; that he has not landed or permitted to be landed any alien at any other time or place than that designated by the Immigration officers of the United States; that he has not by himself or another, brought, landed or imported or attempted to bring, land or import into the United States any alien who is afflicted with a loathsome or dangerous contagious disease, or one who has been convicted of a felony or other crime or misdemeanor involving moral turpitude, or one who is a polygamist, or any woman or girl for the purposes of prostitution; that he has not held or attempted to hold any woman or girl for the purposes of prostitution in pursance of such illegal importation; that he has not aided or abetted the importation of any person or persons in violation of the terms of the Contract Labor Laws of the United States; and that he has not violated any provision of an Act of Congress, entitled "An act to regulate the immigration of aliens into the United States," approved March 3, 1903; and the said affidavits reciting and affirming the truth of every material fact requisite for naturalization, having been recorded, and he having now here in open Court taken and subscribed the oath required by law to support the Constitution of the United States, and to renounce and abjure all allegiance and fidelity to every foreign Prince, Potentate, State or Sovereignty whatever, and particularly all allegiance which he may in anywise owe to *George I King of Greece* whereof he was heretofore a subject;

IT IS THEREUPON CONSIDERED, ORDERED AND ADJUDGED BY THE COURT, That the said *John Allison* be admitted to all and singular the rights, privileges and immunities of a naturalized Citizen of the United States, and that the same be certified by the Clerk of this Court, under the seal of said Court accordingly.

By order of the Court.

IN TESTIMONY WHEREOF, The seal of the said Court is hereunto affixed this *ninth* day of *March* One Thousand Nine Hundred and *twenty one* in the [illegible] year of our Independence.

[illegible] Clerk.

By [illegible] Deputy.

Figure 6.1 John's Citizenship Papers.

➢ PHOTO OF JOHN

I found an unusual photo of John at about this age (see image at beginning of this Section). It's on glass, rather than under glass, and is surrounded by an ornate, carved wooden frame. It's been broken, so the picture of John fits together like a puzzle constructed of pieces of shattered glass. You can tell that he's still a very young man. He's thin, and wears a suit, vest, high collared shirt and smart bow tie. He's cleanly shaved, except for a neatly trimmed mustache. He appears proud and confident. He must have looked something like this when he married, six years later, in 1909.

➢ PHOTO OF MARGARET

Figure 6.2 Margaret.

When I was young, I tried, and failed, to learn something about his wife, my grandmother. My father told me nothing, and I knew I shouldn't ask. Steppy told me that her name was Margaret, and that she'd "run away" when my dad was still a baby - because John was so "mean" to her. A few years later, she asked my father if she could give me a copy of a photo he had of his mother. He acquiesced, and she very thoughtfully did so. The lovely young woman in the picture looks to be about twenty years old. Her long, upswept hair seems more light brown than dark, and her bare shoulders are wrapped in a delicate wispy material. I hung this copy of a photo with those of the rest of the family, and silently told Margaret that she hadn't been completely forgotten.

➢ MARRIAGE CERTIFICATE

At the farm, after my father died, there was absolutely nothing to hint at her existence - until I unearthed (literally) this marriage certificate:

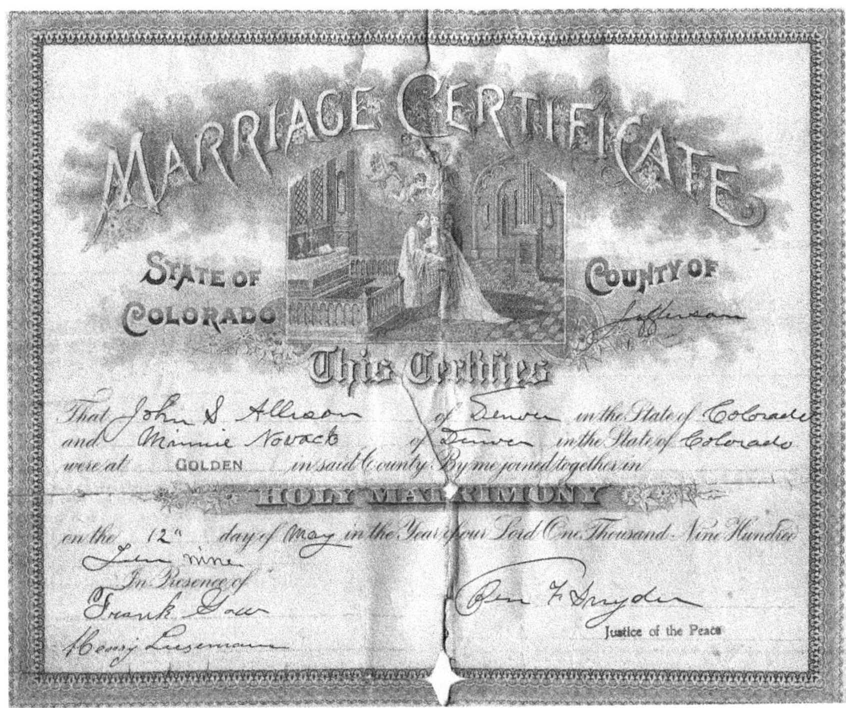

MARRIAGE CERTIFICATE

STATE OF COLORADO

COUNTY OF Jefferson

This Certifies

That John S. Allison of Denver in the State of Colorado
and Minnie Novack of Denver in the State of Colorado
were at GOLDEN in said County By me joined together in

HOLY MATRIMONY

on the 12th day of May in the Year of our Lord One Thousand Nine Hundred
[illegible] nine

In Presence of
[illegible]
[illegible]

[illegible]
Justice of the Peace

Figure 6.3 John and Minnie Marriage Certificate.

So, her name wasn't Margaret. Could Minnie be a nickname for Margaret? I don't think so. And what's the ethnic origin of the name Novack? My mom says it might be Jewish. People often assume that I'm Jewish - perhaps that's why. Steppy thought that she was German, but perhaps she was a Jewish person from Germany. Whatever. I'm just happy to know her name!

➢ NEWSPAPER CLIPPING

With the marriage certificate was a newspaper clipping, undated, with a photograph of my grandfather and an article entitled, "John Allison - Candidate fur Commissioner of Property." The photo shows a very prosperous looking gentleman who's beginning to thicken a bit around the middle. The article's written in German - note the "fur" of the title. Did Minnie write this news to her family in Germany, and did they have the information printed in their newspaper? Or perhaps Minnie subscribed to a German language newspaper here in Denver? I think there are some definite ties to Germany, at any rate.

> ### PHOTO OF MINNIE

John was 32 years old at the time of this marriage, but I'm assuming his wife was quite a bit younger. And with the marriage certificate and the news article, I found another beautifully matted and framed photograph of Minnie. In this one, also, she looks very young - certainly not more than 25 years old. She poses with her hands folded gracefully in her lap. She's of medium build and wears a strand of pearls and a watch. Her dress is an empire waist, with a scooped neck and ties at each shoulder. Her hair is light brown. She has a calm and composed demeanor. And so, it seems Grampa did save a few keepsakes from his marriage to Minnie.

> ### ENVELOPE WITH HAIR

During my visit with Titsa, some months after finding these things, I asked her if she could tell me anything about John's wife. She had never known Minnie Allison, but could remember hearing that she had beautiful hair - hair that people talked about long after she was gone. I bet that's whose hair is in that envelope marked "Millie", that I found at the farm. She thought that perhaps she had been an actress at the Tabor Theater in Denver.

However she came to be in Denver, she didn't stay long after becoming John's wife in 1909.

> ### BUSINESS LETTER

A letter that he sent early the next year, suggests that Brother John was financially secure at the time of his marriage:

Denver, Colorado
March 25, 1910

Frederick R. Ross Esq.,
715 17th Street
Denver, Colorado

My dear Sir:

I hereby transmit for your favorable consideration the following offer, viz:

I will lease stores at 1762 Curtis and 930 18th streets respectively, for a term of five years at the following rental:

First and second years, $150.00 per month, third year, $160.00 per month, fourth and fifth years $185.00 per month; and will pay you four month's rent ($600.00) in advance, beginning May 1st, 1910; and also the additional offer, at your option, of $200.00 per month for an additional five years, if accepted at this time.

In consideration that the following improvements be made to the said store at 1762 Curtis Street, viz:

A modern glass front; the floor to be lowered to the level of the sidewalk; an addition to rear of said store about 16 x 16 feet, one story in height, to connect the said stores, and papering or finishing same.

Hoping you will be able to accept my proposition, I remain,

Very Respectfully,
John Allison

One day, long after we thought we'd been through all the farm stuff, Ken found an another old wallet belonging to John. At one time, it must have been a very nice wallet. His name is engraved on the inside. But it's very well worn - in fact it's worn out. It's strange, though, because it contains many items you'd think he would have removed to place in his new wallet:

- **BUSINESS CARDS**

  There are several business cards that read:

Figure 6.4 Business Card.

Established 1893? John couldn't have started this business when he was seventeen years old. This must be the "Finest Confectionery in the West" that Brother George founded a year after he arrived in the United States. So now Grampa owns it - with a new slogan, "All Goods Fresh and Sweet". I love that. Evidently Mr. Ross accepted Mr. Allison's terms for rental of his properties.

- **PHOTO OF CHURCH FOUNDERS**

  Previously, I found a photo of Grampa, (right front, figure 6.5) at about this age, sitting with a group of men at a large table. Dressed in fine suits, each wearing a boutonniere, they look toward the camera over their glasses of beer. A large picture of the king and queen of Greece can be seen over their shoulders. Titsa said that this photo was taken at John's candy store at 17th and Curtis. The "table", which is covered with a white cloth, is, in fact, the marble block used to roll out candy. She said that, at this meeting, these men founded the Greek Orthodox Church of Denver, and that John became the first secretary.

Figure 6.5 Founders of the Greek Orthodox Church of Denver.

We now have a pretty good picture of Brother John, and his life, in March of 1910. He was a successful businessman, civic minded - running for the position of commissioner, and serving as the secretary of his church, and had been married ten months. A few months later, he became a father. John was 33 years old when his son was born on September 27, 1910. Minnie's age is unknown.

And so, now we can welcome Stephen John Allison - into the world, and into this story.

As a child, I never even knew the date of my father's birthday. And in my life, I never once celebrated the day with him. As an adult, I sent him cards on September 27th for nearly thirty years. Although they were seldom acknowledged, I think he was glad I remembered. I'd always marvel that, nine times out of ten, the weather on that day would be perfect - a quiet, yet glorious, autumn day. Surely, he was born on one of the most beautiful, golden days of the year. Nowadays, on his birthday, I sit for awhile at the cemetery, in the gentle September sun, and remember him.

The infant Steve's time with his mother was short. According to Steppy, because John was so mean (abusive?) to her, Margaret/Minnie had run away - *leaving her husband and child, shortly after Steve was born.* That always made me sad - that she'd left her child.

Therefore, I was happy to hear a different version from Titsa during her recent visit. First she asked if I'd found any papers with the name "Wilbur" on them. Of course I had - those letters from Ella Wagner, the one's that seemed to refer to my dad, but called him by many variations of Wilbur. Titsa explained that in the Greek tradition, John and Minnie's first son was named after his paternal grandfather. But Minnie had wanted to name him Wilbur - and although she was overruled, she always called him that. She went on to say that shortly after Steve/Wilbur was born, *Minnie took him, and ran away.* I'm so glad, for my dad's sake, to hear that she took her baby with her! I wonder if he ever knew.

Titsa showed me pictures of several Greek Americans she had known growing up. One was of Brother John's good friend, George Beskus. Titsa said that it was George Buskas who went after Minnie when she ran away - that he took Steve from Minnie and brought the baby back to John.

My father never mentioned his mother to me, except to say that she had run away when he was very young. But I don't think he ever saw her again.

Titsa told me that, once, "after the war", my father drove with her and her sister and brothers to a Greek American convention in Chicago. On the way, they stopped at a house "outside of Joliet", where he attempted to initiate contact with his mother. His cousins waited in the car while he went into the house. He wasn't gone long, and came back disappointed.

And Steppy told me that she and my dad went to California once, in the 1960's sometime, hoping to make contact with his mother. Steve spoke with her sister, who told him that Minnie couldn't and wouldn't see him - because she'd never told her second husband and children that she'd been previously married, much less had a child.

But, back to the wallet and its contents...

➢ IDENTIFICATION CARD

CERTIFICATE OF IDENTIFICATION No 48463

IDENTIFICATION COMPANY OF AMERICA

July 18-1912

PRES.

Name John S. Allison,

Denver, Colo.

32 Weight 185 Height 5'8"

Color of Eyes Brown Color of Hair Black

Identifying Marks None stated.

SIGNATURE

Figure 6.6 John's ID Card.

And so John becomes a single father, quite a unique situation in those days, I would think. An identification card dated July 18, 1912, found in the aforementioned wallet, gives us a physical description of him at the time. It says that John Allison is 5 feet 8 inches tall, weighs 185 pounds (he's gained a lot of weight in the last two years) and has black hair and brown eyes. It lists his age as 32. That's odd.

➢ OTHER BUSINESS CARDS

Other cards in the wallet are from a real estate agent, a lawyer, the camp commander of his old army unit, and one that seems to indicate that he had more than one candy store (see image at beginning of this Chapter).

➢ PROMISSORY NOTES

In the bill compartment were several notes concerning money borrowed from John, with interest rates ranging from 1% to 8%. They are very difficult to read, as the writers had a hard time forming and connecting the individual letters. Here's a sample few:

Nov. 4th 1910

On or before six months after date I promise to pay to the order of John S. Allison Two Hundred fifty Dollars... with the interest at the rate of 2 1/2 % per month.

D.J. LeMaster
2368 Emerson St.

August 9th 1911

On Demand after date I promise to pay to the order of John Allison Five hundred Seventy nine Dollars... with interest at the rate of 1% per month...

Tony Premountors

August 1st 1910

On demand for value received, I promise to pay to the order of George Psilas, the sum of thirty five Dollars, payable at First national bank of Denver, Colo. with 6% per annum interest payable annully

Nicholas C. Friar

The note above had been signed over to John Allison on October 25, 1912.

June 11, 1914

Two Years after date, for value received, we promise to pay to the order of John Allison seven Hundred and Twenty five Dollars. at 1761 Market Street, Denver with interest at the rate of 8% per annum, payable annually.

Nick Buskas
Gust Spiropulos

Who were these men? We know that Nick Buskas was John's friend – the person who retrieved baby Steve. Were the others less fortunate immigrants, perhaps, or businessmen and/or shopkeepers like the Allison brothers?

➢ PHOTO OF SHOPKEEPERS

Speaking of shopkeepers, I found, at the farm, a photo that gave me a real feel for the times, and the men in my grandfather's world at the time. Seven men are standing in front of a store. All but one wear long white aprons. The sign above the door says “Flood’s”. Sides of beef and plucked chickens hang in front of the store. Next door, round bushels hold many types of foods that are offered for sale. Two bicycles are parked on the street. In my mind, I can almost hear the street noise and distinguish the competing smells.

We’ve learned that John and George purchased “the farm” in 1916. George never lived there as far as I can tell, and I don’t think John moved there until the 1930s. They must have rented it out, or paid someone to farm it for them. And they stayed in town - probably appearing much like the men of commerce pictured in that photo.

➢ HUNTING AND FISHING LICENSE

The last item found in that dilapidated wallet, inserted behind a plastic window, was a hunting and fishing license issued to John on August 14, 1916. (I didn’t know they had plastic eighty years ago.) According to infomation on the back of this permit, which cost a dollar, he continues to gain weight, lose height, and be different ages:

1916
RESIDENT HUNTING AND FISHING LICENSE
STATE OF COLORADO
DEPARTMENT OF GAME AND FISH

This certifies that John Allison
whose signature appears hereon, and who represents himself to be a resident of Denver, Colorado, is entitled to hunt and fish in the State of Colorado in conformity with law, during the season of 1916.

This License is not good after December 31, 1916, and Must Be In Your Possession When Hunting or Fishing.

Date AUG 14 1916 C. O. B. Fraser
Paul Steuc
Commissioner

Issued by 1127 SEVENTEENTH ST.

At DENVER, COLORADO

$1.00 (See Other Side) Nº 59687

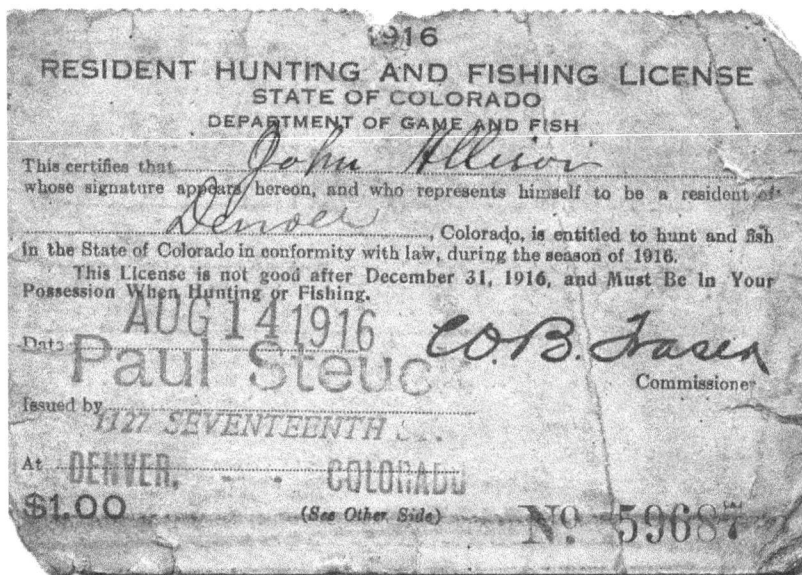

Figure 6.7 John’s Hunting License.

Age:	*38*
Color of Eyes:	*Dark*
Height:	*5’ 7*
Color of Hair:	*Dark*
Weight:	*219*
Sex:	*Male*

And then there was the Great War. I did find two 1917 Liberty Loan buttons, but interestingly, John saved nothing that even mentions this great catastrophe. (*We* now know that Brother Nick died on Armistice Day in 1918.)

Likewise, there are no references to, or reminders of, his son during all these years either. Steve is never mentioned in the many letters John receives from Lawrence Massachusetts, Camas Washington, The Silver Bow Candy Company in Butte Montana and Vin Place Nebraska - nor others from many other places in the United States. Perhaps the many letters received by John, written in Greek from Greece, contain some mention of his son.

My father first appears, among the farm stuff at least, when he's eight years old. Ella Wagner's daughter, Josephine, sends a Valentine postcard to "Master Wilburn Allison, 1009 15th St", in 1919. Someone saved it. And Ella invites him to spend Christmas of that year with her family. And then he disappears from this dusty chronology for the next four years.

I wonder what John and Steve's lives together were like during these years. Or were they even together? Steppy always told me that "the nuns raised your father", so I'm not sure. We know that John was becoming rather obese, which couldn't have helped his many physical ailments (as documented in his various veteran's claims). Did this make him grouchy - perhaps unable to care for his son? Was he so busy with his businesses that he had little or no time to spend with him? I don't know.

➢ SCRAPS OF PAPER

I found several scraps of paper, dated throughout April of 1920 that record refunds or mistakes made by sales persons as they rang up candy sales. I wonder why he kept these? Did he dock their pay? The largest amount is for $.40.

➢ HUNTING AND FISHING LICENSE

In 1922, Brother John purchased, and saved, another hunting and fishing license. It's issued from the Bilbrough-Jones Hardware Co., next door to his candy store, and records that he's 43 years old and now weighs 230 pounds.

➢ CAMPAIGN LITERATURE

John saved both Democratic and Republican campaign literature from the 1924 elections. I don't know how he voted.

➢ BROCHURES

In another box, I found two brochures that were very disturbing to me. The Nutshell Publishing Company in Chicago distributed them. One's entitled:

> Catholic, Jew, Ku Klux Klan
> What they believe!
> Where they conflict!

It claims to be:

> a work to outline impartially the fundamental difference of race, religion and belief that separate the groups, and to find out what each stands for in our material and spiritual development, and to present the accusations and replies of each side so that the reader may judge for himself the justice of each side.

It's a very subtle piece of propaganda for the Klan.

The other pamphlet,

> Ku Klux Klan
> Americans Only - On Guard

is anything but subtle:

> We honor the Christ as the Klansman's guide,
> And we hope in His service to so abide,
> That He will always be at our side,
> To approve our deeds, in love and pride..

It gets worse.

I'm ashamed that my grandfather possessed and saved these pamphlets. The KKK was a very powerful force in Denver during these years. My hope is that he was studying the propaganda in order to make an informed decision about it. He would seem a poor candidate to be a "knight". He wasn't Catholic, but being Greek Orthodox is close. And wouldn't a Greek be about as offensive to the Klan as a Negro or a Jew? If he had voted in 1924 for Al Smith, who was a Catholic, then I'd guess that he wasn't sympathetic to the KKK, or worse yet, a participant in it. But I don't know how he voted.

➢ LETTER TO JOHN

In this same year, John saved seven checks that were returned to him because of insufficient funds or closed accounts. They are almost falling apart from being handled and stamped again and again. He must have tried long and hard to collect his money. One is from Geo. B. Robinson and was returned because of a closed account. Mr. Robinson writes John three times apologizing for the problem and explaining his lack of payment. On October 20, 1924 he writes from the Hotel Henning in Casper, Wyoming:

I know you think I have died. Well, I have been almost dead, and yet I'm living. I am going East today, to the Hospital at Rochester, Minn. It will very likely be about November 15th to 20th before I get back, and will be in Denver then, when will reward you for your kind indulgence and patience. Will you kindly await until that time when I can see you. I have, to be frank, forgotten the amount, and anyhow I am afraid I would have to delay much the same.

In haste,
G.E. Robinson

Was Mr. Robinson going to the Mayo Clinic? It seems like people could "turn a phrase" much more effectively in those days. It's perfectly clear, when he writes that - "I have been almost dead, and yet I'm still living." - that this is a man with a very serious illness.

➢ SHAREHOLDERS REPORT

In this same year, John received a report to the shareholders of the Farmer's High Line Canal and Reservoir Company. In the spring, summer and autumn, this irrigation canal has always bestowed a quiet, dreamlike serenity to the farm. Two wooden bridges span it's flow, and leafy tall trees knit a canopy overhead. Birds, rabbits, raccoons and foxes live along its banks. In the past, the water was used for farming. Now it's used mostly for parks and golf courses. Even today, sitting on the bridge on a summer afternoon, looking down at the water or up at the trees, it's close to a perfect place to be. I wonder who was living at the farm, enjoying the banks of the Farmer's High Line Canal, in 1924? Not John and his thirteen year old son. They lived in the city.

Do you think this father and son spent much time together? Maybe they took trips together. I found a "Road and Recreation Map" of Oregon, dated this same year. It's very informative, especially about camping. One picture shows "a roadside camp in a cool forest". What an experience that would have been! Can you imagine the pristine splendor of these magnificent forests when they were first opened up to recreational use by newly built roads?

I hope they went there together. We'll never know, but somehow I doubt it. I don't think either of them ever took very many vacations - plus, I don't think my grandfather ever learned to drive.

- **LETTER FROM STEVE**

In 1925, Steve mailed his father a very touching letter. I'm assuming that, since he mailed it, he didn't live with his father. He was a student a Sacred Heart School at the time, so maybe he lived there, somehow. Remember? Steppy said he was "raised by the nuns"? Sixty-five years after it was written, I cried when I read it:

At School

May 7, 1925

My dear Father,

As Mother's Day is approaching I am inclined to think of my Mother. But I have not known a Mother. You have been both Father and Mother to me.

For the past fifteen years you have taken care of me and have tried to bring me up right and I in turn owe you a debt that cannot be paid. I am starting from this day to try to do better and not cause you trouble and worry. I am old enough now to know what I should do and ought to do, therefore it is my duty to do what is right and to obey you.

May God bless you, the best Father on earth.

Your Son
Steve Allison

Steve addressed the envelope to:

Mr. John Allison
824 18th Street
Denver, Colorado

Since we know that John was renting space at 930 18th St. in 1910, it seems that, in the interim, he's moved, expanded, or added another business next door.

After months as a paper sleuth, I've figured out that it was the "addition" choice above. John operated the Post Office Pool Hall, at 824 18th Street, during the late 1920's. It was across the street from the main Denver post office - a majestic building that, not only still stands, but also is still in use as a post office.

➢ POOL TABLES

In the barn, we gradually came to realize that the sections of beautiful wood that were surfacing were parts of two regulation-sized pool tables. And then we understood the purpose of the huge pieces of slate that we'd previously unearthed. On scorching hot summer days, we extricated these things out from under a half century of dirt and dust and carried them away to be stored. Ken, Chris and Jay probably moved close to a ton of slate alone. It almost broke their backs as well as their spirits. Eventually, we had them refinished, restored and reassembled. Throughout that summer we located and retrieved many other articles from the pool hall - billiard (ivory?) balls, ball storage cabinets, cues, cue holders, scoring apparatus (tabs on a wire thing), coat and hat racks and some very intriguing gaming devices.

Figure 6.8 Jay DeAndrea and the Post Office Pool Hall table (1991).

➢ RECEIPTS

Most of the business papers, as opposed to the personal papers, that we encountered at the farm pertained to this pool hall. I discovered hundreds of receipts related to its operation. After the first time through them, I wrote in my journal:

What a job! For six hours I sat on the floor trying to sort through this box of Grampa's papers. I did get the receipts in order, but didn't even start on the bank statements and canceled checks. Minute pieces of rubber from the original rubber bands cover the carpet - along with dirt, mouse droppings, disintegrating paper (because the mice have been chewing on these things) and hundreds of intact insect skeletons. What a mess!

Many of the receipts were in a leather three-ring binder. Inside the front cover, someone wrote with chalk, "This book is borrowed and practically stolin from P.S." What does that mean?

A few individual examples afford us an impression of the business and of the times.

The Anti-Dust Chemical Company *2861 Walnut Street, Denver*	*$3.25*
Colorado Coca-Cola Bottling Co. *1024 Cherokee St., Denver*	*$2.80*
Cordove Cigar Company *1354 Larimer Street, Denver*	*$10.52*
Cuban Cigar Company *1812-14-16-18 Market St., Denver*	*$6.40*
Denver Nut and Candy House *2611 Josephine Street, Denver*	*$0.75*
General Cigar Co. *1613 Larimer Street, Denver*	*$21.80*
Gump Glass Company *1509 Cheyenne Place, Denver*	*$5.75*
The Italian-American Pub Co.	*$1.75*
Joseph DeRose Real Estate *Rent Sept. 1 - Oct. 1, 1927* *604 Central Savings Bank Building, Denver*	*$225.00*
Joseph DeRose Real Estate (Water Tax) *604 Central Savings Bank Building, Denver*	*$7.00*
LaDez Cigar Co. *2501 Fifteenth Street, Denver*	*$3.68*

The L. Grauman Company *Pool and Billiard Tables and Supplies,* *Iceless Soda Fountains and Carbonators* *1431-39 15th at Blake, Denver*	*$11.60*
Leader Cigar Factory *2950 Yates St., Denver*	*$3.40*
Loose-Wiles Company Makers of Fine Confections	*$4.90*
Metropolitan Cigar Co. *Larimer at Speer Boulevard, Denver*	*$10.54*
The Morey Mercantile Co. Wholesale Grocers *Denver, Colo.*	*$32.09*
The Mountain States Telephone and Telegraph Co.	*$3.94*
National Biscuit Company *1852-1862 Blake Street, Denver*	*$1.63*
The Niles & Moser Cigar Co. *17th and Glenarm Streets, Denver*	*$14.25*
Public Service Company of Colorado *Gas and Electric Building, Denver*	*$25.35*
Rothenberg & Schloss Cigar Co. *Corner 16th and Glenarm Streets, Denver*	*$8.50*
The Standard Bottling Co. *1200 13th Street, Denver*	*$16.50*
The Tivoli-Union Company *1336-1348 Tenth St., Denver*	*$14.80*
United States Tobacco Company	*$4.20*
The Winter Cigar Company *1816 California Street, Denver*	*$3.52*

Although I'm sure John sold a lot of cigars, the above figures are a bit misleading. The actual sales invoices from the cigar companies list many other items - Planters peanuts, Baby Ruth and Hershey candy bars, gum and cakes for example.

But there's nothing misleading about the Tivoli Union figures. Each of the 57 invoices for that company lists twenty, or more, cases of beer received by John Allison, Steve Allison or sometimes R. Javorina.

Last year the Rocky Mountain News printed the following picture, depicting how downtown fires attracted crowds. In the photo, you can see the Post Office Pool Hall.

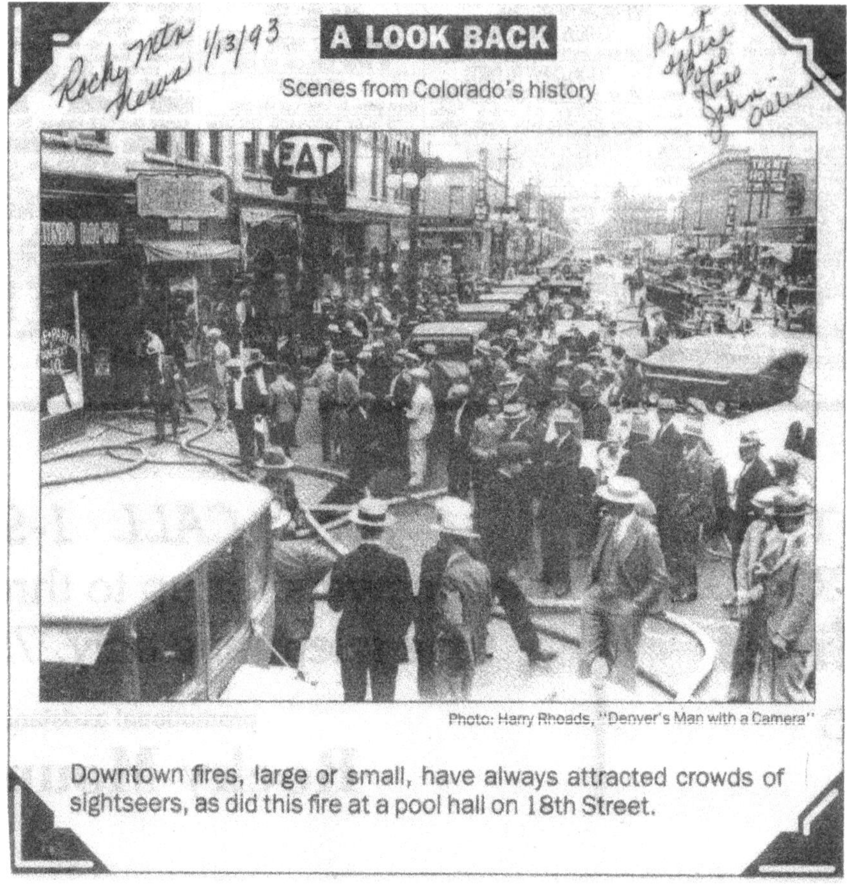
Rocky Mtn News 1/13/93

A LOOK BACK

Scenes from Colorado's history

EAT

Photo: Harry Rhoads, "Denver's Man with a Camera"

Downtown fires, large or small, have always attracted crowds of sightseers, as did this fire at a pool hall on 18th Street.

Figure 6.9 Rocky Mountain New article about Pool Hall fire.

It sounds like a fun place - with lots of cigars, beer, junk food and camaraderie. (Jay has always wanted to own a sport's bar, where he'd feature "Stump Jay - Sports Trivia Night". Perhaps it's in his blood.)

➢ CANCELLED CHECKS AND BANK STATEMENTS

With these invoices were canceled checks and bank statements for the three corresponding years - 1926, 1927 and 1928. The twelve packets of each year were neatly tied together with string. It's pretty obvious from the canceled checks that English was John's second language. For example, he wrote one to the "Colorado Cocolala Bottling Co".

➢ SCHOOL NOTEBOOK

But this is puzzling. Was he also taking classes at this time? A school notebook surfaced from amidst all these business papers. It's filled with class notes, rough drafts of writing assignments, and vocabulary lists - "hatches, ambulatory, font, lampooning", for example.

The subject matter of the writing assignments seems extremely advanced - especially for someone who wrote "Cocolala". In one, he writes of "Austin's self denial and seclusion from the world with the object of promoting the soil", and includes a quote from Virgil showing that "early latin writers had exagerated ideas of what grafting could be done".

This is some pretty serious writing! But it's also in John's handwriting - I think. I'm confused.

➢ FOUR LETTERS

And here are four letters, "asking" for payment, from the National Pepsin Gum Co. in San Francisco. There must have been a misunderstanding about what was purchased and for how much. On May 11, 1927, he received the following letter, addressed to the Post Office Pool Hall.

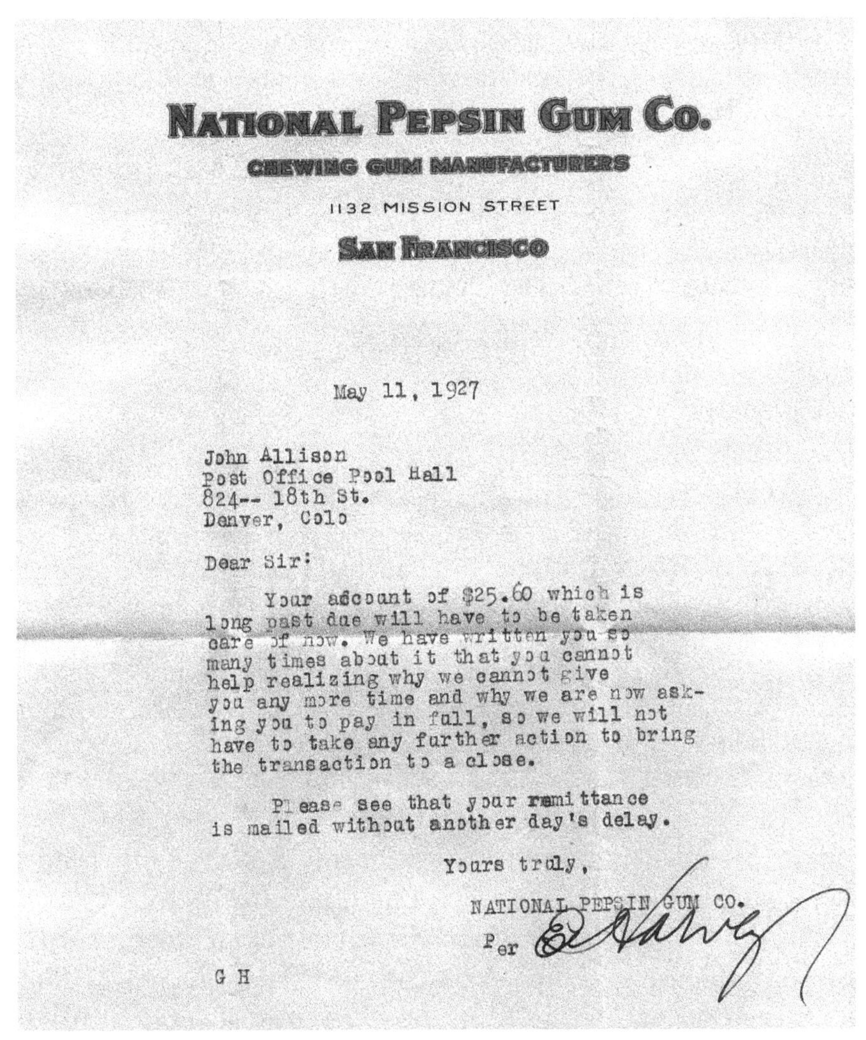

NATIONAL PEPSIN GUM CO.
CHEWING GUM MANUFACTURERS
1132 MISSION STREET
SAN FRANCISCO

May 11, 1927

John Allison
Post Office Pool Hall
824-- 18th St.
Denver, Colo

Dear Sir:

Your account of $25.60 which is long past due will have to be taken care of now. We have written you so many times about it that you cannot help realizing why we cannot give you any more time and why we are now asking you to pay in full, so we will not have to take any further action to bring the transaction to a close.

Please see that your remittance is mailed without another day's delay.

Yours truly,
NATIONAL PEPSIN GUM CO.
Per

G H

Figure 6.10 Collection Letter from National Pepsin Gum Co.

The June 9, 1927 letter informs Mr. Allison that:

> *This is the sixth time we have asked you about that little bill of $25.60 which you have owed us for several months. Your failure to pay shows that you are not taking care of your honest obligations, so there now remains no other course for us to pursue but to protect our interests by instructing our attorneys to take prompt action.*

By July 12, 1927 the account had been turned over to the International Collection Service. The bill must have paid at that point, because that's the last of this correspondence. But I'm sure it galled John to pay it. He saved his original contract with the Pepsin Gum Co., indicating, I think, that he understood the specifics differently than did the gum company.

Since this is the only letter asking for delinquent payment in all these sixty years of business papers, I think that the Allison brothers must have been responsible and reliable businessmen.

➢ OTHER CORRESPONDENCE

Other business correspondence received by John during the 1920's, and throughout the 1930's, make clear that he continued to be heavily involved in stocks and real estate – besides candy and billiards.

➢ PERSONAL LETTERS

He also received many personal letters and photos from family and friends during these years. Someday I'll have the numerous letters written from Greece, in Greek, translated. I would guess that they hold more stories from the hearts and souls of the Krouskos women. From *within* the United States he continues to receive letters from fellow Spanish American War veterans - including many from the very likable J.H. Caloon, whom we met earlier. Another friend sent him a postcard showing the very elegant "Confectionery Section of Marshall Field & Co. Retail, Chicago". It was banded together with several of the Allison Confectionery Store postcards - which picture a wonderland of candy no less elegant and enticing than the one at Marshall Field.

Although it seems that John was certainly a successful proprietor by now, I'm not sure he was as successful as a parent. Before 1926, when he received the above mentioned Mother's Day letter from Steve, there's not one indication from the things John saved, that he even *had* a child. (I'm assuming it was Steve that saved the Valentine card from Josephine Wagner back in 1919.)

➢ LETTER

But one piece of correspondence gives me reason to hope that John at least *tried* to be a good parent. It's a letter, dated May 19, 1927, explaining that he would be receiving a free book from the Grolier Society, as an enticement to buy *The Book of Knowledge Encyclopedia.* Perhaps he considered purchasing the set for his teenaged son - he must, at least, have considered it, since he kept this letter.

Thirty years later, Steve will buy a set for his child - and it could be argued that these books, literally, saved her sanity.

➢ POSTCARD

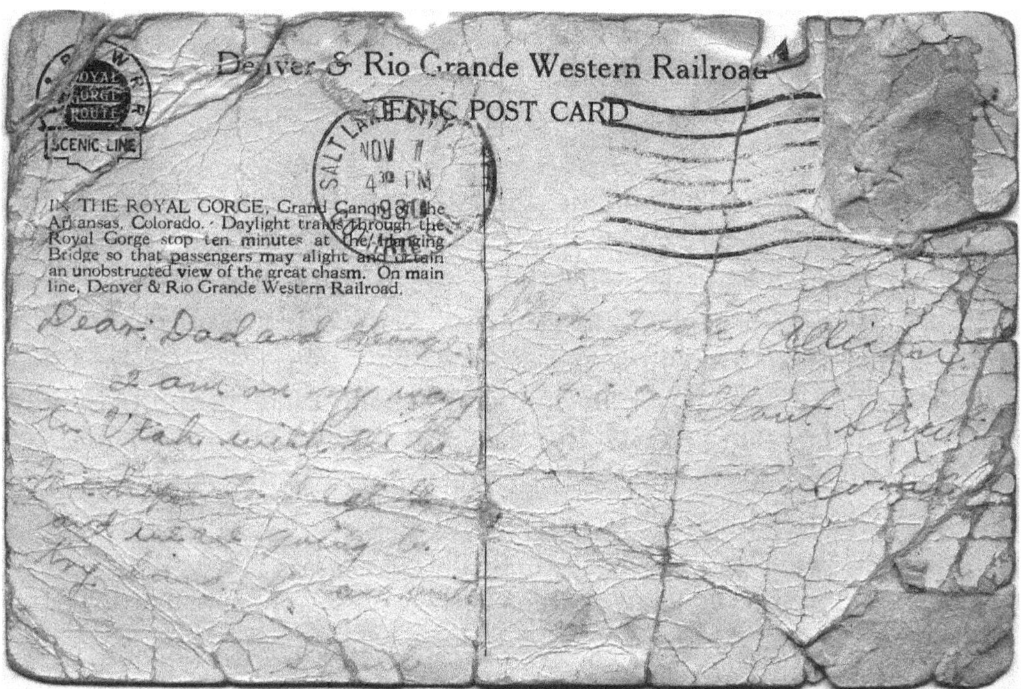

Figure 6.11 Postcard from Steve.

On an autumn day in 1930, John received a postcard, from Steve, that must have meant a lot to him. He not only kept it, but I think he must have carried it around with him for a good length of time - since it's very tattered and worn. Perhaps he even showed it to his family and friends. I hope so. The card, posted from the Royal Gorge in southern Colorado, "spanned by the highest bridge in the world", reads:

Dear Dad and George,

I am on my way to Utah with the team. We hope to beat them, and we are going to try hard.

Please write.
Steve

In high school, Steve excelled in football and baseball; and because of these skills had been offered a scholarship to West Point. Since it was out of state, John refused to let him go. Steve's heart was broken, and it remained broken. It's the only thing my father ever told me about his youth - and he told me the story more than once. He rightfully felt that his father didn't appreciate his athletic talents, and had robbed him of the chance to receive a fine education, for free, while utilizing them.

He accepted instead an athletic scholarship to Colorado College in Colorado Springs. As a sophomore member of that school's football team, he was travelling to Utah for a game when he penned this postcard to his dad and uncle. (And as you'll see, he often wrote to his uncle from college, imploring him to "please write" - meaning, please send money.)

I know that Grampa never understood the importance of sports to Steve, but I think the fact that he saved this postcard shows that he loved him. Like most of us, he probably did the best he could as a parent. If he had, indeed, left home at thirteen – what did he know about being a father? Plus, it must have been difficult, then as now, being a single parent.

I wonder if Steve ever knew that his dad had saved this postcard.

"John S. Allison, Prop'r"

John's business card - circa 1910.

CHAPTER 7

"all his American life"

Ninety-six year old Georgoula, was named "sole heir" when her eldest son, George, died in 1935. Her surviving sons felt that she would need some "guidance" in settling the estate, and decided that John should travel to Greece for this purpose.

➢ JOHN'S LETTER TO HIS BROTHERS

On the day of his departure, he writes this very specific letter to his brothers:

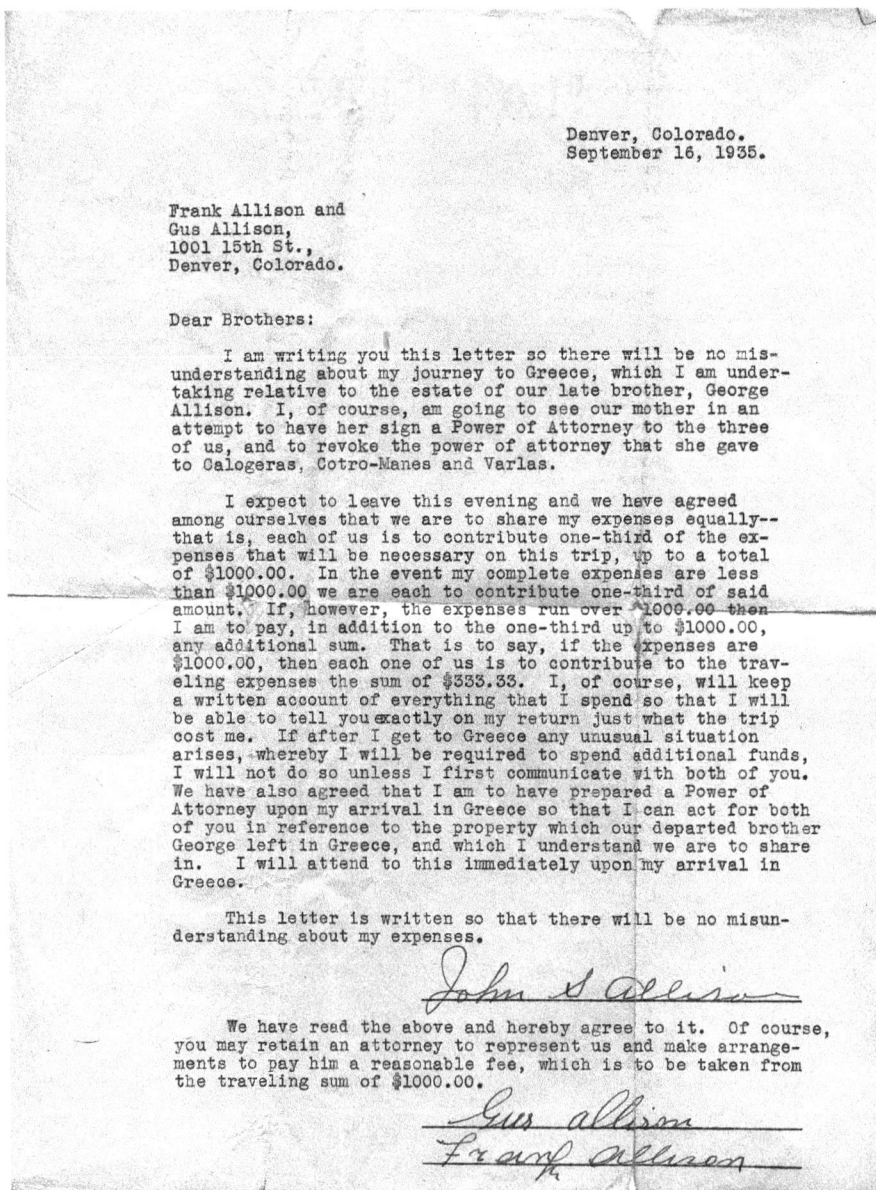

Denver, Colorado.
September 16, 1935.

Frank Allison and
Gus Allison,
1001 15th St.,
Denver, Colorado.

Dear Brothers:

I am writing you this letter so there will be no misunderstanding about my journey to Greece, which I am undertaking relative to the estate of our late brother, George Allison. I, of course, am going to see our mother in an attempt to have her sign a Power of Attorney to the three of us, and to revoke the power of attorney that she gave to Calogeras, Cotro-Manes and Varlas.

I expect to leave this evening and we have agreed among ourselves that we are to share my expenses equally--that is, each of us is to contribute one-third of the expenses that will be necessary on this trip, up to a total of $1000.00. In the event my complete expenses are less than $1000.00 we are each to contribute one-third of said amount. If, however, the expenses run over $1000.00 then I am to pay, in addition to the one-third up to $1000.00, any additional sum. That is to say, if the expenses are $1000.00, then each one of us is to contribute to the traveling expenses the sum of $333.33. I, of course, will keep a written account of everything that I spend so that I will be able to tell you exactly on my return just what the trip cost me. If after I get to Greece any unusual situation arises, whereby I will be required to spend additional funds, I will not do so unless I first communicate with both of you. We have also agreed that I am to have prepared a Power of Attorney upon my arrival in Greece so that I can act for both of you in reference to the property which our departed brother George left in Greece, and which I understand we are to share in. I will attend to this immediately upon my arrival in Greece.

This letter is written so that there will be no misunderstanding about my expenses.

John S Allison

We have read the above and hereby agree to it. Of course, you may retain an attorney to represent us and make arrangements to pay him a reasonable fee, which is to be taken from the traveling sum of $1000.00.

Gus Allison
Frank Allison

Figure 7.1 John's letter to his brother.

Twenty years later, in the 1960s, the nieces will be writing desperate letters to their Uncle John regarding the properties mentioned in this letter. The title I found at the farm, for one of these houses, lists only John. Therefore, I'm assuming that after the relatives in Greece were eliminated from any share of ownership, he must have then purchased his brother's shares.

In yet another box from yet another building at the farm, I unearthed several items that helped clarify the logistics of this trip.

- **PASSENGER LIST**

  John Allison is listed as a passenger in the remains of a small booklet entitled, "Tourist Class Passengers List – R.M.S. BERENGARIA". Mice have eaten about a third of this book, but many interesting facts and figures are still legible.

- **SHIP'S NEWSPAPER**

  The ship's on-board newspaper, "The Ocean Times", was published on the day of John's departure - September 21, 1935.

- **SHIP'S PROGRAM**

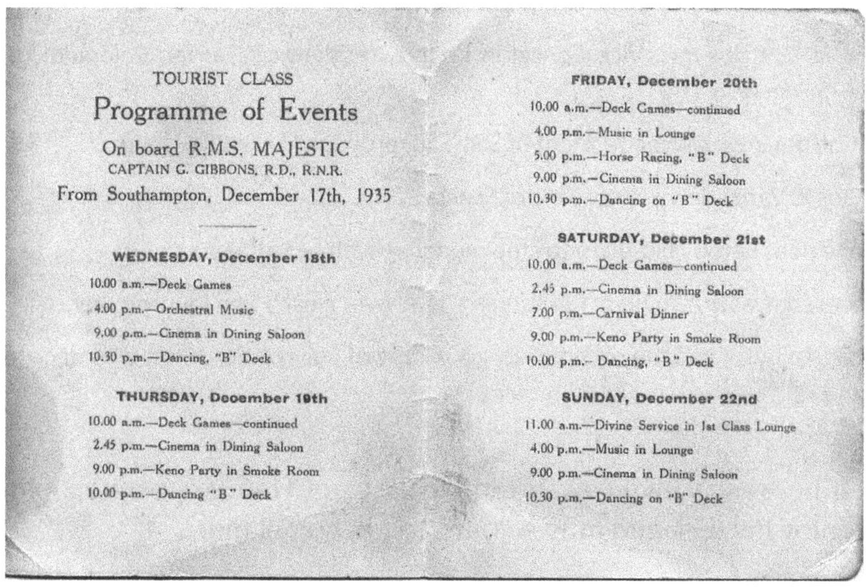

TOURIST CLASS
Programme of Events
On board R.M.S. MAJESTIC
CAPTAIN G. GIBBONS, R.D., R.N.R.
From Southampton, December 17th, 1935

WEDNESDAY, December 18th
10.00 a.m.—Deck Games
4.00 p.m.—Orchestral Music
9.00 p.m.—Cinema in Dining Saloon
10.30 p.m.—Dancing, "B" Deck

THURSDAY, December 19th
10.00 a.m.—Deck Games—continued
2.45 p.m.—Cinema in Dining Saloon
9.00 p.m.—Keno Party in Smoke Room
10.00 p.m.—Dancing "B" Deck

FRIDAY, December 20th
10.00 a.m.—Deck Games—continued
4.00 p.m.—Music in Lounge
5.00 p.m.—Horse Racing, "B" Deck
9.00 p.m.—Cinema in Dining Saloon
10.30 p.m.—Dancing on "B" Deck

SATURDAY, December 21st
10.00 a.m.—Deck Games—continued
2.45 p.m.—Cinema in Dining Saloon
7.00 p.m.—Carnival Dinner
9.00 p.m.—Keno Party in Smoke Room
10.00 p.m.—Dancing, "B" Deck

SUNDAY, December 22nd
11.00 a.m.—Divine Service in 1st Class Lounge
4.00 p.m.—Music in Lounge
9.00 p.m.—Cinema in Dining Saloon
10.30 p.m.—Dancing on "B" Deck

Figure 7.2 Ship's Program.

Returning home, a "Programme of To-day's Events – Cunard, White Star", lists December 17, 1935 as the departure date from Southampton. Mr. Allison could enjoy a visit to the "Cinema in dining Saloon" or "Dancing on B Deck", among other activities.

➢ **SHIP'S NEWSPAPER**

The ship arrived in New York on December 22, 1935, according to another copy of "The Ocean Times".

Brother John's visit home to Greece lasted about three months. During this time he succeeded in having his mother removed as executor of the estate.

➢ **ESTATE DOCUMENTS**

The original documents - revoking the power of attorney that she had somehow relinquished to two lawyers and an official, and conferring it to her sons - are written in Greek, and stamped and sealed repeatedly. The English translations tell us who these men were, but not why they had been appointed. A sampling of certain telling phrases, however, suggest that dear Georgoula had probably signed her X to anything put before her.

In Sparta, this Saturday the 12th of October 1935, in my Office of Notary Public located in the studio of Icaonis Saraciou Katoiotis near Aghessiooce Street...

Appeared Georgia widow of Stavros Krouskos, nee Hioolaou Natiozou, housewife without social profession, resident of Chryasafi and Agriana ....

she does hereby cancel and revoke any and all authority and power conferred by her upon

(1) Nikias C. Calogeras, Vice Consul in Charge, resident of Denver, Colorado, United States of America,

N.G. Cotromanes, lawyer, resident of Sail (Salt, probably) Lake City Utah

Nicolaos X. Varias, lawyer, resident of Sparta ...

And she does hereby bid them to stop meddling with her affairs...

The present was drawn up at her request, read over clearly and loudly to her...

And signed by all and me except Georgia widow of Stavros Krouskos, who declared to be illiterate.

When he wasn't involved in the legalities of George's estate, John found time to enjoy his first and only sojourn to his homeland.

➢ **ENVELOPE WITH PHOTOS**

A large envelope contained several photos that give some idea of people and places that he visited during these three months, including:

1. Middle-aged Georgoula, healthy and robust (photo at the beginning of Chapter 5).
2. Much older Georgoula sits with John and her only daughter (I *think* it's Venetta) in another.

Figure 7.3 Venetta, Georgoula, John.

3. Venetta and Catherine or Joanne.

Figure 7.4 Venetta (seated) and Joanne or Catherine.

4. A man in traditional Greek dress – a skirt and tights like those still worn by the guards at the Tomb of the Unknown Soldier in Athens.
5. A very dapper looking man with a handlebar mustache, wearing a suit and a cap.
6. The Hotel de Ville in Sparta.
7. This dusty envelope also contained a small photograph of John, taken, I believe, for his passport. The photographer at the Morganti Studio captured the image of a well dressed, mature gentleman of about 60 years of age. His full head of hair and his mustache are still black. Since I found, also, an enlarged and framed copy of this photo, I think that Grampa must have been pleased with how he looked in it.

Figure 7.5 John's passport photo.

➢ LETTERS FROM AMERICA

John received several letters from his brothers and his son during his overseas stay. Many were opened and then resealed with a "opened and examined by …" sticker, because of the civil unrest in Greece at the time. Steve's letters will appear later, in his part of this story, but two points are worth mentioning here. He says that he misses visiting his dad at the farm, so John must have been living there by 1935; and he mentions several times that John has failed to write - things hadn't changed much, it seems.

Tucked away, with obvious care in an old trunk in the attic of the farmhouse, we found an article from the December 30, 1935 issue of *The Denver Post*, concerning John's visit to Greece.

A prominent photo of John, accompanied by the words, "Says Greek King Won't Last.", heading the article. The caption under it reads, "John Allison, retired Denver manufacturer, who returned Sunday after four months in his native Greece. He predicted eventual collapse of the newly-revived Greek monarchy."

The article, in its entirely reads:

COLORADO MAN AMAZED TO FIND COPY OF DENVER POST IN GREECE

Retired Candymaker Returning From Visit Abroad Predicts Short Life for Monarchy in Native Land; Saw Signs of Discontent.

John Allison, retired Denver candy manufacturer, returned to his farm home near Broomfield Sunday with two dominating impressions from a visit to Greece. It had been his first visit to his native land in forty-seven years.

'The newly revived monarchy in Greece is not going to last long.' he said. That's the first impression.

'I found a copy of THE DENVER POST in a barber shop in the province of Sparta.', he declared. 'THE POST certainly covers the world.' That's the second impression.

Allison left Broomfield four months ago. He had heard that his mother, who is 96, was seriously ill. He had not seen her since coming to America forty-seven years ago.

COULDN'T FIND BOYHOOD SCENES

'It was a great relief to find she was well,' he said, 'but then it was a shock when I failed to recognize her. Everything was different. I had so many pictures in my mind of my boyhood home, but I couldn't find the scenes. I was away too long.'

Allison was in Greece during a most significant period in the country's history, the return of the monarchy after many years of democratic government.

'There was no doubt that the people wanted King George back even before the plebiscite was held.', he stated. 'And they are happy now that they have their king. But I do not think it will last, even tho the king will do his honest best.'

'They have had a taste of democracy, a sour taste perhaps, but it whetted the appetite. Even now, as King George liberally recalls statesmen who originally agitated against royalty, there are rumblings of discontent and the divisions between monarchists and democrats are reappearing.'

GREEKS LIKE PICTURES FOUND IN POST

Allison called at the offices of THE POST to order several copies of the New Year edition for his relatives in Greece.

'I'll never forget walking into a barbershop and finding a Sunday POST on the table,' he said. 'They told me they liked the pictures, and they had a picture of Prizefighter Carnera, clipped from THE POST hanging on the wall.'

With the exception of three years, during which he served in the Spanish-American war, Allison has lived all his American life in Colorado.

Says Greek King Won't Last

JOHN ALLISON,
Retired Denver manufacturer, who returned Sunday after four months in his native Greece. He predicted eventual collapse of the newly-revived Greek monarchy.

"I'll never forget walking into a barbershop and finding a Sunday POST on the table," he said. "They told me they liked the pictures, and they had a picture of Prizefighter Carnera, clipped from THE POST, hanging on the wall."

With the exception of three years, during which he served in the Spanish-American war, Allison has lived all his American life in Colorado.

Figure 7.6 Newspaper Articles.

What a great article!

But it leaves me wondering about a few things. First, it states that John left home forty-seven years before, which would have been in 1888. The papers from Ellis Island record that Brother George entered the United States in 1892. Did Brother John, then, come to America *before* George? And does that mean, then, that *he* was the older of the two?

Secondly, The Post says that, "Allison has lived all his American life in Colorado." He enlisted in the army in 1898 from Denver Colorado, but before that didn't he live in New York (selling chewing gum on the street corners)? For perhaps many years? If so, he didn't mention the fact to the reporter.

And lastly, the vocabulary and language in general, don't sound much like my grandfather. He wouldn't use words like 'revived', 'whetted', or 'liberally', for example. The paper presented his words as direct quotes, but surely they were often paraphrases. Even so, the piece gives us a touching, but accurate I think, picture of John and his return to his homeland.

A letter written by Brothers Frank and Gus, soon after George's death, suggests that John felt some real concern about receiving his fair share from the estate. It's addressed to the public administrator in charge of the proceedings and reads, in part:

> You are to recognize the claim of John Allison for the sum of $2500 represented by a check in the deposit box of the above decedent, and to sell the one half interest in the Jefferson County farm to John Allison for said sum of $2500.
>
> You are to recognize the claim of Frank Allison for $350 for monies advanced and to pay the same in cash.
>
> You are also to recognize the claim of John Allison to the lots in North Denver which belonged to him, but were in the name of the above decedent, and you are also to recognize the claim of John Allison to the diamond ring which is in the safety deposit box of the above decedent.

So, John somehow received $2500.00 from George's estate and then used it to purchase George's half of the farm. Hmm ... That's strange. And John now owns outright the North Denver lots that were in George's name. *And* there's the diamond ring that Titsa spoke about during her recent visit – the one John allegedly gave to his daughter-in-law. Titsa felt that her uncle shouldn't have ended up with it, but according to this paper, her father agreed that John should have it. But did he deserve to have it? Obviously, some thought not.

In my father's papers, not my grampa's, I found the final settlement of George's estate. As you can see, John's claims were acknowledged and affirmed. But, I have an uneasy feeling about how this was accomplished. Certain disclaimers within the document lead me to believe that might have forced his mother's hand in this regard. I've included here a few brief passages from this very lengthy record:

WHEREAS, George Krouskos Allison, died on or about the 1st day of May, 1935, at the City of Denver, State of Colorado, and,

WHEREAS, decedent is survived by his mother Georgoula, widow, Stavrou Krouskou, residing at the Village of Agrianon, Sparta, Republic of Greece, and the following brothers and sister; John Stavrou Krouskou, Frank Stavrou Krouskou, and Gus Stavrou Krouskou, all residents of the City of Denver, State of Colorado, and Veneta George Kryiakoulia, Nee, Veneta Stavrou Krouskou, resident of the Village of Agrianon, Sparta, Republic of Greece, and,

WHEREAS, the said Georgoula Stavrou Krouskou is the sole heir of the whole of the estate of said decedent by virtue of the laws of the State of Colorado, and,

WHEREAS, the said John Stavrou Krouskou the brother aforementioned claims that the estate is indebted to him in the sum of $2,500.00, by virtue of business dealings which he had with the decedent, and,

WHEREAS, in addition to the sum of $2,500.00, aforesaid, the said John Stavrou Krouskou claims a certain diamond valued at $700.00,

and certain lots described as follows...., which lots said John Stavrou Krouskou claims are his own property, and that the decedent was holding the same in trust for him, and,

WHEREAS, said decedent was joint owner with said John Stavrou Krouskou of Certain farming lands located in and about the County of Denver State of Colorado, and particularly described as follows... and,

<u>WHEREAS, it is the desire of the heir at law, the said Georgoula Stavrou Krouskou to settle and compromise out of Court any and all disputes with her said son John Stavrou Krouskou, and,</u>

NOW THEREFORE, in consideration of $l.00, and other good and valuable considerations past by and between the parties herein, the following agreement has been entered, to-wit

[Several paragraphs follow, detailing how Georgoula gives up all claims to the estate.]

It is further agreed and understood by and between the parties herein, that in making this settlement, the heir at law, the said Georgoula Stavrou Krouskou does not in any way admit the legality of the claim of her said son John Stavrou Krouskou, but this settlement is made in order to satisfy her son and the other heirs at law.

But wait! Here's a "Final Report" dated August 24, 1937, and it makes me feel much better about the whole affair. It states that John does purchase the other half of the farm property with the $2500, and is recognized as the owner of the ring and the lots at W. 29th Ave. and Grove St., but, evidently he didn't unfairly hog *everything.*

Not only does Brother Frank receive the $350, "which is a debt to him from George before his death", but the brothers also:

> AGREE AND ACCEPT that the candy store which is now located at the corner of 15th and Curtis Sts. in the City and County of Denver, ... belongs to the brother Argyros (Frank) Krouskos, alias Allison, the valuation of which was paid to the brother George before his death.

And, *most importantly*, this report makes clear that the old mother and her family in Greece were not completely excluded from the fruits of George's labors:

> To Georgula Krouskas, mother of said deceased,
>
> - $420.00
> - 10 Shares Great Western Hog Co. Stock
> - 600 Shares Pacific Wireless Telephone and Telegraph Co. Stock
> - 21,000 Shares Cresent Petroleum Co. Stock
> - 1 cameo ring and 1 gold pin
> - Certificate of deposit #A484209 of National Bank of Greece, for 1,393,684 drachmas, maturing May 30, 1938.
>
> Value $12,961.26.

Whew! That's good. It looks like Georgoula received everything that didn't have a prior claim against it. And $13,000 must have been worth quite a bit in 1937. Hopefully the Krouskos family in Greece was able to enjoy some improvement in their lives as a result of George's successes in America.

But, now what? What's this?

It's a copy of a lawsuit, instigated by John's son Steve, dated May 29, 1940. I think it must have been precipitated by Georgoula's death. (At 100 years of age!) It's a "complaint to quiet title", and the defendants are *his grandmother, his aunt, his uncles and his father!* It lists Steve as full owner of the lots in town and half owner (with his father?) of the farm. For some reason he feels that his holdings are in jeopardy though. It reads, in part:

The plaintiff complains and alleges:

1. That he is the owner and in the actual possession of lots numbered twenty-five, twenty-six and twenty-seven, block numbered thirty-one, Highland Park, in the City and County of Denver, Colorado and also that he is the owner and in the actual possession of an undivided one-half interest in and to the northwest quarter of section twenty-four, meridian, Jefferson County, Colorado.

2 a) That he is informed that the defendent Georgula Krouskas, is dead but that he has no positive proof of her death.

b) That the defendent Veneta Kyriakoulia may be dead.

3. That the defendants herein ... claim some right, title or interest in and to said real property.

4. That the claims of the defendants ... are without any right whatever.

I found nothing else pertaining to this lawsuit. It must have turned out okay for Steve though, since he ended up with both the properties in question.

John lived at the farm for the next 25 years.

He ordered, read, bundled and stored away numerous publications concerning farming. Most of these were from the U.S. Department of Agriculture.

We found detailed records of his wheat crops as well as notes and letters to and from his farm workers and associates. One letter reads:

Dear Sir:

I would like for you to get that wheat emptied out just as soon as possible as the mice are getting into the sacks. And you know the sacks belong to the Broomfield Mill, and what are destroyed will have to be paid for. I would empty them in the house but you know I have the house full now. I would like for you to get them out this week if you can.

Yours Truly,
Frank Arens

A Columbia Savings envelope held numerous photos that record ongoing visits to the farm by various members of the Allison family. Nephew Chris visits, looking very smart in his Air Force uniform. Chris's brother, Steve, also pays his uncle several visits. Sometimes he's dressed in his military uniform and sometimes in civilian clothes. A 1943 snapshot captures John (middle), Brother Gus with his wife Mickey, Brother Frank and his wife, Anthenia, and two of their children, Titsa and Chris. John's son, Steve, stands to the right with his third wife, Shirley.

Figure 7.7 Allison family at the farm on Christmas Eve 1943.

Sixty-eight year old John became a grandfather for the first and only time in 1944. Linda Lee, or Linna Lee, as he pronounced it with his accent, delighted him and brought him much happiness. There are several pictures of a laughing John holding his laughing infant or toddler granddaughter (see Figure 31.1). These visits soon ended however. He next saw his Linna Lee ten years later.

John saved this 1950 postcard from his son, postmarked Cleveland, Ohio:

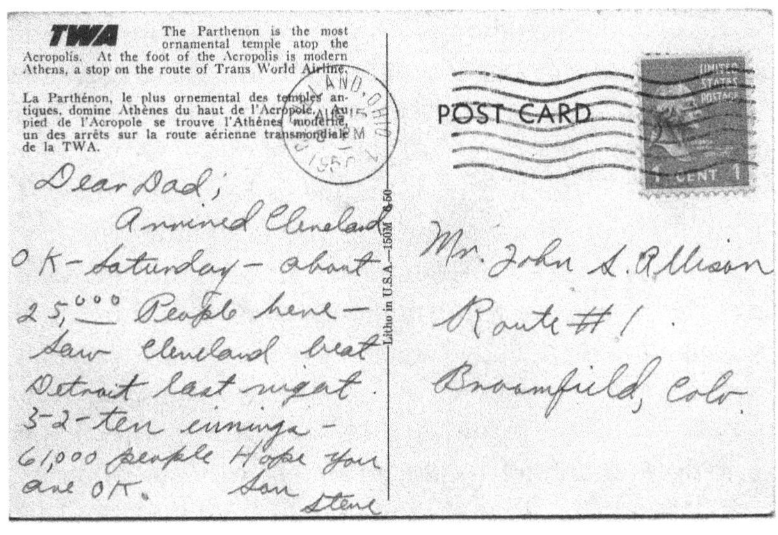

TWA The Parthenon is the most ornamental temple atop the Acropolis. At the foot of the Acropolis is modern Athens, a stop on the route of Trans World Airline.

La Parthénon, le plus ornemental des temples antiques, domine Athènes du haut de l'Acropole. Au pied de l'Acropole se trouve l'Athénes moderne, un des arrêts sur la route aérienne transmondiale de la TWA.

Dear Dad;
Arrived Cleveland OK - Saturday - about 25,000 People here - Saw Cleveland beat Detroit last night. 3-2 - ten innings - 61,000 people Hope you are OK. Son Steve

Litho in U.S.A.—150M 6-50

POST CARD

Mr. John S. Allison
Route #1
Broomfield, Colo.

Figure 7.8 Postcard from Steve.

My first memories of my grandfather date from about 1956. I'd been absent from his life for many years, and even after my return, my visits were few and far between. Nevertheless, he was always so happy to see me!

At first, my father and I, and sometimes my father, stepmother and I visited him at the farm. We always spent the day. Broomfield was considered way out in the country in those days. While Steve attempted to keep up on general maintenance around the property, John would tell me about every aspect of his beloved farm. He told me about the bees he raised and the honey they produced, about his huge garden, about the many farm cats that were his companions as well as his friends, and about the tracks of foxes, raccoons and snakes.

The inside of his house was very old, very dark and very cluttered. It wasn't very clean either. I don't think he had indoor plumbing. I remember the pump outside the door and the outhouse down beyond the garden. He spent most of his time in the kitchen and in the small bedroom just off the kitchen, seldom entering the other rooms of the house. The kitchen held his most treasured possessions. All his military photos, certificates and medals hung there, as did numerous photos of the baby Linda Lee. In his bedroom was a lamp made from his army rifle – an intriguing contraption. It was one of the things that brought tears to my eyes when I once again encountered it, many years later, after my dad died.

I wonder if he was lonely at the farm. He never remarried and lived there alone until about 1961.

He left then, only because he was dying.

When I spoke with my father's cousin Titsa over coffee some time back, she questioned Steve's care of his father in John's last years. She might be somewhat justified in her misgivings. Steve's journals, uncovered at the farm after his death, reinforce my belief that he tried always to stay close to his father and to please him. But probably, in the very end as John was dying, Steve could have done better.

It was at about this point that John began receiving those heart-rending letters from his nieces in Greece. Do you remember them? By 1964 he had received no less than 28 of them, each describing the hardships they are enduring - their brother, with the consent of their mother, has thrown them out of their houses. They beg their uncle, who evidently owns the houses, to write to the "president of the community" that he might intercede. But John was either unaware of their predicament, or unable to answer their letters, much less their pleas. Finally, in 1966, Steve sends a legal affidavit stating that Joanne can stay in the house in Agrionoe. But I found nothing stating that Katherine (she of no dowry) could stay in the house in Hrisafa.

I wish that John could have spent his last years at the farm. But that wasn't to be. He was in his eighties when he left the farm for the last time. He had been a diabetic for several years, but had never learned to monitor and regulate his illness. That took its toll. By 1961, he was suffering from serious health problems and had been hospitalized several times. After one hospital stay, he was told that he wouldn't be going back home to the farm. He needed to go to a place that could better care for him. He cried.

Steve placed his dad's valuables in two safe deposit boxes. Ken and I came across inventories for them during our clean up of the farm years later. Listed were stocks and bonds, bank account passbooks, property abstracts, coin collections, boxes of jewelry, several deeds transferring the farm and the city properties back and forth between John and Stephen over the years and the 1916 deed to the farm.

Many of the stocks, bonds and passbooks listed were in my name, which touches my heart. I'm reminded of how much John loved his Linna Lee. I wonder what happened to the actual stocks, bonds, and bank accounts?

At first John stayed in private homes. He'd sit all day, everyday, alone in his room. When I'd visit (which was very seldom), he'd try to talk to me, but couldn't - because of his teeth. How he suffered with his teeth! After finally ridding himself of his own aching teeth, he could never get used to their replacements. Tears would run down his weathered cheeks when he'd force himself to leave them in his mouth for more than a few minutes. It was a sad thing to see. It broke my heart.

And then he stayed at institutions. After a time at The Golden West Nursing Home on West Colfax Ave., he spent some time at the Mullin Home for the Aged, located on West 29th Ave. at Lowell. This quality institution was run by the Little Sisters of the Poor. I was in high school at the time and several times took the city bus across town to visit him there. But by now his mind was often confused and he sometimes thought that I was his long-gone wife of long ago. That was sad and somewhat uncomfortable. But then something went wrong about his placement there, and he had to leave. Was his behavior too disruptive? Did they raise the price? Was there a disagreement about payment? I just remember Steppy telling me that "the old man" had been "kicked out."

Things went downhill from there. It was back to private homes - and not good ones. It makes me shudder to remember. I was in college when last I visited him - at his final "home", #4 Pennsylvania Street. He had a tiny room there, where he sometimes sat, but mostly slept away, the last few months of his life.

I was married in April of 1965, but there was no question of Grampa attending the wedding. He was almost gone.

On August 28, 1965, Steppy called to tell me that he had died.

Here is John's death certificate, which I found carefully saved in a drawer in the house.

State of Colorado 7446

State File No.

Registrar's No. 3945 Dist. 54

CERTIFICATE OF DEATH

1. PLACE OF DEATH a. COUNTY: Denver
b. CITY, TOWN, OR LOCATION: Denver
c. LENGTH OF STAY IN 1b: 70 years
d. NAME OF HOSPITAL OR INSTITUTION (If not in hospital, give street address): #4 Pennsylvania St.
e. IS PLACE OF DEATH INSIDE CITY LIMITS? YES ☒ NO ☐

2. USUAL RESIDENCE (Where deceased lived. If institution: Residence before admission) a. STATE: Colorado b. COUNTY: Denver
c. CITY, TOWN, OR LOCATION: Denver
d. STREET ADDRESS: 3100 W. 38th Ave.
e. IS RESIDENCE INSIDE CITY LIMITS? YES ☒ NO ☐
f. IS RESIDENCE ON A FARM? YES ☐ NO ☒

3. NAME OF DECEASED (Type or Print) First: JOHN Middle: S. Last: ALLISON
4. DATE OF DEATH (Month Day Year): August 28, 1965
5. SEX: Male
6. COLOR OR RACE: White
7. MARRIED ☐ NEVER MARRIED ☐ WIDOWED ☐ DIVORCED ☒
8. DATE OF BIRTH: Mar. 22, 1877
9. AGE (In years last birthday): 88 IF UNDER 1 YEAR Months Days IF UNDER 24 HRS. Hours Min.
10a. USUAL OCCUPATION (Give kind of work done during most of working life, even if retired): Owner
10b. KIND OF BUSINESS OR INDUSTRY: Candy Store
11. BIRTHPLACE (State or foreign country): Greece
12. CITIZEN OF WHAT COUNTRY? USA
13. FATHER'S NAME: Stephen Allison
14. MOTHER'S MAIDEN NAME: Unknown
15. WAS DECEASED EVER IN U. S. ARMED FORCES? (Yes, no, or unknown) (If yes, give war or dates of service): Yes Span. Amer. War
16. SOCIAL SECURITY NO.: 523-54-0647
17. INFORMANT: Stephen J. Allison, 3100 W. 38th Ave. Denver, Colo.

MEDICAL CERTIFICATION

18. CAUSE OF DEATH [Enter only one cause per line for (a), (b), and (c).]
PART I. DEATH WAS CAUSED BY: IMMEDIATE CAUSE (a): cerebral vascular accident — INTERVAL BETWEEN ONSET AND DEATH: 3 hrs.
Conditions, if any, which gave rise to above cause (a), stating the underlying cause last. DUE TO (b): arteriosclerosis — ?
DUE TO (c):
PART II. OTHER SIGNIFICANT CONDITIONS CONTRIBUTING TO DEATH BUT NOT RELATED TO THE TERMINAL DISEASE CONDITION GIVEN IN PART I(a): diabetes mellitus
19. WAS AUTOPSY PERFORMED? YES ☐ NO ☒
20a. ACCIDENT ☐ SUICIDE ☐ HOMICIDE ☐
20b. DESCRIBE HOW INJURY OCCURRED. (Enter nature of injury in Part I or Part II of item 18.)
ROBT. B. SKINNER, M.D. By [signature] Deputy
20c. TIME OF INJURY Hour a.m. p.m. Month, Day, Year
20d. INJURY OCCURRED WHILE AT WORK ☐ NOT WHILE AT WORK ☐
20e. PLACE OF INJURY (e.g., in or about home, farm, factory, street, office bldg., etc.)
20f. CITY, TOWN, OR LOCATION COUNTY STATE
21. I attended the deceased from 8-28-65, to 8-28-65 and last saw him alive on NEVER
Death occurred at 9:35 a.m. on the date stated above; and to the best of my knowledge, from the causes stated.
22a. SIGNATURE: [signature] (Degree or title): M.D.
22b. ADDRESS: 235 Empire Bldg. Denver
22c. DATE SIGNED: 8/30/65
23a. BURIAL, CREMATION, REMOVAL (Specify): Burial
23b. DATE: 9-1-65
23c. NAME OF CEMETERY OR CREMATORY: Fairmount Cemetery
23d. LOCATION (City, town, or county) (State): Denver County, Colo.
24. FUNERAL DIRECTOR: [signature] ADDRESS: Moore Mortuary, Denver, Colo.
25. DATE REC'D. BY LOCAL REG.: AUG 31 1965
26. REGISTRAR'S SIGNATURE: Fredy L. O'Bryan

STATE OF COLORADO, City and County of Denver, SS.

I hereby certify that the above is a true, full and correct copy of the certificate, in my custody and now on file in my office.

Witness my hand and official seal at Denver, in said State, this 1st day of September, A. D. 1965.

Robt. B. Skinner
Registrar of Vital Statistics
City and County of Denver, Colorado

Fredy L. O'Bryan
Deputy

Figure 7.9 John's Death Certificate.

Steve and Steppy's address is listed as John's "usual residence". He never lived with them – at that address or anywhere else. She would never have permitted it - not that my father would have asked.

And there's still some confusion about John's date of birth. Was it 1877 as this document states, or 1876 as others have recorded?

He died alone in his tiny room at 4 Pennsylvania. He was buried next to Brother George.

Christopher John DeAndrea was born on October 18, 1965. We chose his middle name in honor of his great-grandfather, John Steven Allison. Decades later, I came also to know him by his birth name, Ioannou Stavros Krouskos. The names reflect his life - a son of Greece who died an American.

I remember him with love.

"all his American life"

The Denver Post - 1935.

SECTION
- III -

STEPHEN JOHN ALLISON

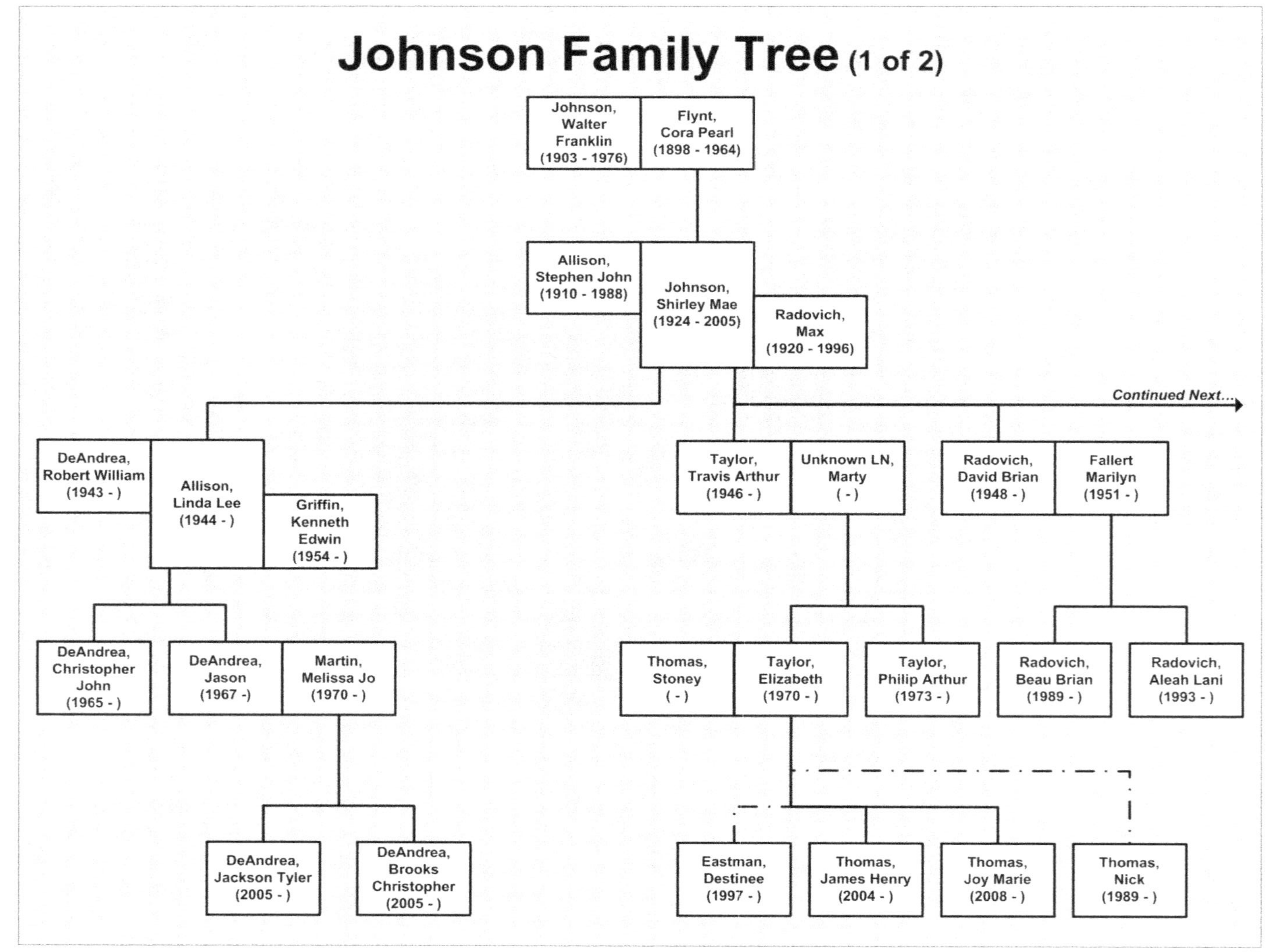
Johnson Family Tree (1 of 2)
Johnson, Walter Franklin (1903 - 1976)
Flynt, Cora Pearl (1898 - 1964)
Allison, Stephen John (1910 - 1988)
Johnson, Shirley Mae (1924 - 2005)
Radovich, Max (1920 - 1996)
Continued Next...
DeAndrea, Robert William (1943 -)
Allison, Linda Lee (1944 -)
Griffin, Kenneth Edwin (1954 -)
Taylor, Travis Arthur (1946 -)
Unknown LN, Marty (-)
Radovich, David Brian (1948 -)
Fallert Marilyn (1951 -)
DeAndrea, Christopher John (1965 -)
DeAndrea, Jason (1967 -)
Martin, Melissa Jo (1970 -)
Thomas, Stoney (-)
Taylor, Elizabeth (1970 -)
Taylor, Philip Arthur (1973 -)
Radovich, Beau Brian (1989 -)
Radovich, Aleah Lani (1993 -)
DeAndrea, Jackson Tyler (2005 -)
DeAndrea, Brooks Christopher (2005 -)
Eastman, Destinee (1997 -)
Thomas, James Henry (2004 -)
Thomas, Joy Marie (2008 -)
Thomas, Nick (1989 -)

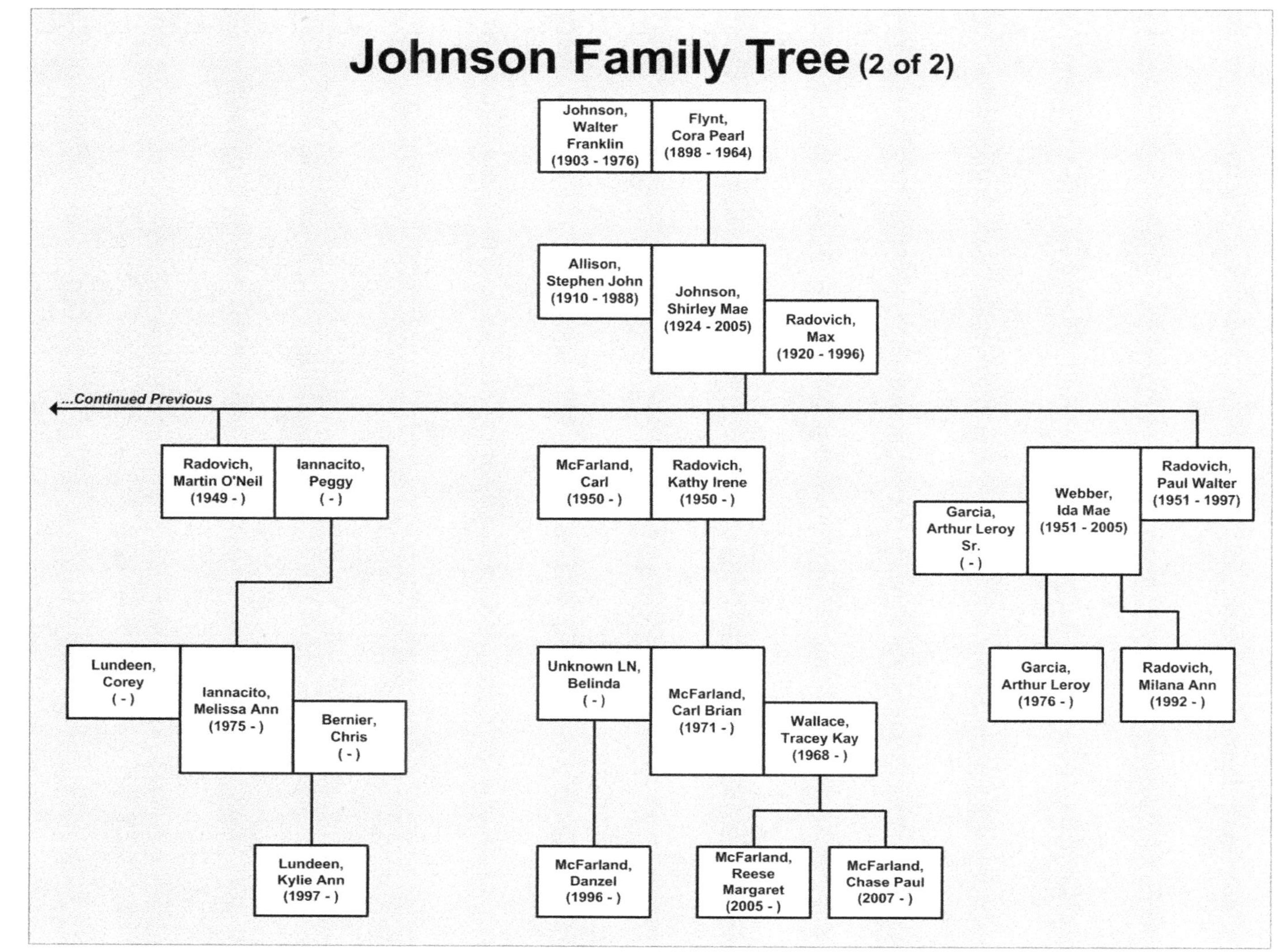
Johnson Family Tree (2 of 2)
Johnson, Walter Franklin (1903 - 1976)
Flynt, Cora Pearl (1898 - 1964)
Allison, Stephen John (1910 - 1988)
Johnson, Shirley Mae (1924 - 2005)
Radovich, Max (1920 - 1996)
...Continued Previous
Radovich, Martin O'Neil (1949 -)
Iannacito, Peggy (-)
McFarland, Carl (1950 -)
Radovich, Kathy Irene (1950 -)
Garcia, Arthur Leroy Sr. (-)
Webber, Ida Mae (1951 - 2005)
Radovich, Paul Walter (1951 - 1997)
Lundeen, Corey (-)
Iannacito, Melissa Ann (1975 -)
Bernier, Chris (-)
Unknown LN, Belinda (-)
McFarland, Carl Brian (1971 -)
Wallace, Tracey Kay (1968 -)
Garcia, Arthur Leroy (1976 -)
Radovich, Milana Ann (1992 -)
Lundeen, Kylie Ann (1997 -)
McFarland, Danzel (1996 -)
McFarland, Reese Margaret (2005 -)
McFarland, Chase Paul (2007 -)

CHAPTER 8

"Little Wilburn/ Wilper/ Wilburt/ Wilbur"

When I think of my father, I think of a sad man.

Although he never said as much, at least not to me, I think he felt his life was very hard - that he was often misused and his abilities, for the most part, under-unappreciated and under-rewarded. I'm not sure his feelings reflected reality, but I think that's how he perceived his life.

He was fifty-five years old when his father died. What had his life been like until that point? And what would it be like for the next twenty-three years, until *his* death in 1988? From my scant memories, from a few conversations with his cousin Titsa and from the dusty remnants found at the farm, I'll try to chronicle his years and better understand his heart.

I have a photo of baby Steve that I treasure (see chapter title page). It was taken at The DeLux Studio of Denver. I'd guess he's about three months old in the photo, propped up in a chair with pillows. He wears a long dress, a knit sweater and a bonnet that ties under his chin. His little hands beg to be kissed. And he's laughing - out loud! What a darling baby. Not much of this kind of happiness survived - he sure didn't laugh much during the part of his life when I knew him.

John and Minnie's son must have started life confused as to his name, and by extension, as to his identity. We know from Titsa that at his birth on September 27, 1910, his mother had wanted to name him Wilbur. Since this would have been breaking with the Greek tradition of naming him after his grandfather, she didn't get her wish.

However, people must have called him that (or some variation thereof). At least some people, some of the time, did. A Happy New Year postcard dated December 20, 1919 is addressed to "Mr. *Wilper* Allison". Someone has crossed out the "per" and written "*Wilburt*" above the word. The salutation reads, "Hello *Wilper*". This time the name is crossed out and rewritten as *Wilbur.* "Little Nick Lewis" in Joliet Ill sent this postcard to eight year old Steve. And, Ella Wagner, the lady who worked in George's candy store, often wrote of "Little *Wilburn*" in her letters, remember?

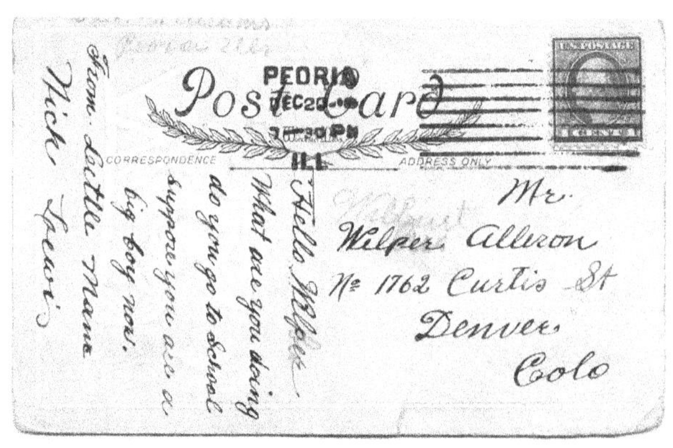
Post Card
PEORIA DEC 20 ILL
CORRESPONDENCE
ADDRESS ONLY
Hello Wilper
What are you doing
do you go to school
suppose you are a
big boy now.
From Little Nick
Lewis
Mr.
Wilper Allison
No 1762 Curtis St
Denver,
Colo

Figure 8.1 Postcard from Little Nick Lewis.

By whatever name, this child was soon a "motherless child". I think Minnie was gone before his first birthday. He lived alone with his father, a single parent, and a male one at that – which must have been an unusual situation in those times. I know nothing about his early childhood, but I'd guess it was a lonely one. John probably put most of his energies into his various small businesses, leaving little time for his young son.

When Steve was twelve or thirteen years old, he saved a tiny snapshot of himself (see Figure 8.2, far left, second row) and his classmates. The girls wear shifts or middies - kind of like sailor dresses, the boys, jackets and ties. They look to be on the brink of adulthood, these young people standing in front of their school. But what school? I was never able to figure out where Steve attended school through the seventh grade. Tetsa told me that, because they were "teased" in the public schools, Uncle George sent his nieces and nephews to Catholic schools. I'm assuming this arrangement included my father also. And, since Steppy told me that "the nuns practically raised your father", I'm almost certain that he too, attended a Catholic elementary school.

Figure 8.2 Steve Elementary School Class.

A caring teacher or acquaintance may have recognized a need for some peer companionship and/or adult guidance for Steve at this time of his life. John received this letter from the Boy Scouts of America dated April 10, 1923:

Mr. M. S. Allison, Sr.,
1333 Stout Street

Dear Mr. Allison:

At the request of Mr. Frank H. Rice, we are giving you, herewith, information with reference to Scout Troops which are, because of their close proximitey to your residence, desirable for your boy to join.

Troop No. 10 meets Friday night, 7:30 at the Grace Community Church, West 13th Avenue and Bannock, L.A. Vizien, Scoutmaster.

Troop No 23 meets Tuesday night, 7:00 at the St. Mark's Episcopal Church, 12th and Lincoln, E.L. Show, Scoutmaster.

Troop No. 80 meets Thursday night, 7:30, Colfax Community Church, 1155 West Colfax.

Application blank is enclosed herewith.

Sincerely yours,
(signed) S.W. Hopson
Scout Executive.

With this letter is an application for membership. Since it sits here today on my desk, it seems pretty certain that Steve didn't join the Boy Scouts. I wonder why? Was he uninterested? Did John forbid it? I'd bet on the latter. It was among my father's things, not my grandfather's; indicating that Steve saved it. It's at this point that he begins to document his own life, and I think he kept the letter and application because they were meaningful to him. Did they represent one of the early disappointments of his life? Maybe.

Chronologically, the next item he saved was a copy of the "ADELPHIAN". It's a school newspaper, "Issued the First Friday of Each Month by the Pupils of Sacred Heart High School, Denver, Colorado". This issue is dated December 5, 1924, and Steve would have been an eighth grader at the time. But didn't high school begin with the ninth grade? I'm confused. Although he made several mistakes in completing the crossword puzzle - I'm impressed. It's very difficult. For example, one clue is "Fallaciously subtle". I'm sure I wouldn't know!

10¢ Per Copy — $1[00] Per [illegible]ar

ADELPHIAN

Issued the First Friday of Each Month by the Pupils of Sacred Heart High School, Denver, Colorado

Volume IV — DECEMBER 5, 1924 — Number 3

The Spirit of Christmas

Ages upon ages have passed into oblivion. Generations after generations of men have entered the great beyond, and left no monument. But along the stream of time, the Great Architect of the universe has reared a memorial to His birth, the significance of which cannot be obliterated by the worldliness of man.

Of all the festivals which crowd the Christian calendar, there is none that takes possession of mankind as Christmas does. It is the birthday of one whose priceless contribution to the human heart and mind was His message of boundless, universal love. No other holiday has such a rich heritage of old customs and observances; and no other feast calls forth so vividly the memory of early affections. The Yule log is hauled to the open fireplace. The graceful evergreen with a waxen angel swinging on its topmost bough is bedecked with gold and silver fruit, and draped with snowy popcorn and glittering tinsel.

During the holiday season we spend much time in the crowded downtown districts. We start out early in the morning to avoid the crowd, but we find the crowd is equally determined to keep out of the jam. We hang by straps in crowded trolleys, jostle along conjested sidewalks, and rush madly through the revolving doors of department stores. Intent on remembrances for our friends whose names appear upon our shopping list, we spend a harassing day, after which we return home fatigued, bending under a load of paper parcels, yet thoroughly content to be a part of the mad carnival of generosity.

There is no necessity to plead for the observation of Christmas. It is good to think of all the joy of the fair outside show of the halcyon days; of the glitter and brightness of hospitable tables with dear ones gathered about them. It is pleasant to see the happy school boy and the gentle grandmother side by side. It warms and cheers to feel the cordial handshake of a friend. But there is something better than the mere observ-

[Continued on Page 2]

Class Leaders

BOYS

Grade 1	Lawrence Collins
Grade 2	Paul Cella
Grade 3	Edward Gessing
Grade 4	John McCarty
Grade 5	M. D. Currigan
	Francis Coyle
Grade 6	Charles Byrne
Grade 7	Lionel Gore
Grade 8	Leon Plamondon
Grade 9, 1st Div.	Ferdinand Telgman
Grade 9, 2nd Div.	Emil Parkes
Grade 9, 3rd Div.	Edward Connolly
Grade 10, 1st Div.	Fred Kirk
Grade 10, 2nd Div.	Joseph Carey
Grade 11, 1st Div.	Milton Luther
Grade 11, 2nd Div.	Lionel McCarty
Grade 12	Frank McNamara
	William Sanders

GIRLS

Grade 1	Kathleen Wade
Grade 2	Margaret Toohey
Grade 3	Anna Marie Wade
Grade 4	Loretto Hebert
Grade 5	Margaret Mary Devine
Grade 6	Inez Feld
Grade 7	Margaret McHugh
Grade 8	Agnes Reidy
Grade 9, 1st Div.	Kathleen Dinan
Grade 9, 2nd Div.	Alice Reidy
Grade 9, 3rd Div.	Elizabeth Barkhausen
Grade 10, 1st Div.	Margaret Grinstead
Grade 10, 2nd Div.	Winifred Caughman
Grade 11, 1st Div.	Dorothy Clifford
Grade 11, 2nd Div.	Anna Theison
Grade 12, 1st Div.	Rose Mary Dolan
Grade 12, 2nd Div.	Mary McCarty

Education Week

A beautiful "Education Week" program was presented in Adelphian Hall on Friday, November 21, by the high school students.

As Father McDonnell was absent, Father Harvey gave an interesting talk to the student body, impressing on our minds the need and importance of an accurate education in Latin. He gave us, also, several examples, wherein Latin was the dominating factor, and charmed us with his eloquence and simplicity.

There followed several interesting talks by high school pupils, each dealing with a different phase of education. John Dinan spoke of "Catholic Education," while Joseph Germanprez talked about "Our Country." Edward Garlick and Miss Dorothy Dooley presented to us the different school teaching systems found in the public and parochial schools. Raymond Connell talked on "True Nobility," while Miss Catherine [illegible]ackus proved, for our benefit, the [illegible] value of a musical education. We had also a real "oratress," namely, Miss Alice Honhart, whose talk concerning "The Teacher, the Hope of America," was quite convincing.

The Misses Dorothy Clifford, Marie Cella and Margaret O'Conner furnished piano selections of great beauty. Miss Bernice McGroarty added to the entertainment by an exquisite violin solo.

This entertainment was completed by a play presented by members of the Senior Class.

The play, "Bookland," was the story of a young girl who thoroughly detested literature. She fell asleep, and three fairies, one of whom remained with her, appeared and promised to make her love literature. There then appeared out of a large book, the different characters of literature, who proved most interesting to her, and made her realize the true value of literature. The cast was as follows:

Girls of the Sen[illegible] Class: Marie Cella, Ruth Winters, Agnes Ire[illegible], Margaret Gallagher, Ruth Genty, Margaret [illegible], Catherine Quinlan, Rose Mary Dolan.
[illegible]lied [illegible]
Queen Love.......... [illegible] ....Anna Schlereth
Happy Smile.......... of ....Verne Amolsch

[Continued on Page 2]

Figure 8.3 Issue of School Newspaper.

A sampling from the "Notes for Sophomores" reflects the more innocent mindset of adolescents of that era:

We all regret the recent bereavement of our classmate, Dorothy Welsh.

Wonder how Mgt. Gruninger enjoyed the Denham?

We wonder how the pupils of the sewing class enjoyed the experience of being sent to the cellar.

Grace O'Brien has improved her looks by adding shell-rim glasses.

We wish to inform our Freshies that self praise is no praise.

Who telephoned C. Dolre at 5:45 p.m.? We wonder.

If the team played like the Sophomores root, they could beat Notre Dame.

We elected our class officers and the members chosen were:

President - Joseph Germanprez
Vice President - Fred Kirk
Secretary - Hadassah Bridges
Treasurer - Frances Copland

However, some "jokes" in the newspaper reflect a more unsettling aspect of adolescent reality in the 1920's:

MISTRESS 'Norah, you must always sweep behind the door.'

MAID 'Yes'm, I always does. It's the easiest way of gettin' the dirt out of sight.'

KLANSMAN (returning home after a meeting) 'You almost was the widow of a martyr tonight.'

HIS WIFE 'How did that happen?'

KLANSMAN 'The fiery cross fell on me.

My father was a first generation American, a child learning and living with <u>all</u> that that entailed - the good and the bad.

It was near the end of this eighth grade year, that Steve wrote the poignant letter (discussed in Chapter 6) to John. Since it reflects the relationship between Steve and his father so well, I have included it again here:

At School
May 7, 1925

My dear Father,

As Mother's Day is approaching I am inclined to think of my Mother. But I have not known a Mother. You have been both Father and Mother to me.

For the past fifteen years you have taken care of me and have tried to bring me up right and I in turn owe you a debt that cannot be paid. I am starting from this day to try to do better and not cause you trouble and worry. I am old enough now to know what I should do and ought to do, therefore it is my duty to do what is right and to obey you.

May god bless you, the best Father on earth.

Your son,
Steve Allison

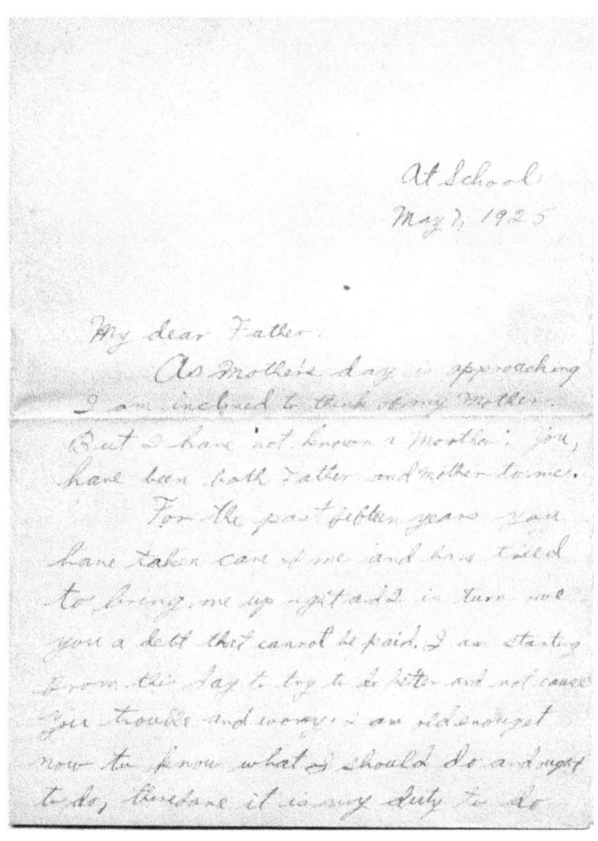

At School
May 7, 1925

My dear Father.
As Mother's day is approaching
I am inclined to think of my Mother.
But I have not known a Mother; you
have been both Father and Mother to me.
For the past fifteen years you
have taken care of me and have tried
to bring me up right and I in turn owe
you a debt that cannot be paid. I am starting
from this day to try to do better and not cause
you trouble and worry. I am old enough
now to know what I should do and ought
to do, therefore it is my duty to do

Figure 8.4 Contents of letter from Steve to John.

These words mark childhood's end for Steve.

"Little Wilburn/ Wilper/ Wilburt/ Wilbur"

Nick Lewis's postcard and Ella Wagner's letters - 1919.

CHAPTER 9

"Steve Allison - Our athletic hope."

The English section of a two-ring binder contains twelve short essays from Steve's freshman year (1925-26). I assume he was still attending Sacred Heart. Technically, they contain many spelling and grammar errors. But they render a touching glimpse of Steve's personality and character, as well as providing a cameo of the times. I love them, and the young person who wrote them. Here, with one image of an original included, are some of the essays.

My First Day in High School

On Friday the 11th awaking but instead of putting on a sweater and pair of pants I put on a good suit and polished my shoes.

I had breakfast and started to school on my `two legadded coupe' (bicycle) on arriving I noticed the faces of new boy and girls.

The first day I was shie on books and tried to study with Joe without sucess. I was very much pleased to see all the boy and girls from last year back and most of all was pleased with my new teacher.

Steve Allison

How I Was Taken for Someone Else

Last spring when the News and Times were holding a field meet at 6th and Bwdy. I happened to be out there and just as I was about to sit down I heard someone calling 'Jack'. He came up to me and said, 'Hello Jack'. At first I thought he was talking to some one else but later found out he was talking to me.

Then he ask me if I were not a member of North Denver High School. I said no then seeing his mistake he walked away.

Steve Allison

"Steve Allison - Our athletic hope."

What I Don't Like in School and Why

Of all the studies that we go thru in school I think that Latin is the most discouraging of all.

This language is about three thousand years old, still it is taught in every American school today. I often tried to think out why we study this dead language instead of studing that which will help us. Altho when I grow up I may find it useful and then will know why we studied it, but by then it may be to late to study.

Steve Allison

The Neighborhood Gossip

Mrs. Jones other wise known as the neighborhood gossip, was a very talkive woman. She is always visiting someone and telling about other peoples business. Her home looks like a place where uncivilized people live because she is always taking care of other peoples business when she should be taking care of her own.

On enterring a neighbors house she will pick out the easy rocking chair and makes herself at home, then she begins her gossip. It is something like this, 'I saw Mr and Mrs Teen going to a party last night and do you know? they never got home until two o'clock, the next morning,' and, 'Mr's Smith drives her husbands motorcycle and also finds time to play checkers'.

When Mrs Jones has told all she know she says, 'Well I must be going now, for I have a lot of house work to do and I am so dreadfully tired that I am about to drop.' As soon as she gets away from her neighbors she says to her self, 'I was never so humiliated in my life! The way Mrs Hooker treated me while I was talking. She diliberity kept on working.' Instead of going home she goes to some other neighbors house where she repeats the same story.

Poor Boys Can Become Presidents

Every person who is born in the United States is eliagable to become president of it, but this does not mean that everyone can become president. Some of the greatest presidents have come from humble homes and poor parents.

Lincoln, who was the son of very poor became the greatest president the United States ever had. He had no one to help him or send him to school and all his education was obtained by hard work. His father had died when he was young leaving him to take care of his mother. At times he would travell miles on foot just to get a book. This shows that one does not have to be well to do in order to become president.

Poor Boys Have Made Excellent Presidents

Lincoln was born of poor parentage and therefore had to work to amount to anything. When he was young he borrowed books from everyone in the country. One day be borrowed a book from someone and that night it rained and water destroyed the book, so young Lincoln worked a week to pay for it. due to the assistance of his mother and his own ambition he became the greatest President the United states has ever had.

Study Serve For Ability

When you find out the real value of studying it well serve for ability. This is shown in early times in such great men as Napoleon Bonaparte, Charlemagne and Alfred I. These men although they lived in hard times and were most of the time at war found time to study and build places of learning. Charlemagne although he traveled all the time and was at war, he established at towns and Orlean... Alfred I divided his day into three parts and one of these was spent in studying, this prepared him for the name England latter bestowed on him which was `The father of English Prose'. He owed his ability to rule England, to the fact that he took every avaiable opportunity to study.

"Steve Allison - Our athletic hope."

School Spirit

School Spirit which is shown in every school of the state is highly recommended as a duty to your school. the best way to show your School Spirit is to protect and defend its colors and to respect those in charge of your school. When the school is to have team you should try out for it weather you can make it or not. This is called School Spirit. If you are not able to play then the next best thing is to cheer for your team and help support it. When the school has a play you should do your part in selling tickets or by helping in any whay you can.

A Bridge

The bridge which crosses the farmer' highland river was built in 1907 by L.R. Semper. It was made of large timbers layed across the river with flat boards layen length wise with a brace extending from each side to the center of bridge. This bridge is still used by the people of Semper County and is known as the bridge of age. A bridge is a very perrity scene as it is surrounded by trees and small bushes. The road that crosses the river is known as lover lane because of the many young couples who pass through on their way home.

Our Family Physician

Dr. W. Jones, who is located in the Steele building, is our family physician. He is considered the best known physician in the West and has a clean and loyal record in the state of Colorado having served in the spanish American war.

He is a well built man, of fourty years of age, with dark hair, large blue eyes and a chin which showes determinating. If you should happen to see him on the street you would think that he was the president of the United States from the way he carries himself. When someone is in need of his help he gladly gives it especially to the poor who cannot pay for treatments. In one case his genorisity was shown when he came across a widow who had a crippled son 'who had to have an operation in the hope of saving his life.' Seeing that he could do nothing for him, the Doctor, at his own expense.

sent him to New York to be operated on by the world's best doctors. this is one of the many cases in which he showed his generisity.

Ice Skating

One December day while I was sitting near the fire reading a book I heard someone nocking at the door and on opening it I found it to be my friend, Tom Kelly. I invited him to come in and get warm as the thermometer registered two below zero. He wanted to know if I would go skating with him and if I had a pair of shoe skates. I told him I had no skates and did not know how to skate anyhow. Kelly said that he could borrow a pair from 'Red' and that he was sure they would fit me. Therefore Kelly and I set out for 'Reds' house which we reached at ten o'clock in the morning and in ten minutes we were again on our way. Arriving at the Small Lake in City Park at 10:30 o'clock we proceeded to put on our skates. When the skates were on Kelly tried to teach me how to skate and here is where the fun began. The first thing that happened was that I forget I was not on solid ground and started to walk to where Kelly was. This first accident was well remembered. After a hundred spills and a hundred sores I advised Kelly that if we didn't quit right away I would not be able to go home, as it was I could hardly walk. Therefore Kelly and I proceed home. As this was my first time on skates I almost made a pledge that I would never try it again, but in two weeks I was able to skate well.

Spring

Springtime, the most beautiful time of the year starts with the disappearance of the snow, the air becomming warmer and the many spring showers. this is followed by summer which is welcomed by everyone. In spring the robbins reappear from their long southern journey, and the sparrows and magpies begins to built their new homes in the barns and different trees. boys are seen on vacant lots playing marbles and baseball. The girls are out jumping rope and playing jacks. these and many other signs show that spring has come.

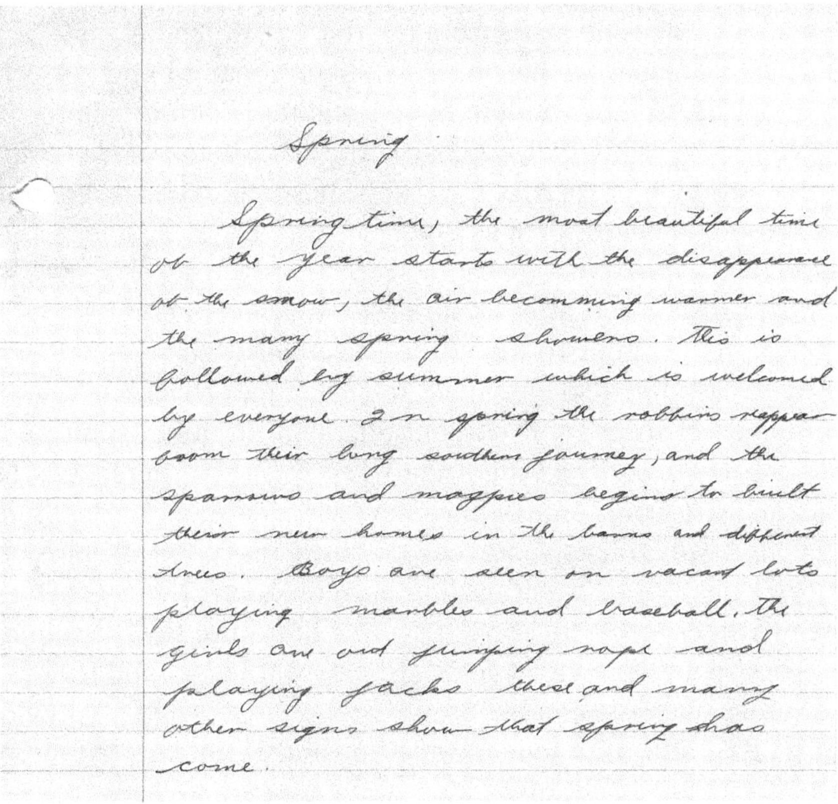

Spring

Spring time, the most beautiful time of the year starts with the disappearance of the snow, the air becomming warmer and the many spring showers. This is followed by summer which is welcomed by everyone. In spring the robbins reappear from their long southern journey, and the sparrows and magpies begins to built their new homes in the barns and different trees. Boys are seen on vacant lots playing marbles and baseball. The girls are out jumping rope and playing jacks these and many other signs show that spring has come.

Figure 9.1 Short essay on Spring.

Fifteen-year-old Steve paints a colorful word picture don't you think? Although the times he depicts may appear *simpler*, I know that they were not necessarily *easier*. I can picture him, setting off to school in his "good suit" and polished shoes, that fall day so many years ago. He hops on his "two legadded coupe" to begin a new chapter in his life.

Of all the studies he must "go thru", the study of Latin is "the most discouraging of all". He's often "tried to think out" why he has to study this dead language, and can't. But he figures he'd better learn it anyway, because it might, somehow, prove useful in the future.

While Steve's at school, the neighborhood gossip begins to make her rounds. She stops by a neighbor's house, chooses the most comfortable chair and begins her reporting. "Mr's Smith drives her husbands motorcycle and also finds time to play checkers." Meanwhile the lady of the house tries to continue her daily chores. The gossip's house, on the other hand, "looks like a place where uncivilized people live", because she is seldom there to do her work.

History was straightforward and patriotic.

The Semper Bridge still leads from the road, now 92nd Avenue, across the Farmer's Highline Canal to the farm. It's been repaired and restored many times since Charles Semper built it, but it's still there. I took photos from this bridge, looking down the canal, one day at the farm, before it was sold in 1989. The pictures are indeed "perrity", as they show the water surrounded by a bower of trees and bushes. Just as Steve described.

As I read the piece about ice-skating, I could see the boys' frosty breath and imagine Steve's discomfort after a "hundred spills and hundred sores". I've no doubt though, that within two weeks; he was indeed "able to skate well".

The English section also contained ten short reports about The Merchant of Venice and its characters, five about Silas Marner and its author and two assignments concerning The Call of the Wild. They are simply written pieces (barely adequate, I would think), but Steve records their grades in detail on a complex chart which lists sentence structure, unity, parallel structure etc. I've included only two of these writing assignments – they reflect a diligent Steve trying his best to write about a type of literature that he found of little interest. They're written with a fountain pen, of course, and there's not one erasure or cross out. You can bet Steve had made *at least* one previous copy of these. Yet they still contain many spelling and grammar errors:

Disappearance of Dunstan

When Dunstan stoled the gold from the floor of Silias cabin he did not have in mind that he was going to meet his maker the same night. After leaving the cabin he fell into the sand pits and was drowned, this ended his conquest for gold.

The disappearance of Dunstan was not looked upon by the people as peculiar because he had quarreled with his father and had run away not comming back for two or three mounths so this did not make him a suspicious character. Durring his absence the people though he had ran of and joined the army but when his body was found in the sand pits, it was proven that he had not left the village and that he was the one who stoled the gold of Silias.

Bassonio

Bassonio, one of the friends of Antonio was wise, honest, loyal and generous. He exhibits his intellegence in choosing Portia as his wife and proved his dertemnation by winning her although he was not rich like the other suitors. The honest of Bassonio is displayed when he tell Antonio about himself and that he has been a spendthrift. In the trial scene Shakespeare reveals to us Bassonios love for his friend Antonio when he is willing to give up anything in the world even his wife in order to save Antonio from the hands of Shylock. Shakespeare discription of Bassonio is good and the way he fits his thoughts into his characters is beyond criticism.

Even though this writing is very basic, to say the least, I don't think a professional writer could better describe Shakespeare's ability to get his point across - *"the way he fits his thoughts into his characters is beyond criticism."*

In another unlabeled section of the notebook, perhaps for history or religion, there's a report on the Crusades, with accompanying maps illustrating the crusade routes and the various countries involved. There's also a detailed drawing of a castle with all the different architectural sections labeled, as well as a diagram of a Catholic alter with the parts of the mass listed.

It's obvious that he put a lot of work into all of these assignments. As you'll see, schoolwork never did get any easier for him. But he tried so hard! Steve, I'm so sorry that I never knew about you and your life and times, and that I therefore never loved you properly. I do now. Life is sometimes tragic on the small scale, as well as the large.

And here's a mystery that I haven't been able to solve. Where did Steve go to school during his sophomore and junior years?

I found a report card from Sacred Heart for the school year 1926-27, which I assumed meant that he attended school there during his sophomore year. He was absent only 1/2 day all year! His grades are mostly B's and C's, with a few D's in Latin. We know how much he loved Latin! Pretty cut and dried - Sacred Heart, right?

SACRED HEART HIGH SCHOOL
DENVER, COLO.

Report of Stephen Allison

Grade 10 1926 1927

		Sept. Oct.	Nov. Dec.	Jan. Feb.	Mar. Apr.	May June Sem. Grade
Christian Doctrine Church History 80	B	B	B	B	B	B
Geometry 65	D	C	C	B	B	C
Trigonometry						
Algebra						
English Literature						
Rhetoric 85	C	C	B	C	C	C
Composition	C	D	B	C	C	
Physics						
Chemistry						
First Year Science						
Ancient History						
M & M History 87	B	C	B	B	B	B
American History						
Civics						
Latin 72	D	D	C	C	C	D
Spanish						
Dramatic Art	C		C	AA		B
Mechanical Drawing						
Sewing						
Stenography						
Typewriting						
Penmanship						
Deportment		A	A	C	B	
Application		B	A	A	A	
Absent					1/2	

Sister Ellen Marie Teacher

AA, denotes 95 to 100 per cent; A, 90 to 95 per cent; B, 85 to 90 per cent; C, 80 to 85 per cent; D, 70 to 80 per cent; E, below 70 or failure.

Figure 9.2 Steve's Sophomore Report Card.

But wait. He also saved many typed and handwritten tally sheets with baseball statistics from Loyola High School for this same year. His name and statistics are recorded on each one! For example, "THE LOYOLA MIRROR, Final Edition" of September 7, 1926 lists Steve Allison as second in batting average at 491, second in fielding with 974, first in runs scored with 28, and first in stolen bases with 21. The pages of fielding statistics list him as first or second in all categories (put outs, assists, etc.). Is it possible that he attended Sacred Heart but played sports for Loyola?

Final Batting Averages of the Loyola Jrs.

	Names	AB	H	PER	2B	3B	HR
1.	T. KELLY	60	25	.425	4	0	2
2.	S. ALLISON	53	22	.418	6	2	5
3.	M. COCHRAN	54	19	.361	4	0	0
4.	W. HAYES	13	4	.308	0	0	0
5.	C. LASSERI	57	17	.306	6	1	2
6.	H. HARMER	51	14	.280	3	0	0
7.	J. KANE	54	14	.252	3	1	1
8.	A. LARSON	59	14	.238	1	0	0
9.	R. CONNELL	56	13	.234	2	0	2
10.	D. WALDRON	5	1	.200	0	0	0

Figure 9.3 Layola 1926 Baseball statistics.

Whatever. The main thing, the important thing, is that he's now playing team sports – and that means he's happy. I believe that my father enjoyed only one period of real happiness in his whole life - the years when he played competitive team sports. He was a very skilled athlete and he loved to play baseball and football!

So tenth grade was the beginning of the "good times". These newspaper tally sheets are fragile and yellowed and have obviously been folded and unfolded and refolded many times. He must have been so proud. And yet his father either could not, or would not, take one bit of interest in these endeavors or recognize any value in them. (He who came from the area of Olympia, Greece!) The boy in every man wants his father to be proud of him. This was one of Steve's major disappointments in life.

During the summer following his sophomore year he participated in the "BABE RUTH CONTEST" sponsored by the city papers - "Sixty-one regional sandlot sluggers made circuit clout Sunday in the opening week of the Babe Ruth home run contest".

The news clipping lists the contestants by category from juniors through semi-pro. Steve Allison is registered as a junior (upcoming?) from *Loyola* – adding to my confusion about where he attended school. So, even if John saw no value in sports, he at least let Steve play – even in the summer.

The front cover of (another) very well used notebook declares, in Steve's handwriting:

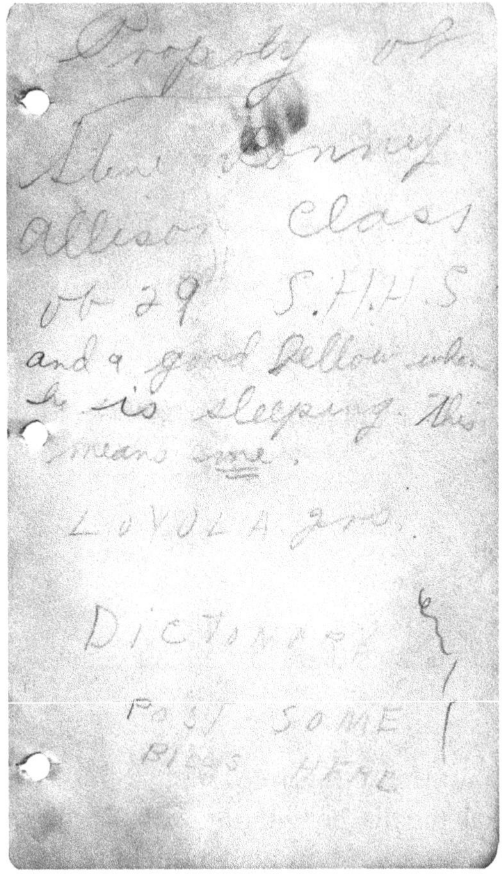

Figure 9.4 Front cover of Steve's Notebook.

Property of Steve Bonney Allison, class of '29, S.H.H.S., and a good fellow when he is sleeping. This means <u>*me*</u>*.*

Okay... Bonney? - Beautiful, handsome? Who knows what that means.

This *Sacred Heart High School* notebook also holds several pages of typed statistics, including one listing Steve's home runs at rival *Loyola High School* in 1926 and 1927. Which school did he attend?

Although they played several schools, Loyola played many teams sponsored by businesses that year - teams like Shavers Drug, Majestic Tea, Snappy Pharmacy and De's Creamry. They went 20/4 for the season. Not bad!

Sixteen year old Steve also kept his work schedule, with times and amounts earned, in this notebook. We know that he signed some of the receipts at the Post Office Pool Hall during this year, so I'm thinking the work schedule is for the pool hall. Whatever he was doing, he was working hard – at least during two weeks in December of 1926, when he worked 122 hours.

Dec 14	420 – 834 – 314	1.	95
Dec 15	(428 – 853) 923 – 1048) 550	3.	25
Dec 16	412 – 934) (1007 – 100) 817	5.	20
Dec 17	(403) 1131) 728	4.	55
Dec 18	(1101) (310) 343 – 1105) 1131	7.	15
Dec 19	(1203) (501) (739) – 953) 9.12	5.	85
Dec 20	(1105) 609) (645 – 553) 12.56	7.	80
Dec 21	(1104) 605) 641 – 1215) 12.35	7.	80
Dec 22	(1103) (602) 623 – 849) 9.15	5.	85
Dec 23	428 – 632 12.00	7.	80
Dec 24	(446 – 929) 16.43	10	40
Dec 25	441 – (11 – 48) 6.07	3	90
Dec 26	Did not work		
Dec 27	(733 – 424) 851	5.	20
	total 116 hr and 359 min or 121 hr 59 minutes		

Figure 9.5 Steve's Work Schedule.

And here's the topper! At the end of his junior year Steve receives a *West High School* yearbook! Under "CHRONICLES – JUNIORS", it names, "Steve Allison - Our athletic hope."

CHRONICLES—JUNIORS

Irene Adair—*A senior aspirant.*
Steve Allison—*Our athletic hope.*
Ruth Ball—*A social bud.*
Chester Young—*A screen "papa."*
Elizabeth Atnip—*Just missed catnip.*

Melvin Lindquist—*Ours by inheritance.*
Edward Lipan—*Turkey in the straw.*
Lorita Lowe—*Was buried once.*
Don McDaniel—*Golfer and skier.*
Ray McDonnell—*Another inheritance.*

Figure 9.6 Page from West High School Annual.

Did he attend three schools in one year? If so, he must have transferred to West very late in the year, as he's mentioned nowhere else in this annual, nor does any photo appear. But his new classmates must have known of his involvement in sports, since he was their "athletic hope".

This yearbook captures a telling glimpse of the times. For example:

- Golfers wear knickers and long sleeved shirts and ties.
- Denver neighborhoods were pretty segregated, and only two students of African American descent attend this large inner city school. Each young man is involved in an extra-curricular activity - Radio Club and Track Team. I'm hoping this indicates that they were comfortable and happy in their school. Considering the heavy influence of the KKK locally during this period, I'm a little worried that this might not have been the case.
- "Modesty, charity and sociability" appear in the motto of "The Domestic Art Club for West High Girls". This organization "tries to promote worthy friendships, establish high ideals, cultivate courtesy and develop pleasing personalities. Many friends have given talks at the regular meetings. Miss Betty Dee Winburn of the Denver Dry Goods Company, spoke at a tea the club held at that store. A beauty talk was given by Mrs. Frances Fisher. 'A Budget for Life' and 'Choosing a Way' were topics on which Mrs. Howard Cooper spoke. Mrs. Sweet emphasized hospitality, and Mr. Sass and Mr. Turner sang solos at some of the meetings."

Since he came to West High School late in the year, he probably didn't know many students well enough to ask them to sign his yearbook. Only one did: "Dearie, Elta Mae Griffin, '29".

However, several members of the faculty signed it, including the principal, Harry V. Kepner. Thirty years later, Steve lived with his third (or fourth?) wife and daughter on South Osceola Street, one mile from Kepner Junior High

School. If we had been a normal family, he might have told me that the school was named after his high school principal. But we were anything but normal.

Did Steve transfer to a public school for sports' reasons? He and John lived in the same area of downtown during these years, so it's unlikely that he changed schools because they moved. Happily, he remained at West High School for his eventful senior year.

His two ring binder from this senior year is empty; but the notations on the inside cover tell much about his state of mind. Clearly Marguerite Gentry was an important part of Steve's life. Other words of wisdom:

Marguerite Gentry - My Sweet Heart Where cupid shoots his arrows. I hope he hits you.

ORDERS TOOK FOR GRAVE STONES

YOU ARE A BOON TO HUMANITY AND GARDEN TRUCKS

DUNCE SA

the higher the mountain

the cooler the breeze

the shorter the dresses

the cooler the knees

PROPERTY OF STEVE ALLISON '29'

SNARE

BA-BY

megalo-ciphalic

metical term

meaning big head

ALL-CONFERENCE

QUARTER BACK '28'

STEVE ALLISON

The above would indicate that Steve was a somewhat immature eighteen-year-old. But don't judge his character solely by his notebook cover. It was a good year for him, no doubt, especially at school. He was all-conference quarterback and, as you'll see, very much in love. But, his senior year was not all roses, either.

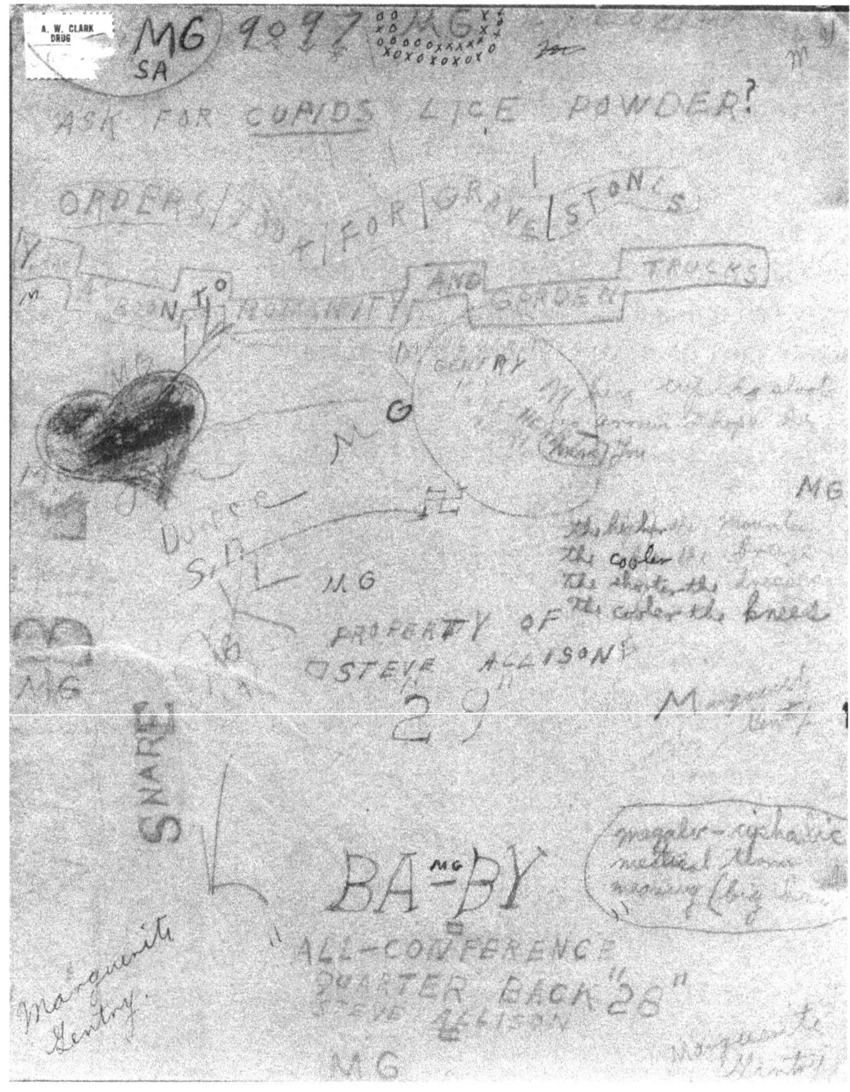

Figure 9.7 Inside cover of Steve's 2-Ring Binder.

A journal that he kept intermittently during his senior year, 1928–1929, was actually a calendar year journal for 1928. Making the best of what he had, Steve modified the dates in the early months to represent 1929. Some of the entries don't have modified dates, and for these an actual date can't be determined. However, it does seem clear that the events occurred in chronological order throughout the school year.

The entries show a more thoughtful young man. The first of several journals that he will keep during his lifetime, it documents disappointments, insecurities, sicknesses and small and large traumas - as well as the good times. I've included most of them:

"Steve Allison - Our athletic hope."

September 1928

20 Senior Picknic, Rock Mt. Lake

22 Loveland beat West 24-6 first game of season

27 Edna's Birthday and mine

January 1929

2 Edna Walton, 261 Fox St. Denver Colo.

3 Went to game with MG, Brother And mother in quarrel when got home.(didn't kiss me good-night)

4 TR and MG went to dance p.m.

5 Iris spoke to MG at dance, Iris mother found locked in room undressed with "DR"

6 Had my pitchers taken, 6 views for annual

7 M called up and said she was going to show with her mother, I called up later and she didn't know me on phone at first and said she didn't know what she was going to do tonight

10 Social, didn't attend, MG was sick

14 We beat North Hi 25-24

15 Went to see LG at hostipal, MG and TR went to dance P.M.

16 Didn't practice Basketball, went over to MG house

17 Pitchers taken of Basket-ball team, We beat Barns Business School 29-24, I made 5 baskets.

18 Went to see Parhoical Games, MG and TR went to see TR's father

19 Fellows got cought diching school, I wasn't with them

20 Went to social. Failed an English test. Found out what (nice) kind of Guy LG was. Mother (M) not home

February 1929

2 Basketball team defeated by South 44-30, made 2 points, played 8 min

3 Father got sick, temp of 104 degrees, My Girls birthday

12 MG mother tried to des. herself

14 Girl went to Show in AM alone; trouble with MA, visited her in afternoon

15 Boulder Prep defeated W 44-29, got in for 2 min, Girl and I both sick

17 visit MG in evening, MG and TR went to dance in afternoon

18 Walked home with MG

20 PM visited MG

21 W Defeated Glen Y 34-26, Played 1 Q

22 SOCIAL with NORTH, Attended, MG danced but I didn't, Eat supper at MG house

23 W defeated by Manual 30-26, Was introduced to Dutch Clark and Van DaGolf

24 Visited MG in afternoon, went to show, LF got $1.40 from MA for date and spent it on pool

25 Went home with MG, had some dancing lessons, Altha came over for visit, MG got mad, step on toe

27 Went to my first dance with MG

29 Went to school play with MG TR LG DN

March 1929

1 East Beat W 25-23, played 6 min, made 2 points
3 Went to show with MG, MG and Nadine went to Areana at PM
4 BaseB pratice started, Walked home with MG, RY and LG about cars
5 Walked home with MG
6 Went to a dance, MG in Finals in Contest, Walked home with MG
7 Walked home with MG, PM I went to America
8 Danced at the Social, Walked home with MG, Came in 2nd in contest
9 Visited MG in Afternoon, then we went over to "arts" PM, Heard Radio
10 MG And Mother and I went for a ride in afternoon, PM MG and I went to a show
11 Walked home with MG, GG had my sweater on
12 TR and MG went to show PM, GG was raided, I was home and didn't call me up
13 Late two school, Eat supper at MG house, walked home with her
14 Walked home with MG (tried too), went home early with LG
15 Got out Early: Dad's Birthday, Marguerite went to see "property", I stayed home
16 Visited MG in Afternoon, MG and N went to the Appolo in PM
17 Went to show in Afternoon with MG, Worked PM at Telephone Exchange
18 MG made up with Iris
19 MG stayed home from school, I went over to house after school, dance pracice
20 Started BaseB practice, Was supposed to have a date with MG at her house
21 MG wore Sweater, she had toothache, I was with her in PM, School play, didn't go
22 MG had toothache, left school and seen Dr, I went over there after Practice
23 Visited MG in Afternoon, She was sick, I stayed with her til 10 PM
24 Worked, Stayed home in Afternoon, PM went to a show. MG and girlfriend spent day together

April 1929

1 MG didn't go to school, I went over after school, MG and SJ ______ on front for l hr
5 MG and I went to social, she danced with WO and DY, I was sore

June 1929

22 Bought my ford, $100.00

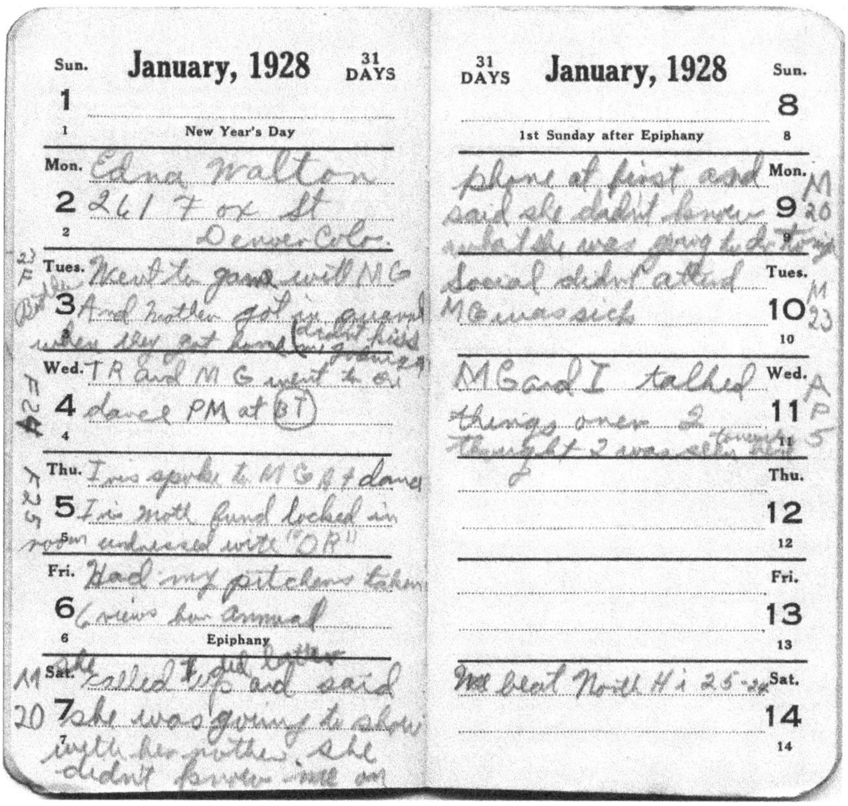

Figure 9.8 Steve's Journal.

Marguerite seems to have been the most important thing in Steve's life during his senior year. But, although they spent a great deal of time together, it doesn't appear that they were ever a "steady" couple. She taught him to dance and actually wore his letter sweater once, but she also often hurt him and made him "sore". She was definitely the less committed of the two. I'm not sure just what they were doing "on front for 1 hr" on April 1st, but I can guess.

And it wasn't just the young folks. How about Iris's mother in the locked room, undressed, with the "DR"? Pretty wild.

On February 12th, Marguerite's mother tries to "des herself". Destroy?

In that same month, Steve notes that his father is sick, with a high temperature. Perhaps this was an episode brought on by the disabilities he suffered as a result of his military service. I'm touched that Steve makes note of John's 52nd birthday in March.

Next to Marguerite, Steve's attention is taken up with sports. He evidently wasn't as successful in his basketball endeavors as he was in football. No wonder, he was barely 5'10". In February, he meets one of his sport's heroes

– Dutch Clark. He couldn't know it at the time, but he'll soon be spending a great deal of time with this man.

Judging by the journal entries, the academic part of his school life was of the least interest to Steve. Failing the English test earned an entry, but that's it! Oh, and he did note that he *wasn't* one of the "fellows" who "got cought diching" on January 19th.

An April 30, 1929 copy of the school newspaper, "The Rodeo", contains articles that hardly seem dated at all - as evidenced by such headlines as, "Try-Outs Held for Senior Play", or "Orange and Black Day Tomorrow", or "Cowboys Squelch East Angels 9-2".

And the author of one editorial envisions a future that hasn't quite materialized. Headlined, "A New Department to Meet New Wants", it reads in part:

> The pupils of West are proud to think that their school is one of the most up-to-date in the United States. Taken at large it is. It prepares the student for present day life. But there is nothing in the curriculum to prepare him for the coming mode of transportation - Aviation. The Denver High Schools should all be equipped with Departments of Aviation. Auto Mechanics Departments are maintained - why not an Aeroplane Mechanics' Course?

Did the writer think that soon we'd all be flying around in our own private planes?

A quaint phrase in an article about the senior prom, on the other hand, shows just how much things did change in another area - that of teen-age music appreciation. The author reports that "Hume Everett and his band furnished the syncopated melodies for dancing."

Syncopated melodies! Makes me smile!

And here's why my father saved this newspaper:

Cowboys Squelch East Angels 9–2

West Outplayed Angels the Entire Game; Entire Team Stars

West defeated East 9 to 2 at the D. U. Stadium, Tuesday, April 23. The West High Cowboys overwhelmed the East High Angels in one of the most sensational games of the season. Steve Allison clouted a home run in the first inning with Davis and Hayes on base. Steve Allison is one of the hardest hitters in the league and the homer that he hit is said to be one of the longest ever made in the Denver-Boulder High School League. Ed Barton showed his ability as a star hurler by holding the Angels to two runs and allowing them only seven hits. Two-baggers were made by Clay Davis and Leslie Elson. Clay Davis was the star hitter of the game. He hit three out of four.

Figure 9.9 Newspaper article about Allstar Game.

West defeated East 9 to 2 at the D.U. Stadium, Tuesday, April 23. The West High Cowboys overwhelmed the East High Angels in one of the most sensational games of the season. Steve Allison clouted a home run in the first inning with Davis and Hayes on base. Steve Allison is one of the hardest hitters in the league and the homer that he hit is said to be one of the longest ever made in the Denver-Boulder High School League.

How proud he must have been!

In the midst of this baseball season, Steve received this letter. It's from his coach I assume:

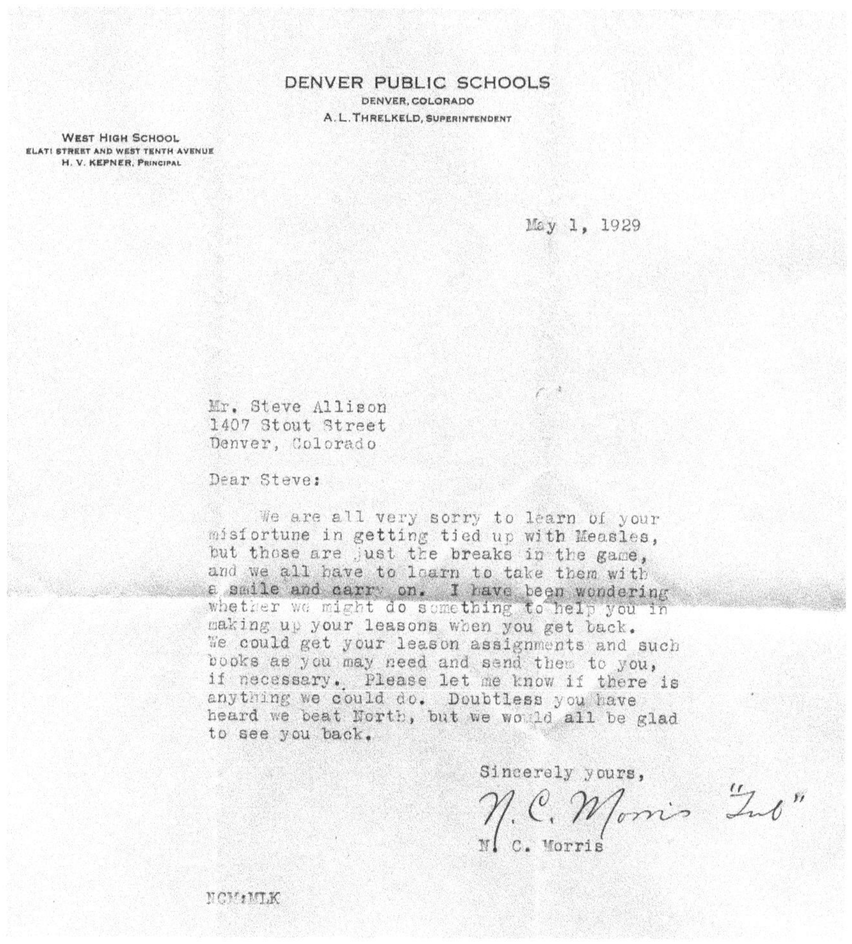

DENVER PUBLIC SCHOOLS
DENVER, COLORADO
A. L. THRELKELD, SUPERINTENDENT

WEST HIGH SCHOOL
ELATI STREET AND WEST TENTH AVENUE
H. V. KEPNER, PRINCIPAL

May 1, 1929

Mr. Steve Allison
1407 Stout Street
Denver, Colorado

Dear Steve:

We are all very sorry to learn of your misfortune in getting tied up with Measles, but those are just the breaks in the game, and we all have to learn to take them with a smile and carry on. I have been wondering whether we might do something to help you in making up your leasons when you get back. We could get your leason assignments and such books as you may need and send them to you, if necessary. Please let me know if there is anything we could do. Doubtless you have heard we beat North, but we would all be glad to see you back.

Sincerely yours,

N. C. Morris

NCM:MLK

Figure 9.10 Letter from Coach.

Obviously, since he saved it, this letter must have meant a lot to Steve. I bet the coach's concern was as important to him as were his peers' tributes. Perhaps it made up some for his father's lack of interest and concern.

We know that John saw little value in his son's athletic accomplishments. And, at this time, he made a decision that brought Steve bitter disappointment and heartbreak. Because of his football and baseball skills, West Point recruited Steve during this, his senior year. But Grampa refused to let him accept the scholarship they offered. He made him turn down a free college education at a prestigious school – one with a proud military tradition, at that. (We know how proud he was of his *own* involvement with the military establishment!) For some reason, he thought Steve should stay in Colorado. I'd always assumed that it was because John needed his help on the farm, but I know now that they didn't even live on the farm during my father's youth. John's decision caused Steve much distress. He was crushed.

Although Steve tells us in his journal that he "Had my pitchers taken, 6 views for annual" on January 6, 1929, and then had "Pitchers taken of Basketball team" on January 17, I don't think he was able to purchase an annual at the end of the year. At least I never found one.

At the farm however, all those many years later, I did find a copy of the photo he had taken on January 6 (one of six "views") for the annual. It's very small, only about 2 by 3 inches. A young version of my father looks out from the cardboard frame. He wears a fine three-piece suit with a white shirt and widely striped tie. He has a beautiful smile. It's the photo at the beginning of Section Three.

With it, I found a page from the yearbook – the page showing Steve with the football team (see image at beginning of Chapter 9; Steve is in the back row, second from left). Did he tear it out of someone else's annual - like steal it?

West High School graduation exercises were held in the school auditorium at 8:00 p.m. on June 7, 1929. Steve saved two of the engraved announcements. With them were two Roman Catholic holy cards - one of Jesus and one of Mary ("Oh Mary! So beautiful and amiable, I love you and I place all my hopes in you."). Perhaps they were from the nuns at Sacred Heart or Loyola - the parochial school (s?) he attended until his junior year.

After his graduation, Steve carefully packed away his mementos from high school.

Recently, I learned that West High School has a very active alumni association. I gave them some of Steve's West High School memorabilia – including his letter sweater and practice jerseys. Combining these with yearbook pictures, school newspaper articles and game programs the association created a special showcase at the school - highlighting Steve's football accomplishments there. Ken, Ken's mom (who graduated from West about 20 years after Steve), Chris, Jay and I went to see the display on Alumni Night. Steve would have been so pleased.

On June 22, 1929, Steve purchases his first car. He was always very conservative with his money, and I'd bet that such was the case even at age 18. (In the senior year journal are three two-cent stamps. One's been carefully removed from a letter in hopes of being used in the future.) He had, no doubt, worked very hard for the $100.00 and had done a lot of shopping around before buying "my ford".

Having packed away his mementos and his disappointments, Steve "Bonney" Allison leaves behind his childhood - and looks toward the future.

"Steve Allison - Our athletic hope."

West High School annual – 1928

CHAPTER 10

Allison

"I haven't even ten cents to buy shoestrings."

Steve's immediate future, happily, held sports - and more sports.

In the fall of 1929 he's a student at Colorado College, a private school in Colorado Springs, Colorado. He must have received some kind of athletic scholarship, since I'm sure that John would not (and perhaps could not, had he wanted to) pay tuition for his son to attend a private college. Chronologically, the first souvenir that I found from Steve's college years is a menu from the Annual Tiger Football Banquet. The Colorado College Boosters Club, whose motto is, "We are behind the Tigers - win or lose", hosted this dinner that was held on December 5, 1929 at the Antlers Hotel. Steve attended as a member of the freshman football team.

I have no doubt that he excelled on the field; but as his mid-semester grade card shows, his academics were not as impressive:

Span.	*1*	*E (conditional)*
Biol.	*1a*	*C-*
Eng.	*1*	*D+*
Math.	*3*	*C*
Bible	*18*	*B-*

Besides athletic endeavors, Steve's time was being taken up by fraternity rush and pledging. The menu of the Annual Norris Dinner of the Chi Sigma of Phi Gamma Delta, held on February 22, 1930, lists Stephen John Allison as a "Neophyte". This dinner, too, was held at the Antlers Hotel.

Lots of fun, but very little studying going on it would seem. The grade card for the semester ending February 1930 is looking very bad:

THE COLORADO COLLEGE

COLORADO SPRINGS, COLORADO

Semester ending February, 1930

Allison, Stephen John

SUBJECT	HOURS	GRADE
Span. 1	3	F
Biol. 1a	3	D+
Eng. 1	3	D-
Math. 3	3	D-
Bible 18	3	D+
Phys. Educ.		a

Remarks

A, A–, A+, very superior ability; B, B–, B+, good; C. C–, C+, average; D, D–, D+, passing, below average; E, condition; F, Failure; Inc., Incomplete.
JOSEPHINE MORROW, Registrar.

Figure 10.1 Steve's Report Card, 1930.

Somehow, nineteen-year old Steve made it through his freshman year, although he must have been on academic probation, I'm sure.

And somehow he saved enough money to purchase an annual, which we found at the farm, still protected by its dust cover. In it, Steve Allison is listed as a freshman (no photo), a Phi Gamma Delta (no photo) and as a member of the freshman football team (nice photo). There's also a photo of him with the basketball team, where he's listed as an equipment manager. Basketball never was his best sport.

He'd been burning the candle at both ends - trying to keep his head above water academically, while competing in sports and being a fraternity guy. His friend and fraternity brother, Bill Hinkley, humorously summarized the results, on the back page of this yearbook:

For he's sleepy and he's lazy

You might even call him crazy

And his good, old, slow wrist watch is his pet,

But even though he's lazy

And some folks say he's crazy

He picks 'em up at short stop like a vet.

Steve must have been sleepy a lot, and late a lot. But he played a mean short stop.

Bill Hinkley's major was Political Science and his "credits" include:

Treasurer of the Junior Class
Phi Gamma Delta
'C' Club
Koshare
Question Club
Baseball 1,2,3
Basketball 1,2,3
Football 1,2, 3

This young man eventually became Superintendent of Aurora Public Schools - as I learned from his recent obituary in the local newspaper. It was then that I realized that my nephew had attended a school named after my father's college friend - Hinkley High School in Aurora, Colorado. Small world.

Another friend, Bill Van Dyke, has also signed this annual. He too was in the fraternity with Steve, in lots of school activities and in sports. His photo is found in places throughout the book. He and Steve are pictured as managers of the All-Conference basketball team - which included Bill Hinkley and Ernie Waters.

Ernie Waters signs, "Your old Phi Gamma Buddie", under this basketball entry:

Ernie Waters, diminutive forward, was the 'fightinest' player on the squad this season. What he lacked in avoirdupois and altitude, he more than made up in scrap. He has two more years.

Avoirdupois?

Super-achieving Bill H., handsome Bill V., scrappy Ernie and sleepy Steve must have been quite a foursome.

I picture them in black and white, like in an old movie - college high jinx, school spirit "win one for the Gipper" and all that. The annual and the other mementos remind me of raccoon coats (ouch!), twenty-two skiddoo (whatever that meant) and a more innocent time. I know, of course, that no time is truly 'innocent', and that hard and bad things are always happening. This was the year of the stock market crash and the beginning of the Great Depression, so if things were looking rosy, they wouldn't stay that way for long.

And do you remember the postcard from Steve, dated November 7, 1930, to his dad and Uncle George? The one Grampa saved? Steve writes that he's on his "way to Utah with the team. Hope we win."

The program for the University of Utah's homecoming game on November 8, 1930 gives a mini-portrait of my father on that fall day during his sophomore year. There he is, on the varsity squad, pictured in his uniform - a *leather* helmet and hardly *any* padding, and listed in the roster as:

No 5	Allison, Steve (Position)		halfback
	(Home)		Denver
	(Age)	20	
	(Exp)	0	
	(Wt)	160	

How proud he must have been! And perhaps John was also a little proud, since he saved the postcard. I hope so.

Later in his life, Steve remembered with pride his days with two famous men - Dutch Clark and Byron "Whizzer" White. He made note, in his high school journal, of meeting Dutch Clark, who's now an assistant coach for his college team. He's listed on this program as such - followed by an impressive biography.

The glories and camaraderie of football were blunted somewhat by Steve's constant struggles - academically and financially. This letter, saved by his dad, but addressed to his uncle sounds pretty bleak:

Colorado College
February 9, 1931

Dear Uncle:

How are you today and how is everything in Denver? Have you been out to see dad lately, is he all right.

My boss took his wife down to Denver last Monday so I didn't get to come down at all as I had planned. I have received the grades for my last semesters studies and find that I have passed in all of my subjects. I have started on my new lessons and find them interesting. But my books cost $18.50 for this semester and my fee's were $16.00 and after paying on my fraternity bill I find myself broke and in need of some money. did you make any deals yet for that property? Business is qite here and things aren't moving fast .

The football team goes out for spring practice tomorrow but I'm afraid I wont be there as I cannot find time to practice.

Well I had better close as I have some studying to do and its getting late. Tell dad hello. And please send me some money as I haven't even ten cents to buy shoe-strings.

Hoping to hear from you real soon.

Your Nephew
Steve Allison
1122 N. Cascade
Colorado Springs

P.S. Tell dad I passed all of my classes. And tell him to write me please.

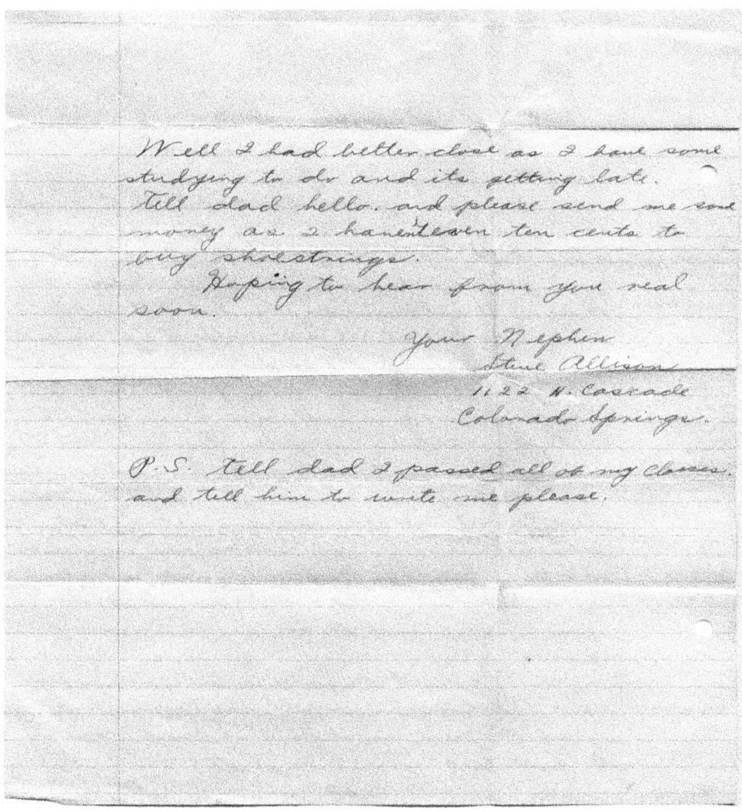

Well I had better close as I have some studying to do and its getting late.
Tell dad hello, and please send me some money as I haven't even ten cents to buy shoestrings.
Hoping to hear from you real soon.

Your Nephew
Steve Allison
1122 N. Cascade
Colorado Springs.

P.S. tell dad I passed all of my classes. and tell him to write me please.

Figure 10.2 Letter from Steve to his uncle.

Steve sent this downcast letter to 808 15th Street, Denver. This is the address of the candy store that his father managed back in 1919. But perhaps John's already living at the farm - since he asks his uncle if he's "been out to see dad lately?" Speaking of his boss, Steve says that "Business is qite here and things aren't moving fast." I wonder what kind of job he had. I hope he really didn't have to give up football because of lack of time (working? studying?). We'll soon see. He tells his uncle that he's passing all his classes, but neglects to add - barely.

But his grades do begin to improve:

THE COLORADO COLLEGE
COLORADO SPRINGS, COLORADO

Name Allison, Stephen John
Class Sophomore Date February, 1931

SUBJECT	HRS.	GRADE MID. SEM.	GRADE FINAL
Eng. 201	3		D-
Hist. 101	3		D
Span. 101	3		D-
Bus. 309	3		C-
Psych. 201	3		D-
Phys. Educ.			B

Remarks

A+, A, A-, Very superior ability. B+, B, B-, good; C+, C, C-, average. D+, D, D-, passing, below average. E, Condition; F, Failure; Inc., Incomplete.
JOSEPHINE MORROW, Registrar.

THE COLORADO COLLEGE
COLORADO SPRINGS, COLORADO

Name Allison, Stephen John
Class Sophomore Date March, 1931

SUBJECT	HRS.	GRADE MID. SEM.	GRADE FINAL
Hist. 102	3	D+	
Span. 102	3	D-	
Graph. 101	2	B	
Graph. 305	2	B+	
Civil 102	3	B+	
Geol. 202	3	D-	
Phys. Educ.			

Remarks

A+, A, A-, Very superior ability. B+, B, B-, good; C+, C, C-, average. D+, D, D-, passing, below average. E, Condition; F, Failure; Inc., Incomplete.
JOSEPHINE MORROW, Registrar.

THE COLORADO COLLEGE
COLORADO SPRINGS, COLORADO

Name Allison, Stephen John
Class Sophomore Date June, 1931

SUBJECT	HRS.	GRADE MID. SEM.	GRADE FINAL
Hist. 102	3		D
Span. 102	3		C+
Graph. 101	2		B
Graph. 305	2		B+
Civil 102	3		B-
Geol. 202	3		D-
Phys. Educ.			a

Remarks

A+, A, A-, Very superior ability. B+, B, B-, good; C+, C, C-, average. D+, D, D-, passing, below average. E, Condition; F, Failure; Inc., Incomplete.
JOSEPHINE MORROW, Registrar.

Figure 10.3 Collection of Steve's Report Cards in 1931.

So perhaps he did quit sports so he could spend more time on his studies…

He must have found the time and the money for at least one extra-curricular activity though. With these grade cards was an admission ticket to the Colorado College "C" Club Dance, which was held on "Saturday Evening, February 14, 1931, after the Wyoming Game". Admission was 50 cents.

He did come up with the money to buy a yearbook, but once again couldn't afford to have his photograph taken for the sophomore class and fraternity sections. But he's prominently featured in the *football* (see image at beginning of Chapter 10) and *baseball* sections; so he must have managed to successfully juggle work, study and team sports.

Top Row—VANDERHOOF, MANAGER; COOL, COACH; WEIDMAN, HAYDEN, HARTMAN, ALLISON, REID, HETER, REA, INGRAHAM, WARNING, DEHOLCZER, VAN DE GRAAFF, COACH.

Second Row—ROARK, E. STARBUCK, OWENS, IRWIN, WEAVER, MARTIN, L. STARBUCK, MCGRORY, FREIS, VANDEMOER, JONES.

Front Row—STILLMAN, BLAINE, DEUTSCH, THOMAS, MATHESON, POMEROY, HINKLEY, RYAN, STAPLETON, MCCLURG.

Figure 10.4 Football Team Photo (Steve is #5).

The narrative on this page tells of a tragic happening:

> Downright tough luck dogged the Tigers' heels throughout the 1930 season, striking its first and hardest blow when Akin, speedy young halfback, received injuries in practice which caused his death.

Left field is Steve's position in baseball. Evidently his skills were more offensive than defensive.

Here is the baseball team photo from this annual:

Front Row—Allison, Hill, Hinkley, Ingraham, Chaney, Butler.
Back Row—Walt Hughes, *Coach*, Sprenger, Clark, Owens, J. Reid, Pomeroy, Mercer, Grant, *Manager*.

THE SQUAD

Pomeroy (*Captain*)	*cf.*
Hill	*2b.*
Owens	*ss.*
Clark	*p, cf.*
Ingraham	*lf.*
Butler	*3b.*
Blunt	*1b.*
Allison	*lf.*
Hinkley	*c.*
Chaney	*p.*
Reid	*c. p.*
Sprenger	*p., lf.*
Mercer	*p.*

Figure 10.5 Baseball Team Photo (Steve is in the front row on the left).

Steve appears without a letter sweater in the "C" Club photo. That must have been a big disappointment for him. We know that he treasured his high school letter sweater.

In the "Puns" section of this 1931 yearbook, there's a weird and very offensive, attempt at humor. It involves the theory of evolution, and is entitled, "The

Cycle of Evolution, or, Fish is fish, even if it does have curly hair". It's long and very involved, and it shocked the heck out of me! That someone came up with such bigotry is sad, but somewhat believable, given the times. That it was included in the annual is hard to comprehend.

And on that unfortunate note, we'll take leave of Colorado College. In the fall of 1931, as he enters his junior year, we find Steve at the University of Colorado at Boulder.

How had that come to pass?

Had he gone to CC on an athletic scholarship, and lost it because of his poor grades? If so and if he was now forced to pay his own tuition - CU, a public university, was much less expensive than CC, a private college. I very much doubt that he *wanted* to change schools.

But once he got to CU, Steve embraced it as his own. He saved many mementos from his time there, including a CU Buffaloes belt buckle. But it was, I fear, the beginning of the end of the happiest time of his life. He didn't play any sports during his time in Boulder. If he had, I'm sure he would have saved some documentation of his involvement in those activities, and there's none. I know that must have broken his heart.

I doubt that academics got any easier for Steve at CU. However, since neither actual grades nor number of students in each class are recorded on the scholastic notices he received, it's hard to tell. It appears that he took "a full load" only one quarter and that he changed his major each quarter:

Form 478. 8-31-12M

UNIVERSITY OF COLORADO
Office of the Registrar
RECORD OF SCHOLARSHIP

Allison, Stephen John

College of Arts and Sciences

3d Quarter, 19 31 -19 32

SUBJECT	RANK	CREDIT
Educ. Psychology	75	3
Inorganic Chemistry	77	4
Criminology	70	2
The History of the U. S.	70	3
American Government	78	3
		15

Fred E. Allen

(OVER) NOT FOR TRANSFER OF CREDITS

Figure 10.6 Report Card from CU Boulder, 1931/32.

Later in his life, my father would be known as Steve Allison, the policeman. He would have a twenty-year career in the field of law enforcement. Perhaps he already felt some interest in this area, hence the course in Criminology that he took in the spring of 1932. Interestingly, neither that course, nor *any* of his third quarter courses are recorded in a letter he received from the Office of the Registrar dated July 15, 1932:

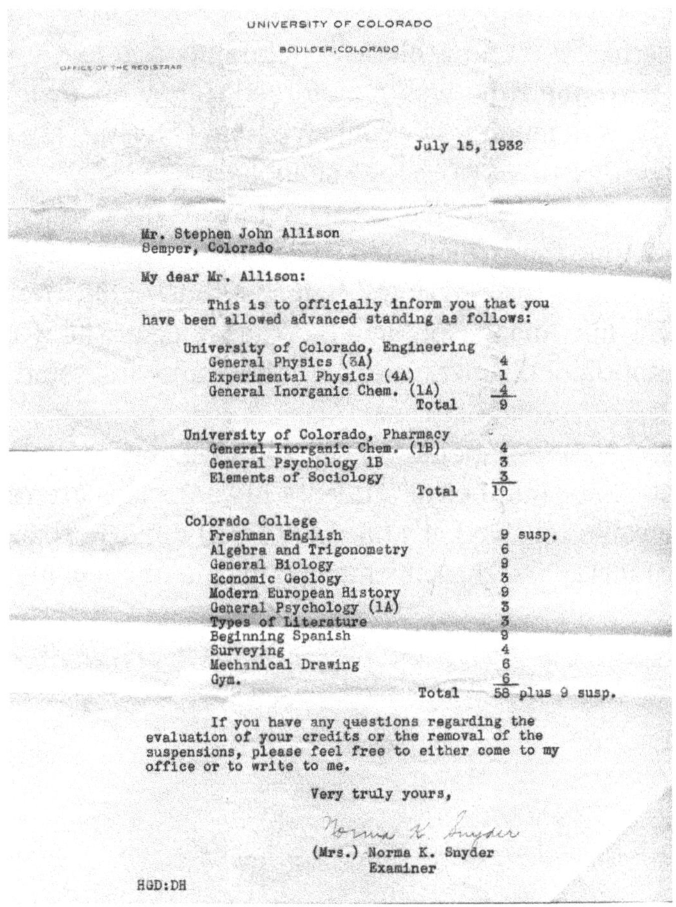

UNIVERSITY OF COLORADO
BOULDER, COLORADO

OFFICE OF THE REGISTRAR

July 15, 1932

Mr. Stephen John Allison
Semper, Colorado

My dear Mr. Allison:

This is to officially inform you that you have been allowed advanced standing as follows:

Course	Credits
University of Colorado, Engineering	
General Physics (3A)	4
Experimental Physics (4A)	1
General Inorganic Chem. (1A)	4
Total	9
University of Colorado, Pharmacy	
~~General Inorganic Chem.~~ (1B)	4
General Psychology 1B	3
Elements of Sociology	3
Total	10
Colorado College	
Freshman English	9 susp.
Algebra and Trigonometry	6
General Biology	9
Economic Geology	3
Modern European History	9
General Psychology (1A)	3
Types of Literature	3
Beginning Spanish	9
Surveying	4
Mechanical Drawing	6
Gym.	6
Total	58 plus 9 susp.

If you have any questions regarding the evaluation of your credits or the removal of the suspensions, please feel free to either come to my office or to write to me.

Very truly yours,

Norma K. Snyder

(Mrs.) Norma K. Snyder
Examiner

HGD:DH

Figure 10.7 Letter from the Office of the Registrar.

Having taken nine credit hours of Modern European History, I wonder if Steve had any inkling of the carnage and destruction that that would soon envelop that continent.

Judging from the three-ring binder he saved from this school year, I'd say his thoughts were of a more superficial nature. Except for his name and address, 1500 Broadway, it's covered with nonsense. CU is written all over it, as are Greek letters that represent fraternities and sororities.

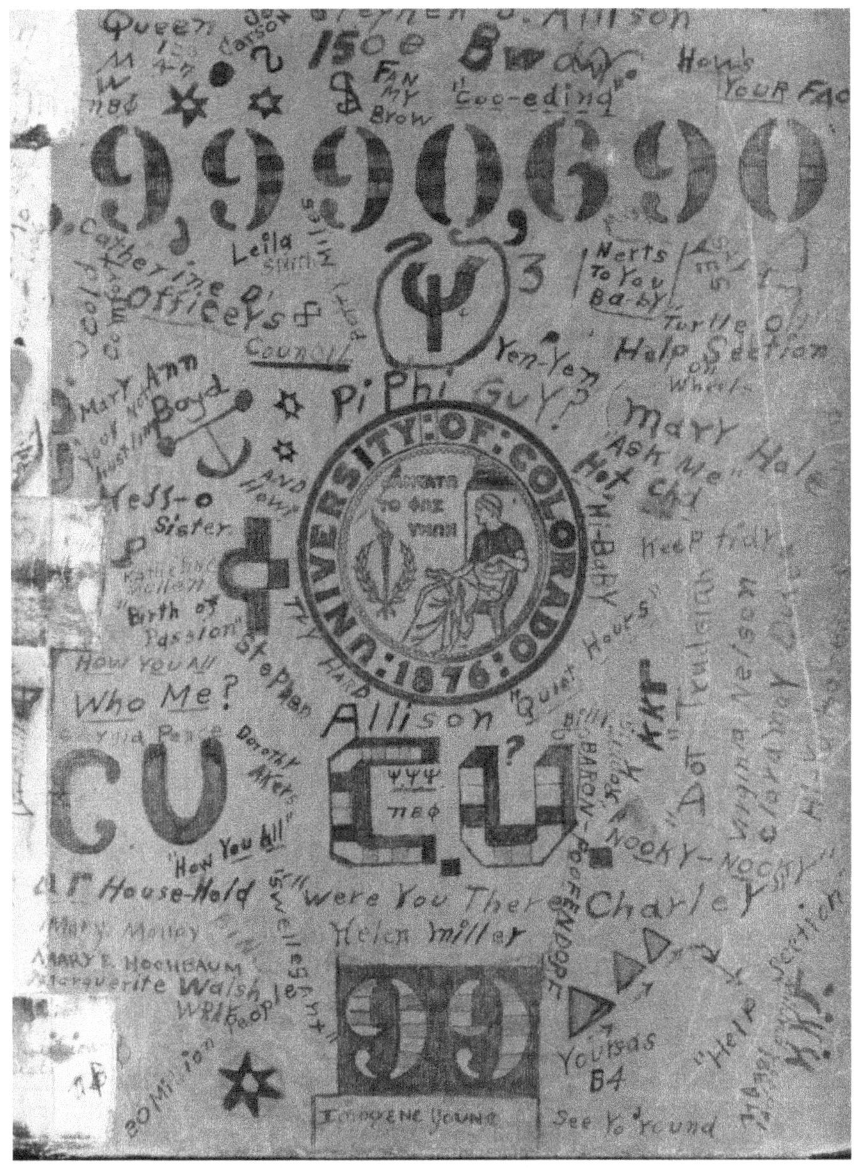

Figure 10.8 Steve's 3-Ring Binder.

Here's a sampling of some of the other tidbits:

Pi Phi Guy?
Katherine Mullin
Yen-Yen
Birth of Passion
Keep tidy
Try Hard
Mary Hale, Queen
Hi-Baby
Jo Carson
How You All?
coo-eding
Who Me?
Georgia Pence
Dorothy Akers
Cold Comfort
Leila Smerl
Mary Molloy
Betty Miles
Nerts to You, Baby
Swellegant
Say Yes
Were You There?
Turtle O
BARON-POOGENDORF
Help Section
Bing
On Wheels
NOOKY-NOOKY
Council
Dot Trudgian
Virginia Nelson
99,990,690
ClaraMay Duke
Mary Ann Boyd
Hi-Ya
Your not Hustling
MARY E. HOCHBAUM
And How?
Marquerite Walsh
30 Million People
Helen Miller
IMOGENE YOUNG
Birmignham Bertha
NO RATS ALLOWED
Rasputin
I'm no angel
I gave you my soul - you heel
Okeydoke

There are several illustrations, including a dog, labeled Ozzie, and a really dumb looking guy labeled Steve. This stuff seems awfully childish to me. Steve was 21 years old. He'd not had an easy life. You'd think he'd be more mature.

Steve really loved popular music. When we cleaned out the garage at the farm, we found at least 3,000 records - the big kind, 78 RPMs. And as you can gather from the names on the cover of this notebook, he also really loved women. Some young woman (it certainly looks like a woman's handwriting) did a very neat job of cataloguing his record collection in this notebook. The recordings are listed alphabetically, with one page per letter. For example the "D" page reads:

D.

Doctor, Lawyer, Indian Chief	H. Carmichael	ARA	109
Drip Drip Drip (Sloppy Lagoon)	Spike Jones	Victor	20-1733-
Day By Day	Les Brown	Columbia	36945
Doctor Lawyer Indian Chief	Les Brown	Columbia	36945
Don't Be a Baby-Baby	Tommy Dorsey	RCA Victor	20-1842-
Day By Day	Martha Stewart	RCA Victor	20-1828-
Don't Let the Sun Catch You Crying	Louis Jordan	Decca	18818 B
Don't Worry 'Bout That Mule	Louis Jordan	Decca	18734 A
Don't Forget Tonight Tomorrow	Frank Sinatra	Columbia	3685

Figure 10.9 Steve's Music Collection; Songs starting with "D".

His love of music and his love of women are two things that will remain constant throughout the first half of his life.

And his love of football will remain constant throughout *both* halves of his life.

Somehow my father gave me the impression that he'd played football with Byron "Whizzer" White. In his dreams perhaps. A newspaper article published a few years ago about Judge White's retirement from the United States Supreme Court stated that he started playing for CU in 1934 - two years *after* Steve left that institution. A program from a football game Steve attended - University of Colorado vs. Colorado Agricultural College, on October 22, 1932 - lists *Clayton* White as a CU player. The retirement article mentioned that

Byron's brother, Clayton, had indeed played football at CU in 1932. So, I guess Steve attended school with the less famous brother.

And speaking of dreams, yes, Steve does leave the University of Colorado in the spring of 1932 - his hopes of ever again playing college football and baseball abruptly ended. And he must know at this point, surely, that he'll never realize his cherished dream of playing these sports professionally.

And at that moment, I think, so ended his youth.

"I haven't even ten cents to buy shoestrings."

Steve's letter – 1931

CHAPTER 11

"Everything is OK in Denver."

I know very little about the next ten years of my dad's life. He saved very little from these years.

I wonder why he had to leave college? I'd guess money was the main reason - or lack thereof. In the midst of the depression, perhaps the family businesses were not doing so well.

We next hear from Steve in 1935, after his Uncle George's death. While in Greece administering George's estate, John received, and saved, two letters from his son. The return address on the envelopes is the TWENTIETH AVENUE GARAGE at 1971 Downing Street, Denver, Colorado. My mother remembers this garage and told me that it was owned and operated by "the Allisons". Perhaps Steve was working there. If so, I doubt he was doing anything mechanical. I don't think he was mechanically inclined – at all. Maybe he was managing it. Well, from this address he writes to his dad by way of their Greek lawyer:

October 19, 1935

Dear Dad,

Hope you are feeling O.K. and that you are having a good time. Have sent 2 post cards to you and received no answer from them so guess you did not get them.

Everything is OK in Denver. It is very cold today. We had a very early frost it came the day before my birthday Sept. 26, Gus and I have been bringing in tomatoes and selling them. The early frost hurt them somewhat but we sold them all.

The reason I did not write you a letter before this is because, there is a chance to get a good job as radio operator at the city hall the job pays $160.00 per month to start with. You work for 20 years then get $90.00 a month pension.

There are 104 applying for the job and all of us have to take both physical and mental eximination because the job is under Civil Service. I have been studying real hard and so far have passed the physical eximation but have not heard yet how I came out in the mental eximination. I have been up to see Mayor B Stapleton he said he would do what he could and that I have to pass both eximanations first then he said he would see. He is very busy and I did not get to talk to him very much. saw Rugg Williams Deputy Chief he introduced me to Chief Carland and they both said they would help me but couldn't do nothing now until they see how far up I got on the examination list. The eximanation lasted five hours and boy I sure had a headache my head was busting. I studyed real hard and feel pretty confident of passing. and am now anxiously awaiting for the returns on the eximanitation. I wish you were here to talk to Stapleton. I know I would get the job then. Stapleton is the head man.

I sure do miss you. I go out to the ranch and you are not there. I kinda expect to see you there and the place don't seem the same with-out you. I do hope you will not get mixed up in the war and hope you will get back here as soon as possible because you never know what will happen when there is a state of war existing between countries. I have been worried about that and do hope you will be O.K.

Everyone says to tell you hello. Gus, Frank, The Bee-man and his wife, Shelter and Mr. Jack.

Please tell my grand-mother and the folks that I would give anything to be over there so I could see them and talk to them. Although I guess I couldn't understand them nor they understand me. Frank received the telegram and he said everything is OK I don't understand the full meaning of it.

Please write me soon and tell me if you plan to come back soon.

I'll close now hoping to hear from you real soon as I sure do miss you. Goodby and good luck.

Your Son,
Steve Allison

P.S. Everything is OK here. so don't worry about anything. Jones was just up and want's me to pay one of the old bills. I told him absolutely nothing doing I wouldn't pay nothing.

They may try to get a judgement against me for it but I don't think they can. Please write soon as possible.

Steve

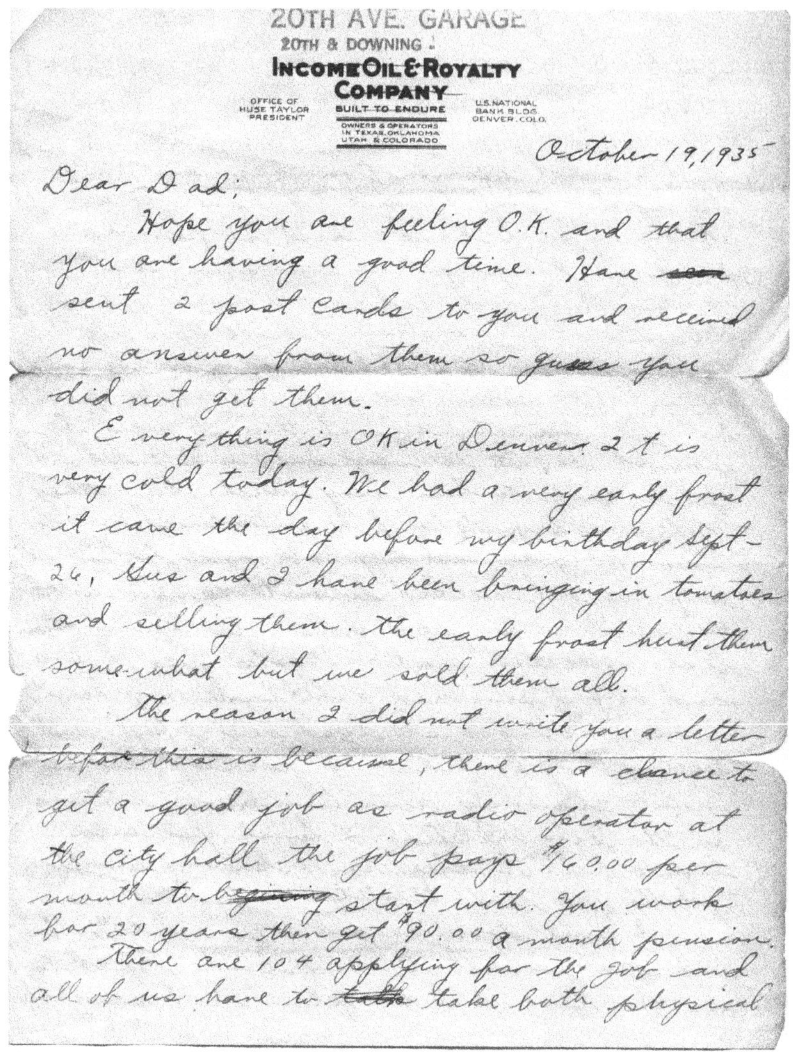

20TH AVE. GARAGE
20TH & DOWNING
INCOME OIL & ROYALTY COMPANY
OFFICE OF HUSE TAYLOR PRESIDENT — BUILT TO ENDURE — U.S. NATIONAL BANK BLDG. DENVER, COLO.
OWNERS & OPERATORS IN TEXAS, OKLAHOMA, UTAH & COLORADO

October 19, 1935

Dear Dad;

Hope you are feeling O.K. and that you are having a good time. Have ~~seen~~ sent 2 post cards to you and received no answer from them so ~~guess~~ you did not get them.

Everything is OK in Denver. It is very cold today. We had a very early frost it came the day before my birthday Sept-24, Gus and I have been bringing in tomatoes and selling them. the early frost hurt them some-what but we sold them all.

The reason I did not write you a letter ~~before this~~ is because, there is a chance to get a good job as radio operator at the city hall the job pays $160.00 per month to ~~begining~~ start with. You work for 20 years then get $90.00 a month pension.

There are 104 applying for the job and all of us have to ~~take~~ take both physical

Figure 11.1 First letter from Steve to his father, 1935.

Good grief! How many ways did Steve find to spell "examination"? I hope he did better on the "mental" part of the exam than his spelling and grammar in this letter might indicate. Perhaps not though, because I don't think he got the job. I sure never heard him mention being a radio operator at "city hall".

Seems Gus is taking care of the farm while John is away. This letter mentions tomatoes and bees - two things I'll always associate with my grandfather. He had a huge garden at the farm and grew the most delicious tomatoes. Also, he always kept bees - lots of bees.

It makes me smile when my dad mentions that Stapleton is the "head man". He talked to John like that – using the same kind of old country phrasing and terminology that his father and uncles used.

He wrote this second letter to his dad in November 1935:

Dear Dad:

Gee it seems you have been gone for about ten years I sure wish you would hurry and get back as I sure do miss you. You said in your letter to Gus that you were feeling sick I hope you feel all-right now.

Have been busy here and working hard. I thought maybe I would find out how I came out on that examination for the Radio Operator. Was suppose to know to-day. Rugg Williams sure is pulling for me. sure is a nice fellow.

Gus is getting along ok on the ranch and things are going along O.K. Wheat price is around $1.02 which I think is high. We have been having a lot of snow and the wheat on the dry land look's very good.

This fellow Roadmer is sure a very nice man. I get things for Gus such as bread and tobacco and roadmer is more than glad to take them out. gus has three tons of coal that I ordered for him so he can be warm. I got Gus a good police dog named "Prince" sure is a good dog.

Frank sure is doing good business at the store. Gus and Frank were very happy over the letter you sent to Gus. Gus sticks close to the ranch and doesn't go away from the ranch much. He seem's very interested in raising chickens.

Business isn't much better with me we are getting along and that's about all.

Secaratery of State Carr resigned this morning. they have been having him up for impeachment for a shortage of about $22,000 on liquor and whisky tax collections.

Would sure like to know when you plan on starting back. Everyone ask's about you Dr. Butterfield gives his regards to you.

Gus read your letter to Havenfien and Epstein and they seemed very much satisfyied with what was in the letter. They both wish you a speedy return. The letter took 16 day's to get here we were all anxious to hear from you. Hope you can finish up and come home as soon as possible as we all sure miss you.

Well Dad I guess I have said enough for this time so I'll close hoping to hear from you real soon.

Your Son

Steve

P.S. Take good care of yourself and write soon. I have your October and November government checks in safe.

Steve

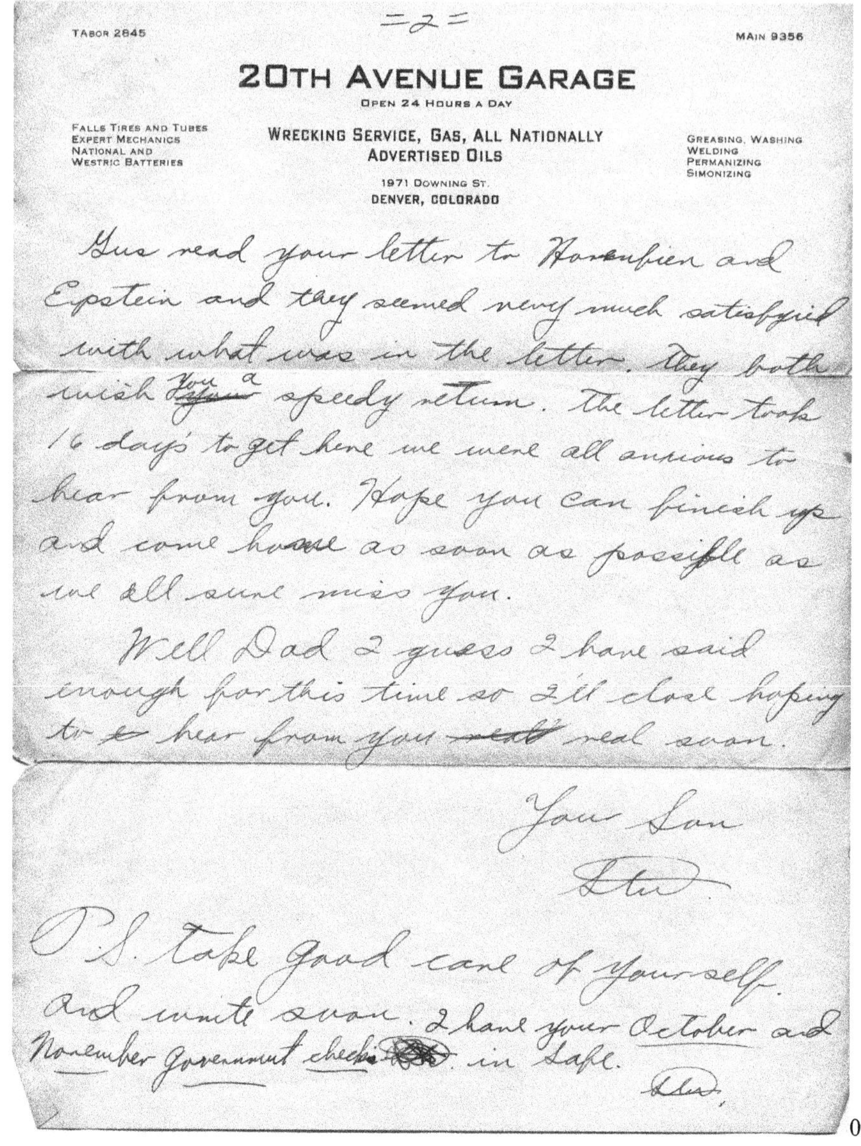

=2=

TAbor 2845

MAin 9356

20TH AVENUE GARAGE

OPEN 24 HOURS A DAY

FALLS TIRES AND TUBES
EXPERT MECHANICS
NATIONAL AND
WESTRIC BATTERIES

WRECKING SERVICE, GAS, ALL NATIONALLY
ADVERTISED OILS

1971 DOWNING ST.
DENVER, COLORADO

GREASING, WASHING
WELDING
PERMANIZING
SIMONIZING

Gus read your letter to Horenfien and Epstein and they seemed very much satisfyied with what was in the letter. They both wish you a speedy return. The letter took 16 days to get here we were all anxious to hear from you. Hope you can finish up and come home as soon as possible as we all sure miss you.

Well Dad I guess I have said enough for this time so I'll close hoping to hear from you real soon.

Your Son
Steve

P.S. take good care of yourself. And write soon. I have your October and November Government check in Safe.
Steve

Figure 11.2 Second letter from Steve to his father in 1935.

He was such a good son.

Is Steve referring to the garage when he writes, "Business isn't much better with me. we are getting along and that's about all."?

Or perhaps to his marriage? According to my mom and Steppy, he was married four times. I can find record of only three marriages. If there was a fourth, *his* first, it must have taken place at about this time…

Two years later, he left this note for his father at the farm:

Dad

We were here and waited for you for two hours. We will be back either tonight or tomorrow morning.

Gus said to read this letter over and then for you to re-write it and send it to your mother. Gus also wants the bill for the hospital which amounts to about 50.00. I think he gave it to you and you have it somewhere.

Steve

On November 11, 1938, Steve attended a pro football game between the Pittsburgh Pirates and the Los Angeles Bulldogs at Will Rogers Stadium at the Broadmoor Hotel in Colorado Springs. Byron White was a player, and he signed Steve's program.

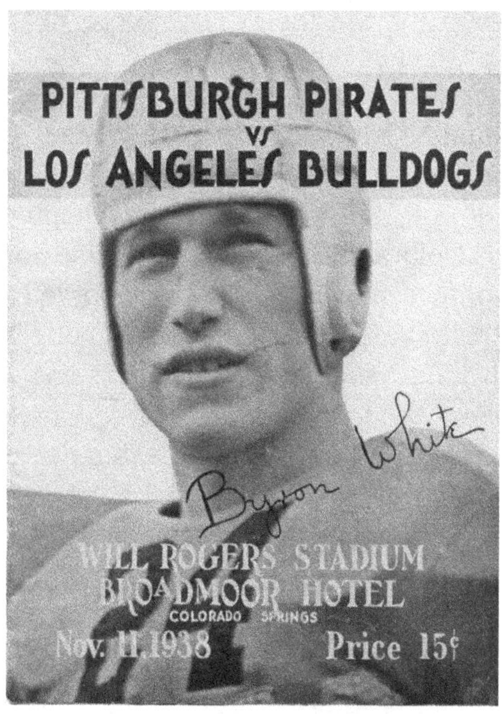

Figure 11.3 Game Program signed by Bryron "Whizzer" White.

It contains a "portrait" of White that also mentions Steve's other athletic hero - Dutch Clark, his coach at CC. Here are a few excerpts:

> Colorado's greatest athlete since Earl "Dutch" Clark - - Byron `Whizzer' White - - entered college under conditions quite different from those which the Dutchman faced when he enrolled at Colorado College. When Clark entered C.C. fall of 1926, he was the state's most famous high school athlete - - all-state in football and basketball, all-American in high school football.
>
> While Byron was making football history, he was achieving an ambition in which football did not figure. He was elected to Phi Beta Kappa the week before his team played Utah; he won a Rhodes scholarship after the football season was over.
>
> With his brilliant football record, White was the most sought after college athlete in America when professional football moguls went after talent. Art Rooney, owner of the Pittsburgh Pirates, drew White's name in the National League draft and began negotiations. White said he would not play pro football if it meant forfeiting his Rhodes scholarship - - and stuck to this even when Rooney offered him an unprecedented $15,000 for one year.
>
> Then, almost on the eve of his departure for England, White learned that he could enter Oxford January 1 without imperiling his scholarship. That made it possible for him to accept Rooney's offer of $15,000 and still carry out his dream of attending Oxford.

While his heroes made headlines and money, Steve played amateur baseball in and around the Denver area.

An 8x10 team photo of him at beginning of Chapter 11 (back row, third from the right) and his Colorado Blue Print team was probably taken at about this time. Each person has signed the photo. George Hotchkiss and Gasper Herrera signed both their names, but the others signed their first or last names only. The batboy, Bob, looks just like Jerry Mathers on the television program, "Leave it to Beaver".

Three newspaper clippings describe games that Steve played in during the summer of 1939. I can't figure out if he played for one, two or three teams. See if you can. The colorful commentaries read in part:

> *5/26/39*
>
> *Cap Eberle's double with Pete Ley and Steve Allison on base brought White House a 2 to 0 victory over Red Shields*

7/10/39

Seven Up and Davis & Shaw went into the seventh with the score 2-2, but Steve Allison's line drive over the left-center fence with two mates aboard quickly put an end to the proceedings. York pitched four-hit ball for the Seven Up aggregation

PUBLIC SCHOOLS WALLOP GOLDEN GATE BY 14-1 SCORE

7/10/39

The National leaguers, some of them hitting to the sky and the rest blowing to it, put another quartet of softball settos into the record book Monday night at City park.

Public Schools opened the program by slapping out sixteen basehits while walloping Golden Gate 14-1. The winners had only two idle frames, the second and third, but they made up for lost time in the third by denting the rubber for eight runs. Spellman did the throwing for the Schools and was touched for only three bingles.

Seven Up and Davis & Shaw went into the seventh with the score 2-2, b Steve Allison's line drive over the left-center fence with two mates aboard quickly put an end to the proceedings. York pitched four-hit ball for the Seven Up aggregation.

Montgomery Ward and Western Slavonics beat home plate as tho it was a dirty rug as Wards finally won, 12-8, in nine innings. The oddity of this contest was that the winners scored eight runs in the first inning and then didn't score again until the ninth, when they chased four more across. Both rallies were aided and abetted by eleven errors by the losers.

Telephone company and First Federal played a listless game that wound up in favor of the Phone team, 9-2.

The line scores and schedule:

Public Schools... 1 0 0 8 1 2 2—14 16 1
Golden Gate...... 0 1 0 0 0 0 0— 1 3 3
Spellman and Niblo; Martin, Kanta and Kanta, Martin.

Seven Up.......... 0 0 0 1 1 0 3—5 10 1
Davis-Shaw........ 0 0 0 2 0 0 0—2 4 1
York and Schrieber; Niblo and Brigham.

Wards........ 8 0 0 0 0 0 0 0 4—12 7 2
West. Slavs. 0 0 0 3 5 0 0 0 0— 8 11 9
Allison, Mullinax and Cox; Roy and Horvat.

First Federal...... 0 0 1 1 0 0 0—2 4 6
Telephone.......... 0 2 0 4 2 1 *—9 10 1
Scott and Blanche; Graves and J. Graham.

23d and Welton

A three-run rally in the seventh inning enabled Red Shields to break a 7-7 tie and whip United Fuel, 10-7, in the softball feature at Twenty-third and Welton Monday night.

Brooks Sports whipped Five Points, 9-5, and East Denver Merchants pummeled Christian Center, 14-3.

The results:

R. H. E.
Brooks Sportswear. 2 0 4 0 0 0 3—9 11 4
Five Points ...... 0 0 1 2 0 2 0—5 11 1
Tomanage and Duran; Rogers and Riley.

R. H. E.
Red Shields ...... 1 4 2 0 0 0 3—10 10 3
United Fuel ... 2 4 0 1 0 0 0 0— 7 7 3
Pappas and Cox; Grande, Ford and Romero.

R. H. E.
Christian Center.. 0 0 0 0 3 0 0— 3 2 6
E Denver Merch. 6 3 1 1 0 3 0—14 9 3
Hall and La Blanche; J. Williams and Shorty.

Games Tuesday.

George's vs. New York Furniture.
Dixie Gas vs. Wangers.
Welton St. Yanks vs. Curtis St. Cards.

Overland Park

All of Overland park's softball winners Monday night piled up easy victories except Kroonenberg, which copped a 4-2 decision from Buchanans in the feature tilt.

Sovereign laced Tramway, 11-4; City Employes thumped Save-a-Nickel, 11-3, and Cosmopolitan socked Texaco, 13-5.

The results:

R. H. E.
Kroonenberg ....3 0 0 0 0 1 0—4 7 0
Buchanan's ....0 1 0 0 0 1 0—2 3 0
J. Camping and Kamp; Montoya and Hayward.

Sovereign ....0 0 0 5 2 0 4—11 11 4
Tramway ....1 0 0 1 0 2 0— 4 5 4
Herrera, Jennings and Vine; Woodruff,

Figure 11.4 Newspaper Clipping about Steve and his Seven Up Baseball Team playing Davis & Shaw.

What a great writer! I've italicized my favorite phrases from this article:

> The National leaguers, some of them hitting to the sky and the *rest blowing to it*, put another quartet of softball settos into the record book Monday night at City Park.
>
> Public Schools opened the program by slapping out sixteen basehits while walloping Golden Gate 14 - 1. The winners had only two idle frames, the second and third, but they made up for lost time in the third by *denting the rubber* for eight runs. Spellman did the throwing for the Schools and was *touched for only three bingles..*
>
> Montgomery Ward and Western Slavonics *beat home plate as tho it was a dirty rug* as Wards finally won, 12 - 8, in nine innings. The oddity of this contest was that the winners scored eight runs in the first inning and then didn't score again until the ninth, when they chased four more across. Both rallies were *aided and abetted* by eleven errors by the losers.

7/26/39

Cook-Alpert remained undefeated in the American Softball League at City Park by trimming White House Cleaners 7 to 2 last night in one of four games witnessed by 2,500 fans.

ALLISON HITS HOMER

Steve Allison hit a homer over the left field fence for the Bottlers.

In other tiffs, Colorado Blue Print eked out a 1-to-0 thriller from the Mantle Club, Bottlers won from Public Schools 2 to 0 and Western Slavonics thumped Davis & Shaw, 2 to 4.

C-A Trims White House

2,500 Witness Softball Games

Cook-Alperts remained undefeated in the American Softball League at City Park by trimming White House Cleaners, 7 to 2, last night in one of four games witnessed by 2,500 fans.

In other tiffs, Colorado Blue Print eked out a 1-to-0 thriller from Mantle Club, Bottlers won from Public Schools, 2 to 0, and Western Slavonics thumped Davis & Shaw, 6 to 4.

Johnson Is Injured

C-A took a 2-run lead off Pug Johnson in the first two innings, then wound up with five in the sixth off Sam Levine. Levine replaced Johnson in the third when the latter twisted his knee while delivering a pitch.

Pug walked two in the first, then wild pitched and Caruso LaGuardia scored. In the second, Jiggs Langton tripled and scored on another wild one.

Irwin Hendler homered over the left field fence in the sixth. Human homered for White House in the seventh.

Allison Hits Homer

Blue Print scored in the first frame when Bud Martin filled the bases with walks and Redel scored during a double play.

Steve Allison hit a homer over the left field fence for the Bottlers.

The scores:

Score by innings:		R.	H.	E.
Bottlers	000 100 1	2	6	2
Schools	000 000 0	0	2	0

J. York and Schrieber; Spellman and Niblo.

Score by innings:		R.	H.	E.
Mantle Club	000 000 0	0	2	2
Colorado Blues	100 000 *	1	2	0

Martin and Goolsby; Cowger and Tolve.

Score by innings:		R.	H.	E.
Davis & Shaw	020 000 2	4	7	1
Slavonics	020 103 *	6	7	3

Niblo and Brigham; Roy and S. Mauser.

Score by innings:		R.	H.	E.
White House	000 000 2	2	6	1
Cook-Alperts	110 005 *	7	5	0

Johnson, Levine and Human; Milner and Kesiel.

Figure 11.5 Newspaper Clipping about Steve and his Bottlers Baseball Team.

I'm trying to picture 28 year old Steve, in this summer of 1939. He's obviously a pretty good amateur baseball player. But, I'd like to be able to picture him with a friend, and so I've nominated Meyer Shapiro. Remember him, the original owner of Steve's high school notebook? Well, after ten years, his name resurfaces – in the above article of 5/26/39:

> Clothiers Win 4th Straight
> Shapiro Homers For 3 - 1 Triumph
> Meyer Shapiro's homer over the left field wall last night was good for three runs and brought the Clothiers a 3 - 1 victory over Denver Boosters....

And with the article is a photograph of a young man, holding a cat. (The original Molly?) Although he's at the farm, he wears a three-piece suit, a tie and a hat. I've decided that this is Meyer Shapiro. I can feel their elation as he and Steve slam homers over the left field wall, to the cheers of a thousand fans.

Figure 11.6 Meyer Shapiro? at the farm.

But in trying to picture Steve further, I come up short. How did he support himself? What kind of work did he do? Did he live alone? Or did he have a wife - as I suspect? Did he and his friends worry about the Japanese and German encroachments that would soon lead to World War II? He leaves me no clue.

A pamphlet tucked away with these baseball clippings might indicate that Steve was experiencing some inner struggles at this stage of his life. It's about self-consciousness, and is very hard on people suffering from this affliction. I've included a small portion of it below. If he was, indeed, "self-conscious", I'm sure that he must have felt even worse about himself after reading this treatise:

> SELF CONSCIOUSNESS (Bashfulness)
>
> A Serious Handicap Yet Easy to Overcome
>
> Do you ever feel embarrassed before strangers? Are you ever bashful in a crowd? Do you ever become confused when you meet people for the first time? If so, it is because you are self-conscious. It is because you constantly think of yourself, of your own words and actions, rather than the words and actions of the people you meet. Self-consciousness can be easily overcome if you know how to go about it.
>
> Self-consciousness means painful consciousness of being observed by others. When people are self-conscious, they are unduly sensitive to the opinions and thoughts of those around them. They undervalue their own judgment and attempt to act in conformity with the judgment of others. Self-conscious people dread criticism. Not only spoken criticism, but mental criticism. A cross look or a mocking laugh can paralyze them. They fear criticism so greatly that they often suspect it where it doesn't exist.
>
> Self-conscious people will go to any lengths to avoid unfavorable notice or attention of any kind. In thus attempting to avoid notice they are often guilty of foolish actions which attract more attention than if they had acted naturally.
>
> There is only one fundamental, underlying cause of self-consciousness and that is a faulty and impaired Nervous System. Men and women with strong nerves rarely suffer from self-consciousness while those with delicate or deranged Nervous Systems are never wholly free from it. The Nervous System is the seat of all emotions. Since self-consciousness is an emotional weakness, it is in the Nervous System that we must search for its cause and cure. The person with strong nerves may feel emotions just as strongly as the nervous one, but he is able to remain calm even in the face of great crises. He does not tremble. He does not lose control of himself. Why? Because his nerves - the tiny channels through which his impulses flow - are strong and in good order.
>
> From this, it can be seen that the only natural way to banish self-consciousness is to build up your Nervous System; to strengthen your nerves and make them function normally.
>
> The first thing to do is to regenerate your lost Nerve Force -to build up strong, sound nerves. No tonic or magic system of exercises can do this. You need a knowledge of the action and abuses of nerves; an understanding of the natural laws of nerve fatigue, of mental and physical relaxation and Nerve Metabolism, such as my course of instruction covers.

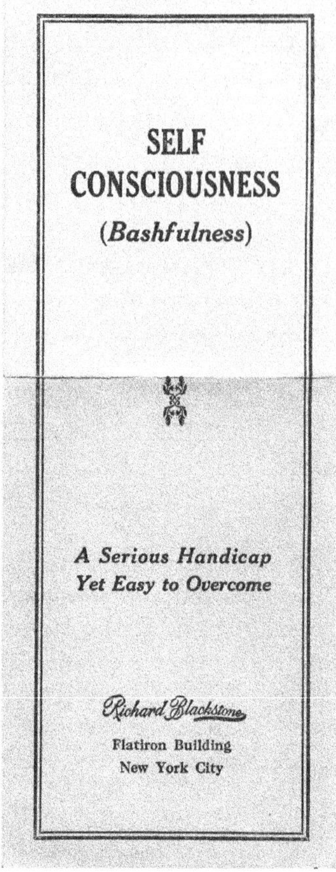
SELF
CONSCIOUSNESS
(Bashfulness)

A Serious Handicap
Yet Easy to Overcome

Richard Blackstone
Flatiron Building
New York City

Figure 11.7 Self Conciousness Pamphlet.

Good grief! Pretty hard on shy people, huh? Pity the poor souls with "delicate or deranged" nerves - they suffer because they think only of themselves, don't you know? And how about that Nerve Force and Nerve Metabolism that the author knows all about?

I hope my dad didn't get too down on himself after reading this. He'll need a healthy mental attitude as he enters the next decade of his life.

"Everything is OK in Denver."

Steve's letter – 1935

CHAPTER 12

"two years of blissful married life"

One day, early in the summer of 1989, while I sorted through the more important things in the farmhouse, Ken was working his way through the less important things in the garage.

Or so we thought. I was working with personal papers, antique jewelry and vintage books for example, and he was dealing with thousands of 33 and 45 records, boxes and boxes of tools, building supplies, fishing tackle and the like. But he found something more.

Tucked into an opening in the wall was what looked to be a small metal toolbox, about 6" - 12". No, it didn't contain cash, or jewels, or stock certificates. But it did contain a valuable gift that Steve had left for his daughter. Inside, just under the lid, was an envelope on which he'd written, "For L.L.". As it would turn out, finding this envelope was the main impetus for me to write this book.

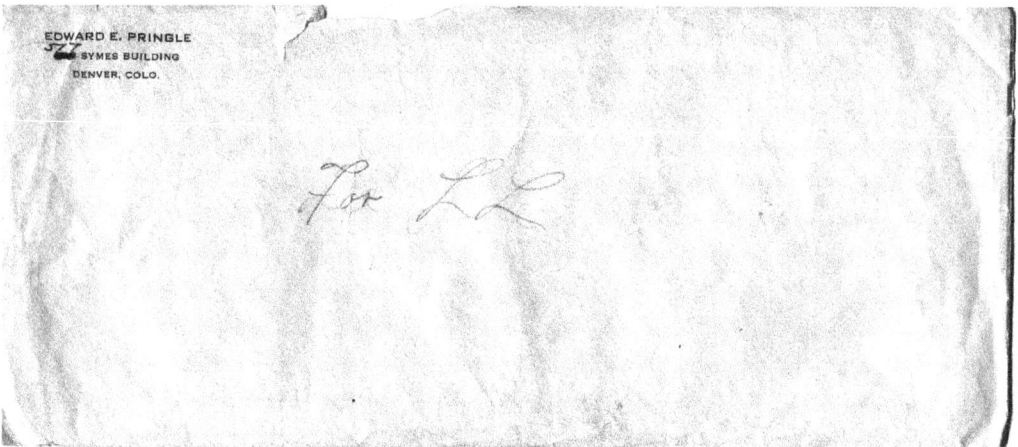

Figure 12.1 THE Envelope.

As we briefly looked through the contents, it was clear right away that it held things of great import to Steve. I put The Box in a safe place, to be looked into more carefully some time in the less harried future.

Which turned out to be a few years later. At that time I found that it did hold, contrary to what I said above, some cash – although it just wasn't very usable cash. There were some paper monies from the Confederate States of America, some franc notes from the Banque De L'Algerie, and a 500,000 drachma note from Greece. There was also, a rosary, a holy card and several postcards picturing Uncle George's elegant "candy emporium" (see Figure 5.6).

Figure 12.2 Paper monies from the Confederate States of America.

There was also a marriage certificate, signed by the Justice of the Peace in Longmont, Colorado, that recorded the marriage of Stephen Allison and Margaret Dunn. It's dated January 9, 1940. Both Steppy, and later, Shirley had told me about red headed Margaret – Steve's second wife. In trying to picture this newly wed couple and their surroundings, I remembered that it was in May of 1940 that Steve filed a lawsuit against his grandmother, his uncles, his aunt and his father concerning ownership of the farm and city lots at 29th and Grove Street. Did he and Margaret live in the house on Grove Street? If so, they didn't live there long. With the marriage certificate, was a newspaper announcement of divorce petitions filed on January 23, 1941, one of which reads: "Stephen J. Allison against Margaret A. Dunn". That was quick.

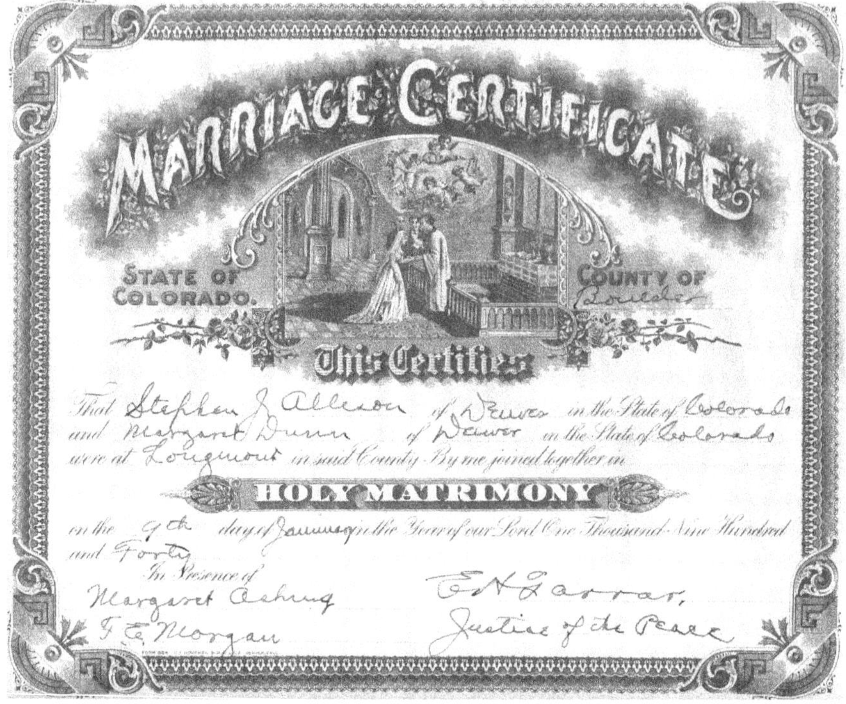

MARRIAGE CERTIFICATE

STATE OF COLORADO.

COUNTY OF Boulder

This Certifies

That Stephen J. Allison of Denver in the State of Colorado
and Margaret Dunn of Denver in the State of Colorado
were at Longmont in said County By me joined together in

HOLY MATRIMONY

on the 9th day of January in the Year of our Lord One Thousand Nine Hundred
and Forty

In Presence of
Margaret Ashing
F. E. Morgan

E. H. Farrar,
Justice of the Peace

Figure 12.3 Marriage Certificate for Steve and Margaret.

And then there were the journals - his and my mother's. He included these, I think, hoping they'd help me better understand my parents - both of them. I think he wanted me to know, by reading these journals, how hard he'd tried, as a single parent, to care for his child; and to understand how hurt he'd been - first by my mother and eventually by me.

Shirley Mae entered his life first, of course. She and Steve met in 1941, when he was thirty years old – and she was seventeen!

They started dating shortly thereafter and she gave him a portrait of herself - a portrait that he'd keep with him for the rest of his life. When I found it at the farm some 40 years later, I gave it to my sister, who treasures it. In it, a young woman with dark blond hair and brown eyes rests her head on crossed arms and gazes dreamily into the distance. This is how she looked when they fell in love.

But what was she doing just before that, while Steve and Margaret were ending their marriage? Because she kept a diary, and because Steve saved a portion of it in The Box, we have a tiny cameo of seventeen year old Shirley Mae:

March 1941

March 17, 1941 Today is Grampa Johnson's birthday.

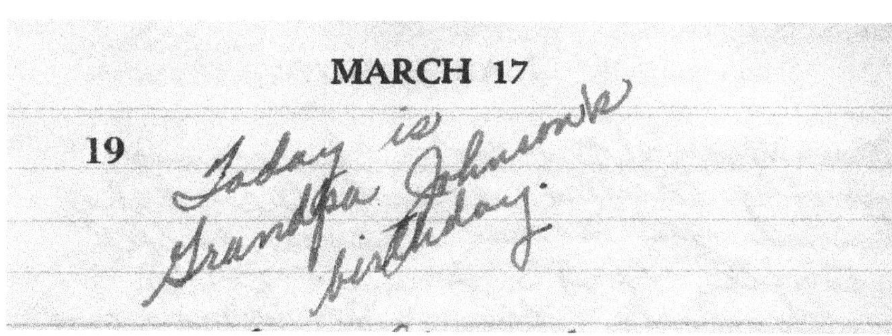
MARCH 17

19 Today is Grandpa Johnson's birthday.

Figure 12.4 Shirley's Journal: March 17, 1941

March 21, 1941	Spring Vacation Am getting ready to go to Pueblo. Went dancing at the Rainbow with Jack and Jimmy.
March 22, 1941	Morton is really worried he sent a Sp Del. today. Had iniation for Sub. Deb. kids at the Pic - met Temple Brooks, a sailor
March 23, 1941	Left this morning for Pueblo at 8:45 A.M. Arrived midst sleet and snow at 12:30 P.M.
March 24, 1941	Went down town and is it ever cold here
March 25, 1941	Went down town again
March 26, 1941	Morton came down for supper. He apologized and tore the picture up. We got stuck in the mud.
March 27, 1941	He was here again today. Sylvia has made the darlingest outfit.
March 28, 1941	Wrote letters all day. Went over to hospital to see J.
March 29, 1941	Took me to the hospital at 10:00 P.M. this evening with acute appendacitis, operated on at 12:30 A.M. Morton got there at 12:00 and Mom and Daddy at 2:20 A.M. Dad Dawley came to see me before they operated.
March 30, 1941	Don't remember much. Mort and Dad had to leave this afternoon, Mom is going to stay till Fri.
March 31, 1941	Still don't feel so good.
April 1, 1941	Feeling lots better Getting all sorts of fan mail.
April 2, 1941	Morton's Aunt and Uncle came to see me today
April 3, 1941	They took out the guard stitches today. Sylvia is sick in bed, too!
April 4, 1941	Job's Daughters were here today, they took Mother to the train
April 5, 1941	I got flowers from Lodge, Jobs Dau. Mom & Dad, Mort and Wilber. Dad Dawley came and spent about 2 hrs with me today, he told me all about Ray's death & I had to cry.

April 6, 1941	Surprise, they brought me home in the back of Lloyd's car, I still have the stitches in me Its keen to be home
April 7, 1941	Doc Brown came over today, great guy

How did it happen that 13 months later, this young girl would marry twice divorced Steve? Who was she, and how did she come to be that person? To answer that, one could of course, write a book – which I hope to do someday. But for now, we'll only briefly visit Shirley's first eighteen years.

In Denver, on January 14, 1924, a baby girl was born to Mr. and Mrs. O'Neill. They named their little daughter Mary Irene, signed the papers giving her up for adoption and returned to their existing family in Kansas City.

Walter Johnson, a Denver policeman, and his wife Pearl adopted the infant Mary Irene and renamed her Shirley Mae. A full term baby boy, born to them five years later, died at birth. After that Pearl was either unable or unwilling to become pregnant again. Shirley Mae remained their only child.

Growing up, she never knew that she was adopted.

Walter, called Bud, adored his blond little daughter. He and his extended family lavished love and affection on her. Pearl, on the other hand, found it difficult to show, if she indeed *felt*, these things for her child. She was a perfectionist and also very aware of what "people might think". She set high standards for Shirley and was often frustrated with, and disappointed in, her daughter. The attention Shirley received from Bud was probably an additional source of aggravation to Pearl.

As Bud moved up the career ladder on the police force, Pearl pursued her interests in her Christian Scientist religion, music (she was an accomplished singer) and maintaining an attractive and well-run home. Tthe towels in the linen closet were tied up with ribbons, for example. The Johnson family moved several times while Shirley was growing up, and so she attended several different public schools in different parts of the city. As the years went by, her father continued to delight in her company, and her mother continued to judge her with a very critical eye.

By her senior year in high school, when Shirley wrote the above diary entries, she had been treated all her life as a princess by the man in her life. But she was more than ready to escape a mother whom she could never please. And that's when she met Steve Allison.

Steve was a Denver police officer. It's unclear when he had actually joined the department, but at about the time of his divorce from Margaret, he was assigned to be Bud Johnson's personal driver. In short order he met Bud's daughter Shirley and they fell in love - whatever that meant to each of them at that moment of their lives.

The other day, my mother introduced me to a friend of hers from high school. Shirley and Idella had recently renewed their friendship after more than fifty years. Idella gave me a photo, dated October 12, 1941, of Steve and Shirley from their courting days. A smiling couple is pictured, and really, the age difference is not at all apparent. She's very poised and stylish in her wide brimmed hat, and he's a very refined looking suitor in his suede jacket over white shirt and tie.

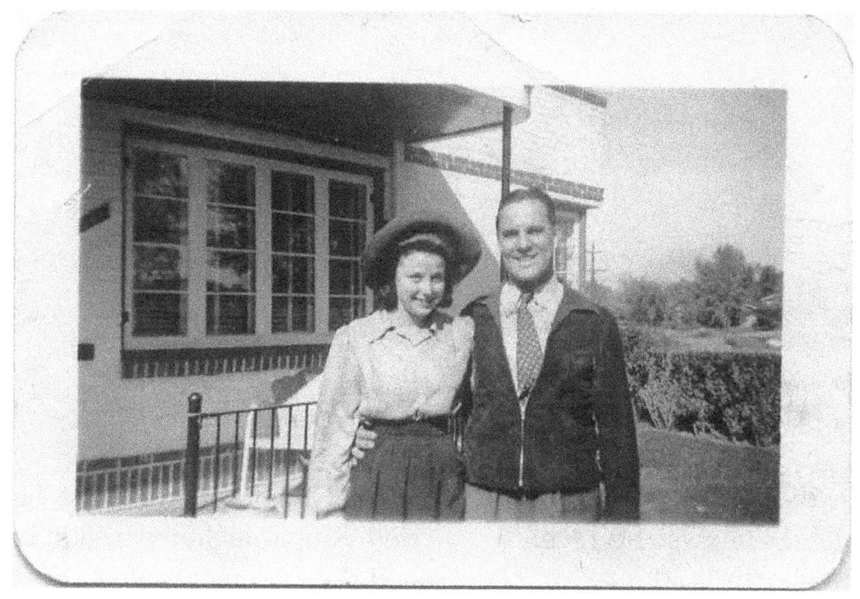

Figure 12.5 Shirley and Steve, 1941.

On November 25, 1941 Steve, Bud and about 40 other policemen posed for a photo in some type of law enforcement class. I wonder if Bud knew then that Steve would soon be his son-in-law, and if so, how he felt about it.

My parents' marriage certificate wasn't in The Box, because, I think, it was too large to fit without bending and folding. I found it in the house, carefully preserved in its original brown envelope.

It states that, with Uncle Gus and someone named Callie Cannon as witnesses, thirty-one year old Stephen J. Allison married eighteen year old Shirley M. Johnson on May 28, 1942 in Littleton, Colorado. Can you imagine a marriage less likely to succeed?

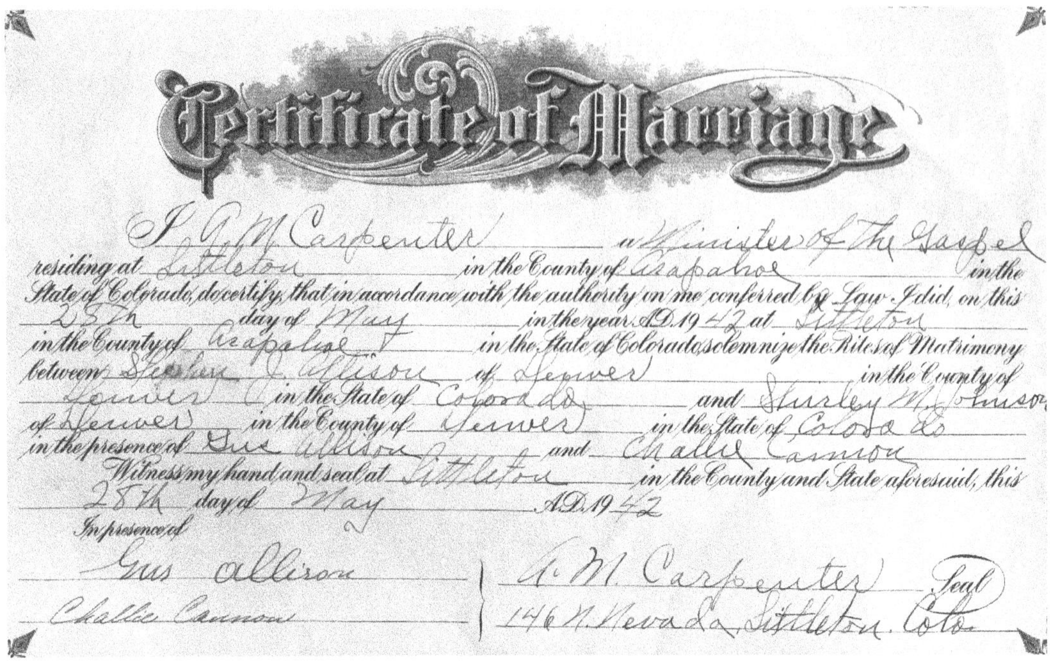

Certificate of Marriage

I, A. M. Carpenter a Minister of The Gospel residing at Littleton in the County of Arapahoe in the State of Colorado, do certify that in accordance with the authority in me conferred by Law I did, on this 28th day of May in the year A.D. 1942 at Littleton in the County of Arapahoe in the State of Colorado solemnize the Rites of Matrimony between Stephen J. Allison of Denver in the County of Denver in the State of Colorado and Shirley M. Johnson of Denver in the County of Denver in the State of Colorado in the presence of Gus Allison and Challie Cannon

Witness my hand and seal at Littleton in the County and State aforesaid, this 28th day of May A.D. 1942

In presence of

Gus Allison | A. M. Carpenter (Seal)

Challie Cannon | 146 N. Nevada Littleton, Colo.

Figure 12.6 Marriage Certificate for Steve and Shirley.

But it did *endure* - for quite a while really. The photo at the beginning of Chapter 12 shows the recently married couple at her parents' house. In the photo shown in Figure 7.07 they joined the Allison family at the farm on Christmas Eve 1943. They lived in north Denver, in the house at 29th and Grove Street.

Figure 12.7 House on Grove Street.

When next we meet them however, a year and a half later, their marriage sounds a bit shaky - as evidenced by this letter Shirley wrote to Steve (which he saved in The Box):

Dec. 9, 1943

Dear Steve:

I have been thinking about a lot of things since you left this evening, I mean really thinking, and I have come to the conclusion that you are right and I have had the wrong attitude during the last two years, I haven't been anything but a little girl, I haven't grown up a little bit since I left home, so I will honestly and truly see if I can't straighten out myself beginning right away. I'm sorry I haven't made a home for you as I should have, but I will try to from now on. Will you have faith in me once more?

Mr. Larcom called, he said he had heard you had been ill and he wanted to find out how you were getting along, nice of him wasn't it?

Virginia Belle called, and she is being married the 19th of this month in a big church wedding, there will be about 250 guests, and guess what I am going to be the receptionest, and then after the wedding all the guest have to sign the book the precher gives the bride and groom, and I have to sit up in the front and have the guests sign it. Isn't that going to be lots of fun. I'm going over there tomorrow night while you are in school and help write the wedding invitations. Her wedding dress is going to cost $100 dollars.

Love,
Shirley

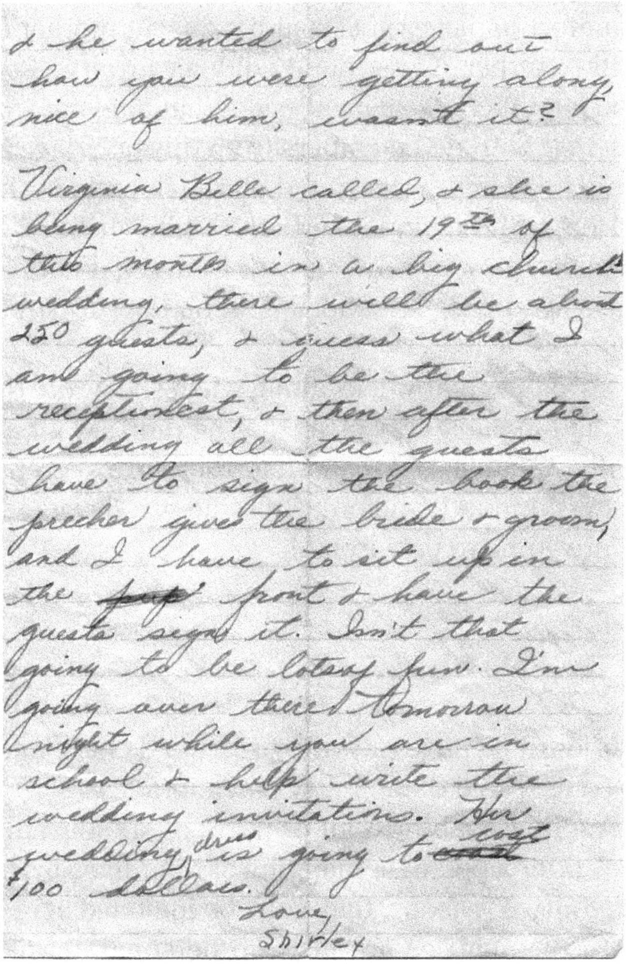

& he wanted to find out how you were getting along, nice of him, wasn't it?

Virginia Belle called, & she is being married the 19th of this month in a big church wedding, there will be about 250 guests, & guess what I am going to be the receptionist, & then after the wedding all the guests have to sign the book the precher gives the bride & groom, and I have to sit up in the ~~frup~~ front & have the guests sign it. Isn't that going to be lots of fun. I'm going over there tomorrow night while you are in school & help write the wedding invitations. Her wedding dress is going to ~~cost~~ cost $100 dollars.

Love
Shirley

Figure 12.8 Letter from Shirley to Steve.

Poor Shirley - she still sounds like *such* a young girl. She's often told me how exasperated my father would become with her housekeeping skills. One of the few things she can remember about this marriage is his frustration with her for having *several* opened jars of mayonnaise in the refrigerator at the same time. Prior to this letter, evidently Steve has yet again pointed out her shortcomings. And she, yet again, is really sorry and will try to do better. Her excitement about her role in the upcoming wedding is endearing - but pretty immature.

It's all so clear. Emotionally, she's about fifteen years old, and experientially, Steve's about fifty years old. Yet he needs a wife that can give him the nurturing and comfort he never got from his absent mother and she wants a husband who will treat her, as her daddy did, as royalty. I doubt very much that Steve treated her much like a princess. What a mismatch.

Another thing that Shirley remembers from this marriage is that Steve was sick a lot. She said he would "roll around on the floor, hollering" in pain from his ulcers. So. Here's Shirley in La La Land, while stressed out Steve is *still* trying to finish college (now at University of Denver), do his police work, *and* keep track of the mayonnaise situation. And oh boy! *Just wait till she tells him she's pregnant.*

I figure she was about eight weeks along when she wrote this letter. Surely she knew. Steve had made it very clear that he didn't want any children, but Shirley had decided that she did – and had therefore secretly stopped using her diaphragm several months before. I bet he was beside himself when he found out they were going to be parents!

Shirley's other journal entries, always bright and cheery, cover five months in 1944, and I've transcribed them pretty much intact.

In addition, The Box contained all or parts of six journals kept by Steve. And although they offer a poignant mapping of their lives in the coming years, I've realized that, for two reasons, they can't be included here in their entirety.

For one thing, some entries are just too personal, intimate or revealing to share without permission from those concerned, and so I've not included them.

Secondly, most of the entries would soon become repetitious, tedious and downright dull to anyone other than myself.

So, I've tried for a happy medium. I've included journal entries that make it possible to follow the lives and times of Shirley and Steve, while excluding those that might cause disquietude for those involved – or that are just too boring.

Three weeks after Shirley wrote the above letter, Steve begins his journal:

CENSUS 1940—*Continued*

Troy, N. Y.	70,304	W. Haven, Conn.	30,021
Tucson, Ariz.	36,818	West N. Y., N. J.	39,439
Tulsa, Okla.	142,157	W. Orange, N. J.	25,662
Tuscaloosa, Ala.	27,493	W. Palm B., Fla.	33,693
Tyler, Tex.	28,279	Wheeling, W. Va.	61,099
Union City, N. J.	56,173	W'te Plains, N.Y.	40,327
Univ'ity City, Mo.	33,023	Wichita, Kan.	114,966
Upper Darby, Pa.	56,883	Wich. Falls, Tex.	45,112
Utica, N. Y.	100,518	Wilkes-Barre, Pa.	86,236
Waco, Tex.	55,982	Wilkinsburg, Pa.	29,853
Waltham, Mass.	40,020	Williamsport, Pa.	44,355
Warren, Ohio	42,837	Wilmington, Del.	112,504
Warwick, R. I.	28,757	Wilmington, N. C.	33,407
Washington, D. C.	663,091	Win.-Salem, N.C.	79,815
Washington, Pa.	26,166	Woodbridge, N. J.	27,191
Waterbury, Conn.	99,314	Woonsocket, R. I.	49,303
Waterloo, Ia.	51,743	Worcester, Mass.	193,694
Watertown, Mass.	35,427	Wyandotte, Mich.	30,618
Watertown, N. Y.	33,385	Yakima, Wash.	27,221
Waukegan, Ill.	34,241	Yonkers, N. Y.	142,598
Wausau, Wis.	27,268	York, Pa.	56,712
Wauwatosa, Wis.	27,769	Youngstown, Ohio	167,720
West Allis, Wis.	36,364	Zanesville, Ohio	37,500
W. Hartford, Conn.	33,776		

	1940	1930
Alaska	72,524	59,278
American Samoa	12,908	10,055
Guam	22,290	18,509
Hawaii	423,330	368,336
Panama Canal Zone	51,827	39,467
Puerto Rico	1,869,255	1,543,913
Virgin Islands	24,889	22,012
Military, Naval, etc., abroad	118,933	89,453
Philippine Islands	16,356,000	13,513,000
Territories and Possessions	**18,951,956**	**15,664,023**
Continental United States	**131,669,275**	**122,775,046**
Total United States	**150,621,231**	**138,439,069**

JANUARY 1944

Saturday 1 Worked, accident
New Year's Day Prev. Bureau
7 am to 3:00 Pm.

Memoranda

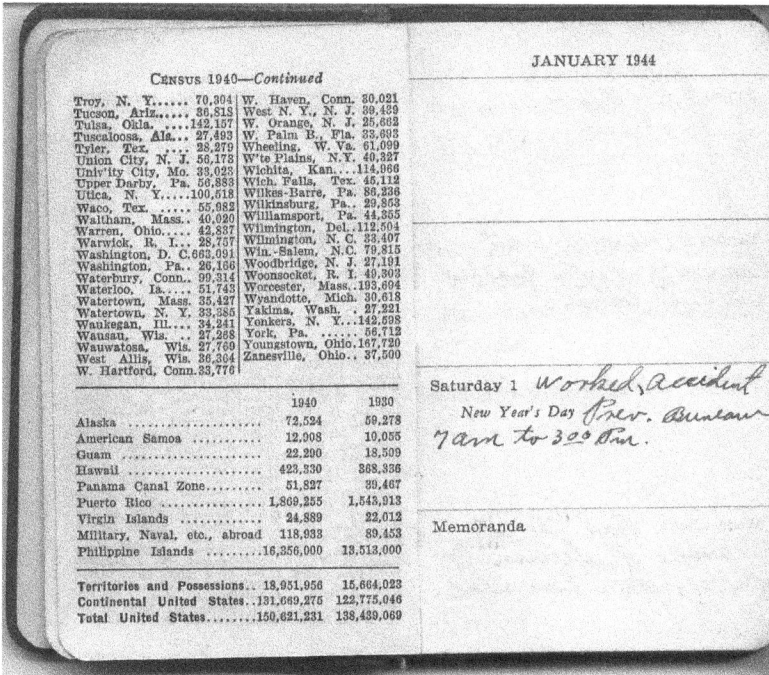

Figure 12.9 Steve's 1944 Journal; Beginning.

JANUARY 1944

Sunday 9 Ranch
Studied – Day Off

Monday 10 Worked Acc-
Prev. Bureau

Tuesday 11 Worked in Acc.
Prev. Bureau
7:00 to 3:00 Pm.

Wednesday 12 Worked in
Acc. Prev. Bureau
7:00 3:00 Pm

JANUARY 1944

Thursday 13 Hanebuta's wife
some what better.
Monty's birthday.

Friday 14 Shirley's birthday.
Micki's birthday
Supper at "Bob's"! talked
to Miss Cutler D.C.-Credit.

Saturday 15 Capt's Campbell's
picture in picture hall
of fame (Post)

Memoranda

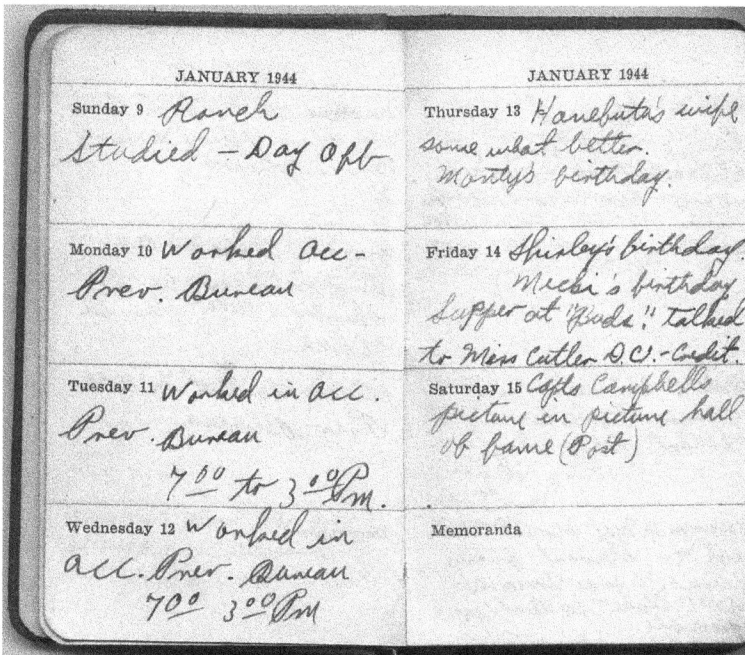

Figure 12.10 Steve's Journal; January pages.

January 1944

1 Worked, accident prev. Bureau 7 am to 3:00 pm

3 Attended first class of Winter quarter in Univ.

5 Read 'The City Manager Profession' by Ridley

7 Shirley's teeth cleaned by Reed.

9 Ranch. Studied - Day off

13 Hanebuta's wife some what better. Monty's birthday.

14 Shirley's birthday. Micki's birthday Supper at 'Bud's'. Talked to Miss Cutler D.U. - Credit.

15 Capt. Campbell's picture in picture hall of fame

18 Dad came in, we saw Economy. School rest of day.

20 Talked to P. DIKEOU.

21 had diner at Uncle Bob's ranch 'Study'

22 Stock Show Shirley talk with Capt. Davis – Sgt Cook - JIM ADAMS - KIRCKOFF - STIMSON - mentioned.

23 Ranch and show with Shirley. Visited Bud and Mother.

25 Talked with Sgt. Beubow, says he will retire July 1st, 1944. 'Just sit still' his advise

26 Attended banquet Eddie Hohns.

28 Efficiency Shoot - 93

29 Teeth cleaned worked on income tax return

30 Had dinner at Bud's' house Visited Uncle George's grave

31 Talked with Dr. Brown - I need 59 Credit points – I will have 39 Points after this quarter if all 'B's.

February 1944

5 Uncle Frank's Home, Georgia's birthday. 26 yrs old.

6 Had dinner at Bud's house, went to the farm

13 Went to ranch, studied.

14 Valentine's Day send card.

17 Received Grade of 95 in Mid-term exam in Johnson's class. Morey going to army Sat.

19 Went out to Ranch Gus and I talked about business

21 Street car acc at 9th Hazel Ct 20 injured

24 Attended Class Dad called from ranch.

25 Snowed all day - Studied

26 Had supper at Bud's' house. Show with Shirley

27 Studied all day - Never left the house

28 Efficiency Shoot 91

March 1944

3 Show with Shirley (Rialto) L.C. Jones went home injured.

4 Ranch (Dad)

5 Studied all day. Did not leave house

9 BUD'S BIRTH DAY DINNER AT BUD'S SEE PROF. LOREN MILLER AT D.U.

11 Fire extinguisher obtained, studied

12 Studied Went out to Uncle Bob's. Finished lesson 15 in extension course

14 Mike Carroll in acc. At 38th Federal Blvd.

15 CAMPBELL TO TAKE MY PLACE IN TEN DAYS IN BUREAU

16 William Clark retired. Final exam in Johnson class Received an 'A' in the course.

18 Worked from 7 am to 11 pm Shirley went to a party. (Idella's)

19 Went to Ranch

23 Norman Williams to be made a sergeant 4-1-44 Saw Uncle Gus.

25 Sgt. Johnson picked his driver for Cr 60 - COWGILL Went out to dad's ranch. Shirley and I visited Virginia and Bill.

26 Bud and Mother were over for dinner, studied

27 Attended first class of spring quarter, was class in police work attended by about 70 officers. Dad called from ranch, Ted and I solved (H - R) Jan Worthington

30 Efficiency shoot – 93

April 1944

1 7:00 am to 3:00 pm worked on car 74 Snowed.

2 Shirley and I had dinner at Buds house.

3 Worked Car 62 - Captured a horse - attended school in the evening.

4 Worked car 62 - was sick most of the day.

5 Day Off - Brought dad in from the ranch.

9 Worked Car 74 (2) accidents Bud and Mother were over for dinner.

14 Chris reported missing

16 Dinner out with Flossie and Shirley. Day off.

22 Worked Car 62 Snowed most of the day Went out to the ranch.

23 Day off, Ted Brooks and wife came over

25 Attended Policeman's Ball with Flossie and Shirley

29 Shirley and I had dinner at Bud's house Grand-dad and mother arrived from Hot Springs N. Mex. Paid William T. Lankin $6.00 for 44 dues.

Steve's journal reveals an on-task and goal oriented man. Go to work, go to school, go to the farm and then study. Then study some more and do it all over again.

He worked in the Traffic Division of the police department during the day, sometimes in the office and sometimes in a patrol car - he and his partner even captured a horse once. And he studied for his extension courses and attended classes at the Denver University at night. I found several written assignments that he saved from these classes.

But he did remind himself to send a card to his young wife on Valentine's Day, and it appears that he tried to make time for them to spend together. They often dined with her parents, sometimes visited with friends, and took in a movie about once a month. They attended the Policemen's Ball with Flossie, an older woman who lived next door to them. She and Shirley became close friends. She was more like a mother to Shirley, I think. She appears often in Shirley's diary – as does Idella, the woman who recently gave me the "courting" photo of my parents.

He mentions several family members. His cousin Chris, who's missing in action, is Brother Frank's son. Uncle Bob, whom they visit twice, is Bud's brother who owns a farm south of Denver. "Grand-dad and mother" are Bud's parents. They were, according to my mom, a very unique set of grandparents. They were, for example, vegetarians, which was pretty unusual for that time. They also rode their bicycles everywhere - again, pretty unusual for an elderly couple in the 1940's.

Steve never mentions Shirley's pregnancy or their impending parenthood.

But Shirley does. Her diary tells of the preparations she's making for the arrival of their child. She's excited about "the baby" and about life in general. She's always been that way. She's a genuine optimist with a huge enthusiasm for life, and for all the people and events that make it so intriguing. Today, in her eighth decade, her enthusiasm remains constant – matured and refined, but just as true. However, as you'll see, there's a bit of doubt and worry that surfaces every once in a while in her mostly cheerful summaries. I think that, subconsciously at least, she was beginning to realize that their marriage wasn't quite what she'd dreamed it would be.

Since her diary entries reflect so well her youthful, good-natured hopefulness (which sometimes comes across as naïve wishful thinking), and since they're all that Steve saved, I've opted to include them in their entirety. *Well, almost in their entirety.* Although she and Steve enjoyed a *very* fulfilling life of intimacy, I've omitted all references to their lovemaking. I'm not quite sure why - except that it seems the right thing to do. Probably it's just a matter of respect.

Her diary reflects, I think, a pretty accurate image of twenty-year-old Shirley Mae Johnson Allison:

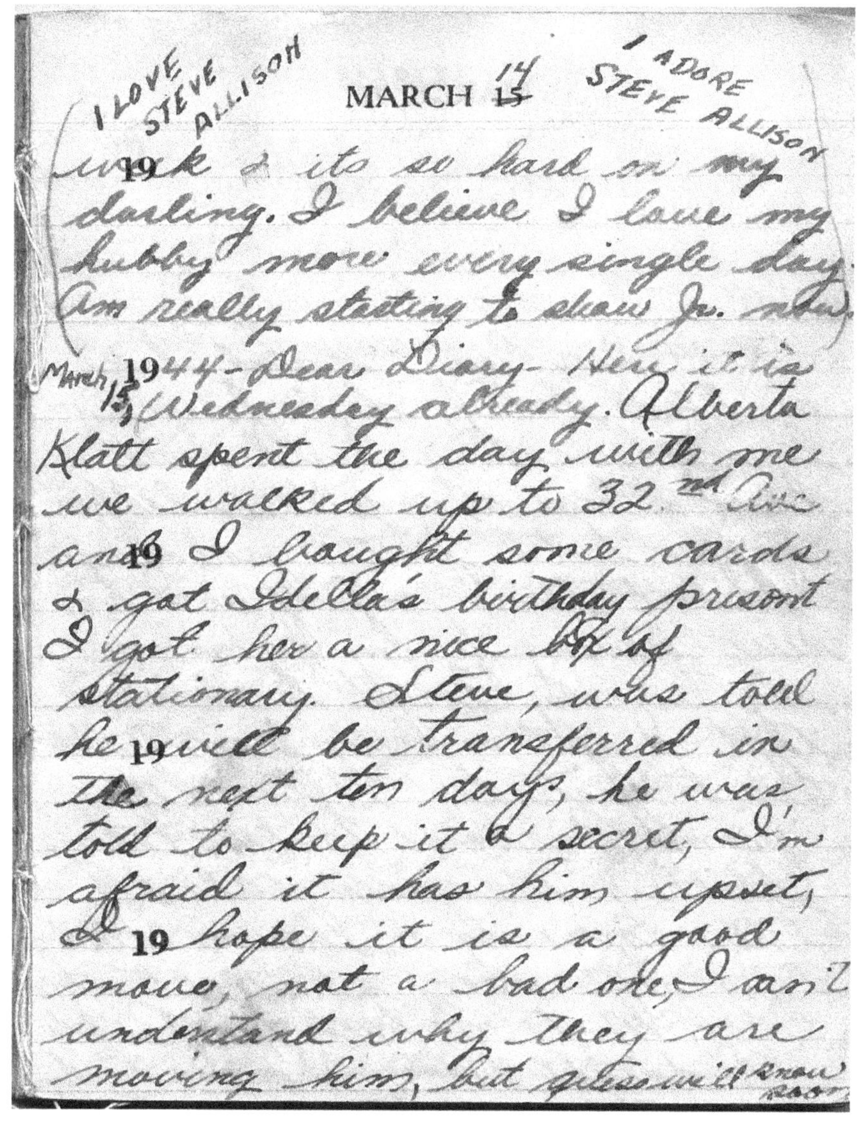

I LOVE STEVE ALLISON

MARCH ~~15~~ 14

I ADORE STEVE ALLISON

19

work & its so hard on my
darling. I believe I love my
hubby more every single day.
Am really starting to show Jr. now.

March 15, 1944 - Dear Diary - Here it is
Wednesday already. Alberta
Klatt spent the day with me
we walked up to 32nd Ave
and I bought some cards
& got Idella's birthday present
I got her a nice box of
stationary. Steve, was told
he will be transferred in
the next ten days, he was
told to keep it a secret, I'm
afraid it has him upset,
I hope it is a good
move, not a bad one, I can't
understand why they are
moving him, but guess will know soon

Figure 12.11 Shirley's Journal; March.

March 1944

March 14, 1944 I LOVE STEVE ALLISON I ADORE STEVE ALLISON I believe I love my hubby more every singe day. Am really starting to show Jr. now.

March 15, 1944 Here it is Wednesday already. Alberta Klatt spent the day with me. We walked up to 32nd Ave. and I bought some cards and got Idella's birthday present. I got her a nice box of stationary. Steve was told he will be transferred in the next ten days, he was told to keep it a secret, I'm afraid it had him upset, I hope it is a good move, not a bad one, I can't understand why they are moving him, but guess we'll know soon.

March 16, 1944 Worked like a horse today, did four big lines of washing. fixed lima beans and ham and a jello salad for supper, tasted pretty good. I hope I didn't strain myself as I am sure having funny pains in my tummy. Shirley Marymee called this morning and Sharon called this afternoon, she left at 2:30 P.M. to go back to Pueblo. Goodnight Diary I'm dog tired.

March 17, 1944 Well lets see today I did nothing but bake a cake and sleep, I was really worn out. Baked the cake for Idella's birthday party tomorrow. We went over to Mother and Daddy's tonite and Mama sewed on my dress, it is almost finished. She helped me decorate Idella's cake real fancy. It is snowing like heck afire tonite. Got a letter from little Steve today, he seems pretty thrilled about the baby. Steve got some exams back, 4 A's and two B+'s. Goodnight diary. It is 11:58 P.M.

March 18, 1944 about 1:00 A.M. Didn't do anything all day today but rest. Steve had to work on a hit and run case tonite, so he took me over to Idella's at 6:15 P.M. We talked and messed around, then at 8:45 P.M. the girls all came, they all got in the house without her hearing them, she was the most surprised little girl you ever did see. Everyone was there but Penny, there was Sydney, Reba, Mary Mankin, Rae Marie, Betty Jean, Viryl, Margaret Hayes. We really had fun. Steve came about 11:00 P.M. and we stayed till Idella lent me two of her maternity dresses. Idella got a lot of nice presents. We took Sydney home with us. Came home and went to bed.

March 19, 1944 Today is Sunday and its been a bad day all day for me, Stevie says I have been going to much and have tired myself out, anyhow I have wanted to cry all day and carry on like a dummy, Steve has been so good to me. Alvina had a fight with her mom so she is here to spend the night, it is now 12:30 A.M. and I have to wash and go to bed yet. Poor Vina is certainly mixed up, I sure hope Steve and I talking to her helps a little bit. I love Steve. He was so good and kind to me today because I didn't feel good. I love him so much. Goodnite diary.

March 20, 1944 First Day of Spring. Cleaned up the back porch thoroughly today and cleaned up rest of house. Alvina sat and read a magazine while I cleaned. Defrosted the ice-box. Her boyfriend is here again tonite, it is kind of a nuisance, I don't mind her but don't like him hanging around. They did my dishes for me tonite and they have gone to the drugstore to get some ice cream. I am going to wash my dress and put up my hair and go to bed as I am really all in. Steve is out working on that hit and run case tonite again. Am going to the show with Vina and Shirley tomorrow.

March 21, 1944 Over 16 inches of snow, worst storm in 25 years. Boy oh boy did it ever snow last nite and today, its at least a foot deep. Alvina went home today. we couldn't go to the show on account of the storm. I didn't do much of anything except to look out of the window and watch all the cars that got stuck. Talked to Daddy today. Stevie shoveled all the walks when he got home then took a real hot bath and is now lying down on the couch.

March 22, 1944 This is Dad Allison's birthday. Straightened house up a little, spent remainder of day writing letters and working on my Scrap Book, I finished it today, now all I'll have to do is add things as they come. Talked to Aletha's mother, my Mom and daddy and to Sydney Jean on telephone. Am certainly hard to get along with the last few days, don't know what makes me so irritable, I will have to try and overcome it, as it is wholly unnecessary for me to act that way.

March 23, 1944 Shirley called and Wesley is here until Monday, was certainly surprised to hear him, they are coming over tomorrow afternoon. Then Steve called and they made Norman Williams a Sergeant, that makes Steve 3rd up on the list, really 2nd since Dill is in the Navy. And at 5:15 P.M. tonite I layed down for a few minutes and I could see the baby kick which was a thrilling moment as I have felt nothing up to now. Received congratulatory notes from Grandpa and Grandma.

March 24, 1944 Straightened up the house and did my shopping for the week-end. Shirley and Wes couldn't come out today. It is snowy weather out again. Talked to Daddy and Mother, Daddy doesn't feel good. Steve and I put up the card table and he studied while I wrote the list of whom to send birth announcements. I figured it will cost $3.36 including the stamps. Talked to Virginia Belle, we are going over there tomorrow nite and play cards. Thats about all I did today, diary, except talk to Steve about naming the baby.

March 25, 1944 Cleaned house, Steve went out to Dad Allison's, he is fine. I got his birthday card back because I sent it to Semper. We went over to Virginia Belle and Bill's, we sat and talked we looked at her O.B. book all about having babies. She is expecting in September. Talked to Idella on the phone, she wants me to come over next week and get that dress. Got home at 12:45 A.M. and took a bath and went to bed.

March 26, 1944 Slept until 9:00 A.M. The baby woke me up kicking real early. (Steve) slept then til 10:30 while I fixed breakfast and cleaned up the house and washed out some things. He washed his hair. Mother and Daddy came over for dinner, we had a ham dinner I fixed, it was good. Mom brought the dress over she made, it fits fine. Daddy and Steve talked shop all day. They left at 8:00 P.M. Layed on couch and talked to Steve till 10:00. Ironed his police shirt and went to bed.

March 27, 1944 Today is Aunt Persis's birthday. If this weather isn't the most terrible I've ever seen, its snowing again. I wanted to wash today and then it snows. So I washed my hair instead. Oiled my nails and fixed them and read a story to Steve after he got home from school. We were talking about Linda Darnell, the actress, and we hit on the name Linda Lee Allison if its a girl, do you like it, diary, I do, and Steve does too its the first girls name either one of us has mentioned that he really liked. Talked to Mom, Dad, Virginia Belle and "Pa".

March 28, 1944 Washed a few things out today and mended my girdle, cleaned the house. Today was the coldest day we've had all winter 3 degrees above zero. Steve got two A's and 1 B on his report card. I am going to go to bed at 9:00 P.M. starting tonite as when I go to bed at 11:00 or 12:00 I want to loaf the whole next day. If it is nice tomorrow I think I'll go down town and see Mr. Galvin. Steve and I had a little argument, he's so tired and I'm so irritable that its bound to happen once in a while. It was my fault. Am sorry. P.S. it is 11:45 A.M. Steve and I made up.

March 29, 1944 Today, 3 years ago, I lost my appendix in Pueblo. Went down town with Virginia Belle, charged a dozen diapers, a baby nite gown and kimona, and charged myself a new Spring hat, I am going to try and save the money to pay for them if I can so I won't have to worry Steve about it, I think I can. Had lunch with Steve at the Columbine we saw Uncle Frank and Georgia and Titsa. Am tired from walking.

March 30, 1944 Well we at least had a part of a day of nice weather. I took Stevie's uniform out and aired it and washed his pajamas for him. He took me over to Idella's and got my dress, sure is cute, it will go perfect with the hat I got. Steve is on the war path cause we stayed over there so long and he had an examination to study for. He and I have both been so nasty the last few days, he has reason to be. I don't know why I am, I'm going to try to stop it. Aunt Persis called me.

March 31, 1944 I LOVE STEVE ALLISON. I WORSHIP STEPHEN ALLISON. I love my Stevie more than anything in this world. Washed blinds in kitchen, breakfast nook and dining room, hung dining room drapes out to air. Washed some underclothes for myself and Stevie, got his uniform ready to wear tomorrow. We decided to go down town and window shop tonite, we rode down on the bus, got back at 9:30 P.M. I'm so tired I want to bawl at every thing. Steve gave me $5.00 to buy a maternity brassiere. "Pa" just called. Boy am I tired out, I guess I'm getting old or something. Baby moved today and tonite.

April 1944

April 1, 1944 APRIL FOOL'S DAY. Well we really had April showers for the first day of April. Steve worked North Denver today so he had lunch at home with me, he stopped in three or four times. A radio repair man took our big radio down to have it fixed. I cleaned the back bedroom thoroughly and moved the furniture around, helped Steve carry the Cedar Chest into the front bedroom, hope I didn't hurt the baby. Steve is asleep on the couch, I'm going to wake him up and make him go to bed.

April 2, 1944 Steve had to work today so I went over to Mom's and Daddies, Steve got there about 3:30 P.M. and we had a nice dinner, then went out back and enjoyed the nice sunshine till evening then played pinocle, after which Steve and Daddy went and got some ice cream, then we came home, it is about 10:30 P.M. and I am half dead I'm so sleepy, had a nice day and now I hope I go to bed and have a nice sleep. Nightie night diary.

April 3, 1944 Washed clothes today, I had 15 Turkish towels, boy did I ever get a back ache from it, I couldn't even do the supper dishes I had to go to bed. Took my books back to the library and got four others. It was really wonderful weather out today. Goodnight.

April 4, 1944 Cleaned house. Washed five sheets, eight pillow cases, 1 dress, a brassiere and a pair stockings. Mended some hose, mended Stevie's police shirt, Washed hair and put it up. Stevie was home twice during the day. He fixed a parking ticket for virginia Belle and her Mother. He went to bed at 6:30 P.M. sick, thank goodness he's off tomorrow so he can relax. It is 11:00 P.M. and I still have to wash my hair and put it up, so better be on my merry way. Am so tired I can't see straight. Bambi has something in his eye.

April 5, 1944 Went out and got Steve's dad and brought him in by the house and then down town he went and saw all his Greek friends and got his hair cut. Micki went with me and I got a maternity brassiere, it sure fits swell. I have to sleep in it. got a slip, too. Paid cash for brassiere and charged slip, certainly hope I can save enough money to pay for it out of grocery money. Miss Flossy came over and we talked until 9:00 P.M. I'm going to take a shower and go to bed now.

April 6, 1944 Well this has been a lazy day. I've had a sore throat all day so slept most all day. Steve went to school tonite. I am lonesome or restless tonite for some reason. I am going to write little Steve a letter and go to bed. Steve and I got a Easter card from Uncle Gus and Aunt Micki today. I sent one to Mother and Dad, Idella and Gus and Micki, and one for Steve.

April 7, 1944 Good Friday. Washed some more clothes. Sprinkled clothes tonite so I can iron a few tomorrow, wanted to iron tonite but Flossie came over and we got to talking. she helped me do dishes, she's going to help me fix Steve's shirts. I got a Easter card from Mom and Daddy and so did Steve. Stevie's Dad called. Washed my Chinelle robe. It washed nice but can't hardly get into it. Also washed a dozen tea towels, collar and cuffs, police shirts, house dress, apron, pants. It is ten of eleven so nite diary.

April 8, 1944 Oh man what a day, cleaned house, washed and ironed, dyed Easter eggs, baked cake, cooked ham, went to store twice, mended and it is now 11:00 P.M. and I still haven't washed my hair and I'm not going to. I am going to bed. Fixed real cute place cards out of eggs for tomorrow. Flossy came over and sewed collar and cuffs on maternity dress and she fixed the bow on it, just precious, she helped me dye the eggs, I sure like her - she lent me a table cloth for dining table and pads.

April 9, 1944 EASTER SUNDAY. Well we certainly had a rainy Easter, it rained the whole blessed day. My table looked lovely with the pretty basket of eggs and egg place cards, the dinner seemed to be well enjoyed, the ham was done to a "T" Steve had to handle an accident so dinner was delayed til 4:30 P.M. Mom and Daddy went home at 8:15 P.M. I have to put my hair up as I washed it this morning. Mother got a rose plant from Uncle gus and Micki. I'm going to take a shower and go to bed as it is almost 10:00 P.M. and Steve has a day off tomorrow. it is snowing something fierce now, wunnerful "Spring" weather. Night diary, I'm tired and awfully sleepy. I love my Stevie.

April 10, 1944 Today was Steve's day off and we slept most of this snowy day away, we just enjoyed each others company, we sat around and talked, and took cat naps. its a good thing he's not off more often or neither one of us would get anything done. He went to school tonite, and I went over to Flossie's, we looked at her beautiful paintings till 10:30 P.M. It is now 11:00 P.M. and I have to polish Stevie's shoes yet and even tho' I haven't done anything all day I am tired. I certainly do like Flossie. I never have met anyone as nice, she certainly is artistic. Here comes Stevie. Nightie night!

April 11, 1944 Yours truly is doing her dernest to catch cold so I'm going to go to bed after I take a shower. Mother came over after church and got stuck in the mud and Daddy had to come get the car out. I took her over and introduced her to Flossie and showed her all F's paintings. Flossie says she is going to teach me to draw, I pray I can learn. Daddy came back for dinner and then took Steve to school and Mother went home, it is now 7:30 P.M. and I'm going to go to bed and see if I can't feel better. Idella called.

April 12, 1944 Cleaned house and got my supper all ready to cook, then went over to Flossie's and sewed button on steve's overcoat and made new ironing board cover and took my first lesson in drawing. Steve went to school tonite. I took a bath and have been piddling around waiting for him to come home, it is 10:00 P.M. I have a dilly of a cold and to be perfectly frank I feel absolutely awful. Nite.

April 13, 1944 Flossie and I went down town at 10:30 A.M. and got home at 3:00 P.M. She paid my way on the bus and took me to lunch, she bought me two more baby nitegowns. We looked in every baby shop in denver. We sure had fun. Steve went to school. Flossie came over and helped me do the dishes and talked a few minutes and went home. Mother sent me the nicest dish cloth, it is black and white. Steve got home at 9:10 P.M. and we've been sitting here enjoying each others company, we're going to bed now it is now 10:30 P.M. Steve is so all in. He is writing a 20,000 word thesis. It has rained and snowed today. *(It really does say 20,000 words!)*

April 14, 1944 Today was a very unhappy day for us. Chris was reported missing in action, he has been missing since the 29th of March. The whole family tried to keep it from me which I think was awfully sweet of them, Steve finally told me this afternoon. I feel terrible about it but there is still hope and I pray to God he is alive. Steve and I went down town and tried to see Uncle gus but couldn't find him. Steve went in to see Uncle Frank, I stayed in the car as I was afraid of crying. Steve said he was taking it awfully hard and had been crying all day. Steve bought me an ice cream sundae on the way home.

April 15, 1944 Did my Saturday cleaning. washed some clothes. Ironed til 10:30 A.M. I am trying to get all my clothes that are too small now washed and ironed and mended, and put them away so that when I get back to normal I will have all my clothes ready. Talked to Georgia and Aunt and Mother and Daddy on phone today. Aunt Anthenia was feeling terrible. Steve is in bed, he studied about 3 1/2 hours this evening and he is really tired and sleepy. He was about to cry this afternoon because a wee little puppy died in his arms. Forgot I talked to Aunt Ester as this is her birthday, she is forty years young. Well I have to set the table and get breakfast started for in the morning, and take a shower yet, so I'm off.

April 16, 1944 This is my Stevie's day off. We got up at 8:00 A.M., had breakfast and Steve went back to bed. I polished all his badges and buttons and shoes and Sam Browne, and washed his shirt. He got up and washed his hair and studied, then he took Flossie and me out to dinner at Betty May's (I had a whole short cut steak) then we went for a ride out by the air-port and Lowry Field, Flossie was just floored by all the new additions and by all the airplanes. We took her down by five points ... she really enjoyed it. We got caught in an awful blizzard. After I got home I finished my ironing, it is now 10:30 P.M. so guess I'll get to bed.

April 17, 1944 Went to see Dr. Butterfield, I am doing just fine except I'm gaining too much weight. No starches! Got some goods to make myself a dress at J.C. Penney's. Steve found out I charged $10.00 at May Co. my was he irritated with me and to top that off I didn't do a speck of work and the house looks like a mess. I have to finish my dishes before Steve gets home or he will be mad. the baby will be born in 90 days.

April 18, 1944 Cleaned the house and washed two sheets and five pillow cases. Flossie cut out my dress and sewed the front already. We walked to the library tonite and then looked at birth announcements, I picked the one I want her to make me. Steve didn't go to school tonite, he worked on his thesis. it is after 10:00 P.M. and I have to put my hair up yet. I am going to Shirley's for lunch tomorrow so will have to get up early. Talked to Mommy and Daddy on telephone. Felt miserable all day. I love Stevie.

April 19, 1944 It snowed all day today, I didn't do anything except read and lie around. I was supposed to go visit Shirley, but it was too snowy. Hope to go Friday. Stevie was home for lunch today. Flossie took some darts in my black dress that Mother made and it fits a lot better in the shoulders. I think Mother forgot to put the darts in. Flossie sewed on my maternity dress too, tonite, its going to be a honey. Steve stayed home and studied tonite. He doesn't feel good a bit. He is so sweet and I love him so I wish I could be perfect for him. Talked to Mother and Daddy and Virginia and Shirley.

April 20, 1944 Whee, I have a brand new maternity dress and it is darling, gee can that Flossie sew, I just love her. I don't know whats been the matter with me today, I have felt just as blue and miserable as can be. Got the baby's crib today, it is darling, it sure matches my furniture. Daddy came over to see it, he sure liked it. Steve is going to sleep in the back bedroom and the baby and I will be in the front. I am so tired, I'm going to bed now and get up early and wash my hair. It is 9:35 P.M. Am going to start housecleaning Monday.

April 21, 1944 Went over and spent the day at Shirley's house, we didn't do much but talk. Had lunch there. we walked up to Englewood and did some shopping and then back. About 5:00 P.M. I took the streetcar over to Mommy's and met Stevie there, we had a real good supper, and visited with Mom until about 9:00 P.M. and then came home and Steve went to bed he was so all in. I feel so blue tonite. I don't have any reason to, but he gets so much on his mind that I feel kinda left out in the cold sometimes, I'll be so-o-o glad when he gets done with school. I love him so much. I want to be close to him all the time. Its 10:30 P.M. Steve's dad called and we talked about fifteen minutes.

April 22, 1944 Oh boy am I tired. Cleaned house. Got salad and sandwiches ready for this evening. Steve went out to his Dad's after work. Virginia Belle and Bill came over, we played records and then played Monoply. Bill and I won. Steve was so tired he was kind of cranky. I'm sleeping in the front bedroom from now on. Mr. and Mrs. Brooks are coming over at 2:30 tomorrow and I've got to bake a cake. Clean the house up get dinner, get myself cleaned up all before 2:30 P.M. it is now 1:30 A.M. Oh dear what a life.

April 23, 1944 Wotta day - Wotta day. Stevie and I had a battle royal all day, we both ought to be ashamed. Mr. and Mrs. Brooks came over, they are very nice people, wish we could have become acquainted before now as he is going into the navy. That's about all that happened today. Flossie is fixing Steve's shirts. Night.

April 24, 1944 Washed 2 sheets, 15 towels, six pair pajamas. Cleaned out petunia bed. Sprinkled clothes down ready to iron. Steve was home for lunch. Every thing is hunky dory now. Flossie came over tonight and brought a shirt she fixed for Steve. She is coming over early tomorrow morning and we're going to start cleaning the basement out, as Steve will be working nights next month and I want to get through before then. Steve took my suit, blue dress, black slacks, brown skirt to the cleaners. Am trying to get everything in order before I go to the hospital.

April 25, 1944 Flossie and I started Spring housecleaning downstairs today. I did four lines of washing while she scrubbed and cleaned the fruit closet. We got all the canned goods washed and put in there. I did quite a bit in the store room, but will finish it tomorrow. We took Flossie down to the Policeman's Ball. we sat with Mother and Aunt Sylvia. I couldn't even march in the Grand March the price of having a baby, I guess. We got home at midnite.

April 26, 1944 I guess I over did it yesterday cause I felt awful all day, so I just sorted over the stuff for Tuck a Way Home, and hung all the clothes out that were in the store room closet and Flossie scrubbed it, we found a housedress that will fit me with a few alterations so Flossie sewed on it this after noon. We walked up to 32nd and I got my shower invitations and some groceries. Steve studied tonite and I wrote two letters. Oh I forgot, I layed down with Steve and slept a whole hour and 1/2 and I really mean slept. Night.

April 27, 1944 Didn't do too much today, cleaned a little more of store room, will just have to finish tomorrow so I can get my washing and ironing done before Steve starts working nights next Tuesday. Shirley called Tuesday. Stevie is down in the dumps tonite. Flossie and I walked to the library tonite after supper and I stayed over at her house and talked til 8:45 P.M. while she sewed on my dress, she finished it so now I have a house dress. Steve is taking a shower and then we're going to bed early for once, its just 9:15 P.M. now. Mother got a birth announcement from Uncle Frank and Aunt Helen and they have a boy.

April 28, 1944 Finished cleaning basement. Ironed three shirts, one pair slacks, one tablecloth, and a night gown after dinner and I'm tired. Stevie and I went to 32nd after he got off work, and got our groceries, and went to Penney's and got a gift for Shirley's shower, got Steve two pair shorts and shirts, and got our expected heir another nite gown, and I got a bottle of fingernail polish. Flossie didn't feel good today she has a cold. Steve came home for lunch. I emptied all the trash tonite as I don't want to have to do to much tomorrow as I am really worn out tonite, it is 10:15 so I guess I'd better take a bath and scoot.

April 29, 1944 VIRGINIA BELLE'S BIRTHDAY. Washed four lines of clothes, and cleaned both bedrooms thoroughly and straightened rest of house. We went over to Mother's for chicken dinner, as Grandma and Grandpa Johnson arrived home today, they are both looking swell. Aunt Persis and Uncle Charles and the kids were there too, we visited until 9:30 P.M. and then everyone went home and mother and I did dishes. Stevie and I got home at 11:00, and I stayed up and read til midnite. Don't feel so good.

April 30, 1944 Haven't felt a bit good all day. Stayed in bed til 10:00 A.M. Stevie worked until 3:00 P.M. I straightened the house up and did a tiny bit more ironing, and got up a nice dinner, just lazed around rest of day. Steve washed his hair. I think I'd better take it easy for a few days, as I feel awful. Steve's Dad called and gave me 'hell' for not stopping and talking to Uncle Frank when I went by there Tuesday nite on my way to the Policeman's Ball. Oh dear! I didn't mean to slight Uncle Frank, but it was raining cats and dogs and I had Flossie with me and I was supposed to be there on time. Uncle George passed away nine years ago today at four A.M.

Let's pause for a moment, here at the end of April 1944, and look a bit closer at Shirley and her life.

Like Steve, she never mentions the day to day events of the war. The subject never comes up until they learn, on April 14, 1944 that cousin Chris is missing in action. I would have thought it to be an important subject, one very much on everyone's mind. Maybe they just took the wartime atmosphere and its effects as a given. Of course they didn't know at that time, that millions of European civilians were being frozen, starved, worked to death, shot or gassed - in addition to the military casualties they did know about.

Do you get the feeling that she was continually doing household chores and then resting because she had done too much? Doing laundry was certainly hard work and time consuming in those days - waiting for a sunny day, washing the clothes (sounds like Shirley did hers by hand), hanging them out to dry, bringing them in, sprinkling the stuff that needed ironing (even her nightgown!) and then doing the ironing. And she's constantly trying to stay ahead of her other housework – and barely does so. I had to smile when she writes of the help she gets from Flossie in this area. Shirley has always been able to find people who are willing to help her do her housework. It's hard to explain. The helpers are truly happy to do her work for free or for a very small payment. She gives them herself in return, I guess. So I'm sure Flossie was happy to help Shirley, because Shirley, in turn, genuinely and sincerely liked and admired Flossie.

We've seen that Steve works, goes to school and supports them financially. Shirley cooks, takes care of the house and makes sure his clothes are in tiptop shape. But she's at his mercy as far as money is concerned. She hopes to save $3.36 out of her grocery money for birth announcements and stamps. She also needs to save enough from the grocery money to pay for the slip she charged.

And yet she doesn't seem to be bitter about what she does without. In fact, then, as now, she seems to get a whole lot of happiness from very insignificant things. She celebrates life, whatever that brings. She's thrilled to have two maternity dresses (three, if one counts the housedress they altered). And she's so pleased with her Easter table. Nothing's changed there either. My mom has always loved seasonal tablecloths, centerpieces and decorations.

Shirley was somewhat pampered though, in ways very indicative of the times. She'd have a hard time keeping up with today's wives/mothers who work eight hours a day, exercise throughout pregnancy and lead a full social life. She couldn't even participate in the Grand March at the Policeman's Ball for goodness sake! And the family hesitated to tell her about Chris being missing in action - because of her delicate condition. And was it also indicative of the times that she was still wearing a *girdle* when she was six months pregnant? Yikes!

Speaking of intimate things, "pitching woo" seems to be a mutually satisfying aspect of their marriage. Part of its allure for Shirley, perhaps, was a result of her upbringing by such a puritanical mother. But mostly, I think, she felt it to be a wonderful bonus in expressing her love. Even though once in a while she feels "blue" and "kinda left out in the cold", mostly she just wants to be a good wife to Steve. She wants "to be close to him all the time", and wishes she "could be perfect for him".

It's hard to tell how Steve feels about her. He doesn't often mention his wife or their lives together. His journal entries continue to record for the most part, the details of his studies and his job. But only the details - unlike Shirley, he seldom mentions how he *feels*. He doesn't mention, for example, the puppy that died in his arms.

Here's a small sampling of his notes from the next two months:

May 1944

1 Bud sent letter to Glendale, Calif: attended school

3 Worked in Bureau Attended Baines funeral talked to Jim Dikeou
6 Luther on Vac. I will work in his place as clerk 3:00 Pm to 12
7 Day Off, Shirley, Flossie and I went out to the ranch. Put in a bridal wreath plant in back yard
10 Worked in bureau. had meeting Dikeou, Mayor OK.
11 Chris reported to be a war prisoner
14 Day Off. show with Shirley
15 Flossie called Dutton, Bud talked with Jim Dikeou. Flossie called Blakely.
18 Worked Car 73 with M. Young - Talked with Capt. Davis
19 Shirley and I - dinner with Butterfield.
21 some talk with Sgt. Nevin
22 Day Off attended meeting with Chanceller Cheavington Shirley and I went out to the ranch.
23 5 of us met who are on the eligible Sgt.'s list.
24 5 of us met with the Civil Service Commission on petition
25 Talked with Stamison and Dikeou also Dr. Nelson.
29 Day Off, Shirley and I went out to my Dad's ranch.
30 Worked 5 hrs extra on Memorial Parade

June 1944

1 7 AM - 3 PM Car 61
2 Rec cap and Gown from D.U.
4 Day off - Mother-Bud over for dinner.
5 Car 61 with J. DAY Handed in term paper 7350 words for Banks class
7 had dinner at buds house
10 Graduation exercises at Audit. received my college degree after 7 yrs of work had party at our house after exercise received many gifts. Mayor attended the exercise.
11 Day Off Went out to ranch.
14 Went out to Ranch, worked at Cosmo hotel. Car 61 - also Fed Court Buckley field with Shirley and Flossie. Returned cap - Gown to D.U.
17 Day Off - Jim called said Dick saw the Mayor. Favorable. Flossie called him also - Favorable.
18 Dinner at Country Kitchen
19 Dinner at Country Kitchen
22 dinner at Bud's Degree taken in to be framed - 6.75 was very sick at night.
23 Was too sick to go to work
24 Sick - did not go to work
25 Day Off, was sick most of the day. Went out to ranch.
27 talked with Jim Dikeou Sent letter into World Ins. Co. Ivan Eldher in St. Lukes
29 Efficiency shoot - 99
30 Meet and talked with Mr. Bundy. Very good man. very impressive

JUNE 1944

Sunday 4 Day off - Mother - Bud over for dinner.

Monday 5 Worked Car 61 with O. DAY - Talked to Capt Dons and Capt Campbell - Handed in term paper 7350 words for Burke's class

Tuesday 6 Worked Car 61 with Officer Day.

Wednesday 7 Worked Car 61 with Officer Day, had dinner at Bud's house,

JUNE 1944

Thursday 8 Car 61.

Friday 9 SHOOT Car 61

Saturday 10 Worked Car 61. Graduation exercises at Audit. received my college degree after 7 yrs of work had party at our house.

Memoranda after exercises received many gifts - the mayor attended the exercises.

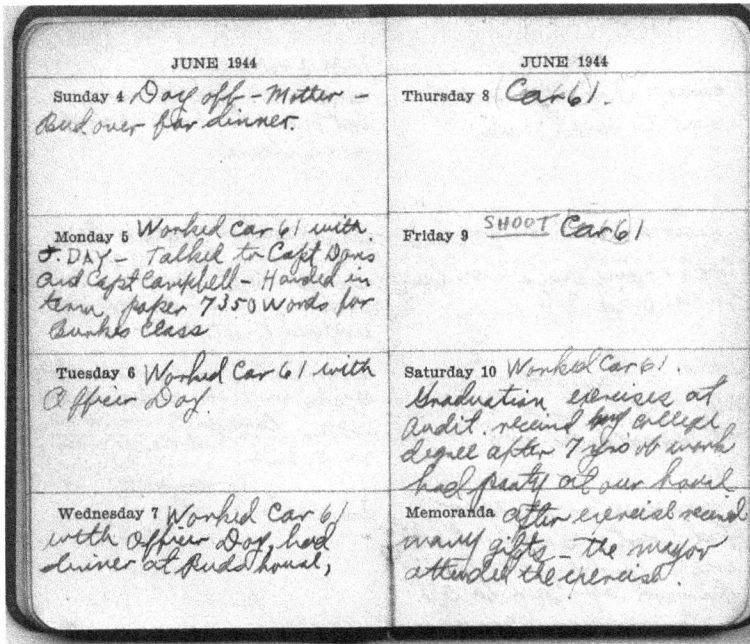

Figure 12.12 Steve's Journal; June.

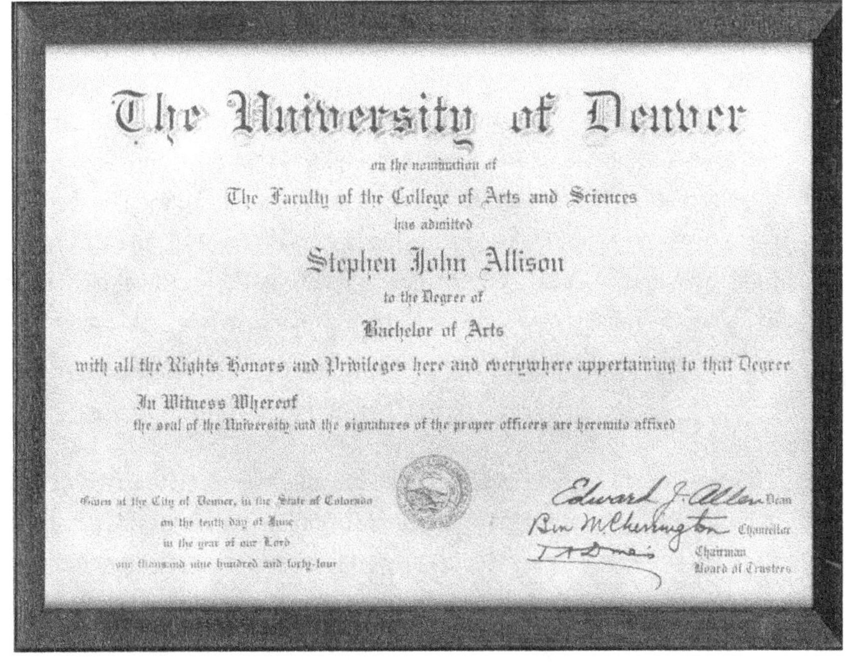

The University of Denver

on the nomination of

The Faculty of the College of Arts and Sciences

has admitted

Stephen John Allison

to the Degree of

Bachelor of Arts

with all the Rights Honors and Privileges here and everywhere appertaining to that Degree

In Witness Whereof

the seal of the University and the signatures of the proper officers are hereunto affixed

Given at the City of Denver, in the State of Colorado on the tenth day of June in the year of our Lord one thousand nine hundred and forty-four

Edward J. Allen Dean

Ben M. Cherrington Chancellor

Chairman Board of Trustees

Figure 12.13 Steve's Diploma from the University of Denver.

Returning to Shirley's diary, here's what she's been up to during these same two months of 1944:

May 1944

May 1, 1944 Well, I've been gadding all day, went down town and saw the Bond rally parade, I walked about 5 or six miles just shopping around. Stopped in and saw Georgia, Titsa and Uncle Frank and explained why I didn't see them before now. Bought a rubber sheet and a shirt. Waited for Stevie, he had to work late, so Daddy brought us home in Cruisor 60 - had supper and Steve went to school and I went over to Flossie's and we talked til 9:30 P.M. I came home and took a shower and read some magazines I don't know what time it is now, around 10:30 I guess. Stevie said he would be late as he wanted to see Uncle Gus. Nite, I AM TIRED.

May 2, 1944 Steve and Rex Hunt and Uncle Gus got stuck in a bar somewhere last nite and Steve didn't get home until 12:45 A.M. and he was feeling good. It was thundering and lightening so badly, and I am so scared of it that he made me sleep with him. He is so sweet. We had breakfast and the rest of the day we played records. We had a good time. I didn't do a thing around the house. Went to Shirley's shower and she got just loads of nice things. Flossie finished the dress for Shirley and oh it was darling. I didn't get home til 12:45 A.M. just now, and Stevie is very put out at me for being out alone, oh these lovable men.

May 3, 1944 Got up at 9:00 A.M. and went and layed with Stevie and told him all about the shower and then we had breakfast. Steve left around 11:00 A.M. and went out to D.U. and then he and Uncle Gus went to Charles Baines funeral and then he went to work, he came home for supper. I've just been lazy today, I feel like I'm catching cold so have tried to avoid that. It is 11:00 P.M. now and I'm waiting for Steve to come home. I just put up my hair and took a shower. Mother went down town and bought some flannel to make me a dozen diapers. Am going to fix my nails now. Paid $1.00 on Drug Store account, I paid $1.12 so I owe them $3.00 exactly.

May 4, 1944 I love Stevie. Stevie and I laid around till this afternoon, and then we went down town and I got my cards for Mother's Day, and Stevie went to work and I got a street car and went over to Mother's and Daddy's, we talked and then ate dinner, then sat around and gabbed til 10:15 P.M. then I met Steve down town at 11:00 and we went and saw Uncle Gus. It is now 11:45 P.M. and I have to take a bath and put my hair up yet so I'd better get busy. Saw Grandma and Grandpa for a minute.

May 5, 1944 Whew am I glad Stevie doesn't work this shift every month, I just can't get any thing done in the day time when he's here. I didn't do a thing today except straighten up the house a little bit, I'll just have to pitch in and do double tomorrow, I have a washing and ironing to do and the house has to be cleaned thorough tomorrow. I'm going to get up early tomorrow and see if I can't do some of it before he gets up. I went in and slept with him until 10:15 this morning, and then we went outside and mowed one side of the lawn and raked it etc. and I had to have lunch at 12:30 so he could meet Uncle Gus at 1:00 P.M. and after he left, I just didn't have ambition to do anything so I washed up the dishes and went over to Flossies. We talked awhile and then walked up to Lowell and got some ice cream. Its after 9:00 now and I want to take a bath and get to bed so I can get busy early tomorrow. Talked to Stevie just now on telephone. I love my Steve so much. Have had pains in right side since yesterday.

May 6, 1944 Washed 4 lines of clothes, cleaned house thoroughly, ironed quite a bit. It is now 11:05 P.M. and I have to wash my hair and I'm all in I can hardly see straight.

May 7, 1944 Slept till 9:30 A.M. and got up and ironed my dress and apron. got breakfast. Steve dug up the bridal wreath over at Flossie's and transplanted it over here under the garage window. Flossie made me the cutest apron today. I didn't even know she was making it. we took Flossie out to Pa Allison's and all the Frank Allison's were there, too. We came back and had chicken dinner and then played Chinese Checkers. It is now 10:20 P.M. I have to take a bath yet so better scoot.

May 8, 1944 Slept until 8:30 A.M. when Daddy called, then went and slept with Stevie until 10:00 A.M. We got up and ate breakfast. Then my Stevie studied while I straightened up the house and then we laid down until 1:30 P.M. and then I got him ready for work and he left about 2:45 P.M. Then I went over to Flossie's and we walked up to 32nd to the store. Then we came home and did Flossie's dishes and had some ice cream. I came home and put up my hair and laid down to listen to the radio. Now I'm going to take a bath as Steve should be home soon, it is after 10:00 P.M. Flossie fractured her finger and it sure is swollen, I hope it gets better as she can't paint with it.

May 9, 1944 Today Stevie and I worked out in the yard all day, he really got a lot done today. I went over to Mother and Daddy's for supper and then Grandma and Grandpa took us down to Lodge and we saw a movie, and then played Bingo. I won a little Memo Pad and a dozen napkins and a beautiful red rose bud. Steve came out about 10:00 P.M. and stayed till 11:00 P.M. It is now midnite and I want to take a shower yet so Nite.

May 10, 1944 Slept this morning until 10:30 A.M. Got our breakfast and then we took Flossie to the Doctors to look at her finger. Then we went to the Market and got our groceries, came home and fixed lunch and Steve went back down town. I cleaned house and defrosted the ice box. I bout scared myself, Steve and Flossie to death down at the store, I was standing waiting for Stevie to get some milk when water started running down my legs, but it stopped so guess it wasn't anything. Talked to Mr. King, and Morey has been here since a week ago Sat. he leaves again tomorrow. I am to go over there the 18th and take care of the nursery for Faye. Am going to bed now it is 9:30 P.M.

May 11, 1944 Stevie and I worked out in the yard all day until he went to work, then I straightened up the house, and went over to Idella's for supper, Morey left today again. Just got home it is 11:00 and I have to take a bath yet. The Allison's got a telegram at 11:00 P.M. tonite that Chris is a prisoner of war in German territory.

May 12, 1944 Slept til 9:00 A.M. and Mother called, went back to bed til 10:30 A.M. and then Dick Penner called, he is in town on a furlough til Tuesday. Steve and I worked outside til 1:30 P.M. then Daddy came over and we came in and talked til time for Steve to go to work, then I cleaned house and got supper ready as Idella was coming over, she got here at 6:00 P.M. and left at 9:30 P.M. we had a nice visit. Stevie just called and wanted me to go to bed early so am going to take a shower and scoot as I am tired. The baby is pressing against my ribs till I can hardly breathe.

May 13, 1944 Have been sick all day, stayed in bed didn't even do my dishes, will have to get up early in the morning and get my work done now. Stevie cut the Evergreen tree for Flossie and dug a lot of dandelions in our yard. I don't know what made me sick but something certainly did. I got a Mother's Day card from Flossie today. Am going to take a bath and get back to bed now. Nite.

May 14, 1944 Mother's Day - Slept til 9:30 A.M. got breakfast and then went outside with Steve. Came in and laid down for awhile, then got cleaned up and went to the Federal and saw "Memphis Belle" and "Madame Curie" I liked them both very much. today is Mother's Day, and I got a box of chocolates from Bambie and Steve. We gave Flossie a box of candy too. We went to bed and listened to radio for awhile, I couldn't sleep so got up and walked the floor for awhile, my legs bother me something terrific.

May 15, 1944 Got up at 9:30 A.M. and did my washing. Steve slept till 10:30 A.M. and then ate breakfast, we went outside and I pulled weeds while he mowed the lawn, we went over to Flossie's and they talked for awhile, she talked to Mr. Dutton the Mayor's secretary today. I cleaned the house up spic-and-span, did my ironing and did a lot of watering besides. it is now 10:45 P.M. and I still have a shower to take. It has been unbearably hot today to me - maybe its because I'm so heavy. Talked to Mama and Daddy today. Stevie picked up our clothes from the cleaners today.

May 16, 1944 got up at about 8:00 and had breakfast. We went down to Public Market and did our shopping for the week and wandered around town til about 11:00 A.M. then came home and worked in yard and mowed it until 12:30 P.M. then laid down til 2:00 P.M. had lunch and Stevie went to work. Straightened up and then laid down and read till 7:00 P.M. then went outside and talked to Cunio's til 8:00 P.M. Came in and brought my scrap book up to date and finished tracing another dozen announcements, it is now 9:25 P.M. and I have a notion to wash my hair as it is dirty. so better get busy Steve went out on Car 73 today.

May 17, 1944 Worked outside till my Stevie went to work cleaned house from top to bottom. Spiva's came by for a few minutes. Locked myself out this afternoon and Stevie had to come bring me the key. Flossie and I went down to the Chinese place on Curtis and had a full portion of chow mein, um was it good and then we went and saw Uncle Frank, then walked from Curtis to Glenarm and back down to Stout window shopping, it really did me good, I feel 100% better. have to fix hair and take bath yet it is 11:00 P.M.

May 18, 1944 Left at 11:30 A.M. and went over and stayed with the kids at Mrs. King's until 5:00 P.M. then went over to Mommy's for dinner she got some new rugs and a new bedspread today down town, her house sure looks pretty since they got it done over. She sent out my shower invitations tonite. Stevie just got home a little after me it is just about 11:00 P.M. I am really tired tonight. I have to take a shower yet so I'd better get started I guess. Had a nice day.

May 19, 1944 Stevie and I went down town at 10:00 A.M. first we paid the Telephone bill and Steve got a hair cut. then we went to see Uncle Gus and he bought me a dish of youdi [?] and then we took him down to the O.P.A. and back to the place then Steve took me to meet Jim Dikeou, he certainly is a highly educated man we took him to the Shirley-Savoy to a meeting, then went to Doctor Butterfield's and Dorothy was there, and we all went to lunch together, then she spent the rest of the afternoon here at home with me. Jack says he thinks the baby will be born in June, everything is perfect my blood pressure etc. Talked to Mrs. King tonite and I'm going to take my huge washing over to her house Monday and do it in the washing machine. Nite. Talked to Mama tonite.

May 20, 1944 Got up at 8:30 A.M. we worked out in yard till Steve went to work at 2:30 P.M. then I cleaned house thoroughly and washed out a lot of dirty clothes. helped Flossie paint some of my announcements. Then watered yard good. i must be old cause I'm all in, its not 10:00 P.M. yet so I want to put up my hair and take a bath and hit the hay cause I am awfully tired, we didn't go to sleep til 2:00 A.M. and Cuneo's radio woke us up at 7:45 A.M. Nite.

May 21, 1944 Stevie and I worked outside till he went to work, we cleaned the inside of the Ford with the sweeper and then washed. After Steve left I cleaned kitchen real good, and

Stevie came home at 10:00 P.M. and brought some ice cream and cake from Aunt Reba's wedding and we went to bed, and read til midnite, then went to sleep.

May 22, 1944 Got up before Stevie and ironed his police shirt and my dress. Fixed his breakfast and straighted up house. Went to town and got his Dad some bread, meat and seeds, then went out to farm and brought Dad Allison back to town and stopped here at home and had some lunch then went out and got some tomato plants. The car got stuck out in country, and Stevie had to hurry to get out to D.U. in time for the meeting with Chancellor. Flossie and I walked up to 32nd and got some ice cream. Nite.

May 23, 1944 I cleaned house and then fixed Steve's lunch and then went over to King's and took care of the kids while Faye went to a party. had supper over there and got home about 9:00 P.M. Idella and I played with the kids and talked all evening. It is 10:30 P.M. now and I have to get ready for bed. Talked to Virginia Belle and to Mother, the Allison's aren't coming to my shower, guess they are still mad at me. Faye washed 22 shirts for me. Am going to start from today and start growing my nails long again.

May 24, 1944 Cleaned house. Steve and I worked outside again this morning. He had a meeting with Civil Service Commission today. I hope it was a good one. Marion Horner called and she's going to take me to Mother's Friday nite. Everybody that is invited is coming except Aunt Ella and Elsie and they sent me presents over. the Allison's may come if Aunt feels better. Flossie and I went down and had some chop suey and walked around. it is 9:30 P.M. now and I want to take a bath and go to bed early as I am tired. i love my Stevie so much.

May 25, 1944 Didn't do anything but sleep till Steve left. Talked to Marion Horner, Mother, virginia belle on telephone. After Steve left I got busy and cleaned both clothes closets, put all our winter clothes away, and cleaned both chest of drawers, took all Stevie's clothes into back bedroom. Took baby's things and put them all where I want them and packed some of the suitcase. Washed a few things and Flossie pressed them for me. My hay fever has been bad today. Was going to wash my hair but I'm too tired.

May 26, 1944 We went to store and got weekend groceries, and stopped over at Kings and got bassinette and toilet. Came home and baked a cake. marion came over and picked us up (Flossie), and we went to my shower. There were fifteen there. virginia Belle and her mother were there, Idella and her mother, Shirley Marymee, Marion Horner, Aunt Ester, Aunt Reba, Aunt Persis, Grandma Clutter, Grandma Johnson, Flossie Higman and Aunt Sylvia. Aunt Ella, Aunt Micki and Elsie Peterson all sent me presents as they couldn't be there. I got a bathinette from Mother and Grandma Johnson and loads of other nice things. Virginia Belle got a crib just like mine. Every one had such a good time. Stevie brought us home. Am so tired I won't be able to sleep.

May 27, 1944 Didn't do much but rest today, I straightened the house up and put away all my presents. It is now 9:30 and I'm going to take a bath and paste some things in my scrap book and try and get some letters written before Stevie comes home. Flossie came over for awhile this evening and we gabbed for some time. Dominic Crow was made a Sergeant so that leaves Stevie next, cross your fingers diary. talked to Mother and Marion and Virginia Belle on the phone. I don't know why I should be so all in but I am.

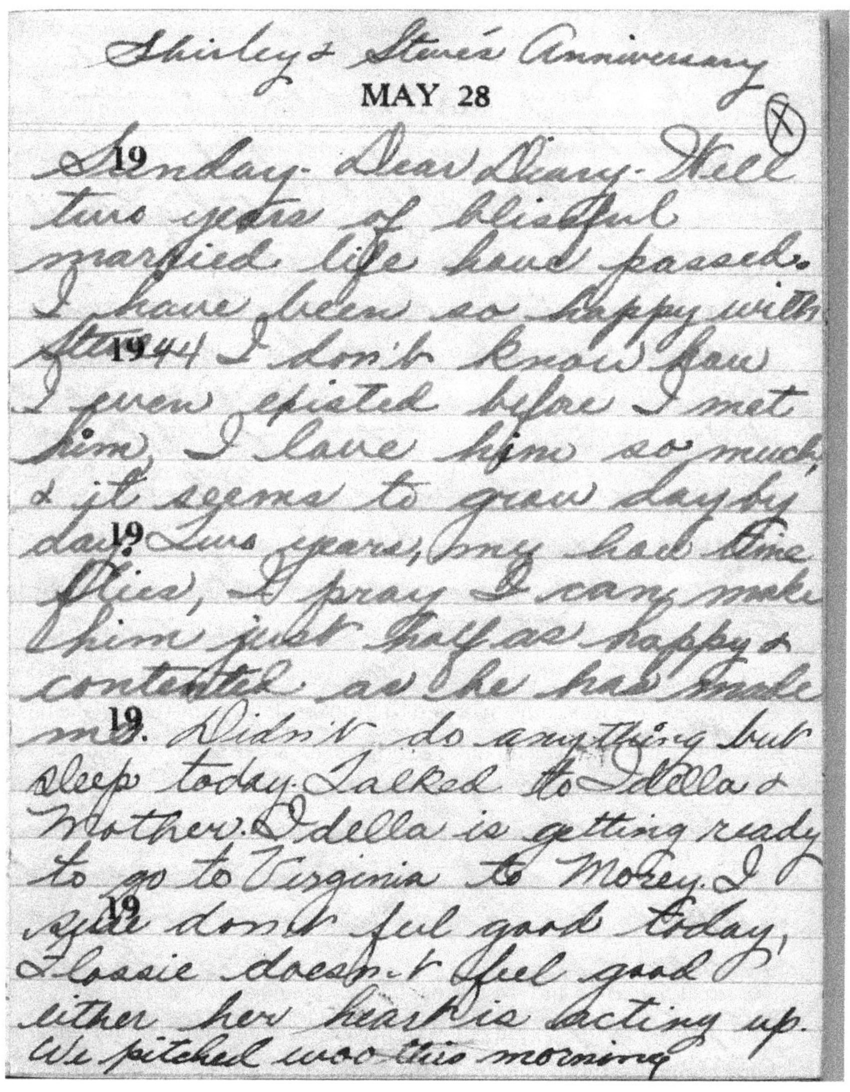
Shirley & Steve's Anniversary
MAY 28
Sunday - Dear Diary - Well two years of blissful married life have passed. I have been so happy with Steve 1944 I don't know how I even existed before I met him, I love him so much & it seems to grow day by day. Two years, my how time flies, I pray I can make him just half as happy & contented as he has made me. Didn't do anything but sleep today. Talked to Idella & Mother. Idella is getting ready to go to Virginia to Morey. I sure don't feel good today, Flossie doesn't feel good either her heart is acting up. We pitched woo this morning

Figure 12.14 Shirley's Journal; May.

May 28, 1944 Shirley and Steve's Anniversary. Well two years of blissful married life have passed. I have been so happy with Steve I don't know how I even existed before I met him, I love him so much, and it seems to grow day by day. Two years, my how time flies, I pray I can make him just half as happy and contented as he has made me. Didn't do anything but sleep today. Talked to Idella and Mother. Idella is getting ready to go to Virginia to Morey. I sure don't feel good today. Flossie doesn't feel good either her heart is acting up.

May 29, 1944 Today was Steve's day off, I straightened up the house while he mowed the lawn then we went out to his Dad's and had a nice visit. We got Flossie some tomato plants and onion sets and came home. then we went down town and got some groceries. Stevie went to school tonite and I watered and ironed a shirt and dress. We got a beautiful tablecloth and napkins from Aunt Micki and Uncle Gus for our anniversary. It is almost 11:00 P.M. so I want to take shower and get some shuteye. Stevie bought me two ice cream cones today and Flossie brought me a dish of it. I love my Stevie with all my heart and soul.

May 30, 1944 Memorial Day - Slept until 11:30 as Stevie went to work at 3:00 A.M. got up and cleaned house from top to bottom and got lunch ready. Then Stevie laid down for a few minutes before going back to work. Virginia Belle and her mother and Grand-mother stopped by and we went out to cemetery. Poor Mrs. Carson is really lonely, I gave her some of my iris to put on his grave. We got home at 5:00 P.M. and I went over to Flossie's for supper and then came home and watered and picked all the dead buds off iris.

May 31, 1944 Went down town early this morning with Stevie and Flossie, we bought some goods to make blankets out of, and some yarn to make a soaker, then my Stevie took us to lunch at Bennetts. Came home and straightened up the house and laid down till 6:00 P.M. Flossie and Nell came over and Nell looked at my baby things, she has started my soaker already. We walked up to 32nd and got some shampoo and eye wash for me. we also had a strawberry sundae. Came home and Flossie washed my hair for me. It is now 10:30 and I have to take a shower yet. I love my Stevie so much.

June 1944

June 1, 1944 Got up at 5:45 A M and fixed breakfast for Stevie as he starts the 7:00 A.M. to 3:00 P.M. shift today, then I got some of my washing out but couldn't finish as the wind blew something terrible, went to store came back and straightened up the house and then Virginia Belle came, we had lunch and walked up to 32nd and got some yarn, came back and she went to sleep for an hour while I started supper, Bill came about 5:30 P.M. and we had supper and then we all four sat out in back and gabbed, it is now almost 10:00 P.M. and I am so tired I can hardly move. Dominic Crowe was made a Sergeant today. I love my Stevie so much.

June 2, 1944 Slept till 11:00 A.M. then straightened up house. Mother called. I wrote all my Thank you notes this afternoon. Did two lines of washing, and then started on the birth announcements after supper, I am just quitting and I haven't got but half of those done and its after 10:00 and I have dishes to do and my hair to put up and my shower to take. I wrote 16 thank you cards they are just darling, Flossie painted a tiny rose on each one. Mrs. King and Gary rode over for a few minutes this evening on their bycycle. Nite. Idella called too, she's not pregnant.

June 3, 1944 Slept til 9:30 A.M. Then walked with Flossie up to 38th and Federal to Save-A-Nickel. Cleaned house throughly and cleaned vegatables Steve brought home. Washed some of his clothes and the two bedroom rugs and the bath mat and toilet seat cover. Got Supper. Ironed until 10:15 PM. Flossie came over and cleaned my chicken for tomorrow and made me some noodles. It is now about 11:00 P.M. and I am have to put my hair up and take a shower. Stevie worked extra at the Shirley-Savory tonite. Mother and Daddy are coming over tomorrow so I'd better get ready for bed and try to get some rest.

June 4, 1944 Woke up at 5:30 and read paper, then Idella called at 9:00 so got up and sprayed rose bushes and went to store and then fixed breakfast. Cleaned house up and prepared dinner. Mother and Daddy got here at 3:45 P.M. and we had dinner and then went outside and Daddy fixed the lawn mower and we took turns mowing. Came in at 6:30 and did dishes then Steve went and got us some ice cream and Flossie came over and had some, then we played pinocle until 10:00 P.M. and they went home and I'm tired.

June 5, 1944 Went to Bob Coursey's wedding at 9:30 A.M. at St. Catherine's - it was a beautiful wedding. Met Virginina Belle at 1:00 P.M. and we had lunch at the Columbine then I went and got Steve a pen and pencil set for graduation. Went to see Doctor Butterfield's and everything is O.K. then went down and X-ray's taken of my tummy and I got to see the pictures of our baby, Doctor Brandeburg says he thinks it will be three or four weeks before it is born. Didn't get home till 5:30 P.M. fixed supper and went over to Flossies. It is 10:15 P.M. now and I have to put up my hair and take a shower yet.

June 6, 1944 Slept till 10:00 A.M. got up and straightened up house. Went over to Flossie's and we walked up to 32nd Ave. Came back and Steve was home, he brought home the X-ray's of the baby. We worked out in the yard til dinner then after dinner we worked outside until 8:00 P.M. then Steve laid down and he just woke up and it is 10:00 P.M. so I guess he'll go back to bed now. I finished writing my birth announcements while he was asleep. Mary Flannery came over and she's going to have another baby in December. Talked to Idella and Daddy. D-DAY The Invasion of Europe started today.

June 7, 1944 Stevie let me sleep this morning, he came in and shut the blinds and kissed me goodbye and shut the door and I slept rite through it. I went over to Mother's early this morning and we went down on Broadway and shopped. Stevie came over for supper and Gramps ate there too, Grandma is lots better although she is awfully weak. Mother and Daddy and Grandma and Grandpa went in together and bought Steve a Masonic Bible for Graduation. It is 9:45 PM. and I've got to fix my hair and take a bath yet.

June 8, 1944 Didn't do much today. slept until 11:00 A.M. then polished some of my dining room furniture and swept the floor real well. Steve laid down at 6:00 P.M. and slept till I woke him up to go to bed, and he went right back to sleep and slept till 6:00 A.M. Flossie came over and we washed my hair and then I went to bed. I forgot to write in you, dear diary yesterday.

June 9, 1944 Cleaned house thoroughly, polished rest of furniture and got house ready for party tomorrow nite. Walked up to 32nd Ave and got myself two dish rags and one case of mascara. Stevie is sure down in the dumps for some reason. he went over and spaded up part of Flossie's garden for her while I mowed the back lawn. Charlie and Marion Horner came over for awhile to get their tickets for the graduation tomorrow.

Stevie gets his degree.
JUNE 10
No more ~~teachers~~ pencils no
more 19 books no more teachers funny
looks. Whoopie! Stevie got his
diploma tonite at the auditorium
He looked so handsome in
his 1944 cap & gown, and the mayor
congratulated him. After graduation
he had a lovely party, &
got so many nice gifts.
19 Guests included Aunt Esther,
Uncle Bob, & Eddie, Marion &
Chuck & Mother & Daddy. Mickie
He got a shirt, tie, brushes
19 desk calendar, pen & pencil
Masonic Bible, Book ends.
Scrap book. He got a card
from his Dad. Mother came
19 over for supper & we went
down together. Flossie was
sick & couldn't go.
I am so happy

Figure 12.15 Shirley's Journal; More June entries.

June 10, 1944 Stevie gets his degree. No more pencils, no more books, no more teachers funny looks. Whoopie! Stevie got his diploma tonite at the auditorium. He looked so handsome in his cap and gown, and the Mayor congratulated him. After graduation he had a lovely party, and got so many nice gifts. Guests included Aunt Esther, Uncle Bob, and Eddie, Marion and Chuck and Mother and Daddy and Mickie. He got a shirt, tie, brushes, desk calendar, pen and pencil, Masonic Bible, Book ends. Scrap book. He got a card from his Dad. Mother came over for supper and we went down together. Flossie was sick and couldn't go I am so happy.

June 11, 1944 I got up at 5:00 A.M. and put my hair up and read the paper then went back to sleep until 8:45 A.M. steve went over and dug up the rest of Flossie's garden while I fixed breakfast. After breakfast I cleaned up the house throughly and then Steve and I laid out in the back yard and took a sun bath. Got a chicken dinner and had flossie over, then we all three went out to the old man's for a while. On the way back we stopped for a few minutes at Charley's and Marion's. Then we came home and had some ice cream and went to bed.

June 12, 1944 Am sitting of all places, on the toilet writing this. It is 9:45 P.M. and I have to put up my hair and take a shower yet before I hit the hay. Shirley Marymee came over and spent the day with me, we had a nice time visiting. We walked up to 32nd and got some groceries. Stevie took her down to Curtis to catch her car on his way to school. Boy, am I tired, shoo, I must be getting old Flossie was over for a minute this evening. Well, I'd better get my business done as I am really all in.

June 13, 1944 Cleaned house. Steve was home for lunch. Didn't do too much as I was tired for some reason. Steve and I went out to his Dad's this afternoon, we stopped and talked to some people we know out on Tennyson St. Took some petunias out to Mrs. King, she hasn't heard a word from Idella. Flossie put in her garden. Stevie is working extra tonight at the Cosmopolitan Hotel at a party for The Dental Assn. He is working 9:30 P.M. til 2:00 A.M. Am going to write some letters now.

June 14, 1944 Slept till 11:30 A.M. Was kinda sick all night with pains in my stomach. didn't do anything but straighten house a tiny bit and walk to 32nd. Steve came home at 3:30 P.M. (Daddy brought him) and Flossie, Steve and I went out to Buckley Field, gee we had a good time, they had open house. We had steak dinner out there, too. We got there about 4:00 and we just got back and it's after 10:00 P.M. I have to take a bath yet so I'd better scoot. Got a letter from Uncle Joe and Aunt Letha today

June 15, 1944 Washed clothes all day today. Stevie mowed the lawn and pulled weeds and watered everywhere. ruth Spiva came by for a few minutes. Flossie cut the top of my hair and washed it for me. I wrote three letters and Stevie addressed his Thank You cards. Flossie made a Get Well card for Grandmother and a Thank You card from me to Nell. Steve brought me home a photostatic copy of his degree for my scrapbook, he's so sweet and considerate. It is past midnite and I have to take a bath yet. Mother called me today, she is fine. Night.

June 16, 1944 Cleaned house and washed some more clothes and ironed. the wind blew something awful all afternoon Stevie came home for lunch. Flossie went out to see Patty. After work Steve and I went and bought $6:00 worth of groceries, we got him a pretty new straw hat. I got a pair of panties, some wave set, a nursing bottle some Mum and some bobby pins. After supper we watered and then looked at the new Collier's magazine. I am going to get ready for bed now as I'm all in.

June 17, 1944 Today was Stevie's day off, we slept till 9:30 A.M. then Stevie took Flossie down town, she talked to the Mayor, and so did Dick McCusker. Sounds very favorable. Stevie put on his trunks and we laid out in the sun all afternoon. We washed and polished the Chrysler. It sure looks pretty. We walked up to thirty second and got 1/2 gallon milk. Then watered the yard. We went over to St. Dominic's carnival, we didn't win anything. There was a fight and Steve helped handle it, gee was it exiting. We saw Ernie Cavaleri and his wife and baby over there. Have to take a bath now.

June 18, 1944 Father's Day - Didn't do anything today. I was over at Flossie's most of the day. She fixed a picture for Daddy with my hair on it, he really liked it. Steve and I, Charley and Marion, Bern and Sylvia and Beverley, Aunt Esther and Uncle Bob and Eddie, Mother and Daddy, went out to a place called Country Kitchen and we ate and ate, you go back and get as many helpings as you want. We went over and visited Aunt Reba and her new husband, they sure have a nice place. It is after 11:00 P.M. and I have to take a bath yet.

June 19, 1944 Washed some sheets and pillow cases today, and cleaned the house. Stevie got home early and slept a while. We had a early supper and then got ready and went down to see Doctor Butterfield at 5 P.M. He said my blood pressure was high and I have to drink two glasses of water a hour. We messed around down town until after 7:00 P.M. then came home and watered till just now it is 9:45 P.M. Am going to bed now as I am really tired out for some reason

June 20, 1944 whew was it hot today. 90 degrees. I went to the store early this morning and cleaned early so I just took it easy this afternoon. I defrosted the ice box and washed and ironed a police shirt for Stevie. Mailed a birthday card to Claire Martin as this is her birthday. Stevie and I watered until just a few minutes ago. It is about 9:30 P.M. now. got a letter from Little Steve. boy oh boy I've just about melted today. Will I be glad to get rid of this extra weight I'm carrying around.

June 21, 1944 The longest day in the year - and the hottest so far this summer. I straightened up my house a little and then went back to bed, I didn't sleep good last night at all, I was sick to my stomach and then it was so hot I just couldn't sleep. I felt kinda sick today too. Gee I'll be glad when our wee one finally gets here. Mrs. King called. Idella is in Blackstone, Virginia. Steve brought me some ice cream this afternoon. We mowed the lawn this evening and watered. It is now 9:30 P.M. I don't know where time flies to. I'm so tired, I'm going to bed right now. Nite.

June 22, 1944 Cleaned the house and washed and ironed a few pieces then got ready and went over to Mother's. We went up to Colorado Blvd. and got some groceries. Stevie came over at 5:30 P.M. and had supper. He called Herb Forsythe and he said they weren't going to hold the Sergeants list over. He feels bad about it but I am sure they will make him before the list goes out. We just got home it is almost 10:00 P.M. and I have to take a bath yet. Had a enjoyable day. Boy is it ever hot outside. Stevie is sick.

June 23, 1944 Boy I wasn't kidding when I said Stevie was sick. I didn't take my clothes off from the time I got home from Mama's til 8:00 A.M. this morning. This is the first time I've ever stayed up all night, he just vomited and vomited, I called Doctor Butterfield. He finally went to sleep when I put on the heat pad. Flossie and I walked to 32nd and got my groceries and took my books back too. Steve is resting now, am I ever glad. it scares the living day lights out of me when he's sick. Daddy came over for a fw minutes.

June 24, 1944 Stevie didn't go to work today as he still doesn't feel too frisky. I was sure glad he was around tho' as I have been miserable all day with my feet. We cleaned the back porch and basement today, oh what a relief, it was so messed up and dirty. Steve felt a lot better late this afternoon and evening. We went and got the bread for the dogs and the bread for his Dad tonite. Steve is so darned sweet to me. He scrubbed the back porch and woodwork for me today I love him so much it hurts.

June 25, 1944 Slept til 10:00 A.M. got breakfast and sat around and talked till noon, then we got ready and went out to the farm. Georgia and Tetsa, Aunt and Uncle Frank came while we were at Dad's. Came home about 3:00 P.M. laid down and slept till 6:00 P.M. got supper. Steve watered I went back to bed, I don't feel a bit good for some reason. My feet and legs hurt something awful. Steve feels a little better but not too good still.

June 26, 1944 Cleaned house and did three lines of washing. Sure got sick for a little while today, but feel lots better now. Talked to Mary Flannery and to shirley Marymee today. the place that Wesley used to work at burned down today, Goldberg's, Steve took Flossie and me over to see it. We went to the Doctor's, and Jack says I'm doing fine and that he expects it any time now. Stevie and I mowed the lawn and watered this evening. it is after ten, and I have just got to write some letters before I go to sleep. Talked to Mama tonite. Got a letter from Idella and from Sharon. Sharon wants to stay here July 1 - 2

June 27, 1944 Boy did I clean house today, I really scrubbed until it shines. Am sure tired tonite tho' and my legs really hurt. Steve and I went over to Spiva's and got the bassinette, gee it's a lovely thing, and she had a pair of knitted booties and a handmade dress in it.

Stevie cut the front lawn tonite and trimmed the big tree in front as the wind broke one of the big branches last nite. We walked across the street and looked at Mr. Smith's roses, they're certainly lovely. Mother is going to Ginger's shower with me and she got my present for me which I greatly appreciate. Wrote to Idella and Sharon today. Walked to 32nd Ave and got groceries.

June 28, 1944 Slept quite a bit today as I was all in for some reason. Cleaned up house. Stevie came home for lunch and brought my robe home from the cleaners. Flossie made me two little sheets for my bassinette. We washed my hair tonite, and I've got it put up already. now I'm going to take a bath and go to bed (it is 9:00 P.M.) as I am going to spend the day with Mother and then we're going to Ginger's shower tomorrow nite. I have to get up early and wash and iron my clothes before going over. Aunt Persis called and talked to Steve.

June 29, 1944 Washed eight of Stevie's shirts, my dress and slip and his socks and underwear. ironed some of it. Straightened up house. Took shower and went over to Mother's. Went over to Grandma's and Grandpa's while Mama fixed supper. Steve was there when I got back. Mother got ready and we went to Ginger's shower, it was a nice party and I won the prize playing Cootie, it is a pair of tile wall plaques. it is almost midnite and I must put my hair up as it is stringing down my neck, it got rained on today.

June 30, 1944 Just piddled around all day. Walked up to 32nd and did my shopping for over the holidays. Stevie came home and brought me some eggs. daddy came over twice. Charley Lutter came over for a few minutes. Steve watered and dug weeds, and then took Flossie and me for a little ride down by Sloans Lake and around. It is now 9:30 P.M. and I'm having cramps in my legs.

Sweet, naïve and immature, Shirley.

Sweet? Positively. She's truly a *good* wife, daughter and friend. She never has an unkind word or thought about anyone and is genuinely appreciative of, and thrilled with, any small kindness shown to her.

Immature? Somewhat. She writes of her terror during a spring storm - at a time when millions of women throughout the world are trying to survive the real, nightmarish terror of World War II. (She however, unlike Steve, at least makes note of D-Day.) Later in her life, my mother would certainly come to know real fear, of real things. But at this point, she's such a child.

Naïve? Probably. She's happy with her pregnancy and *seems* completely contented. (What a nice incubation period for her baby - carried by a mother who loves her husband, has good sex, gets lots of sleep, is pretty pampered, enjoys good friends and has a happy attitude about every new day. Lucky baby.) So *why* then, did she walk away from all this *just nine months* later?

I'm reading these diary entries, in their entirety, for the first time as I'm typing them. It's hard not to skip ahead to see what happens, in a very short while, to destroy this marriage. But even at this point, Shirley's left us a few clues. But, *I* think that perhaps she was *already* a lonely wife - needing more involvement with her husband than she was getting.

On April 21, 1944, for example, she writes, "I feel so blue tonight. I don't have a reason to, but he gets so much on his mind that I feel kinda left out in the cold sometimes."

And it would seem that she *also* needed more involvement with *life* than she was getting while married to Steve.

Later, she could never remember much about her time with him, but always spoke passionately about her life with Max, her second husband - especially their early days together. She would recall, and still does - in great detail, all the *interesting and exciting* things they did. For example, he took her dancing at elegant ballrooms several times a week, to dinner often at the Ship's Tavern in the Brown Palace Hotel and on many romantic out of town trips.

Her days with Steve, on the other hand, were spent "straightening" up the house, washing, ironing, getting groceries, and preparing meals. Spending time with an older neighbor, Flossie, going to a few movies and going to the farm were about the most exciting things she did in that marriage.

Speaking of Flossie, I recently asked my mom to tell me more about this friend from her Grove Street days. She had always spoken of her with great fondness and I wanted to get a clearer picture of their friendship. Shirley told me that at the time of these diary entries her friend was probably between 45 and 50 years old and had never been married. She was a very talented artist and was also a very kind and giving person. She was very active in the Democratic Party. That's probably why Steve asked her to speak to the Mayor about his sergeant's promotion. According to Shirley we visited Flossie sometime after our reuniting in the 1960's; but I don't remember that at all. They kept in contact until she died in the 1970's.

During this conversation, Shirley also told me how much she disliked being with her own mother during these years. I told her it sure wasn't evident from her daily notes, but she assured me that such was the case - that their relationship had always been uncomfortable and strained. The subject had come up when she told me that Flossie "couldn't stand my mother." It does seem that, during these years at least, Flossie was more of a mother to Shirley than was Pearl.

Shirley's diary conveys so well her life as well as her time. When she records that she "walked up to Save-A-Nickel", I can visualize her daily routine, but am also reminded that people actually walked to the grocery store in those days. I think it's great how much she walked. It's a good thing she did too, because she and Steve sure ate a lot of ice cream! (I wonder why they didn't buy enough to have it at home - in the "ice box" - instead of going out to buy it every time.)

And she didn't have a washing machine! Too much work! At one point she says she's going to take her laundry to King's (the parents of her friend Idella) and use their washing machine to wash, among other things - 22 shirts! Good grief, that's a lot of shirts - especially since she has only *three* dresses.

Idella and Shirley's marriages will both become extremely unsettled in the near future, and both will end. The Spivas, whom Shirley mentions on May 17 and June 15 and 27, will, in less than a year, open their hearts and home to her infant daughter. But of course in June and June of 1944, she has no inkling that her marriage will soon end. On May 29, 1944 she writes, "I love my Stevie with all my heart and soul." and on June 24th that she loves "him so much it hurts."

I came across something last week that reminded me anew of the age differences between my parents at the time of their marriage. While cleaning in our basement, Ken found a football program that Steve had saved from 1937. It prompted me to wonder anew just what he'd done, besides attend football games, in the decade - that's a long time! - after leaving CU and marrying teenaged Shirley. This program is for a Thanksgiving Day match between CU, his old university, and DU, the university from which he would eventually graduate.

Glancing through it, I am taken to a time and frame of mind very removed from our current experience. An ad for New Method Cleaners reads, "A Football Game is symbolic of true sportsmanship. Good sportsmanship in life means satisfactorily shouldering a responsibility."

I wish more of today's college and professional athletes felt this way. They often face criminal charges as a result of their unwillingness to shoulder responsibility.

And there are lots of ads for cigarettes. On the back cover Carole Lombard endorses Lucky Strike. She says, "When I had to sing in a recent picture, I considered giving up smoking. But my voice teacher said I needn't if I'd select a light smoke - Luckies."

We were so gullible.

But back to Steve's "present" life, in May and June of 1944. It doesn't seem to hold much happiness - at least as reflected in his (and Shirley's) journal. He works, worries a great deal about his possible promotion to sergeant, takes care of the yard, studies, finally graduates, has dinner a few times with his in-laws, visits his dad at the farm, and takes in a few movies. He sometimes visits the Parkhill Lodge, where he will soon become a Mason.

He seldom mentions his home life. And he never mentions his baby - although he and Bambi, the cat, do give Shirley candy on Mother's Day. I don't think he did anything to commemorate their second anniversary on May 28, 1944 however; which is sad, since she noted that it marked "two years of blissful married life".

Much of his time was taken up with pursuing his promotion to sergeant. I'd bet that most, if not all, of his contacts with Jim Dikeou were concerning this subject. Jim Dikeou was a very successful Greek businessman, who eventually owned the city's minor league baseball team, among other things. He must also have had some political pull that Steve felt he could use on his behalf. My father was always somewhat bitter about the obstacles he faced in trying to advance his career. During one of our few conversations, he told me that he could have been promoted faster and higher if the police department hadn't given extra "points" to men who had been in the military. He thought this very unfair, since it wasn't his choice to remain a civilian. I'm not sure why he didn't serve though. Was he too old? Did he have to look after his father? I don't know.

I felt bad for him that here weren't any Allisons, except dear Aunt Mickie, at his graduation. They didn't come to Shirley's baby shower either. He notes that it took him seven years to graduate. Was that counting all the years at Colorado College and the University of Colorado when he was younger? It had been sixteen years since he started to pursue a college degree. He was 34 years old. You have to hand it to him for hanging in there. I thought it was interesting that he was depressed, "down in the dumps" according to Shirley, on the day before his graduation. Sometimes people do get depressed, instead of happy, as they approach the "pay off" of a long and difficult struggle. Maybe he was sad because his relatives weren't acknowledging this long sought success. I've hung his diploma in our home. I wish he could know that I'm proud of him.

Today I was reminded that I'm also proud of my mother, although in a different way. I'm proud of her ability to live and love life - each and every day of it! In the course of cleaning the basement last week, we ended up with several bags of stuff to take to my mom, who in turn takes them to her friend, who in turn takes them to the homeless shelter. So, I took time out today, writing day, to take them over to Shirley's house this morning. I'd hoped I'd be gone for an hour at most, and then begin writing.

Right off, though, we had to make a trip to the home of another of her friends to pick up something. On the way there we stopped to buy cinnamon rolls to enjoy with the friend. Several stops later we returned to my mom's. While I was there she gave me two magazine articles that she thought might help me with my "writing". One was by a woman writing about her dysfunctional family and the other gave pointers on writing about one's own past. I was touched by her thoughtfulness. And, most importantly, she gave me a letter she had written and had notarized, giving me permission to use in any way I care to, her diaries and letters from the years 1944-45. I really appreciated that. By the time I returned home, it had turned out to be a three-hour outing. However, we had a fun time.

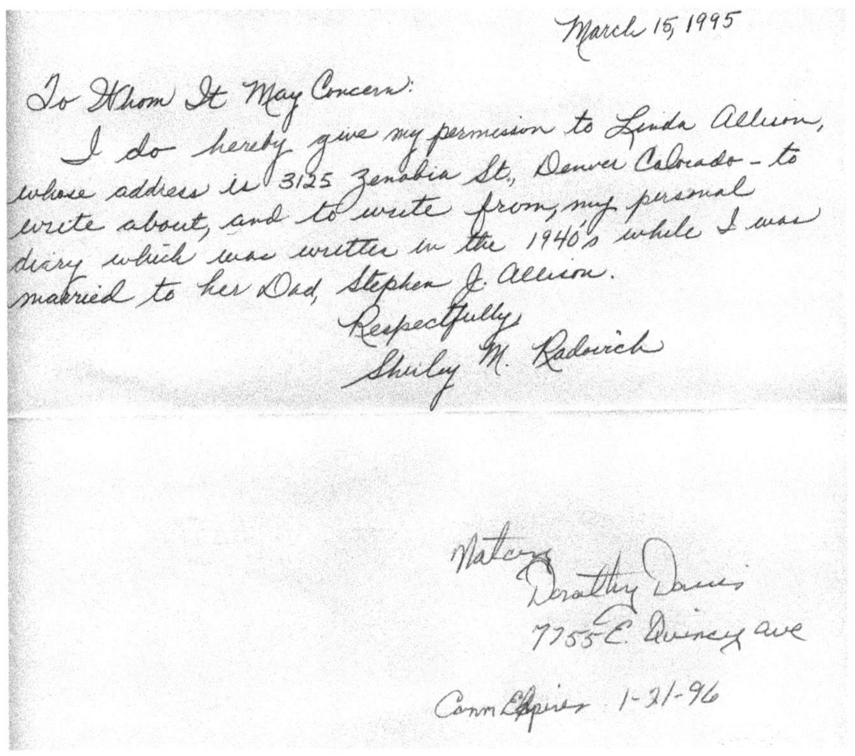

March 15, 1995

To Whom It May Concern:
I do hereby give my permission to Linda Allison, whose address is 3125 Zenobia St, Denver Colorado - to write about, and to write from, my personal diary which was written in the 1940's while I was married to her Dad, Stephen J. Allison.
Respectfully,
Shirley M. Radovich

Notary Dorothy Davis
7755 E. Quincy ave

Comm Expires 1-21-96

Figure 12.16 Letter from Shirley, authorizing the usage of her diary.

Although I'll always have reservations concerning Shirley's care for me as a child, I'll say this - she's a great mother to me now, and has been ever since we "met" in 1967. She's easygoing, very generous and a fun person to be around. I love that she lives each day of her life as if it were a gift - and a new adventure. And no matter what the circumstances, she always looks on the bright side, trying to find joy in each and every day of her life.

"two years of blissful married life"
Shirley's diary - May 28,1944.

CHAPTER 13

"I love my Stevie and my baby."

And now we have a beginning, and an end – the beginning of the story as it includes Linda Lee, who's born on July 21st, but the end of the story as told by Shirley. Her diary entries end on August 6, 1944. Actually, the rest *of the diary itself* is missing - just as the front part was missing. I think Steve decided what part he wanted to save in The Box and then discarded the rest. *That's* probably meaningful.

As we rejoin them, Shirley's awaiting the arrival of their baby and Steve's awaiting news of a possible promotion.

I've paired their entries for this time period - summer days of 1944.

Saturday, July 1, 1944

Washed all the windows, and dusted my blinds in my room. Cleaned rest of house. Sharon came at 12:30 P.M. she slept all afternoon. Aunt Persis and Uncle Charles came over for awhile. Got supper. sharon's boyfriend came and they went out. Steve and I and Flossie went for a ride and had a pop-cycle. Came home and slept for awhile. Put hair up and took a bath and went in and listened to radio in Steve's room until midnite then went to sleep. Paid magazine man.

R.O. Campbell on vac I will work in his place in acc. Bureau 7 a - 3 pm.

July 2

Sharon stayed out all nite. She didn't come home til 6:00 and they have left now. Steve and I went over to Charley and Marions, and then out to the farm to see Dad Allison. We had a flat tire on the Ford, we had to change it right in the crossroads by his Dad's. We watered till now. I have to put up my hair and take a bath and wash Steve's combs. Talked to Mother and Daddy is sick.

Day Off - Ranch with Shirley

July 3

Cleaned house. Washed four sheets, six pillow cases, twelve bath towels. Shirley Marymee called. Dampened Stevie's shirts to iron tomorrow. My feet are swollen something terrible. Talked to Mother, Daddy still doesn't feel very good. It rained something awful today and I can't bring my clothes in because they're so wet, the wind is blowing something fierce, I hope I have some clothes left in the morning. Brought my scrap book up to date tonite while Steve was studying. Am going to put my hair up and go to bed.

Clerk acc. Bureau 7 am to 3:00 Pm

Morgan's Efficiency average for last 3 yrs 87.94.

July 4

Slept till 12:15 P.M. then got up and cleaned house and made a cake, and watered yard. Stevie came home and we had a bite to eat and then laid down and slept, Then we got up and took our baths and we went over to Mother's, we took Flossie and watched the fireworks. Mother had some ice cream and cookies, Daddy is still sick in bed. We played Chinese checkers, and we just got home, it is 12:30 A.M. Aren't we night owls? I love my Stevie.

Worked in bureau Bud sick at home, possible pneumonia.

July 5

Got up about 10 A.M. Flossie and I went up to 32nd and got our groceries. Came home and washed my brown chenille bedspread, Stevie's white turkish bath robe, and a lot of other things. Stevie and I took a nap, then I got supper, did dishes watered the lawn, cleaned out magazine rack. Wrote letter to W.L. Johnson for Stevie. Sprinkled my clothes, and ironed a few. Will have a big ironing tomorrow. Talked to Mother. Daddy is worse, they had the doctor.

Worked in Bureau Wrote letter to W.L.J.

July 6

Cleaned up house. Rested in afternoon. got supper for Steve, then we walked up to the library, then we walked thru Highlands Park and watched some boy Scouts playing, then we walked up to 32nd and Lowell and got some ice cream, on the way home we got caught in a rainstorm, and had to run up on some dark houses porch, we both got soaked but we had fun we giggled all the way home. Its fun to do things like that with the one you love.

Worked in Bureau, delivered letter to W.L.J. Bud still sick

July 7

Went down town at 10 A M and met Shirley M. We went shopping. We walked up to Doctor Butterfield's, he said if the baby didn't start by Monday, he's going to start it. Then we went and had lunch, and went to the show at the Orephium. Came home at 5:00 P.M. and Stevie called and he was at Mother's so I took a bath and climbed abroad a bus and went over there. I had supper over there. We had a nice time. Came home and went to bed.

---

received word from Bundy - favorable.

W.L.J. talked with boss. I talked with Chief Hanebath - no vacancies. Saw Dikeou.

Saturday, July 8, 1944

Stayed in bed till noon, I am definitely tired out. Didn't do a thing untill Stevie came home except iron another shirt for him. We went down town and bought our groceries and came home and had supper. Then Stevie mowed the lawn. I'm going to take a bath now and go to bed. Shirley, Marion, Mother and Daddy, Doctor Butterfield and Stevie called me today. Got two ounces caster oil to take Monday, if Jr. isn't around by then. Oh boy!

Worked in bureau W.L.J. saw boss

Efficiency's
1940 - 77.50
1941 - 82.50
1942 - 86.66
1943 - 89.83

July 9

Stevie went out to ranch and I stayed home as I felt miserable. Got dinner, and I think unless I am mistaken that my labor pains have started. Chuck and Marion were over and she helped me make up my beds, and she took the sheets and pillow cases and two towels home to wash for me. Georgia called, and so did Mother. Boy does my back have pains in it.

Day Off - Ranch   Shirley not feeling so good.

July 10

Well the castor oil didn't bring results so Dr. says we'll just let nature take its course. I called Mr. Galvin and he is helping me. Flossie helped me iron and wash some things this afternoon. The Mayor called and talked to Stevie this afternoon, he still didn't commit himself, we will have to sit tight and wait till the 13th I guess. After supper we rode over to Mother's and visited awhile, Daddy and Stevie went and got us some ice cream and then we came home, it is 10:30 and I have to put my hair up.

Worked in Bureau
Talked with boss by Ph.
W.L.J. talked with No. 1.

July 11

Cleaned house up throughly and went down town and saw Mr. Galvin, we had a nice visit, came right back home. Flossie has mended and ironed all my clothes, gee I appreciate it. Mother came by after church and she and Stevie and myself talked and talked. Got supper. Marion came over and she had washed and ironed my four sheets and two towels, she is sure swell. Stevie and I played records until 10 P.M. Now I have to put my hair up and go to bed. Mickie called tonite. Shirley called, too. We got an address to write cousin Chris. President Roosevelt is going to run for fourth term.

Bud came back to work from being sick.
Jim called me at 6 Pm - said all is OK.

July 12

Didn't do a thing today, I felt so miserable I just stayed in bed and read the Science and Health all day, I guess the exitement is getting too much for me, but we'll know tomorrow whether its Sgt. Allison or not. We went over to Mother's and Daddy's for supper again tonite, They sure have been swell to us thru this suspense. It is after 10 P.M. and I have to put my hair up yet, and I'm really all in.

Worked in Bureau

Talked with #3 - said all is ok

July 13

It is 3:30 P.M. and I am writing in you now as I presumably am going to spend the rest of the night giving my Stevie a Jr. But I wanted to be sure and tell you that Steve will be known from now on as Sgt. Steve Allison,

Well I'm home again, Dr. Butterfield decided we could wait for awhile longer. We went over to Mother's for awhile. Aunt Persis, Shirley, Virginia Belle, and Dad Allison called.

"D DAY" 12:15 - Chief called me in his office Made SGT Dill also made as was Sgt. Cook a Capt

July 14

Cleaned house. Went down town and payed telephone bill, talked to Titsa for awhile. Came home and laid down till Steve came, then we went to the store. Came home and fixed supper. Went outside and watched Stevie mow the lawn. Flossie came over and sewed the stripes on Stevie's shirt for us. We had some ice cream. It is raining. I am so tired all the time, I will be glad when this business is over.

Bought Sgt. Cap thanked No. 1, Mr. Bundy

Talked with capt. Davis to rpt to him 7-16-44 3:15 AM

Saturday, July 15, 1944

Cleaned the house thoroughly, washed Stevie's underwear and socks. Took a nap till he came home, then got supper. After supper Bert and Ed stopped by for a few minutes, they brought me a gorgeus shawl for the baby. Jimmy D. and Brown stopped by for a few minutes too. Stevie went to bed about 7: P.M. I pressed his shirts for him after he went to bed. Poor guy will have to get up at 2:15 A.M. I have my slip, dress, and brassiere soaking so I'd better get them washed and put my hair up and go to bed myself as it is going on 9:00 P.M.

Worked in accident bureau as clerk.

received Sgt. Badge – very happy about it.

July 16

got up at 2:00 A.M. with Stevie, then went back to bed till about 9:00. Got up and cleaned up the house. Stevie got home about noon and I fixed him some lunch. He went out and clipped the lawn and then at 2:00 P.M. we walked down to the Egyption and saw "A Guy Named Joe". Came home and Stevie washed his hair while I fixed supper, he went to bed and I went out and watered then did the dishes, cleaned out silverware drawer and put clean papers in it, then washed the two sheets and five pillow slips and three towels. it is now 11:00 P.M. Have to put up hair. Marion H came over a minute. Six people killed in fire at Elitches

---

Started to work for Capt. Davis as Sergeant on Detail #1. - Capitol hill.

July 17

Cleaned up the house and fixed us some lunch, then we went out to farm and brought Dad in, we stopped here at home for a while then went down town. Saw Uncle Frank and they had two cards direct from Chris today. On the way back to farm Stevie's Dad bought us some ice cream and he gave Steve $5.- to buy sticker for Ford. Mary took me to 32nd to get groceries this morning, Stevie went to bed about 7:30 and I went out and watered till 9:00 then went to bed.

Cr. 20 with Kirtly

Shirley and I went out to ranch, Dad was brought in

July 18

slept till 8:45 AM. got up and straightened up the house, started lunch Mother called and Shirley called. Had lunch and I laid down and slept, Stevie cleaned up the garage and watered, Georgia called.

Cr. 20 –Kirtley

July 19

<no entry>

Cr 20 with Kirtley

Talked to #1

Called W.L. Johnson by Phone

July 20

<no entry>

Cr. 20 with Kirtley

took Shirley to Hosp in Cr 20 at 6:00 AM.

Stayed with Shirley from from 6:00 AM 7-20-44 to 3:30 Pm on 7-21-44

33 1/2 hr's

July 21

Gave birth to a 6# 15 1/4 oz. daughter at 1:05 P.M. Was in labor 34 hrs. Dr. Butterfield had to use instruements to get her.

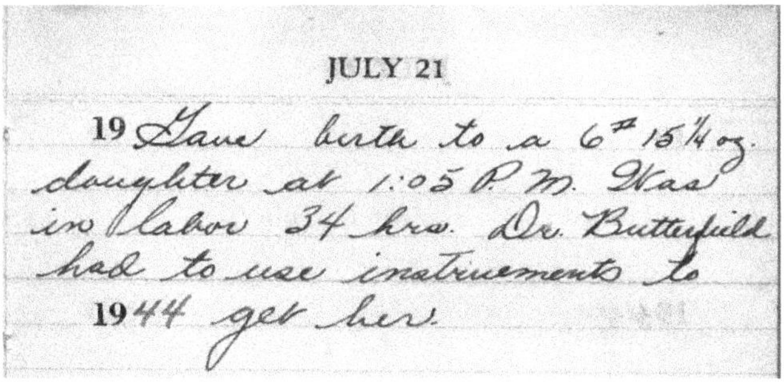

Figure 13.1 Shirley's Journal: July 21, 1944.

Day Off - At Presbyterian hospital Baby girl born at 1:05 PM
Shirley had a hard time, glad it was over
Called my dad.

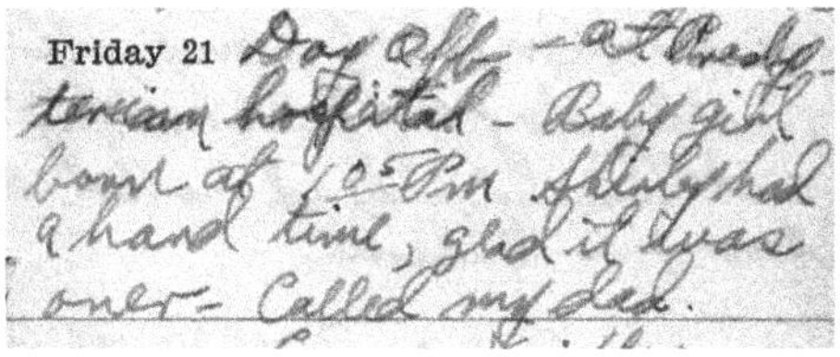

Figure 13.2 Steve's Journal: July 21, 1944.

Saturday, July 22, 1944

<no entry>

Cr. 20 - Kirtley,
saw Shirley, came home cut lawn
sent in preliminary report on Shirley to World Ins Co.

July 23

<no entry>

Cr. 20 with Kirtley,
had dinner at Harris's
saw baby and Shirley at hospital.

July 24

<no entry>

Cr. 20 by myself - Kirtley day Off

saw baby and Shirley Dad called saw Jim Dikeou.

July 25

<no entry>

Dad came in,saw Shirley

Davis said a Capt stated that I was tough, remark originated from radio Room

July 26

<no entry>

Car 20 with Kirtley

July 27

<no entry>

Cr. 20 by self - Kirtley off

Meet Father Hogus for bazzar.

July 28

<no entry>

SHOOT - 77Cr. 20 by myself

Saturday, July 29, 1944

<no entry>

Day Off - Put in pulley whell in ford with Frednegrill aid,

Paper came for Shirley to fill out for World Ins.

Jim Smith called said he was ordered off of land at 37th York.

July 30

Came home from hospital. Went to bed. Am sure weak.

Worked at circus

Brought Shirley home with baby from Hospital

Talked to Butterfield.

July 31

Stayed in bed today too. stevie is working Cole Bros. Circus from noon till midnite. Awfully hot weather. 95 degrees and 100 degrees.

Worked at Circus from 12 noon to 12:00 MID.

August 1

Had to walk floor with Linda Lee all night as she had colic, really all in, I can't even move out of bed. Mother and Daddy left on their vacation tonite they are going to Sweetwater Lake.

Worked Cole Bro's Circus - 12 Noon to 12:30 A.M.

Regular Shift for month is 8 Pm to 4 Am.

August 2

Slept all day and nite.

Worked Cole Bros. Circus 12 Noon to 12:30 A M.

August 3

Feel more like my own self today. got up and got dressed. Hearld Spiva brought us over a fresh homemade cherry pie. Stevie brought a lady over from the circus to see Baby, she gave her $5.00. Then Flossie stayed with Lindy Lee and we went to the circus for awhile and did some shopping. Had my fortune told, hope everything she said comes true. Baby has been real good today Marion called, she has two sweaters for the Punkin. virginia Belle and her Mommy stopped by for a few seconds. Reba W. over too. Steve didn't go to work till 7:00 P.M. as this is the last nite of the circus and he has to stay till it pulls out, it is after 1:00 A M now so guess I'd better go to bed. Nite. I love my Stevie and my baby.

Worked at Cole Bros. Circus 7 Pm - 2 Am

August 4

Took Linda down to see the doctor. We took her down to the hall and all the fellows got to see her. Took her by The University of Denver and let the girls see her. Stopped by Uncle Franks and they all took a peek at her. I hope I didn't overdo it as I've started to flow a little again. Have some diapers to do and the supper dishes to do and it is just midnite. Linda is asleep, I hope she stays that way, I am pooed out. I love Stevie so much, more and more each day.

Worked Cr. 20 - with Chafin.

Saturday, August 5, 1944

<no entry>

Cr. 20 with Chafin

"Hooper's PLACE" and Brown's "place" clean   Saunders "place" run good.

August 6

I ironed all morning while Stevie and the baby slept, then got breakfast and gave Linda her bath. Later we went over to Charley and Marion's for a few minutes, then took the punkin out to see her Grandpa Allison, my, my, did he think she was ever something. Came home, got supper and got Stevie off to work then laid down and slept till now, it is most 10:30 and I have the dishes to do yet, I'll be glad when I don't poo out so. Didn't write in you yesterday as I was too all in. Idella came home the 4th. Saw the Frank Allison's.

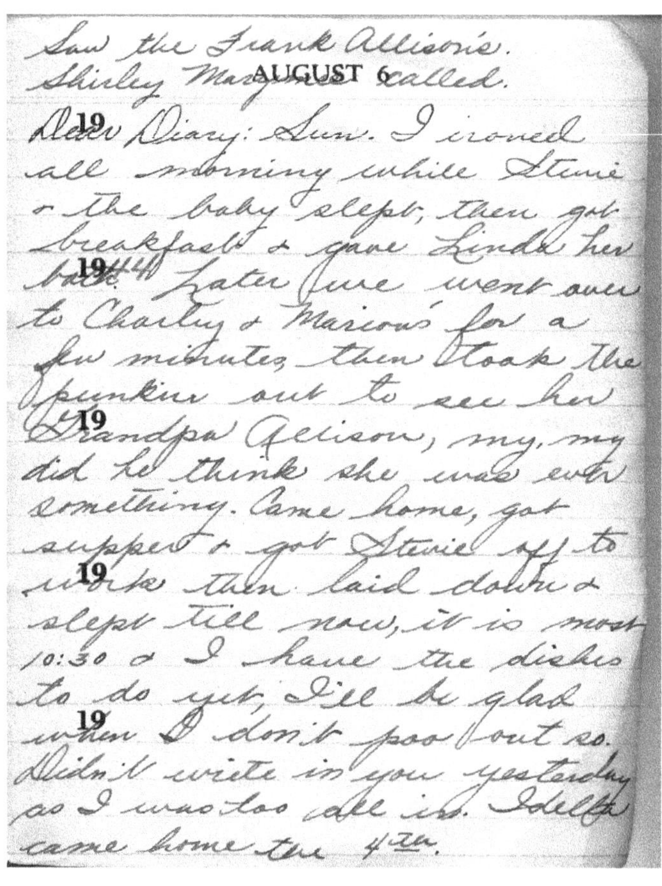

Saw the Frank Allison's.
Shirley Marjorie called.
AUGUST 6
19
Dear Diary: Sun. I ironed
all morning while Stevie
& the baby slept, then got
breakfast & gave Linda her
bath. 1944 Later we went over
to Charley & Marion's for a
few minutes, then took the
punkin out to see her
Grandpa Allison, my, my
did he think she was ever
something. Came home, got
supper & got Stevie off to
work then laid down &
slept till now, it is most
10:30 & I have the dishes
to do yet, I'll be glad
when I don't poo out so.
Didn't write in you yesterday
as I was too all in. Idella
came home the 4th.

Figure 13.3 Shirley's Last Journal Entry: August 6, 1944.

Cr. 20 with Chafin

Shirley paints lovely word pictures of the happy couple before their baby's arrival. For example, they:

- listen to records on a summer evening – going outside now and then to change the hoses,
- run home, arm in arm and giggling, in the summer rain,
- enjoy still (although I've continued to omit these references), a very healthy sex life.

And then they are three. Or four, if Bambi the cat still exists. He's never mentioned again. After their daughter is born, Shirley seems, although exhausted, happy and contented. On August 3rd she writes that, "I love my Stevie and my baby."

If I seem preoccupied with her state of mind, it's because I know what's coming – and soon. And since Shirley of today can't remember anything about these years, I'm trying to understand just what happened to this little family.

She's still trying to keep ahead of the housework. It does sound a bit overwhelming. Imagine washing a "turkish bathrobe" out by hand!

I smile when I read her lists of the people who phone each day. I've omitted many of these notations, for brevity's sake. Recently she told me how much she enjoys her caller identification service. She really likes knowing who's called in her absences. Evidently she's always felt strongly about telecommunications.

On a more serious note, the Christian Scientist religion has always been, and continues to be, a very important part of Shirley's life. It was one very significant gift that she received from Pearl, her often demanding and judgmental mother. She mentions reading the Science and Health publication and of visiting Mr. Galvin (the practitioner, I'm assuming) shortly before her baby is born, and that he "is helping me."

Hopefully her faith helped her through 34 hours of labor a few days later. One of the things Shirley can remember today, from these years, is the difficulty of my birth. Somehow I "got hung up" on her pelvic bone. Because of this anatomical problem, four of her next five children were also born in similar painful circumstances.

I bet she was disappointed that her parents went away on vacation so soon after she had given birth to their first grandchild. From her diary, it's clear that she would have welcomed some help during this time.

And Steve is still mainly preoccupied with his role as breadwinner - and with trying to win his promotion to sergeant. In the days before "D-Day", he contacts several persons who might have some influence with the people making the decision about the promotions.

And then, finally, he is a sergeant! I was so happy to read that! I was holding my breath. He writes that he is "very happy about it". That's the closest he's come to showing *any* emotion in his journal. Even when his child is born, he simply notes that he was "glad it was over".

One of the photos I found is of a group of men standing on the steps of the State Capital Building. It is undated with no notation of any kind. I think these are Denver policemen, and I'm going to arbitrarily say this is at about the time Steve becomes a sargeant.

Figure 13.4 Group of men at State Capital. Likely Denver policemen. Steve is in the second row, third from left.

He was very disappointed, however, later in his life, by his lack of recognition and promotion within the police department. He'll retire 17 years later as a lieutenant, having advanced only one additional rank.

I have several snapshots, which unfortunately I can't find, taken at John's farm from this time. In two of them, Shirley is holding her newborn baby. She's pale and beautiful in her summer dress. In another, Steve encircles her, and their baby that she's holding, in his arms. These must have been taken on August 6, 1944.

Shirley's August 6th entry is her last. That's too bad. Already I miss her. And I'm wondering again why her diary ends here. Did she lose interest and quit writing or did Steve discard the next few months' entries - because they made him look bad? Was he abusive? Was he having an affair? As we know, she can't remember; but perhaps she wrote of things that *he* was doing that might help explain why their marriage will unravel in the very near future… Well, whatever - say good-bye to our friendly chats with Shirley.

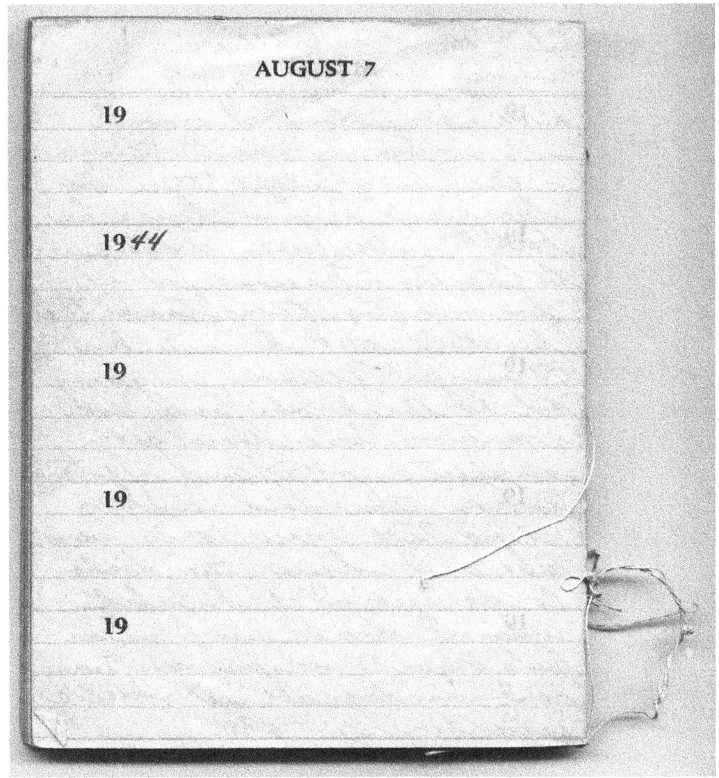

Figure 13.5 Shirley's empty diary.

Steve's daily notations continue to be pretty dry, but with some intriguing exceptions:

August 1944

7 Night off2:00 PM Justice Court Swartz VS Fallaseo. Amt $16.32

8 Cr. 20 with Chafin(A)

13 Day Off, went out to Bob's and Esthers

15 Crow to open Filling Sta

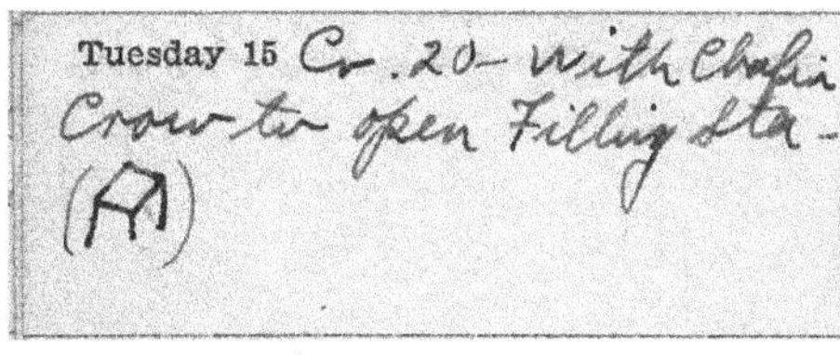

Figure 13.6 Steve's Journal: August 15, 1944.

Steve's drawn what, I'm guessing, is supposed to represent a table. Looking at it closer, I realize that what I thought was a capital A on the entry of August 8th is actually this same symbol – representing a table, or something like a table.

19 Put Major Paul B. age 38 in jail Dist [disturbance?] from Wand Hotel. He was from camp Beal Calif.

20 Day Off Cut lawn.

21 Cr. 20 with Cummings. Bud was over for supper. "Rossonian shooting" 2 arrest.

22 "Shooting" possible at 2739 Lafayettee 3 arrest [Table]

24 Meeting held by Chief Hanabath another disturbance at 23rd Welton - Glenarm

25 Bud received letterOK from Glendale Chief OK's trip.

27 Day Off - Went out to Dad's ranch.

29 [Table]

30 Had two cuttings on 5 points.

September 1944

1 Cr. 20 with Chafin Shift 12 noon to 8:00 Pm.

2 Dist call 5:40 Pm. Myer's Drug Store (3) arrest (2) soldiers (1) civilian.

4 Worked prade 8:00 AM then Cr. 20 with Chafin

6 [Table]

7 Day Off. Bud arrived back from Calif. Bud came out second in Job for Chief of Police - Glendale Los Angeles Capt was first.

9 Man with (2) shot guns at 1837 Pearl captured. Attended Berkley lodge with capt. Davis and Spiva.

10 talked to Jim Dikeou Shirley and baby over at Buds house.

12 SHOOT - 91. James Dikeou took over Devers Cafe.

14 Shimel's case came up, he was fined $5.00 + cost and suspended

15 Comp 724 E. 17th Ave Japanese with fruit stand

16 Examination given for Sgts. and Capt's - Bigelow would not let me take the exam.

19 attend funeral Fire Chief Hawkins

20 [Table]

22 Started to put new roof on garage.

24 Day Off - All went out to Uncle Bob's place for farewell dinner for Grampa Johnson.

25 got off at 3:00 Pm.Attended citiation exercises at Buckley Field for Chris.

27 [Table]

29 worked extra at Mamoth Gardens 8:00 Pm to 11:00 Pm

30 worked extra at Mamoth garden from 8:00 Pm to 11:00 Pm.

October 1944

1 Detail 4:00 A to 12 NOON

2 bought (2) bushels Peaches $5.00, bu of tomatoes for Gus.

5 Day Off Painted garage, worked on car
6 Cr. 20 with Chafin. Charley and I went to football game
7 Day Off painted on house all day. Dad came in from ranch.
10 Efficiency Shoot - 89.
12 Bud and Mother were over for dinner. also Bill and Virginia.
13 Shirley and I went to football game DU vs C C.
14 Day Off - Went down town with Shirley. got Dad's radio back.
16 Shirley and I went to Aladdin theatre.
17 1st day of vac. Painted on house, went out to my dad's ranch.
18 Vacation Worked on inside of house.
19 Vacation Rode with Bud on Cr. 60. Painted on house, supper at Bud's house.
21 Up to Boulder with Butterfields to see C U beat C C, then we went up to Butterfields place in the mountains.
25 Went over to Butterfields new place in Jefferson County.
29 At Butterfields, saw (4) deer's.
30 Returned from Butterfields place in the mountains.

November 1944

1 4 am to 12 Noon Talked to Ben about Sweatbath. [Table]
4 [Two Tables]
5 Day Off went to ranch with G. talked about lots
8 received deer meat from Spiro Cosmos.
9 Took overcoat to Gross tailors. Show with Shirley. [Table]
11 Worked Parade [Two Tables]
12 I went to football game at D.U. visited Capt. Davis at night.
14 Prestone Put in Chrysler. [Table]
17 Saw druggist 28th Fairfax 829 Dexter case solved
21 Meeting held for capts - Sgts; 2:30 Pm Men to rept. for roll call when they go off duty. Men not to go in joints. "Anderson Case" to capt Childers
22 Cr. 20 2 Women (colored) cut by another colored woman at 25th and Wash. [Table]
26 Day Off - Football Game Super bombers 0 - Marchfield Calif 0
28 sold revolver to Klines friend. Went out to my Dad's ranch.
29 Helped Bud move [Table]

December 1944

1 12N to 8:00 McCallister resigned
2 Checked Efficiency at Hdqts – 1944 FEB - 91, MAR - 93, APR - 93, JUN - 93, AUG - 88
3 Dinner at Bud's new house.
5 Dist. call at McCallister's Home would not let us in.
6 McCallister's wife called capt Davis, said Mc was out - in uniform. [Table]
7 High Chair from Englewood.

9 BQ Snow and temperature around 6 degrees above. Dad called from ranch.

10 House trailor's ordered off #26 - Madison. temperature about 2 degrees above last night. Oil drained in FORD Billy G. 17, of 1327 Madison brought in from City Park for dist.

11 Day Off Brought dad in from ranch. Van H and lady friend came over.

12 Ceiling price on Chrysler - $765.00 with radio and heater [Three Tables]

15 Gus in Jail.

17 worked air bond show Stapleton Field

19 BQ [Table]

20 Cr. 20 - with Frednegill efficiency shoot 97.

21 attended R. Herrmann's wife's funeral. Chief Hanebath and R. Smith were there.

22 Visited Capt Wolf, he is about dead from cancer. Worked at Mamoth Gardens

23 Worked at Mamoth garden's.

24 Cr. 20 with Chafin. Dinner at Dome with Bud and Mother.

25 Cr. 20 with Chafin

26 Acting Capt for capt. Madden 1:45 to 3:15 Pm. [Table]

29 Open house capt. Cook's house. Little Steve arrived from S.F. will be at Fitzsimmons Hospital.

31 Saw Steve (cousin)

At the back of this small notebook, in the address section, many police officers are listed - as are a doctor, a cabinetmaker, two roofers, a painter, and a picture framer.

The NOTES section contains his 1943-44 grades from DU. His major was Political Science and his grades were A's, B's and C's. It also lists his 1944 Efficiency Shoot scores and other notes to himself. For example:

Notes

2-22-44 Good book - THINKING ABOUT WAR AND PEACE
'Reading and thinking' by McCloskey
Dow Extension course Vocabulary building

7-7-44 Should have - 1 grey flannel Suit 1 Chalk striped Blue Suit

7-10-44 KUHLMYER - No.1's Secretary.

12-12-44 See Mr. KELLEHER 20th and Arapahoe St, St. Vincent De Paul for 2nd hand furniture.

12-12-44 See HENSLEY 20th and Curtis Service Sta about selling Chrysler.

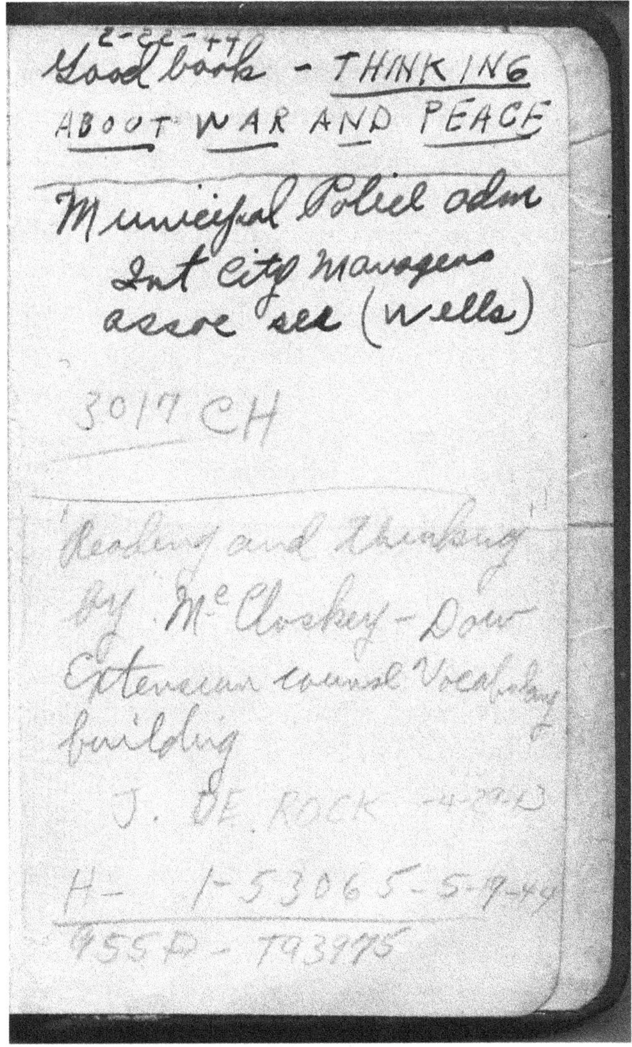

Good book - THINKING
ABOUT WAR AND PEACE

Municipal Police adm
Int city managers
assoc sec (wells)

3017 CH

'Reading and Thinking'
by McCloskey - Dow
Extension course Vocabulary
building
J. DE ROCK

H- 1-53065-5-9-44

Figure 13.7 Notes page from Steve's journal.

If his journal is any indication, Steve wasn't yet a very big part of his infant daughter's life. There are only two entries in nearly five months that even hint of a child. On September 10th he writes that Shirley and the baby spent the day at her parents' house and on December 7th he mentions something about a high chair. I know that his journal has always been concerned primarily with his job but he *does* mention several outings with Shirley and several social outings with friends in the months after he becomes a father, so it's not as if the journal is *only* about his work. According to Shirley, he never wanted to be a father - and I'd guess that, at this point at least, he has minimal interest in the role.

And notations about his police work *do* continue to make up most of his journal entries. I've included less than half. He's very concerned with his shooting scores. They must be an important consideration in the promotion process. On December 20th he shot a 97. I bet *that* made him happy. Way to go Steve!

He and his partners have a pretty rough district to patrol - lots of complaints, disturbances, shootings and "cuttings". (Speaking of disturbances, a fellow officer, McCallister, is causing some of these himself. He resigns shortly thereafter.) On November 21st they're told "not to go in joints". Was that for their safety or for appearances? Do they have only one day off each week? That's a long and stressful week. And why wouldn't Steve's boss let him take the exam for captain? And why does he, a sergeant, want to take it? Don't you have to be a lieutenant before you can be a captain?

He's sure not at home with his family much. He had to work on Christmas day - Linda Lee's first Christmas. From his minimal journal entry on that day it appears there was not much of a family celebration. Did they have a tree? If so, did the baby - and Bambi - love it? Plus, he's doing a lot of moonlighting. Besides keeping order at parades, circuses and bond rallies, he also works at Mammoth Gardens. Mammoth Gardens was a place where they held boxing matches and other sporting events, I think.

He and his wife seem to enjoy a close relationship with each other's extended families. She calls his relatives Dad Allison, Uncle Gus, Cousin Chris, etc., and he refers to hers as Uncle Bob, Grampa Johnson, etc. He even calls his in-laws Bud and "Mother". Since he never knew his own mother, I bet he liked being able to call someone that. Pearl was never very motherly to Shirley, but maybe she was more so to Steve.

Bud applies and interviews for the position of police chief in Glendale, California - but comes in second. Shirley and Steve attend a citation ceremony for Cousin Chris who had evidently been rescued from the prisoner of war camp. Chris' brother, Little Steve, arrives from San Francisco and enters Fitzsimmons Army Hospital. And Uncle Gus lands in jail on December 15th. It was probably for gambling or something connected with gambling. He got into a lot of difficulties because of this habit/addition - debts, questionable schemes to raise money, and threats against his life.

They enjoy a pleasant social relationship with their doctor and his wife - the Butterfields. They spend most of Steve's vacation with them, at their home in the foothills of the Rocky Mountains. Although both my parents will maintain their relationships with the Butterfields after their divorce, Shirley and Max and their four children will, for a few years, actually live at "the Butterfields' place in the mountains". These were the happiest days of my mother's life. She's often told me so.

And *what* about those "table" drawings, if that's what they're supposed to represent...?

Before the Allison family steps into 1945, let me share with you some newspaper articles that Steve saved from the final days of 1944. They offer a colorful and telling peek at this time in his life and the nation's life.

On Thanksgiving Day, November 19, 1944 he saved the entire home edition of The Denver Post - including the comics (Dick Tracy, Little Orphan Annie, Terry and the Pirates, Popeye etc.) This day's news must have held special significance for him - but I'm not sure what, exactly, it was.

The Rocky Mountain News Sunday magazine, "Parade", for November 26, 1944, asks the question: "How Are Your War Manners?" and goes on to advise that, "It is well to check your own public behavior against the changes from peacetime standards."

The article then lists, with accompanying photographs, several examples of declining public morals, such as:

> Women have lowered their peacetime standard of decorum, especially when they carry on conspicuous table-to-table conversation with unfamiliar men in restaurants.

Another interesting change the article decries is that of women wearing work clothes, not only to work - but out shopping, to the movies, or out to dinner.

A section of the Friday, December 8, 1944 edition of The Rocky Mountain News contains an editorial, a letter to the editor and a news article - each of which concerns police and police work. The editorial, by E.D.M. in "This Town" section, pertains directly to Steve's peers, his boss, his employer and his profession:

At a time when juvenile delinquency is becoming an ever graver issue in Denver, it is pertinent to point out a specific example of how police can help combat the growing social menace.

Over on the North Side there are two police officers, Robert Riley and Joseph Hale, who drive a traffic car.

But these two officers feel that their moral duty extends beyond their regularly assigned duty. When they come across a boy or girl whose conduct demands discipline, they handle the case in a fatherly and understanding manner.

These two officers are going far beyond their purely official duties in juvenile work in the North High area. Many parents owe these two men a deep debt of gratitude for the occasions on which they have escorted sons and daughters home late at night.

These officers, for instance, once interrupted a gay party just beginning in which five boys and one girl were the principals. The girl was escorted home. Later, the mother called up the officers and, in tears, thanked them for saving her daughter from a terrible experience.

Suppose that Police Chief Hanebuth poured out his energies and his talents (if he has them) in doing something tangible to aid the battle against juvenile delinquency - suppose he did this instead of disrupting and breaking the morale of the whole Police Department with petty, unfair, unreasonable and needless decrees and sour orders.

Think what good the chief would accomplish if he could impart to the Police Department the zeal and devotion to public service now being exhibited by those two North Denver policemen.

What a wonderful opportunity for real community service a grouchy chief is passing up. It is tragic.

In the "Letters From the People" section, "BERNARD BECWITH, Police Reporter" writes:

News Reporter Points to Police Training

Editor: With all due respect to Safety Manager Robert J. Kirschwing, but at the same time in justice to more than 300 men of the Denver Police Department who hold certificates as qualified to administer first aid, I would like to clarify a couple of points apparently misunderstood in one of Mrs. Mayfield's columns.

Quoting Manager Kirschwing, she said first aid kits are not placed in Denver's police cars primarily because many of the officers do not know how to render first aid. Capt. Ray Shane, head of the personnel division, tells me 372 men of the depart ment took a Red Cross standard course in first aid, requiring 20 hours of schooling, and receiving certificates on its completion. Among these, 25 took and advanced course, requiring 10 hours additional schooling, and qualified as experts. Of the 25, there are five who took still more training and were certified as instructors.

The training was ordered by August Hanebuth, then acting safety manager, in 1942. I talked to Mr. Kirshwing about this, and he said he was not aware the training had been ordered, since it was before his appointment to his present office.

Captain Shane also pointed out that complete first aid kits, including two blankets adaptable to conversion into stretchers, are assigned to each of the 70-series cars which respond to traffic calls. All officers in these cars are certified as experts to render first aid. The others have orders to apply such measures as stanching extreme bleeding, administration of resuscitation and extrication of patient from point of danger, but to undertake nothing else until a police surgeon arrives. Hence, no kits are assigned to these other cars.

I am sure there was a misunderstanding on this all the way around and Manager Kirshwing has told me he, too, misunderstood just what the point in question was. However, a large number of men of the department, with whom I work, have expressed themselves as feeling hurt that their qualifications as first aid attendants were unacknowledged and they all would appreciate it a great deal if the circumstances could be clarified.

Another letter (unrelated to police work), in this same section, offers an interesting proposal from J.D.F. This is a woman (or it could be a man, I suppose) whose thinking is both very much ahead of her time and yet very much a quaint reflection of her times:

Reader Suggests Women Give Up Cigarets to Men

Editor: During the last few days I have read several proposals designed to relieve the cigaret shortage, but it seems to me that no one has hit upon the happiest and most effective plan of all. It is simply this:

Let all of the women give up the manly art of cigaret smoking as a patriotic gesture to their country. Within a matter of hours, there would be sufficient cigarets available for the male population.

The women would derive immediate benefits. Their skin would improve and their voices would benefit. Young mothers would no longer endanger the eyesight of nursing babies or imperil the health of their young sons and daughters with the vile and poisonous fumes of the evil weed.

I realize, of course, that there will be those who will cry that a ban on women smoking would be infringement of their rights, but I am convinced the vast majority of American women would accept such a ban as both a patriotic duty and a boon to their womanhood.

Of course, it would probably be necessary to exempt women who are doing jobs of a masculine nature and such women could be given special cards to permit them to buy cigarets in the event they cannot bring themselves to smoke pipes or use chewing tobacco.

Once the majority of women stopped using cigarets there would be plenty available for men. In that simple fact is the essence of the plan.

Speaking of the roles of men and women during these times – here are a question and answer found in the advice column:

Should Husband Date?

DEAR MRS. MAYFIELD:

This note is in reference to your answer to a letter of a girl, 22, who had been dating a married man. You say it is wrong, that she should confine her dates to single men.

Well, I'm a married man, and have been out at Lowry three months. During that time I've met and dated several nice girls. At our first meeting I always tell them I'm married.

Do you think it would be better for us married soldiers who seek companionship to date girls and let them believe that we are single? I always tell my wife about my date and she approves because she has implicit trust in me as I do in her.

Please tell me what you expect a married man to do? I wish the married gals around here would stage a dance for us married fellows! B.

DEAR B.:

I still think it's a much sounder idea for the single gals to confine their dates to the single fellows. If you married men can get them to date you, that's fine from YOUR viewpoint, and I can't say I blame you when it's all open and aboveboard with the wife. But what about the poor girl who gets involved with a married man (and don't tell me some of them don't). Think how she feels when he comes out with "Sorry, Baby, but I'm already married!" That's really a pretty kettle of fish story, isn't it?

Remember something else, too. You say your wife trusts you, and vice versa, but that isn't true in a lot of other cases. As a result many wives are angry when their husbands take other girls out, start going out themselves, and there you are.

Sometimes it all works out. Other times it doesn't. It's these other times I'm thinking of.

Do you see my point now? M. M.

P. S.: You speak of the married girls giving you married soldiers a party. Perhaps you'd be interested in the "25-and-Over" Club, which meets every Saturday night at 8:30 at the Y.W.C.A. This group is made up of both married and single men and girls, all over 25 years of age. There's dancing, games, conversation, and, generally speaking, lots of fun. You'd be very welcome. M. M.

Figure 13.8 Items from the Advice Columns Page.

And finally there's this report:

Policeman Picks Up Wrong Bottle At Drug Store; Luck Saves Eyes

A Denver policeman who accidentally picked up the wrong package in a drug store Wednesday and took home a vial of powerful acid in belief it was eye-wash, was pronounced out of danger by an occulist yesterday, after one application of the diluted acid to his eyes.

Patrolman Arthur C. Schmitt, 3867 Winona ct., a veteran of 31 years on the Police Department, said he had been bothered by an eye inflamation following a cold contracted several weeks ago.

He visited a drug store and asked for a boric acid solution. Inadvertently, he picked up the wrong bottle from the pharmacists' counter, carrying away, instead, a similar bottle containing hydrochloric acid.

Efforts to Warn Him Are Vain

Schmitt, who was off duty and in civilian clothes, was unknown to the druggist. The latter discovered the mistake a few minutes after Schmitt's departure, but all efforts to identify and warn the unaware buyer proved fruitless Wednesday.

Schmitt works nights at headquarters. He went home with his medicine, poured some into a glass and, fortunately, diluted it heavily with water. He applied it to his eyes. He assumed the burning sensation was a reaction from the inflamed condition and went to work.

He said his eyes began to puff and blisters formed on the lids, but he decided to defer medical examination until yesterday - his usual day off.

Wife Learns Facts

Meantime, Mrs. Schmitt chanced to talk on the telephone with a neighbor, Mrs. Walter T. Lee, 4546 Meade st. She mentioned her husband's eye trouble and added he had bought some medicine before going to work. Mrs. Lee's husband, who is blind as a result of an accident several years ago, had heard of the appeal spread by the druggist in an effort to identify and warn the acid purchaser. He had spoken of it to Mrs. Lee only a few minutes before her phone conversation with Mrs. Schmitt.

Mrs. Schmitt disposed of the hydrochloric and telephoned her husband. An eye-specialist was consulted and examination disclosed that, while the acid had severely burned Schmitt's eye, its dilution had been such no permanent injury should result.

On that happy note, the year 1944 comes to a close.

"I love my Stevie and my baby."

Shirley's diary - August 3, 1944.

CHAPTER 14

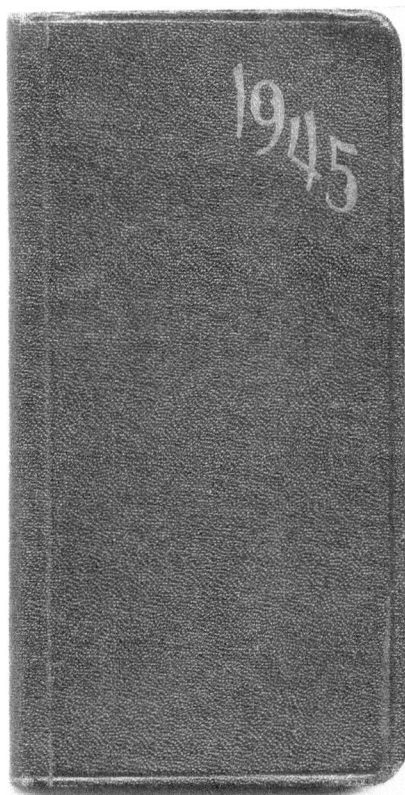

"Shirley did not come home last night."

And now Shirley and Steve's marriage comes to an end.

Only Steve's journal records its demise. Therefore, keep in mind that it's told from *his perspective only.* And since he saved it in The Box, it's obviously the version he wanted remembered. In it, only Shirley is to blame.

As we saw from Figure 13.5, Shirley's diary ends in August of 1944. Additionally, you can see that there are frayed edges and no cover. What happened to the rest of her diary? And, since Steve didn't save any of Shirley's diaries from this point on, and since she can't remember anything about these years, we'll never know her version of the events.

Still, it's a difficult part of the story to relate.

In it, Shirley is *perhaps* guilty of some marital indiscretion. We don't know what might have precipitated these actions - Steve certainly doesn't acknowledge any responsibility on his part - but still they probably happened.

(It's also *very* difficult to tell because it reminds me, uncomfortably to say the least, of the role I played in the demise of *my* first marriage.)

And so I'm hesitant and concerned about what follows.

I don't want to hurt my mother, although she's assured me that it's okay to write about this time in her life - nor do I want to offend my brothers and sister. Shirley is, after all, their mother as well as mine. Hopefully they'll realize that in order to continue with Steve's story, these next few chapters need to be included.

With these considerations in mind, I'll be even more selective in transcribing Steve's journals – while still striving to accurately convey his activities and concerns. The journals themselves become much harder to read – literally. The handwriting is messier and he writes more, so there's a lot squeezed into each day's space.

Sgt. S. Allison
2921 Grove St.
Denver, 11 Colo.

January 1945

1 Jack S. hit Sgt. McCallister [Table]

2 Cr. 20 - Chafin 4A - 12 N

4 [Table]

6 QB Stock Show Sheep skin vest from H.

7 Day Off - Home all day.

9 [Table]

10 To Dad's ranch with Charlies Truck.

12 Auto-Ped Fatality about 49th Cook (H -R) [Two Tables]

13 1st day at Stock show 11AM to 11Pm Kirkpatrick and Burkhart taken to dr's office for sobriety test then they were sent home.
14 Worked Stock show 11AM to 12 Mid.N.
17 Worked Stock show 11AM to 12:00 mid night. Had bad cold.
18 Worked Stock Show Shirley came to show with Idella and JOE DANOS.
19 Worked Stock Show [Table]
20 Worked Stock Show from 8 am to 12 Mid. Kids day.
21 Worked Stock Show Cowboy badly hurt
22 Excused from Work. have bad cold. Cowboy Burks died.
23 Mgr's hearing on Kirkpatrick - Burkhart both got 30 day's fine. [Table]
24 Steve and family over dinner. Henning moved in basement. JOHN AND ANGELO ALSO OVER
26 Henning's mother moved in down\stairs
29 Day Off - Went out to Dad's ranch
31 Day Off Brought dad in to town.

February 1945

1 Cr. 20 Chafin 8Pm to 4 AM [Table]
3 [Four Tables]
4 Day Off Stayed home Charley Horner was over.
5 Cr. 20 alone Basket ball games at Mamouth Garden's
7 [Table]
8 Played 1st basketball game in 14 yr's Cowboy Inn closed.
12 Cr. 20 E. Townsend Basket ball playing at East. Player hurt at Mammoth garden's
15 Obert going into the Army he was later rejected [Table]
17 [Two Tables]
18 Day Off - dinner at Bud's house
19 Talked to Bud about Shirley
20 Played a quarter of basket ball at Manual Hi.
21 QB from JOE [Table]
22 Isadore S. arrested on a cutting
24 [Two Tables]
25 Day Off - To uncle Franks for dinner. Shirley talks about John Zenpathos.
27 Bigelow salary cut by council to $200.00 per Month [Table]

March 1945

1 4 AM - 12 Noon
3 I went out to my dad's place.
4 Cr. 20 Chafin Shirley did not come home last night
5 Shirley did not come home Monday night.
6 Shirley and baby not home when I went to work.

8 Shirley not home when I came home.

9 Talked to Lawyer Mills

11 Spanked Shirley for leaving baby alone (3) hr's baby was sick baby was caffed on leg's

13 Was put in Presbyterian hospital; Stomach

14 Could not get hold of Shirley for (2) days.

15 Shirley came to see me at Hospital. all she wanted was some money. Said she had been having a swell time.

16 She had not seen the baby. I could not call to tell her I was in hospital because she was not home.

17 Baby left at Spivas but only to be left for a few days.

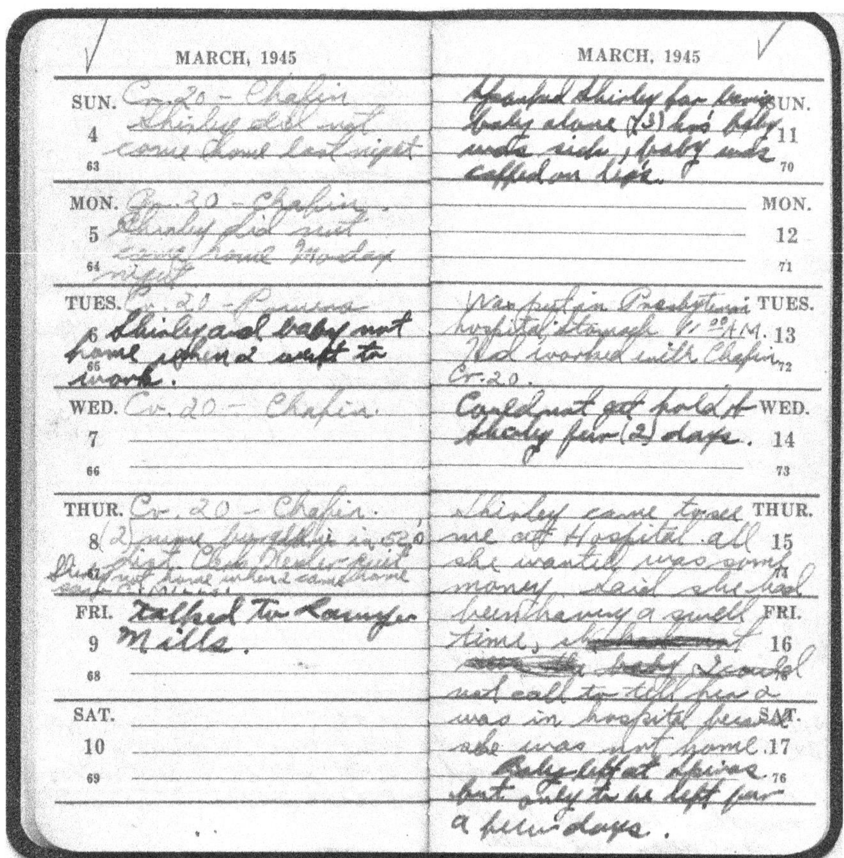

MARCH, 1945

SUN. 4 Cv. 20 – Chafin. Shirley did not come home last night

MON. 5 Cv. 20 – Chafin. Shirley did not come home Monday night

TUES. 6 Shirley and baby not home when I went to work.

WED. 7 Cv. 20 – Chafin.

THUR. 8 Cv. 20 – Chafin. Shirley not home when I came home

FRI. 9 Talked to Lawyer Mills.

SAT. 10

MARCH, 1945

SUN. 11 Spanked Shirley for leaving baby alone (3) hr's baby was sick; baby was caffed on leg's.

MON. 12

TUES. 13 Was put in Presbyterian hospital Stomach 11:00 AM. Had worked with Chafin Cv. 20.

WED. 14 Could not get hold of Shirley for (2) days.

THUR. 15 Shirley came to see me at Hospital. all she wanted was some money. Said she had been having a swell time,

FRI. 16 I could not call to tell her I was in hospital because she was not home.

SAT. 17 Baby left at Spivas but only to be left for a few days.

Figure 14.1 Steve's Journal noting Linda Lee's first move: March 17, 1945.

20 Shirley came to see me stayed for few minutes asked for money.

21 Frednegill came up to see me at hospital

22 Spiro - Gus up to see me at hospital. Chafin called me.

23 Papers served. Got out of Presbyterian hospital. Very weak. Saw Shirley. Said she had been going with ERIC FRIESEN

24 (SAW BABY) She met him at church about 1st of March. Attended A.A.V. basket ball game together.

25 Told me first that she went with Idella with ticket from Carlson Frink, but admitted Eric took her to games while I was sick in hospital.

27 To Butterfield's - 3:00

28 Had hearing Bowman's office, Shirley agrees's to ask for nothing just that I support baby. She had a date with Eric that night.

29 Got back from Butterfields.

31 served papers' for divorce. Shirley said she wanted her freedom.

Well, things sure went to hell in a hand basket during the first three months of 1945. It happened so quickly. Steve suspected something was amiss in January, when Shirley came to the Stock Show, where he was working, with her friend Idella - and Joe. He wrote this entry with a very heavy hand. She must have been behaving pretty erratically by February, at which time he discussed the situation with his father-in-law. And by March, she's flown the coop!

I'm so intrigued as to the WHY of her behavior. I wish, again, that she would talk to me about this time in her life. But she just can't remember it. Although once, quite guilelessly, she did reminisce about "Eric - my boyfriend during the war."

She turned twenty-one years old in January of 1945. Did she start to feel very trapped - married to a much older man, who not only expected her to wash his hair, his clothes, his combs etc., but now expected her to be completely responsible for their baby also? I bet she was overwhelmed, and probably not doing a very good job of any of it. In fact, one of her few memories of this time, as I've mentioned before, is of Steve "bawling me out" for having several opened jars of mayonnaise in the refrigerator at one time. And he was so parsimonious, as we've seen from her diary. She never complained; but did she have to beg for, and account for, every penny he gave her? Did she get into trouble "charging" things?

Had he become physically abusive in his efforts to get her to shape up on the domestic front? We know from his journal that he "spanked Shirley for leaving baby alone (3) hrs" on the day before she left. Maybe this wasn't the first time...

Had he turned away from her sexually after their child was born? That's sure been known to happen. If so, that could have been disastrous, as sexual compatibility had always been a very important component in their marriage. And you know, *now that I think of it,* maybe the "table" drawings in Steve's journal are not tables at all, but meant to represent - BEDS. And do the beds represent sex? The table/beds *do* begin to appear less than a month after Linda Lee's birth. *Was he recording adulterous encounters?*

For whatever reason or reasons Shirley turns away from Steve and their daughter. When Steve is hospitalized, Linda goes to stay with the Spivas, a policeman and his wife who were acquaintances through Steve's work, but "only ... for a few days." Since they had earlier lent the Allisons their bassinet, I'm guessing that they had children of their own, which would have been nice for eight month old Linda Lee.

Until he left the farm in his old age, John kept a photograph of his granddaughter, at about this age, on the large radio that stood in this kitchen. I have it now, and in it, a very bald baby leans happily forward in her high chair and gives the world a very slobbery, toothless smile. It must have been taken shortly before her family disintegrated.

When he gets out of the hospital, Steve stays for a few days with his friend and physician, Dr. Butterfield. Then he went home. He didn't exactly return to an empty house, since "Hemmings" and his mother had begun renting the Allison's basement in January. But, he did return to an empty home.

The next day, he's served with divorce papers. "Shirley said she wanted her freedom."

"Shirley did not come home last night."

Steve's journal - March 4, 1945.

CHAPTER 15

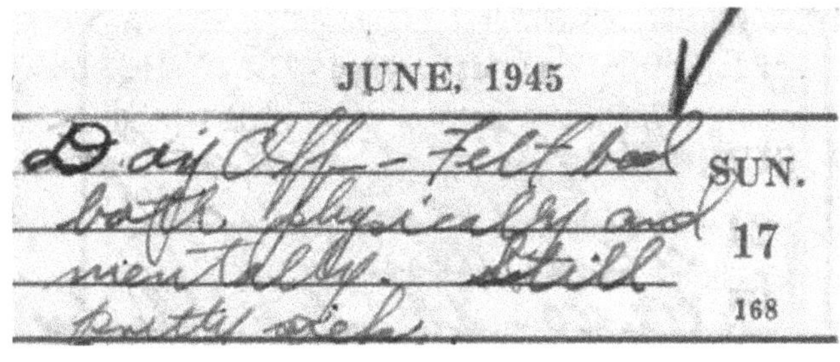

JUNE, 1945

Day Off – Felt bad both physically and mentally. Still pretty sick.

SUN. 17

168

"Felt bad both physically and mentally."

Steve's journals include many notations about Shirley's whereabouts and activities during the next year or so. I've omitted most of them. Suffice it to say that he recorded every action of hers that reinforced his feelings of betrayal and hurt.

The table/bed drawings disappear, but are replaced by initials coupled with an X. Yes, I'm guessing that the table/bed drawings probably *did* represent some type of an encounter with a woman and I'd bet money that now the initials plus "X" represents a similar (sexual) encounter.

Again, for the sake of brevity, I've left out many of Steve's notations concerning his job, i.e. car number, partner's name, details of cases, shifts and departmental happenings. With this in mind, let's see where life now takes Steve:

April 1945

1 Cr. 40 11:00 AM to 7:00 PM Driver Stroup

2 Saw baby.

3 Shirley saw John Zenpathos she say's he love's her very much.

4 Saw Baby. Found a Valentine card to JOHN ZENPATHOS from Shirley with love.

5 Day Off Took Shirley's cloths to Kings. Baby stayd at Grandma Johnson's.

6 Saw baby.

7 Shirley visited baby for first time since 3-17-45

8 I was up most of night very sick.

9 Shirley called now wants custody of baby. Talked to Bud

10 Saw baby.

12 Saw baby. Roosevelt died

13 Day Off Shirley called Had Linda over here. Talked to Mills.

15 Cleaned house somemore

16 Saw baby Met Spaulding.

20 Day Off Saw fights at auditorium.

21 YSX

22 Shirley called said she was adopted at 3 day's Name MARY IRENE O'NEIL

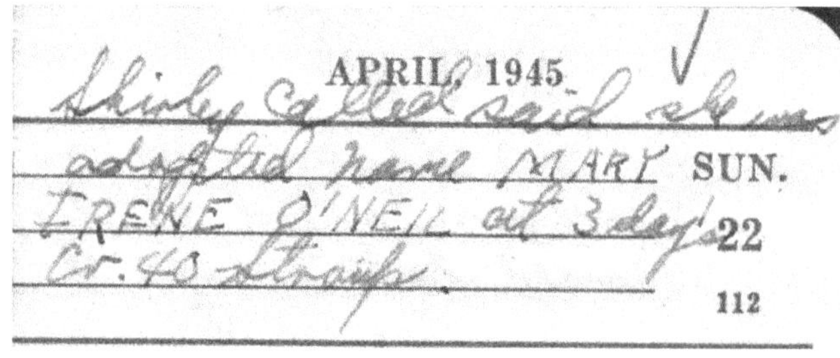
APRIL 1945
Shirley called said she was adopted name MARY IRENE O'NEIL at 3 days
Cr. 40 Stroup
SUN.
22
112

Figure 15.1 Steve's Journal noting Shirley was adopted: April 22, 1945.

23 Saw baby.

25 Saw Baby. Shirley calld YSX

Figure 15.2 Steve's Journal with first usage of "X": April 25, 1945.

27 Mrs King called Mr's King about thru with Shirley. went out to ranch.

28 Saw baby.

29 Mrs Johnson called. Shirley moved home today.

30 Shirley called

May 1945

1 Cr. 40 - Stroup. 2:30 A. to 10:30 A.

2 Shirley was waiting for me 11:00 Pm. We talked til 2:30 AM SHIRLEY HAD BROKEN HER PROMISE.

3 Meet and talk to JOE DANOS.

6 Shirley, Bud and Mother took L Lee out to Uncle Bob's.

7 false alarm on V day Shirley called.

8 VE DAY worked 16 hr's

10 Saw baby. Shirley called said my lawyer had not answered her complaint yet.

12 Seperate hearing to be on custody. Shirley came over about 2:00 PM She wants to come back very much.

13 Was very sick again in bed all day

14 1st day off this month. Shirley came over 6:00 PM to 9 Pm Want to come back.

15 Shirley called, she took care of baby while Spivas were out.

16 Saw baby.

17 Shirley calld said she had a letter from Johnny Z. She was mad because I ask Spiva's to appear in court.

19 Shirley came over, then she took L.L. over to 758 So. Race. wanted me to come over for dinner. Mickie home from Hospital.

21 went out to dad's ranch

22 Day Off Found letter #7 addressed to Johnny Zenpathos. I feld very bad about it.

23 Saw baby.

24 Efficiency shoot 94 Talked to Bud, Shirley called wanted me to go to dinner Came over later with baby.

25 Telegram that Chris liberated. Went out to Dad's ranch.

26 Shirley came over , showed me a letter from Idella

27 Shirley called me. She came over in the rain, then left in Rain.

28 Talked to Bud

30 Parade duty Talked to Bud - he said Shirley felt bad about Monday Dad was in

June 1945

1 saw baby 7 PM to 3 AM Cr. 40 - Stroup

2 Shirley called and came over with baby.

6 Saw baby.

7 Shirley came over; Bud and Shirley came to Dist 4 Sta talked about 2 hr's.

12 Shirley brought baby over to dist. 4 Sta

13 Saw baby. Talked to May Co about 34.69 Bill. to bill her at 758 So. Race St.

14 was very sick - "stomach".

15 Still very sick - "stomach".

16 Shirley called, then came over. said mental cruelty would be all right to charge her Stomach somewhat better.

17 Day Off Felt bad both phyically and mentally. Still pretty sick.

19 Mary Zinn came over to see about job.

20 Mary Zinn started as house keeper Shirley called.

21 Linda Lee brought home from Spiva's Shirley called

Figure 15.3 Steve's Journal noting Linda Lee's second move: June 21, 1945.

23 Shirley came over to see baby; Shirley was with D. Penner. She is going to Elitches tonight with him. She was out with Johnny Zenpathos has a date with him Monday night.

24 Day Off shirley has a date with Dick Penner.

25 Shirley went to Edelwiess, then to Denham, then to Lakeside, then to Club Pelican all with Johnny Zenpathos.

27 Chris got back from Germany

30 Shirley called she has been going with Max RADOVICH. Could not come over to see baby, had to get ready for Max RADOVICH.

I was touched by the entry for April 13th. For the first time in his journal, Steve calls his baby daughter by name - "Had Linda over here".

In April, he also begins to "see" YS. Pretty quick, I'd say. Did the table/ beds above refer to meetings with YS - *before the marriage ended?*

Things seem to have settled down a bit between Shirley and Steve by April. At least they start talking, and on the 7th she goes to see the baby for the first time. Meanwhile, she's staying with Mrs. King, her friend Idella's mother.

In the process of filing the divorce paperwork, Shirley discovers that she's an adopted child. She's often said that this revelation was very traumatic for her and that it eventually led to her being hospitalized. She then moves back home with her parents. She must have been in a *most* confused state of mind.

She starts to call and come over a lot. Steve must have been agreeable to these talks and visits. In fact, on May 3rd, in a three-and-a-half hour conversation at two o'clock in the morning, she confides to Steve that she "hadn't kept her promise".

Later that month she shows him a letter from her friend Idella. After discussing her own serious marital problems, she advises Shirley about a drugstore product that *might* end an unplanned pregnancy. For some reason, perhaps inadvertently, Shirley leaves this letter with Steve. Later, he included it in The Box that he prepared for L.L.. Besides wanting to disclose the mindset of these two young friends, he probably thought it would help explain his feelings of pain and anger.

(Shirley and Idella had been friends since first grade, but after their respective divorces, they lost contact with each other. Recently, as I mentioned above, they reestablished contact - after 50 years. Shirley, Idella and I went to lunch one day not long after. I really liked her. It seems her life has been much like Shirley's - in that her subsequent 50 years of responsible adulthood were very unlike those few heady days of youthful drama. And yet she, like Shirley, hadn't lost *any* of her youthful optimism and spunkiness.)

Shirley received Idella's letter "c/o Mt. States Tel and Tel. Co., General Engineering" in Denver, where she had been hired as elevator operator. By that time, however, she already knows she isn't pregnant.

In May, Steve is often sick. On the 13th, Mother's Day, he's "very sick again; in bed all day". I feel so sad for him. He's never known his own mother. His mother-in-law, whom he briefly referred to as Mother, left his life when his wife did. He's trying to be both mother and father to his child. No wonder he was sick. It breaks my heart.

On May 22nd, for only the third time in his journals, Steve records how he feels: "Found letter #7 addressed to Johnny Zenpathos. I feld very bad about it."

Shirley starts to visit the baby more, and comes to see Steve several more times. On the 27th, after one such visit, he writes "She came over in the rain, then left in the Rain." I wonder why he kept being there for her? Did he still love her and miss her and worry about her? Or did he dislike her and hope to find out things that would be detrimental to her in a divorce? Or neither? Or both? He repeatedly talks to Bud about Shirley, which makes me think that he still cared about her. But I don't know.

He's still sick in June. He feels "bad both phyically and mentally." In the midst of his sickness he interviews someone to care for the baby. I'm sure he was at his wits' end trying to figure out what to do about her. The Spivas had been kind enough to keep her for three months, but they had not bargained on such a long run. Had she learned to walk during those months? Or perhaps to say a few words? That reminds me. Somewhere there's a baby book that I found at the farm. I'll try to find it. Did Shirley write in it? Did Steve? Did Mrs. Spiva?

Titsa recently told me that, at about this time, Steve asked her parents if his daughter could live with them. They were unable to help him out. Not only were her own children grown and gone by this time, but Titsa's mother also had a serious heart condition. It would have been a real hardship for them. And so, Steve hires a stranger.

On June 20th, "Mary Zinn started as housekeeper", and on the 21st, her eleven month birthday, "Linda Lee" was "brought home from Spiva's." I don't know if Mary lived at 29th and Grove, or if she went home when Steve wasn't at work. It must have all been very confusing for little bald Linda Lee.

Shirley keeps telling Steve that she wants to "come back". He must not have agreed. I don't think she knows what she wants, nor exactly what she's doing.

Until she meets Max. Max will prove to be the love of her life - for real and forever.

"Felt bad both physically and mentally."

Steve's journal - June 17, 1945

CHAPTER 16

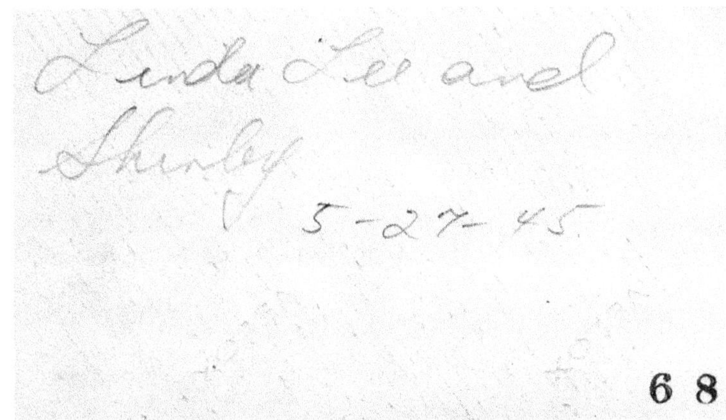

"will let me have L.L."

The last six months of 1945 are as tumultuous for the Allisons as were the first - as evidenced by the remainder of Steve's journal:

July 1945

1 7 Pm to 3 Am.

3 Shirley dancing at Albany Hotel with MAX RADOVICH

4 Shirley came and took baby over to 758 So. Race. Officer HALL shot by Mexican

5 Linda Lee taken to Dr. Danielson – eye's are O.K. Officer V. HALL died 7:06 AM.

7 Shirley came over and brought LL to see me at station.

10 Spiva's over to see Linda Lee.

11 Mary Z tells me she will be leaving soon.

13 Mr. Johnson over.

14 Shirley did not come over or call Max Radovich left Denver.

15 Shirley came over and got Baby to take to RADOVICH HOME

16 Baby did not sleep good last night.

18 Shirley called was over at RADOVICHES. Shirley saw Uncle Gus and cried.

19 Baby taken to Mrs. Spauldings - 9:00 AM. MARY ZINN Left.

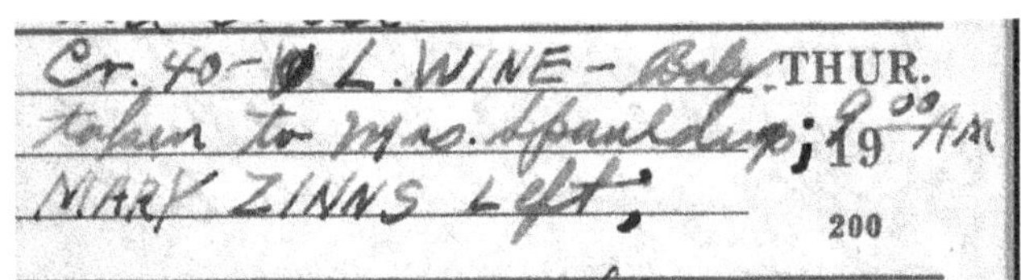
Cr. 40- L. WINE - Baby THUR.
taken to Mrs. Spaulding; 19 9:00 AM
MARY ZINNS Left.
200

Figure 16.1 Steve's Journal noting Linda Lee's third move: July 19, 1945.

21 Saw Baby. to meet me Baby's birthday. Mr's Johnson took baby 11:00 AM to 5:00 PM. Shirley was and give me shoes for L.L. but Max came into town.

22 Saw baby.

23 Shirley bought shoe's for L.L., they were charged to D.D.G., said she would take to L.L. tomorrow.

24 Saw baby, no shoes for baby yet.

25 Called Mr Roswell at May Co. Shirley told him could not pay bill as she is supporting Baby.

26 Saw baby. Shirley had baby from 12:30 P - 2:30. baby received her shoes. Eff. shoot 94.

27 Shirley borrowed .50 to go to Denver theatre. Wants me to start suit against her

28 Day Off. Visited dad at the farm.

30 Mr - Mr's Johnson took LL out to Uncle "Bob" Johnson farm.

31 Saw baby. Shirley called ask me to file counter charges at once. She don't want to appear in court. will let me have L.L..

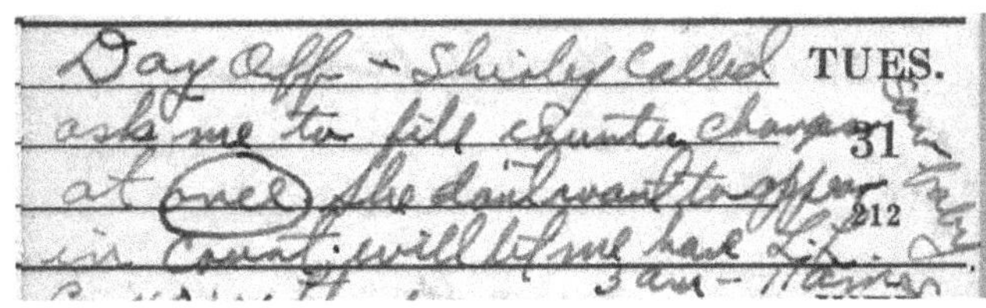

Figure 16.2 Steve's Journal: July 31, 1945.

August 1945

1 Cr. 40. W. Stroup 3 am - 11 am Saw baby. Had Mills start counter suit against Shirley.

2 Shirley came over talked about my counter suit, she took baby to Idella's

3 Saw baby. Baby was taken to Butterfield for shots. Shirley say's she is going to spend week with MAX in Texas.

4 went out to ranch.

5 Shirley had LL from 1:30 Pm to 6:00 Pm.

6 Shirley starts work as elevator pilot - split shift.

7 Saw baby

8 Shirley called want's me to take her back; She had trouble with May Co.

10 We were put on alert, 6 AM for VJ day. HSX

11 Charley H, his dad, brother and I went to Hot Sulpher Springs.

12 Day Off - Hot Sulpher Springs.

13 Cr. 40 - F Lane Very sick stomach

14 still pretty sick. V J day Went back to work 5 Pm till 1 am.

16 Shirley came over with a "Betty"

17 Shirley was over, called Bowman from here saying not to contest the divorce and giving me L.L.

19 Shirley came over, St. Rocco parade.

23 Effic. Shoot 91.

24 HSX

26 Shirley came over, we went to Gothic show

28 Hot Sulphur Springs with Gus

29 Hot Sulphur Springs with Gus

30 Hot Sulpher Springs with Gus. XFD

September 1945

1 6 to 2 Am Cr. 40 - W. Stroup YSX

2 Shirley called. Young woman found dead in Platte river.

3 worked labor parade 3 to 11 am. saw "Bud" Johnson.

4 YSX

7 YSX

8 Saw baby

9 Day Off - Hot Sulphur Springs with Gus, Micki YSX

10 Henning to St. Joseph Hosp. YSX
12 I was sick. YSXS
13 Shirley called me at Station
14 YSX
15 Shirley called
16 Went out to Pa's ranch; Shirley came and got L.L.
17 saw Linda Lee YSX
18 Shirley came over with Linda Lee.
19 called Mills, he said the case is set for 9-21 9:30 A.
20 YSX
21 Divorce hearing Judge Walsh Ct. D.Bowman not present, went out to Ranch.
22 YSX
24 Shirley supposed to have been up in Wyo. for the week end.
29 Shirley called, wants dishes, furniture and L.L. when she get's married again.
30 Shirley had L.L. this afternoon.

October 1945

1 Shirley had L.L. this afternoon. HSX
2 YSX
4 Shirley called, she was working.
5 Saw D U and Oka play football
6 YSXS
7 Saw Games at Regis Stadium
8 YSX
10 YSX
12 (4) People killed in 1 car AA. 38th Subway. Attended football game at D.U.
13 Shirley called me at station. YSXS
14 Football game's at Regis. YSX
15 Day Off - Painted front Storm door. Took R. H. to see Jim Dikeou.
17 Efficiency shoot 84.
18 Shirley called, Butterfield say's she will have a baby the 1st part of April 1946.
19 Shirley called again. Saw J. Dikeou Yvonne still sick.
20 Yvonne still sick. went out to dads ranch. Snowed rather heavy.
21 Attended game at Regis Stadium.
22 Cr. 40 - W. Stroup Capt. Pitt says there is something wrong - no one wants to drive 40; Fight at Mammoth.
24 Took Gus out to ranch.
26 Shirley called YSX
27 Shirley called again, she don't feel so good. YSX
28 Shirley had LL this afternoon football game at Regis.
30 Saw Baby. Day Off - Out to Ranch with Gus.

November 1945

1 YSX

2 Cr. 40 - W. Stroup 4 am - 12 N.

3 Shirley called

4 Attend Football game at D.U. YSXS

5 Shirley called - was in Butterfield's office; Butterfield to tell her family tonight; Max to pay her expenses.

6 saw Butterfield, he talked to Bud. I'm not mixed up in deal at all. Ferrius moved in upstairs. YSX.

8 25.00 from Ferrius for 11-6-45 to 11-21-45.

10 football game D.U. - Aggies. YSX

12 Worked 5 hr's overtime on parade; YSX

13 Day Off - Went out to Dad's ranch.

14 Saw Shirley she got a $1000.00 check from MAX

16 First day of my vacation.

17 Vac. Very sick all day.

18 Vacation YSX

19 Shirley called; she is leaving in about (2) weeks will adopt her baby out. She say's she will not marry MAX. YSX

21 YSXX

22 Football game at D.U. also out to Dad's ranch

23 Ferrius paid 25.00 for period 11-21-45 to 12-6-45. YSX

24 Shirley called twice: She is leaving in about a week for San Antonio, Tex; Bud has the check for $1000.00.

25 Football game at D.U. Very good game.

26 Saw Shirley, she had bad cold. YSXS

27 Out to Ranch YSXS

29 Shirley called - was mad, wanted Cedar Chest etc. YSXS

30 Vac. YSX

December 1945

1 6 pm - 2 Am Cr. 40. W. Stroup Shirley had baby and burned LL Right hand.

3 Shirley called Y.S. Shirley left town.

4 Out to dad's ranch

5 Shirley gave L.L. a bath over the weekend and LL caught cold.

6 YSXS

8 Mrs Johnson had L.L said she was going to box my ear's when she saw me - for keeping some of Shirley's stuff.

10 Rec. letter #1 from Shirley from San Antonio Tex.

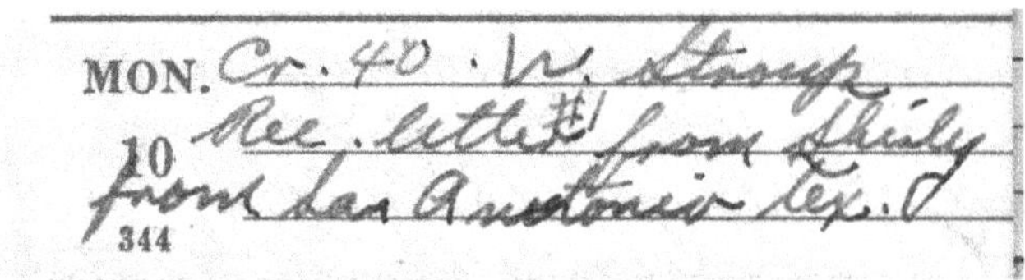
MON.
10 Rec. letter #1 from Shirley
from San Antonio Tex.
344

Figure 16.3 Steve's Journal noting Shirley's letter from Texas: December 10, 1945.

16 Mrs Johnson called Y said she was not going to take LL today.

18 Very cold, not much doing

23 Johnson's had L.L brought her back with a rash. Johnson's to leave 1st of Jan. for 6 week's Vac.

24 Saw L.L. YSX

25 YSXXSS

27 Efficiency shoot 90.

28 Rec. letter #2 from Shirley.

29 Mrs Johnson wanted LL got very smart with Mrs. Spaulding. YSX

30 Saw L.L YSX

Steve received Christmas cards from 32 people, and he's listed them at the back of this journal. They're mostly police officers and their families and Allison family members. In October we learned that YS's first name is Yvonne. Her name and telephone number are written here also, as are Steve's twelve efficiency shoot scores for the year.

From this journal, from letters Steve placed in The Box and from recent talks with Shirley, I've been able to learn quite a bit about my parents' lives during this second half of 1945. In a nutshell:

Shirley

In June Shirley meets Max Radovich, an officer in the Air Force, and falls in love. Although two years will pass before they marry in 1947, this is the beginning of their lifetime journey together. Max returns to duty in Texas in July. By the time she and Steve file for divorce in September, she is certain that she is pregnant.

The baby is Max's, but she continues to confide in Steve. Two letters addressed to Shirley from Max were in The Box. My mom was puzzled as to how Steve came to have them (and the letter to her from her friend Idella). I told her that, according to his journal, she had shared them with him. She couldn't remember, but did say that - if he had seemed sympathetic at the time, it was probably because - "he only wanted one thing." Meaning, sex.

Figure 16.4 Max Radovich with his mother.

The letters, dated July 18 and August 1, 1945, were sent from San Angelo, Texas, where Max was stationed as a lieutenant in the Air Force. Earlier, he'd been a bombardier, stationed in Asia. They make subtle reference to their love. I think perhaps he knew at the time that their son had been conceived on July 4th. They're beautifully written, convey a loving concern and are the words of a true gentleman.

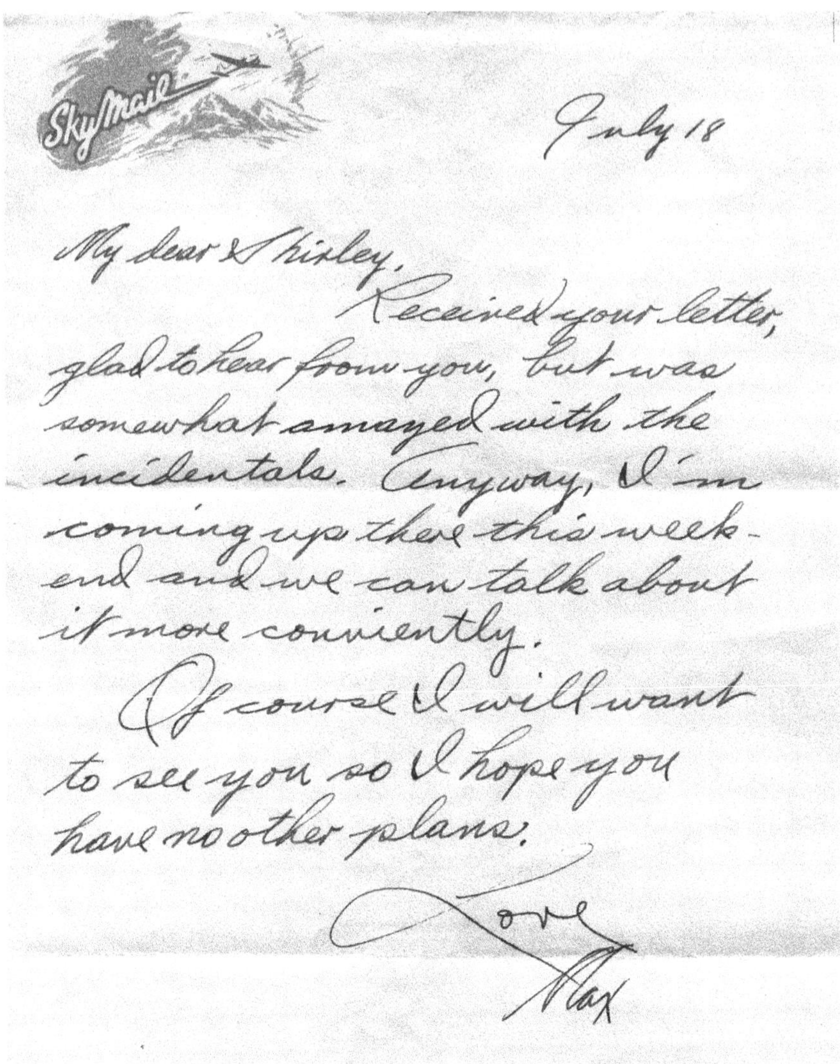

SkyMail

July 18

My dear Shirley,

Received your letter, glad to hear from you, but was somewhat amayed with the incidentals. Anyway, I'm coming up there this week-end and we can talk about it more conviently.

Of course I will want to see you so I hope you have no other plans.

Love
Max

Figure 16.5 Letter from Max to Shirley.

On her job at the Telephone Company, Shirley meets a young woman who becomes her friend and remains so for the next 50 years – becoming Aunt Betsy to Shirley's children. Aunt Betsy has many stories to tell of their madcap adventures during these months. And although her life is most unsettled, Shirley makes an effort to visit often with Linda Lee. However, it seems that she's not planning on being permanently reunited with her daughter. On July 31, Steve writes that she "called to ask me to file counter charges at once. She don't want to appear in court. will let me have L.L." She was hoping to marry Max - and soon.

But Max let her know, gently, yet firmly I bet, that he wasn't ready for marriage. Can you imagine her state of mind? This was not the type of situation a young woman wanted to find herself in – especially in 1945! Trying to find a workable solution, she asks Steve on August 7, "to take her back." But he doesn't.

So what to do? For months the matter remains unresolved, but by November Max and Shirley make their decision. They will allow their child to be adopted by another family. Dr. Butterfield agrees to help her break the news of the pregnancy to her parents. Poor Shirley, I'm sure that her parents were very disappointed, worried and mortified. Max gives Bud a check for $1000.00 to cover Shirley's expenses during her stay at a "home for unwed mothers" in San Antonio. She boards a train for Texas in early December and will remain there until April of 1946. She's told me some very touching stories about her time there. As usual, she had a very positive attitude, which meant that she found as much good in her circumstances as she could, and saw the best in each person she met there.

Steve

About a month after Steve hires Mary Zinn to take care of his house and his baby, she quits. He has to come up with another plan. I guess he gives up on keeping Linda Lee at home, because on July 19 he takes her to live with a Mrs. Spaulding. I wonder who she was? How did he know her? He refers to her as "Mrs.", so I don't think he was very familiar with her, or even knew her previously. Steve visits his daughter there two days later - on her first birthday.

He must have been praying that this new arrangement would work out, and at least initially, it looked good. Since he hadn't wanted a child to begin with, he must have felt incredibly relieved. Whereas he had visited "the baby" about once a week when she was with the Spivas, now he visits her about once every two weeks.

And his journal takes on a whole new tone. It's the beginning of what appears to be a more enjoyable life - at least socially. He sees YS a lot and HS occasionally. In August he goes to a mountain resort to enjoy the baths, massages and hot springs. He goes to the lodge. He goes to the "fights" and to numerous football games throughout the fall.

He's now referring to Bud and Mother as Mr. and Mrs. Johnson. Pearl is angry with him for, among other things, not returning Shirley's cedar chest. So much for her being his mother figure...

And so much for his marriage to her daughter. On September 21, 1945, Steve and Shirley file for divorce. The Box contained this newspaper clipping from the day after:

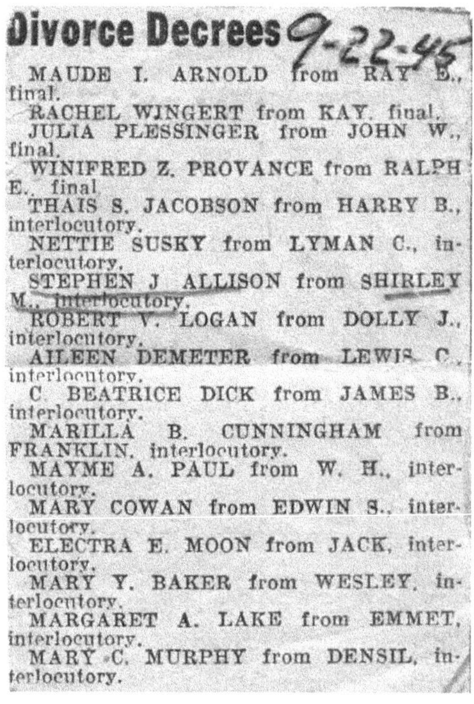

Divorce Decrees 9-22-45

MAUDE I. ARNOLD from RAY E., final.

RACHEL WINGERT from KAY, final.

JULIA PLESSINGER from JOHN W., final.

WINIFRED Z. PROVANCE from RALPH E., final.

THAIS S. JACOBSON from HARRY B., interlocutory.

NETTIE SUSKY from LYMAN C., interlocutory.

STEPHEN J ALLISON from SHIRLEY M., interlocutory.

ROBERT V. LOGAN from DOLLY J., interlocutory.

AILEEN DEMETER from LEWIS C., interlocutory.

C. BEATRICE DICK from JAMES B., interlocutory.

MARILLA B. CUNNINGHAM from FRANKLIN, interlocutory.

MAYME A. PAUL from W. H., interlocutory.

MARY COWAN from EDWIN S., interlocutory.

ELECTRA E. MOON from JACK, interlocutory.

MARY Y. BAKER from WESLEY, interlocutory.

MARGARET A. LAKE from EMMET, interlocutory.

MARY C. MURPHY from DENSIL, interlocutory.

Figure 16.6 Newspaper Divorce Notifications.

My mom told me today that her lawyer didn't even come to the hearing - because he was so "disgusted" with her. He was upset because she wouldn't fight any of my father's "charges", nor ask for a property settlement. She wanted nothing it seems - only out.

On November 6, when Dr. Butterfield talks to Shirley's parents about her pregnancy, Steve notes that he's "not mixed up in deal at all". That's relief you hear. Did no one question that *he* might be the father?

That same day, he rents the upstairs of his house to a man named Ferrius. Did Steve then move downstairs? Was Hemmings (or Hennings - he spells it different every time) still renting the basement? He'd gone to the hospital in September, but Steve still receives money from him in November. It's hard to figure the roommate situation out.

Also in November, he takes his little daughter to have her picture taken - I found the three 11"-14" photos at the farm. Two are professionally framed, and relatively clean, and Steve's written on the back of each, "November 1945,

Baby Linda Lee, Age 16 Months". "Baby Linda Lee". My heart aches when I realize how much Steve loved his daughter and how hard he tried to be a good father.

The third photo, in a store bought frame, he gave to his father for Christmas 1945. He inserted a little Christmas gift card into the corner, under the glass, on which he wrote, "Christmas Cheer, Linda Lee, Age 16 months".

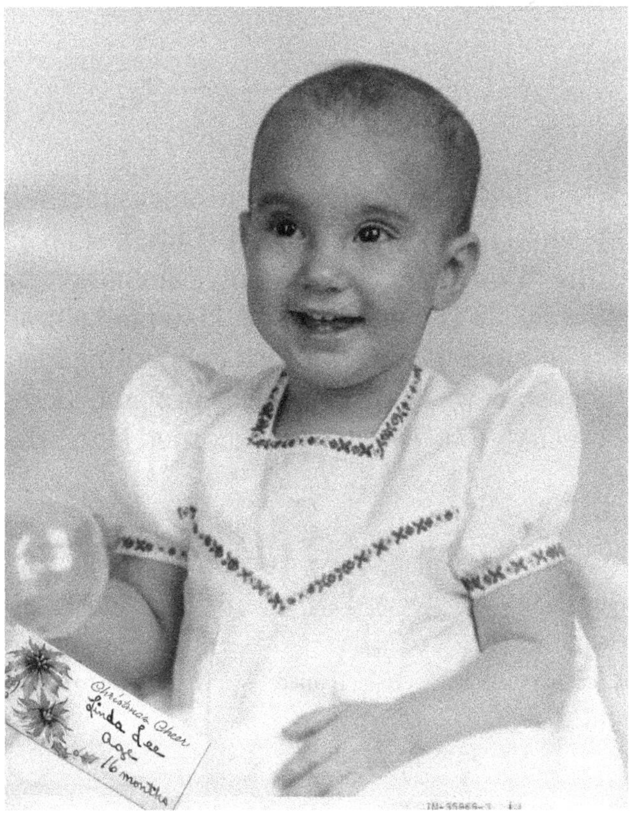

Figure 16.7 Baby Linda Lee, 16 months, 1945.

It sat in my grandfather's kitchen for the next twenty-five years. I know this for two reasons - because I remember seeing it there and because it's filthy. A sure sign. Have I mentioned that my grampa didn't keep a very clean house? In fact, I don't think he ever cleaned his house - to tell the truth. After he died, my father gutted it and redid the whole inside. It was probably easier than cleaning it.

Ever bald Linda Lee wears a simple dress with hand stitched designs in each of the three photos. Who made it for her, do you think? Her lack of hair makes her dark eyes seem very large and weary/wise. In one pose, I can actually glimpse some physical resemblance to Shirley. It's the *only* time. No one would ever guess, then or now, simply from looking, that Linda and Shirley are even *related.* In life, as in photos, this daughter will always look very much like her father.

The entry for December 18th was heartening to me - Steve's actually kind of chatty. He talks about the weather and notes "not much doing". Christmas, however, doesn't seem particularly joyful, although it appears that his time with Yvonne was "merry".

On New Year's Day 1946, Steve begins to chronicle another year. The inside covers of this very small booklet, about 2"-3", contain some printed facts that are pretty interesting. Two in particular, really caught my attention - Denver's population in 1940 was 322,412, and it cost $.03 to mail a first class letter.

As before, I'll omit most of the notations concerning his police activities. Although I find them somewhat intriguing, it's probably better - ethically and in the interest of brevity - to leave them unrecorded here. His year begins:

January 1946

2 Cr. 40. - S. Passanelli 11 am to 7 pm. Received letter #3 from Shirley. YSX

3 Received pictures of L L from Shirley. YSX

4 Went out to ranch.

5 Took L L's pictures to Geo. Rouch to be framed. Sgt. W. Johnson to take 6 week leave of absence starting 1/1/46 Going to Texas.

7 YSXS

8 YSX

9 15.00 Rec. from W. Ferrius 1-6-46 to 1-21-46

13 Shirley has not inquired about L L from Mrs. Spaulding. YSS

14 Mr's Spaulding received a postal card inquiring about L L from Mrs Johnson the first up to this date. YSX

15 Strike called 12:01 AM tonight meat packing Co's. No days off until after strike. YSX

16 attended Fight at the Elks Club.

17 Attended Stock Show

18 Attended fights

19 Attended "Elk's" fight.

21 attended "finals" at the Auditorium of the Elk's tournament.

23 Uncle Frank Allison bought bldg. - Colfax, Olive for $15,000 $1,000.00 down

24 15.00 Rec. from Warren 1-21-46 to 2-6-46

25 Cr. 40 S. Passanelli. Worked late with Sam on Larimer St. on rape case.

26 Cr. 40 S. Passanelli. Talked to MGR. about Sam - no soap YSXS

27 Made (2) arrest on rape case.

February 1946

1 3:00 Am to 11 Am Cr. 40 S. Passanelli. received letter #4 from Shirley. She did not mention L.L. I went out to the ranch.

2 Found moths had ruined (2) pairs of trousers.

3 Frank and Family came over for a few minutes.

4 answered Shirley's letter #4.

5 The Johnson's arrived late this evening from Texas.

6 Johnson's visited L L at Spauldings.

7 Out to ranch with Gus.

9 I was given to understand that the (3) Mexicans Sam and I arrested for the rape of a woman were run thru Police Court for Vag. and were given 90 day's each.

11 Begley and OHRUH shot by a mexican. - Manual Perez - age 18.

12 Day Off Out to Dad's ranch.

13 Cr. 40 A Levinson Passanelli to work S.D. on Begley and Ohruh case.

14 Manual Perez - wanted for shooting of Begley and Ohruh killed the night marshall at Castle rock, Colo. Captured

16 talked to Mueller about Gus Gus came to Denver in 1906 applied for paper's in S. Dak. in 1925. He is 57 or 58 yr's old. Alien married to a citizen does not have to file 1st paper. Candidate need's 3 or 4 good references.

18 Mrs. Spaulding wants to put L.L. some place else.

Monday 18 Cr. 40. A. Levine.
Mrs Spaulding wants to
put L.L. some place else.

Figure 16.8 Steve's Journal noting Linda Lee will have to move again.

20 Received letter #5 from Shirley.

21 Day Off Went out to ranch.

22 Went to Greeley with Sam for fights.

26 Made arrangement to move L L , 3-1-46, to 1377 Ogden St.

27 Ferrius to Move 3-1-46.

28 Dad sold Lots next door for 3600.00 less 5%.

March 1946

1 Cr. 40. S. Passanelli 6 Pm to 2 Am Moved L.L. over to 1377 Ogden

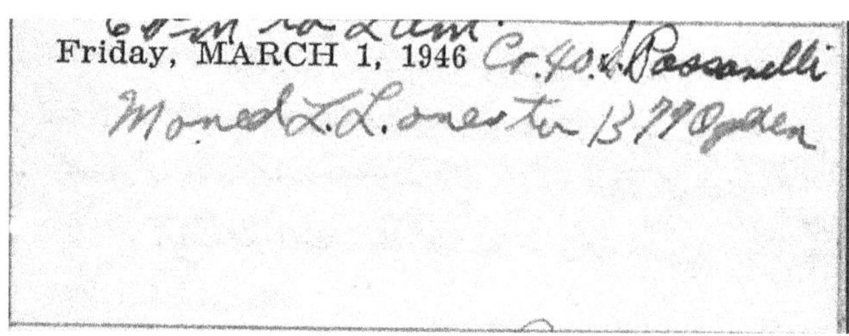

Friday, MARCH 1, 1946 Cr. 40. S. Passanelli

Moved L.L. over to 1377 Ogden

Figure 16.9 Steve's Journal noting Linda Lee's fourth move: March 1, 1946.

4 Saw L.L. Mrs Kartees was neverous about L L Talked to Dr. O.J. about her and L L.

5 YS Told Mr's Johnson about L.L. being moved. LL taken for exam. Dr. Butterfield W - 24 lbs Baby somewhat neverous.

6 Mr's Johnson's came over and stayed at Mr's Kartees house 2 hr's. Said LL was to much bother while she was small. Mrs Johnson slamed Mr's Spaulding terrible.

7 Mrs Kartees told me the Johnson's had called and had been over. Mr. J said Shirley would be back in 3 weeks and would go to ct about L.L.

8 Mr's Kartees "kick" Mrs Johnson out of the house.

9 I went over and saw L.L. Met "JANICE BLAIR" radio and orchestra singer.

11 Went out to Dad's ranch.

12 YS called at 1:05 AM today.

13 Mrs Johnson went over to Mr's Kartees place to see L L the baby did not sleep very good that night.

15 talked to Mrs Laughton, D.G.H. about Kartees. will be OK for her to keep LL.

16 Mr - Mrs Johnson was over to see LL at 1377 OGDEN they stayed about 2 hr's as a result the baby hardly sleep at all that night. The Johnson's are making it tough on anyone I get to take care of LL. It seem's as though Mr's Johnson is "A Mental Case".

17 Met and talked to Mrs. Forte and daughters about taking care of L.L.

19 Mr. - Mrs Johnson had Dr. Butterfield call me about her taking care of L.L. and getting some one to help her. YSXS

20 Mr. Johnson called me as did Shirley from San Antonio TEX. Mrs Martin and Mr. Shore Juevnille Ct officers, sent to 1377 Ogden St by Sgt. W. Johnson.

21 Moved L L to 2805 Perry.

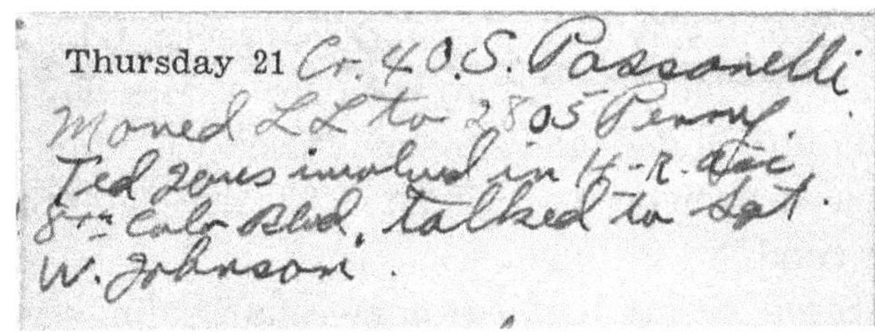
Thursday 21 Cr. 40 S. Passanelli
Moved LL to 2805 Penny.
Ted Jones involved in H-R acc.
8th Colo Blvd, talked to Sgt.
W. Johnson.

Figure 16.10 Steve's Journal noting Linda Lee's fifth move: March 21, 1946.

22 Shirley called from San Antonio TEX Dad's birthday.

23 Divorce final announce in paper. ECSX

27 Lowry field with Chris.

31 saw Linda Lee she look's good. YSX

What to do about Linda Lee?

In February 1946, after caring for the toddler for eight months, Mrs. Spaulding asks Steve to find another place for her.

On March 1, after working his usual shift, Steve moves his daughter to the home of Mrs. Kartees at 1377 Ogden Street. His upstairs tenet, Warren Ferrius, had just moved out the day before. Oiy! What a week!

Linda Lee's placement with Mrs. Kartees is pretty shaky from the start. Two days after becoming the caretaker, Steve reports that Mrs. Kartees is "neverous about LL" - and two days after *that*, Dr. Butterfield finds the "baby somewhat neverous" also.

Yvonne tells the Johnsons about the move and they become very involved. Steve thinks they're *too* involved and "are making it tough on anyone I get to take care of LL." He also notes that, "It seem's as though Mr's Johnson is A Mental Case."

I wonder how it happened that Yvonne was in communication with her boyfriend's ex in-laws? Maybe he wasn't *exactly* her boyfriend at the time – they'd had no intimate contact for several weeks, *if* I'm interpreting Steve's journal correctly.

Bud and Pearl consider having their granddaughter live with them. They also report that Shirley will go to court, when she returns from Texas, to regain custody.

Steve obtains approval from someone at Denver General Hospital for his daughter's continued placement with Mrs. Kartees. However, a few days later, officers from the juvenile court arrive there to investigate. Were they sent by Shirley's father, Mr. Johnson as noted in Steve's journal?

The next day, after a stay of less than three weeks, L L. is taken from the home of Mrs. Kartees and placed into the care of Mrs. Forte of 2805 Perry Street. This is her fifth home - and she's only twenty months old!

But she must have been pretty resilient - a few days later Steve reports that "Linda Lee looks good."

On the job, Steve seems to have numerous dealings with "Mexicans". There's a not so subtle prejudice evident in these notations.

He visits his aging father quite often and spends some time trying to figure out the citizenship status of his Uncle Gus. According to his notes, Gus, the youngest Allison brother, was about 16 years old when he came to the United States.

And he becomes *officially* divorced, I guess. The Box contained this March 23, 1946 newspaper clipping:

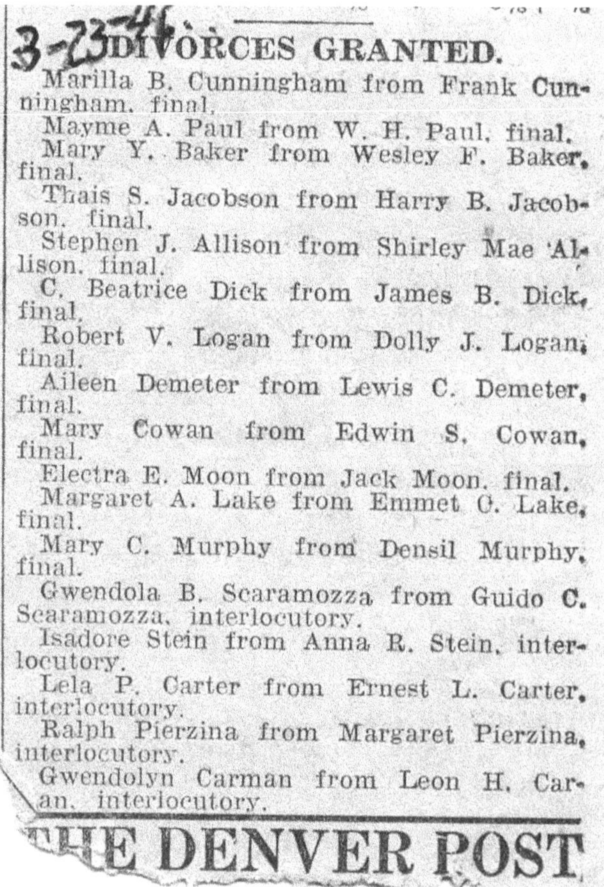

3-23-46 DIVORCES GRANTED.

Marilla B. Cunningham from Frank Cunningham, final.

Mayme A. Paul from W. H. Paul, final.

Mary Y. Baker from Wesley F. Baker, final.

Thais S. Jacobson from Harry B. Jacobson, final.

Stephen J. Allison from Shirley Mae Allison, final.

C. Beatrice Dick from James B. Dick, final.

Robert V. Logan from Dolly J. Logan, final.

Aileen Demeter from Lewis C. Demeter, final.

Mary Cowan from Edwin S. Cowan, final.

Electra E. Moon from Jack Moon, final.

Margaret A. Lake from Emmet O. Lake, final.

Mary C. Murphy from Densil Murphy, final.

Gwendola B. Scaramozza from Guido C. Scaramozza, interlocutory.

Isadore Stein from Anna R. Stein, interlocutory.

Lela P. Carter from Ernest L. Carter, interlocutory.

Ralph Pierzina from Margaret Pierzina, interlocutory.

Gwendolyn Carman from Leon H. Carman, interlocutory.

THE DENVER POST

Figure 16.11 Denver Post "Divorces Granted" Notices.

It's been one year since Steve entered the hospital suffering from stomach ulcers. One year since Shirley dropped Linda Lee off at the Spivas - "to be left for a few days only." Twelve months later, Shirley's in a *home* for unwed mothers, Linda Lee's in her fifth *home* of that turbulent year and Steve's once again *home alone.*

"will let me have L.L."
Steve's journal - July 31, 1945.

CHAPTER 17

Very truly yours,

TEXAS CHILDREN'S HOME FINDING SOCIETY

Mary F. Barrett

(Mrs.) Mary F. Barrett
Case Worker

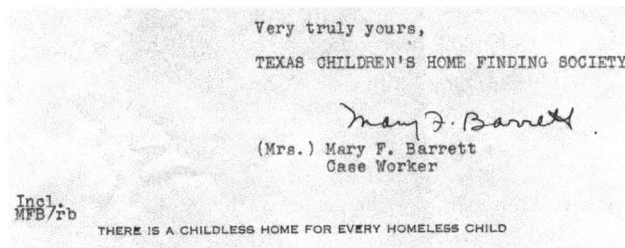

Incl.
MFB/rb

THERE IS A CHILDLESS HOME FOR EVERY HOMELESS CHILD

"THERE IS A CHILDLESS HOME FOR EVERY HOMELESS CHILD"

Once again things are looking up for Steve. His daughter is safely settled with the Forte family - not even a mile from his home - and he can visit her often. On the job he's given some promising new assignments. And his love life blossoms - and becomes much more complicated.

April 1946

1 10 A to 6 PM Cr. 40 Dad completed sale of L's 26-27 for 3407.06. YSXS
4 Mr. Johnson visited L L at 2805 Perry St. YSX
5 I saw Linda Lee.
6 YSX
8 Mrs. Johnson visited L.L.
10 Saw L L she looks good.
11 Cr. 40. F. Cowgill. YSXS
12 Cr. 40. F. Cowgill YSXS
13 Cr. 40 F. Cowgill Resistance and DK call had to go to D.G.H. for "shots".
15 Margaret called, I saw her and her mother.
16 Day Off Lowry and Fitzsimmons with Cris YSX
19 YSX
20 Took L L out to dad's farm. YSXX
21 Officer C. Schofelis shoot man, he died early this A.M.
23 YSX
24 Attended Policemen's ball with Y. YSX
25 I was notified that I will work downtown next month replacing Sgt. Fine. MDX
26 Saw L.L. ECX
27 Saw L.L. she sure looks swell. Went out to Dad's ranch with Y. YSXS
28 Saw L.L. took some pictures of her
29 YSX

May 1946

1 District #1 - Walking YSXS
2 Saw L.L. Shirley called.
3 Shirley visited LL for the first time in a long time. Not impressed too much about seeing her.
4 Saw Linda Lee received some pictures of her YSX
5 ECX
7 Day Off Out to ranch Y and kids.
8 Visited L.L.
11 Saw Shirley She said she never did care too much about L L, but was hurt when Michael was born and she could not keep him, Shirley wanted me to sign some paper's as not being the father of Michael. YSXS
14 YSXS

15 Saw L L. Shirley saw L L yesterday - told Mr's Forte L L did not really seem to be her child.

17 Mr's F. called said she was up all night with L L. Mr's Johnson and Shirley had been over and had upset L L very much. It is too bad they have to upset L.L.

18 Saw L.L. Shirley called twice. Sgt. Johnson to go to N Western for (20) week's of school. YSXS

22 Frank Family got a new Pontiac "8" - cost $1633.00

23 Parmont Show with Y.

24 Day Off out to ranch Y and kids. YSXS

25 Saw L.L. ECX

27 Saw Linda Lee.

30 Walking; (4) hrs on prade duty. YSX

June 1946

1 4 AM to 12 N Cr. 10 M. Lewis Saw L.L. Somebody notified health dept that Mrs Forte had T.B. sound like Mrs. Johnson, Bud is out of town.

3 Saw L.L. went out to Dad's place

5 mary Forte's test "stood" - was OK - she does not have T.B.

6 Saw L.L.

8 I saw L.L. Hot Sulphur Springs

12 Saw L.L.

13 Saw L.L.

15 Went out to the ranch.

16 Saw L.L. - had breakfast at Fortes, Acting Captain.

18 Saw L.L. she has a cold.

20 Saw L.L. Officer Frank Cowgill shot and killed a man named W.L. Cross - 6:29 A.M.

22 Saw L.L. I had to serve paper's on Cowgill at the County Jail.

24 Dad was in.

25 HSX

26 Saw L.L.

28 Hot Sulphur Springs with Gus, Mick, Y YSX

30 Hot Sulphur Springs YSX

July 1946

1 3 Pm to 4 Am Cr. 10. w. russell Saw L.L.

4 Sgt. O'Fannell and Officer Schoeberlin got into an argument.

6 YSX

10 Officer Burkhart excused 12:30 A.M. - had been drinking. Went out to Dad's ranch.

12 Saw L.L. Hearing held in Chief Haneboth's office, officer Broderious cleared of Dk charge. HSX

13 Will attempt to sell front blonde bedroom set and (2) lamps - $160.00 YSX

14 YSX

15 Acting Capt. - Hdqts, capt. Trinnier had day off.

18 Day Off Went out to ranch. YSXS
19 Acting Capt. - Hdqts. Capt. Trinnier sick. Saw L.L.
20 Acting Capt. – Hdqts Capt. Trinnier sick. YSX
21 Acting Capt. - Hdqts. Capt. Trinnier still sick. L L birthday Shirley caused a scene at 2805 Perry St.
22 Acting Capt. - Hdqts
23 Acting Capt. - Hdqts
24 Acting Capt. - Hdqts. saw L L Went out to Dad's ranch.
25 Acting Capt. - Hdqts Attended first Capts Meeting
26 Acting Capt. - Hdqts. Hearing on Pete S. of Corner Buffett - serving Dk's he got 10 day's.
27 Acting Capt. Went out to dad's ranch.
28 Acting Capt. Went out to cut trees at ranch.
29 Acting Capt. Officer M. suspended for drunkness Went out to ranch to cut trees.
30 Acting Capt. L.L. very sick - I called Dr. Butterfield.
31 Acting Capt. - Capt. Trinnier was down for a few hour's. Cut some more trees at Dad's ranch.

August 1946
1 11:30 A - 7:30 P Cr. #10. W. Russell YSX
2 L.L. somewhat better.
3 Saw L.L.
4 YSXS
5 Saw L.L.
8 Saw L.L. YSX
9 Saw L.L.
10 Day Off Hot Sulphur Baths Gus - Micki
12 R. Richardson and Sgt. McLean suspended, both indicated by Grand Jury. YSX
13 Saw L.L.
14 Saw L.L.
16 Day Off Hot Sulphur Springs. FDX
18 Saw L L
20 Saw L L. I talked to Shirley
21 Strike duty at May Co.
22 Strike duty May Co. Shirley called.
23 Saw L.L. Strike duty May co.
25 Saw L.L. - took some pictures of her.
26 ECX
27 Saw L.L. Went out to Dad's ranch.
31 Shirley for the first time since 7-21-46. Shirley was with Mr - Mrs Johnson.

Although Steve refers to it only indirectly, one extraordinary thing happened during these months - my brother, whom Shirley named Michael, was born on April 5, 1946. Shirley was able to love and care for him briefly, but at the end of the month she reluctantly returned to Denver - alone. She tells Steve that "she was hurt that she could not keep him." I know that she truly was.

The Box contained an envelope addressed to Mr. Stephen Allison, Police department, radio division, Denver, Colorado. It's postmarked San Antonio, Texas on May 16, 1946. Inside are two letters. One is typed on Texas Children's Home Finding Society stationary ("THERE IS A CHILDLESS HOME FOR EVERY HOMELESS CHILD") and refers to the papers Shirley asked Steve to sign on May 11:

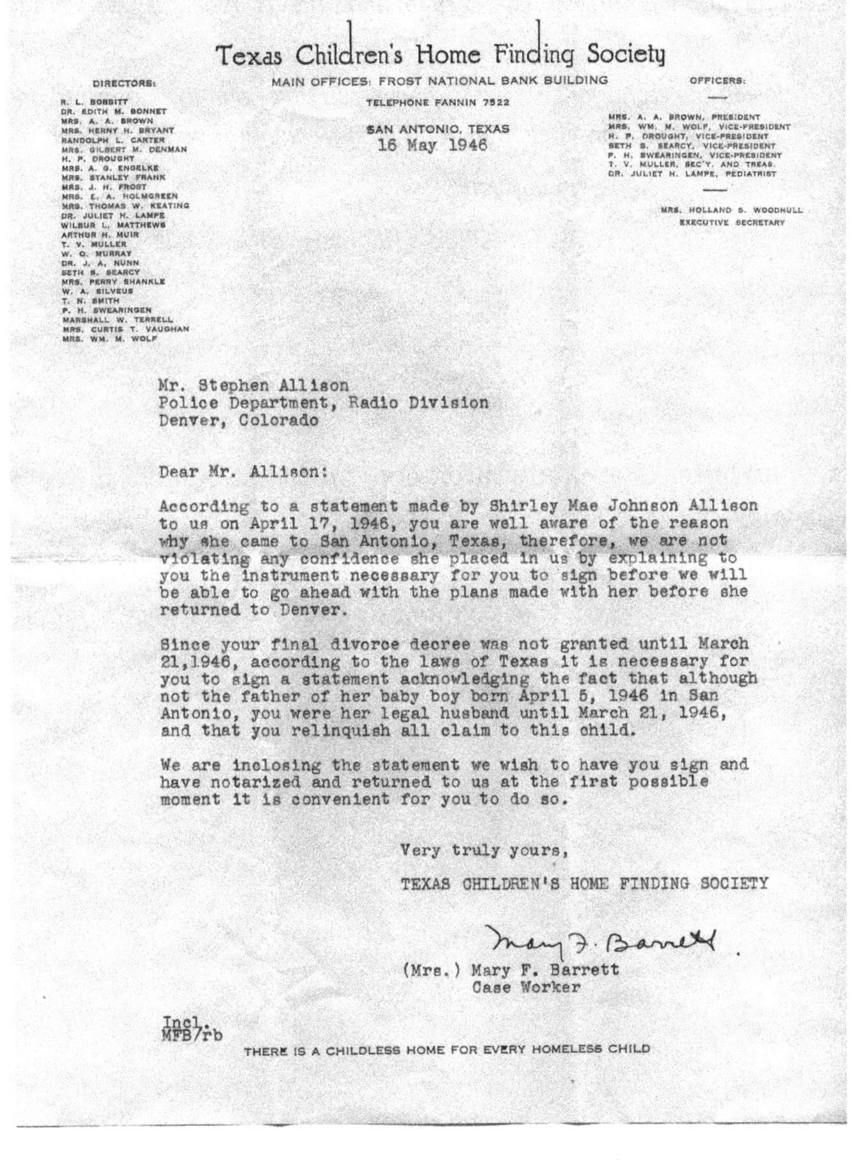

Texas Children's Home Finding Society

MAIN OFFICES: FROST NATIONAL BANK BUILDING

TELEPHONE FANNIN 7522

SAN ANTONIO, TEXAS

16 May 1946

DIRECTORS:
R. L. BOBBITT
DR. EDITH M. BONNET
MRS. A. A. BROWN
MRS. HERNY H. BRYANT
RANDOLPH L. CARTER
MRS. GILBERT M. DENMAN
H. P. DROUGHT
MRS. A. G. ENGELKE
MRS. STANLEY FRANK
MRS. J. H. FROST
MRS. E. A. HOLMGREEN
MRS. THOMAS W. KEATING
DR. JULIET H. LAMPE
WILBUR L. MATTHEWS
ARTHUR H. MUIR
T. V. MULLER
W. O. MURRAY
DR. J. A. NUNN
SETH S. SEARCY
MRS. PERRY SHANKLE
W. A. SILVEUS
T. N. SMITH
P. H. SWEARINGEN
MARSHALL W. TERRELL
MRS. CURTIS T. VAUGHAN
MRS. WM. M. WOLF

OFFICERS:
MRS. A. A. BROWN, PRESIDENT
MRS. WM. M. WOLF, VICE-PRESIDENT
H. P. DROUGHT, VICE-PRESIDENT
SETH S. SEARCY, VICE-PRESIDENT
P. H. SWEARINGEN, VICE-PRESIDENT
T. V. MULLER, SEC'Y. AND TREAS.
DR. JULIET H. LAMPE, PEDIATRIST

MRS. HOLLAND S. WOODHULL
EXECUTIVE SECRETARY

Mr. Stephen Allison
Police Department, Radio Division
Denver, Colorado

Dear Mr. Allison:

According to a statement made by Shirley Mae Johnson Allison to us on April 17, 1946, you are well aware of the reason why she came to San Antonio, Texas, therefore, we are not violating any confidence she placed in us by explaining to you the instrument necessary for you to sign before we will be able to go ahead with the plans made with her before she returned to Denver.

Since your final divorce decree was not granted until March 21,1946, according to the laws of Texas it is necessary for you to sign a statement acknowledging the fact that although not the father of her baby boy born April 5, 1946 in San Antonio, you were her legal husband until March 21, 1946, and that you relinquish all claim to this child.

We are inclosing the statement we wish to have you sign and have notarized and returned to us at the first possible moment it is convenient for you to do so.

Very truly yours,

TEXAS CHILDREN'S HOME FINDING SOCIETY

Mary F. Barrett

(Mrs.) Mary F. Barrett
Case Worker

Incl.
MFB/rb

THERE IS A CHILDLESS HOME FOR EVERY HOMELESS CHILD

Figure 17.1 Letter from the Texas Children's Home Finding Society.

Dear Mr. Allison:

According to a statement made by Shirley Mae Johnson Allison to us on April 17, 1946, you are well aware of the reason why she came to San Antonio, texas, therefore, we are not violating any confidence she placed in us by explaining to you the instrument necessary for you to sign before we will be able to go ahead with the plans made with her before she returned to Denver.

Since your final divorce decree was not granted until March 21, 1946, according to the laws of Texas it is necessary for you to sign a statement acknowledging the fact that although not the father of her baby boy born April 5, 1946 in San Antonio, you were her legal husband until March 21, 1946, and that you relinquish all claim to this child.

We are inclosing the statement we wish to have you sign and have notarized and returned to us at the first possible moment it is convenient for you to do so.

Very truly yours,

TEXAS CHILDREN'S HOME FINDING SOCIETY

(Mrs.) Mary F. Barrett

Case Worker

The second letter is a handwritten copy of the statement Steve wrote, as requested:

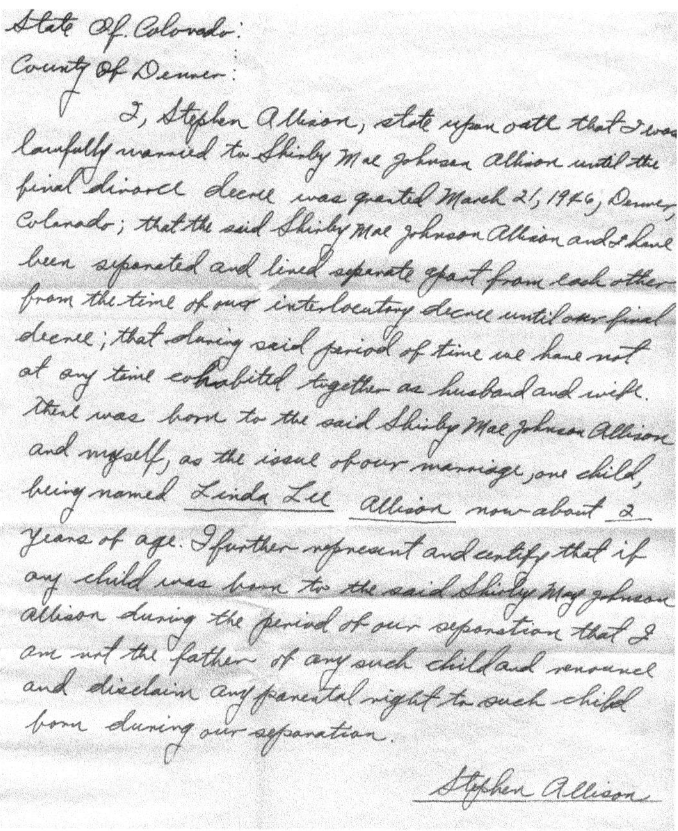

State Of Colorado:

County Of Denver:

I, Stephen Allison, state upon oath that I was lawfully married to Shirley Mae Johnson Allison until the final divorce decree was granted March 21, 1946, Denver, Colorado; that the said Shirley Mae Johnson Allison and I have been separated and lived separate apart from each other from the time of our interlocutory decree until our final decree; that during said period of time we have not at any time cohabited together as husband and wife. There was born to the said Shirley Mae Johnson Allison and myself, as the issue of our marriage, one child, being named Linda Lee Allison now about 2 years of age. I further represent and certify that if any child was born to the said Shirley May Johnson Allison during the period of our separation that I am not the father of any such child and renounce and disclaim any parental right to such child born during our separation.

Stephen Allison

Figure 17.2 Letter from Steve certifying Linda Lee as his only child with Shirley.

State of Colorado:

County of Denver:

I, Stephen Allison, state upon oath that I was lawfully married to Shirley Mae Johnson Allison until the final divorce decree was granted March 21, 1946, Denver, Colorado; that the said Shirley Mae Johnson Allison and I have been separated and lived separate apart from each other from the time of our interlocutor decree until our final decree; that during said period of time we have not at any time cohabited together as husband and wife. There was born to the marriage, one child, being named Linda Lee Allison now about 2 years of age. I further represent and certify that if any child was born to the said Shirley May Johnson Allison during the period of our separation that I am not the father of any such child and renounce and disclaim any parental right to such child born during our separtion.

Stephen Allison

Max and Shirley's firstborn son reentered our lives some 45 years later - bringing much happiness to everyone involved. We learned at that time that he'd been adopted shortly after Shirley returned to Colorado. Mr. and Mrs. Taylor of Lufkin Texas renamed him Travis and raised him with great love and affection.

Although she's definitely not his only paramour, and although their relationship sometimes cools for long periods, I think that Steve is very much in love with Yvonne by this date. They attend the Policemen's Ball together and she and her sons visit the farm with Steve on at least two occasions. Amongst my father's things, were many photos of a lovely young woman – oftentimes posing with two young boys. I think they are of Yvonne and her sons.

In April, Steve met with another of his ex-wives, Margaret.

There are several interesting developments on the job for Steve during these months. He had to "walk the beat" in lower downtown on several occasions during this spring and summer. In those days it was known as Skid Row - not LoDo, as it's fashionably called now. He told me, years later, about many dangerous situations that he encountered there. I wonder why he was taken out of the patrol car and assigned to foot patrol during this time? I don't think he was in trouble - because shortly thereafter he's assigned as acting captain at headquarters several times.

And the real shocker is that his patrol car partner of many weeks, "Officer Frank Cowgill shot and killed a man named W.L. Cross - 2:29 A.M." on June 20,1946. The next day Steve has "to serve paper's on Cowgill at the County Jail." When I first went through my father's stuff at the farm, I found numerous front-page news articles and news photos about this murder. Unfortunately, in trying to decide what was saved and what wasn't, I must have thrown these papers away. I looked for them high and low today, but I didn't find them. I'll look again, later. If I remember correctly though, W.L. Cross was killed at Officer Cowgill's home. I don't think it was a love triangle, but maybe something like a dispute over a card game after a night of heavy drinking. I've omitted most of Steve's notations concerning alcohol misuse by his fellow officers, but in this instance perhaps murder was the result.

Steve enjoys the natural steam baths at Hot Sulfur Springs with Uncle Gus, Aunt Micki and sometimes Yvonne. He accompanies his cousin Chris to Fitzsimmons Army Hospital and Lowry Air Force Base a few times - probably to do with Chris being a prisoner of war and all.

He visits Linda Lee at least once a week. He takes her to see his dad at "the ranch." He takes some photos. On April 27, 1946 he notes, "She sure looks swell." I never knew that he had tried so hard to stay close to his young daughter. And therefore I never appreciated this fact; nor showed him my appreciation. I'm very sorry for that.

Could it be that I remember living with Mrs. Forte? My very earliest, yet vivid, memory is of sitting at a table covered with a red and black checkered "oilcloth". I remember the waxy smell. The table sits beside a second story window. Looking out this window, I watch the trees move in the wind. The large leafy branches sway slowly and sometimes brush against the window. There's an old lady in the kitchen with me. We are both very quiet, because she doesn't like any noise. It's so quiet I can hear the refrigerator, which sits atop four thin legs, as it turns on, runs a bit, and then turns off for a while. I'm eating saltines and drinking milk but I mustn't make a mess with the cracker crumbs because the woman is very strict with me. I look out the window for hours. I'd describe my feelings as "melancholy"- can a two year old be melancholy? Maybe more like sad.

This memory has been my constant companion throughout my life. It's never faded. I "saw" it as a young child, as an adolescent, as a young adult, and as a mature adult - and now it's as clear to this middle-aged woman as my activities of only yesterday. What makes it so strong, I think, is the accompanying feeling of utter loneliness.

On second thought, I don't think this memory is of my time with Mrs. Forte. Steve mentions that he visited with her "and her daughters", so I think she must have been a younger woman than the one I remember from the "quiet house". Perhaps it's from my time with Mrs. Kantee - where I was for three weeks just before my time with Mrs. Forte? But no. That three-week stay was in *March* – before there were leaves on the trees.

This memory, then, must be from even *before* Mrs. Kantee - from my time with Mrs. Spaulding! Could that be? Could a year old child experience, and then remember forever, something that clearly?

"THERE IS A CHILDLESS HOME FOR EVERY HOMELESS CHILD"

Texas Children's Home Finding Society Letter

CHAPTER 18

Archaeology

Time out.

Well, I did return to the dusty boxes in the dusty storage room - looking for the elusive news articles about Officer Cowgill and the murder that, as I remember, took place at his home. After a full day of unsuccessful searching, I unearthed, instead, a box filled with papers and photos that I'd previously overlooked.

As you know, at the time of his death, I hardly knew my father. And I knew even less about *his* father. Five buildings held the jumbled remains of their lives. Every item I found would eventually help me to know them better - their hearts and their times - but only after I'd struggled to fit each item into some sort of chronological order and/or emotional setting. Each time I'd think I had all the pieces in order, within their groupings, and had them committed to paper, I'd find another whole batch of artifacts. Nothing was found in context, as they say in archaeology - as long as we're talking about artifacts.

And now, at this late date, it'd happened again!

This latest discovery included artifacts that concern not only Steve's life from this point on, but also many that dealt with his earlier life, and also with John's life. As I sorted through them, I knew that much of the earlier part of this story would now have to be rewritten - again!

And so it was. It's taken several weeks, but hopefully you'll not have noticed where I went back and placed many of these artifacts in their correct context. Thank goodness for computers.

Concerning John, I found:

- The photo of his mother, Georgoula.
- His photo as a thin young soldier.
- The list recording the members of his seventh regiment.
- His framed discharge papers.
- His photo, as a civilian, at about age 30.
- The photo of his wife (I think), Minnie Novack.
- One franc coin dated 1913.
- The photo of an older, and a "stouter", John - marching with his veteran compatriots (see image at beginning of Chapter 18).
- The letters from George Ellis
- The photos of a military parade.
- A small picture of Charles Lindbergh.
- A two page letter in Greek.
- His framed photo, taken at age 59, which he also used for his passport.
- The newspapers from the ship he took to and from Greece in 1935 - the R.M.S. MAJESTIC.

Do you remember any of those?

Concerning Steve's life, *up to this point* in our story (August 1946), I found:

- The photos of his cousins Chris, Georgia and Titsa.
- The photo of his cousin Chris in his Air Force uniform.
- The photo of Steve and his adult baseball team.
- The photo of Steve in a law enforcement class, dated November 25, 1941.
- A framed copy of Steve's Denver University diploma, dated June 10, 1944.
- The enlarged and framed snapshot of the infant Linda Lee at about five months of age.
- The three studio photos of L.L. that were taken in November 1945.
- A very large photo of the house at 29th and Grove Street (see Figure 12.7).

The sturdy brick house on Grove Street - where Steve lived for many years with and without his little family - is buried under lots of snow. He must have taken this photograph after one of the big snowstorms that he makes note of in his journal.

(We've lived, since 1965, about a mile from this house. I drive by it at least once a week. It still looks exactly the same.)

Any of those ring a bell?

Concerning Steve's life *from this point on* (September 1946), in our story, I found:

- More photos of Yvonne and her sons.

  They're tucked away in a Bri-Tone photo-developing envelope from North Pharmacy at 1279 Marion.

  But wait! The name on the return section of the envelope is *H. Smith* of 1307 Franklin. Which means that - they're *not of Yvonne after all!*

  They're of H.S.! - As in Steve's "HSX" notations of 8/10/45, 8/24/45, 10/1/45, 6/25/46 and 7/12/46.

  Therefore, the other photos (taken at the farm etc.) which I'd assumed were of Yvonne and her sons - are also of *Helen* and *her* sons. I'm very confused.

- Two photos professionally mounted together in one frame.

  On one side is a photo of (I *now* know) Helen Smith. On the back my father has written, "OCTOBER 1947". On the other side is a photo of a very sedate elderly couple. (Steve's long absent mother and her husband?)

- A photo of Steve at the Denver Police Command School, dated February 1949.
- Two large studio photos, taken in 1949, of Linda Lee and Steve together.
- A framed document written in Greek, with only Steve's name in English.
  I think it's from his induction into some type of Greek fraternal organization.

- About one hundred photos and dozens of books containing photos of women in various stages of undress.
  Today we would describe these as soft porn, but which must have been considered pretty pornographic at the time. Evidently Steve had a healthy appreciation of the female form.

Now, back to the story. Let's see where these pieces will fit.

Archeology

CHAPTER 19

ECX DECEMBER 1946

Thursday 5 Cr. 10. W. Russell
Saw L.L. Agreement with
Forte family 42.50 + phone bill
per month — went out to Dad's
ranch.

"42.50 + phone bill"

Late summer of 1946 finds Steve on vacation. In the early fall he celebrates his 36th birthday. As the year winds down, he writes:

September 1946

1 1st day of vacation – sick

2 2nd day of vacation - still sick. YSX

3 3rd day vacation and still sick. Saw L.L. Shirley called. Went out to ranch - Y. Dinner at Tiffin - Y. Elitches later. YSX

4 Vacation. I am still sick. saw L L saw Shirley.

5-11 Vac. - Hot Sulphur Springs

12 Vac. - Took L L with Gus - Micki out to Dad's Ranch. YSX

13 Vac. - Had L L over to the house. Shirley called me. YSX

14 Vac. - Went out to ranch. Dad and I argued. YSX

16 Cr. 10 with Sgt. Stanley. May Co. strike duty Saw L.L.

17 Saw L.L.

18 YSX

19 Saw L.L.

20 Shirley called - said she was in St. Joseph Hosp. for mental check up by a doctor.

21 acting Cap. - Hdqts. Saw L.L.

22 Acting Captain at hdqts. YSXS

23 saw L.L. YSX

27 Saw L.L.

28 Saw L.L.

29 Day Off - Hot Sulphur Springs - Gus, Micki, Wes Head and wife. YSX

30 Day Off - Hot Sulphur Springs. YSX

October 1946

1 7:45 P to 3:45 A. Walking district #1. Saw L.L.

3 Saw L.L. YSX

4 YSX

5 Shirley saw L.L.

6 Shirley called me. ECX

7 Saw L.L.

8 Day Off - Saw L.L. YSXS

9 L.L. sick, I had to call a doctor.

11 Acting Capt. - Hdqts. YSX

13 Saw L.L. YSXS

14 EHX

18 Saw L.L. - went out to Dad's ranch.

19 Shirley saw L.L. - she always tries to upset L.L. - trying to make her cry. Officer O. one year's suspended by Capt. Cook.

20 Saw L.L. ECX

21 Went out to ranch, got stuck in the mud.

23 Saw L.L.

25 Shirley called.

27 Saw L.L. Painting roof of house.

29 Brought Dad in from Ranch.

31 Painted Sheriff Koch called me about Dad having a fight with Vermott.

November 1946

1 Saw L.L. finished painting roof of house Officer C. Clark worked on Model A.

2 Change shifts today - working 11:30 AM to 7:30 PM. 11" of snow on car #14.

3 Snow now 17 inches deep. Saw L.L.

4 Still snowing - now is 27 inches deep.

7 Saw L.L. Order trousers from rose tailors. Shirley called. YSXS

8 Saw L.L. Officer J. C. suspended for fighting.

9 Snowed again - very cold. ECXS

10 Walking - very cold Went out to ranch with officer Clark.

11 Walking - very cold. Saw L.L.

12 Saw L.L.

13 Walking YSX

14 Dad called from ranch.

15 Day Off - Brought Dad in from ranch, we saw L.L. YSX

17 Saw L.L.

18 Saw Shirley.

20 Saw L.L.

21 HSX

23 Day Off - went out to ranch with Gus, with a load of timbers.

24 Saw L.L.

25 Dinner with Yvonne, saw Shirley

27 Found gas smell in kitchen upstairs.

28 Saw L.L.

29 Day Off - Worked on Model A. Ford with Officer Suer. YSXS

December 1946

1 4 AM - 12 NOON Cr. #10. W. russell. Saw Linda Lee.

2 Yvonne bought stove $94.00 YSX

3 HSX

4 Saw L.L. YSX

5 saw L.L. Agreement with Forte family - 42.50 + phone bill per month went out to Dad's ranch. ECX

6 saw L.L. - Account started for L L in Police credit Union. Shirley called.

7 Day Off - Attended football game at D.U. Saw L.L. Got a bad cold.

8 Walked - Was sick.

9 Sick - did not work. Bad cold.

10 Sick. Shirley called.

12 Sick. Fortes' moved in upstairs with L.L.

13 Sick. Shirley called.

16 Cr. 10. W. russell YSXS

19 results Capts Exam 1-Girard 2-Johnson 3-Loan 4-Derby 5-Sawyer

21 Day Off - out to Ranch with officer Suer.

24 Walking. Mr - Mrs Johnson came over to see L.L. Shirley did not come to see L.L.

25 Walking. Shirley called but did not come over to see L.L.

27 Walking.

On the last page of the journal, under "Xmas cards received 1946" Steve lists 30 people - including several that we've met:

- Antoinette and Gus Allison
- Frank Allison & Family
- Shirley A.
- Yvonne
- Darrell Suer & Family
- most of his patrol partners.

The addresses listed tell a sad story in themselves:

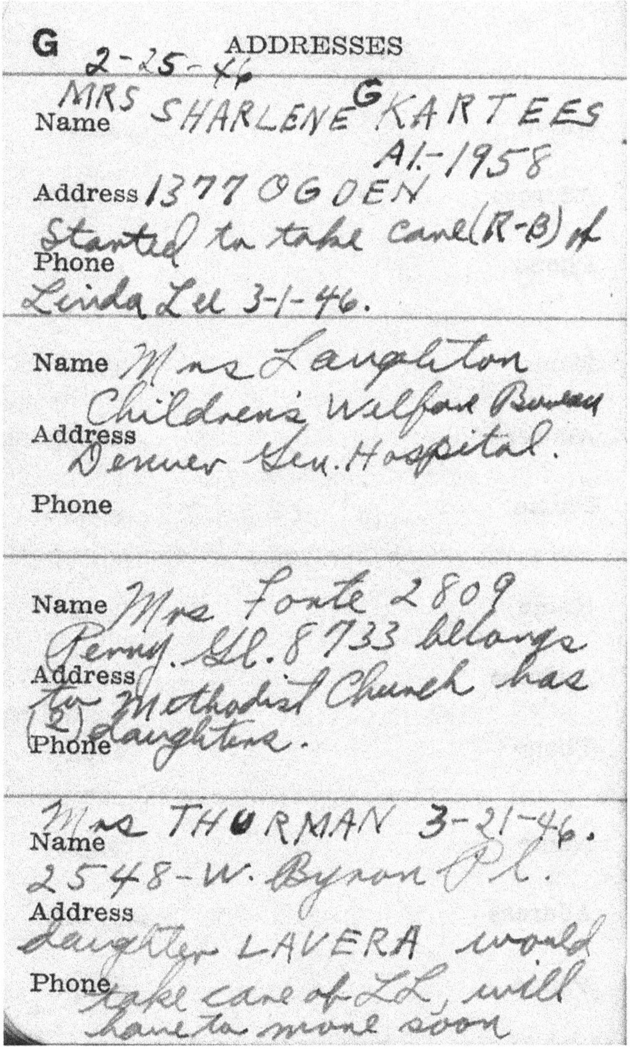

Figure 19.1 Addresses section of Steve's Journal.

ADDRESSES

2-25-46

MRS SHARLENE G. KARTEES

Al.-1958

1366 OGDEN

Started to take care (R-B) of Linda Lee 3-1-46

Mrs Laughton

Childrens' Welfare Bureau

Denver Gen. Hospital.

Mrs Forte

2809 Perry. Gl. 8733

belongs to Methodist Church has (2) daughters.

Mr. THURMAN 3-21-46

2548 - W. Byron Pl.

daughter LAVERA would take care of L L, will have to move soon

Steve and Shirley often talk, and sometimes meet, after her return from Texas. She confides in him a lot, it seems. For instance, she tells him in September that her parents have had her hospitalized for a "mental check up".

Her behavior *had* been erratic, *to say the least*, especially after she discovered that she was adopted. I'm sure that she was a constant worry to her very conservative parents, with whom she was once again living.

Her friend at the Phone Company - Aunt Betsy to us now - often speaks of their adventures from this time. They're stories filled with "jump seats" and wild rides through the night with friends. But, she also says that Shirley was often "unreliable" in those days - like making plans to meet and then not showing up.

While in the hospital, in the name of therapy, Shirley's injected with what she recalls as a "truth serum". What was the reasoning behind such an intervention? What was it meant to accomplish, and how? It's all *very* traumatic for Shirley, and makes a lasting impression on her. (She's often made reference to it - as she does in the letter found in Chapter 2.)

Steve feels that Shirley purposely upsets L.L. during her visits - and yet he's perturbed when Shirley, "did not come over to see L.L." on Christmas.

According to Shirley her visits *were* upsetting to L.L. She's told me that she did visit me faithfully - for a very long time; but that she finally stopped coming because her "visits did more harm than good." Of course she didn't intentionally upset her child - but the visits probably were affected somewhat by her unsettled circumstances and confused state of mind.

I'm curious about Steve's relationship with Yvonne. They don't have much of a social life. They hardly ever even go on a date. You'd think they'd at least spend holidays together. Did she want more?

Grampa, who's 70, seems to be getting pretty quarrelsome. First he argues with Steve in September and then on Halloween he gets in a fight with someone else. Perhaps he was frightened. Perhaps he was paranoid. Probably he was lonely.

L L had been a part of their family for nine months when Steve makes an "agreement with Forte family 42.50 + phone bill per month". I assumed that meant he'd agreed to pay *them* that amount for the continued care of his child.

I was surprised to read in the next week's journal, therefore, that they - with Linda - had moved into the upstairs of Steve's house. I realized then that *they* would be paying *him* that amount!

Now there's yet another grouping of people living at 29th and Grove St. - Steve, Mrs. Forte, the two Forte daughters and Linda Lee. (*I always wonder what happened to Bambi.*)

How long will this arrangement last?

"42.50 + phone bill"

Steve's journal - December 5, 1946.

CHAPTER 20

"L L and I went visiting."

Steve's 1947 journal is primarily an account book of monetary exchanges, expenses and rent income. Although Steve was always very "frugal", money must have been especially tight at this time – he utilizes a 1940 day calendar for his 1947 entries. He records literally hundreds of such notations, but I've included only a few. Interwoven with the budgetary items, however, the real story continues:

January 1947

1 Cr. 10 - W. Russell. 4am to 11:45am.

2 attended Ice Follies, Auditorium. 47.10 on House Frank 24.50 YSX

5 Walking Dist #1 11.00 Frank

6 16.00 Frank

7 Groc – 7.00, gas 1.10, Fortes 42.50 Rent for 1-12 to 2-12-47. Stove 15.00

8 YSX

9 Frank – 15.00

10 Medicine 1.00 Milk bill - 2.94

11 arrested JOE D. – Later fined 106.00. Pol. Ct.

14 went out to Ranch. Uniform cleaned 1.68

15 YSX

19 Day Off - Ranch

20 Donations 1.00

21 YSX

22 Eggs - 2.10

23 IN-TAX 11.70 PEN 5.46 Blue Cross 3.40

24 YSX

25 Bought 7.00 canned grape fruit juice.

27 Officer Belamy suspended. (YS 10.00) bacon - 3.87

28 Day Off - out to Dad's ranch. L L to Dr. Butterfield. G-E. 18.40 Tel – 5.18 Both pd by Fortes. YSX

29 Medicine 1.50

30 Efficiency shoot 88 Sleeper for L L - 2.34.

31 Visited Elieen and Freddy with YS Guarding Trust 4.20 TOTAL YS - 6

February 1947

1 On Cr. 50 alone. Chry. Brakes 20.00. shoe repairs 4.50. PPA 5.00

2 Day Off - Went up to Dr. Butterfield's.

4 gasoline - 1.95. Meat - 3.17. repair Chry. - 5.56. Present - 1.25

5 Phonograph Needle - .75

6 Uncle Frank operated on at Presby. Hosp.

8 Desk Sgt. hdqts. visited Frank at Hosp. twice today.

9 Notified Uncle Frank has Pneumonia. Visited Uncle Frank.

10 Brought dad in from Ranch to see Uncle Frank at Presby. Hosp.

11 Visited Waldron 230 Eudora, with Y.S.

12 Final Exam on 1st aid class 7:00 - 9:30 Pm.

13 Stick up 1225 Larimer

14 Present M W - 3.56 Candy 1.17

15 Desk Sergeant Hdqts. YSX

16 YSX

17 YSX

21 YSXX

22 Desk Sgt. Hdqts

23 TED L. WILLIAMS IS INV. - AUTO THEFT. YSX

24 Day Off. went out to Ranch.

25 10.00 for Car heater.

27 Fruit - Veg. - 8.79

28 Water bill - 5.22 Pd. Cloths for L.L. 2.37 1.00 for Red Cross.

March 1947

1 Desk Sgt. Dist. 1. 4 AM to 12 Noon.

2 To Evergreen with Homer

4 Went out to ranch

5 Day Off. show - Aladdin.

7 went out to Ranch.

8 Shirley came over to see L.L. Ice Cream .72.

9 L L and I went visiting.

12 Day Off. Margie Evans YSX

13 Ham - 12.23 Jello - .62

14 Shirley leaving to get Married at Raton N. Mex tonight.

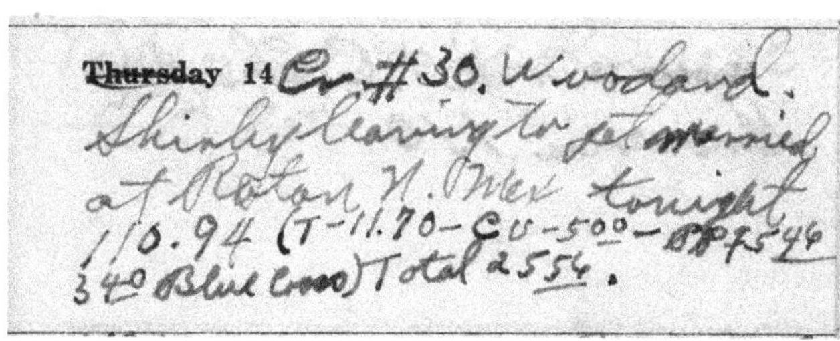
Thursday 14 Cr. #30. Woodland.
Shirley leaving to get married
at Raton N. Mex tonight
110.94 (T-11.70-CU-5.00-BB 5.44
3.40 Blue Cross) Total 25.54.

Figure 20.1 Steve's Journal noting Shirley's marriage: March 14, 1947.

15 Cloths 20.22. YSX

17 IPX

19 Day Off. to Colo. Springs. MEX

20 Prudential 2 mo. 48.18. Stimson Ins "Car" 7.20

22 YSX
24 YSX
25 Attended Greek Ind. Day celebration at Cosmo Hotel with Y. S. Dinner Dance 4.00 Flowers 2.00
26 Margie Evans engaged to Belamy
27 YSX
29 Shirley was over to see L.L.
31 3.10 - Community Chest. YSX

April 1947
1 8 Pm - 4 Am Walking Dist #1.
4 Ruby – 820 21st St. 321 Republic Hotel.
5 Mr - Mrs Johnson over to see Linda Lee
7 Had dad in from farm. YSX
9 IPX
11 Cr 20 C. Chafin Escort Greek Church parade 11:00 Pm.
12 Attended Greek Church
13 Went out to Ranch
14 YSX
16 YSX
17 Ruby Al-6621 YSX
18 Chrysler repainted cost 44.15
22 Day Off - Went out to ranch.
23 YSX
24 Efficiency shoot 96
25 YSSX
26 RWX
30 Day Off - Up to Butterfields with Gus.

May 1947
1 4 AM TO NOON Shirley was over to see L.L. IPS
2 Aunt Micki very sick. YSX
3 Tax refund city 8.32
6 Brought dad in from ranch.
7 shirt material taken to Rose tailors for shirt.
9 HOSSELKUS the man to see at fish hatchery near Deckers, Colo
10 Attended Phi gamma Delta dinner at the University Club. MDX
12 Carl Moss man to see for things at MW - Catologue Dept YSX
13 Took L L out to ranch.
14 Went out to ranch with Chris and his mother.
16 HSX
18 Attended Political meeting at Aphia Temple. Stapleton, Morrissey, Black were there.

20 YSX
21 Newton elected Mayor of Denver. Nick Lewis man to see Wray, Colo. HSX
22 Visited basement 15th Curtis. 10.88 to Lodge
23 Sgt's Johnson, Girard and Sloan made captains.
25 Handled rape case 1425 Williams. MARY S. Age - 17.
26 Broke up with YS.
27 Vegetables - 2.50 HSX
29 Efficiency shoot 88. Ruby left for Calif. YSX

Just a few comments on Steve's bookkeeping:

- He paid quite a bit of money to his Uncle Frank in January.
- Probably the gift he bought at Montgomery Ward for $4.50 and the flowers he purchased the same day, Valentine's Day, were for Yvonne.
- The $3.10 to the Community Chest on March 31 is interesting. Two years later, this organization will help him place L.L. with a foster family.
- Most of the notations concern household expenses. I have a feeling that he's keeping such exact records in order to closely monitor what he spends "on" the Fortes. L.L.'s been a part of their family for a year now - I hope Steve doesn't ruin the arrangement by his financial nitpicking. (Having gotten a feel for the prices of goods and services in the 1940's, I'll omit most of the remaining "expense" notations.)

Speaking of Mrs. Forte, since she and her daughters moved in, Steve seldom mentions his own little daughter. He was probably relieved - and happy to let her be LL's primary parent. He and Linda Lee *do* go visiting on March 9th though. I wonder whom they visited?

Late May was eventful for Steve. On May 22, he "visited the basement 15th Curtis". I'm assuming that this mysterious sounding event had to do with his job. Somehow though, I think it might be related to some very interesting photos, of some very in teresting women, that we found at the farm. I'd describe them as soft-core pornography, but I'm sure they would have been considered pretty shocking at the time. The models in the photos are definitely amateurs, as are the photographers. We found about a hundred of them - along with books touting the many benefits of nudist camps and books on appreciating and drawing the human female "form".

On the 23rd of May several sergeants are promoted to captain - including Sergeant Johnson. I'm assuming this was this Bud Johnson – Steve's ex-father-in-law.

On May 26, Steve and Yvonne break up. But then he records her initials once again on the 29th. If you're following the initials trail, you know that he's not been exactly faithful to Yvonne. ME, IP, RW, MD and HS all make appearances. I wonder if ME is Margie Evans who became engaged to another police officer on March 26, 1947? And is MD his other ex-wife, Margaret Dunn? Does RW designate Ruby - Ruby from the Republic Hotel, who left for California on May 29? We know that HS is Helen Smith - a woman who's been in and out of Steve's life for the past two years and whose packet of snapshots I recently found.

And speaking of "initials", remember when my mom told me that Steve "only wanted one thing" from her? Well, last week she told me something else that makes me think that Steve was probably less than honorable in many of these relationships. In a restaurant over breakfast, she said, "I don't know if it's good - you making me remember some of these things."

Assuming she was upset thinking about her decisions of that time, I said something like, "Don't feel bad—I was totally responsible for my divorce. My actions were thoughtless, hurtful and broke apart our family."

"No," she said, "I mean making me think about things *your father did.* He had sex with me regularly when I was *only seventeen years old* and still living at home! And then, there was this one friend, Shirley M., and he tried to have sex with her *while we were married.*"

She was sincerely upset. It struck me as she recounted these distasteful events, that perhaps she'd "blocked out" so many things from this time, not because of things *she'd* done, but because of things *Steve* had done.

But as of March 14, 1947, she's free of her entanglements with Steve. On that day she and Max are married. Max traveled throughout the west as a cattle buyer. That's probably why their marriage took place in Raton, New Mexico.

Photos of Max from this time show one of the most handsome men I've ever seen. He looked like Gregory Peck – *only better. And* he dressed impeccably. Not only his suits were tailored made - so were his shoes!

Max Radovich was a man of character - a quiet, reflective and gentle man. Although he had served during the war as a navigator and bombardier in the Air Force, he *never* spoke of those years or of those experiences. I think that, for him, they were far too serious for any conversation.

No wonder Shirley fell head over heels in love with him - and remains so to this day.

Although she would have had to go to court to regain custody of LL - a few months after their marriage, Shirley asks Max if this might be a possibility. It isn't. That was probably a wise decision.

"L L and I went visiting."
Steve's journal - March 9, 1947.

CHAPTER 21

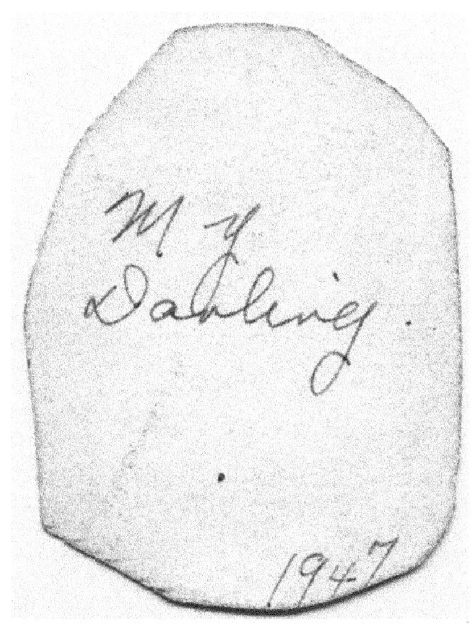

"My Darling, 1947"

Continuing in Steve's 1947 Journal:

June 1947

1 7P to 3A Cr. 30 Hanahran

5 Day Off -Hot Sulphur Springs with Gus Bathe 2.50

9 YSXX

10 Brought dad in from ranch -3 teeth extracted

11 Day Off - Up to Butterfilds with HS HSX

12 Brought dad in from ranch.

13 YSXS

15 Father's day - out to ranch with HS

16 YSX

18 Efficiency shoot – 94

22 Day Off - Mountains with HS and LL HSX

June 1947

24 Doug Spaulding has chicken pox.

25 Police Hat 4.50

29 Day Off - Up to Butterfields with H.S. HSX

July 1947

1 Cr 30 G. Seaton 11AM - 7PM Dad had (3) more teeth pulled. Lake Side with HS

2 Talk to Chief O'Donnell - will be transferred to Dist. 4 7-5-47.

3 Elitches "Les Brown" with Mani Stampty.

6 H.S. birthday Gary, Kent Spaulding sick Chicken Pox.

7 Brought dad in from ranch for teeth.

8 Received phonograph (portable) HSX

10 Rainbow Ballroom, H.S. - Linal Hampton orchestra

12 HSSX

13 Day Off - Hicken's cabin in Mts. HSX

14 Shirley called

15 Talked to YS in Lighthouse - first time I saw her since 6-16-47. She ditched me for Doug E.

16 Went out to ranch with HS and LL.

17 YS left for Chicago did not see her.

19 Shirley came over to see LL.

20 Birthday party for LL at Uncle Gus Apt. HSX

21 HSX Somebody in YS Room - 12 PM LL birthday - Party for LL at HS House Eileen tells me YS has been going with DE

22 Went out to Ranch L L. Somebody in YS Room 11Pm I'm feeling very blue.

23 Day Off - to Central city, Rollinsville with HS. Feeling very blue HSX

Figure 21.1 Helen Smith in Central City.

24 Efficiency Shoot 97 Lights on downstairs 12 Midnight YS

25 Elitches with HS Light in middle room upstairs YS

26 YS to arrive at 8:30 AM on 27th, requested DE to meet her. HSX

27 Day Off - Hot Sulphur HSXX

28 Called YS - I was supposed to get a letter from her. Talked to PAT P. - 1117 Penn. about YS.

30 YS called me HSX

31 YS called me, was very nice. HS left for Nebr - 5 Pm. Talked to Pat P.

August 1947

1 Cr 40 E. Lindquist still on 10 am to 6 pm shift.

2 YS called me feel sick.

4 Received letter form HS. YS called me, she has trouble with her feet.

5 Saw YS this Am 1st since 7-15-47. 10.00 Butterfield - BAL 83.00

6 called HS Sutherland, Nebr. RTX

7 YS called me. Her Dr. say's she has walking heart.

8 H.S. called me from Sutherland Nebr. YS called.

9 HS arrived 10:30 AM from NEBR. HSX

10 Day Off - Rollinsville with HS
11 YS called. HSX
13 Shirley called. YS called.
14 YS called.
16 Acting Capt – Hdqts HSX
17 Day Off - Rollinsville - H. S HSX
18 visited YS at her home.
20 Visited 1170 Jersey St. - a possible place for L.L. 60.00 per month.
22 YS called me. HSX
24 Acting Capt. at Hdqts YS called
26 Day Off - out to ranch.
27 LL fell from Chrysler. YS visited.
29 HSXX
31 Acting Capt. Hdqts. HSX

September 1947

1 1st day of vacation Circus with HS and Jackie HSX
2 Hot Sulphur Spr. with gus, Micki YSX
3 Hot sulphur springs Baths 12.00
9 Out to Dad's ranch. YSX HSXS
10 YSX Fortes moved to 1711 Vine St. - 9.00 to Mary Forte for LL.
12 YSX
14 HSX
15 Broke off completely with YS
16 Cr 10 J. Power's 4 am - 12 noon. HSX
17 Chrysler to Cullen-Thompson complete over-haul Job.
18 Cousin Steve married in N. York.
19 Shirley and YS called.
20 HSXS
24 Police School Called YS

Figure 21.2 Police School. Steve is in the second row, far right.

25 Police School Went out to Dad's farm. Called YS HSX

26 Police School - Camp George West Golden, Colo. Crime Investigation

27 last day of Police school Out to Dad's ranch Birth-day HSX

28 Day Off - Moved LL to Mrs. Thomas Scarry, 5011 Osceola Gl.-8409.

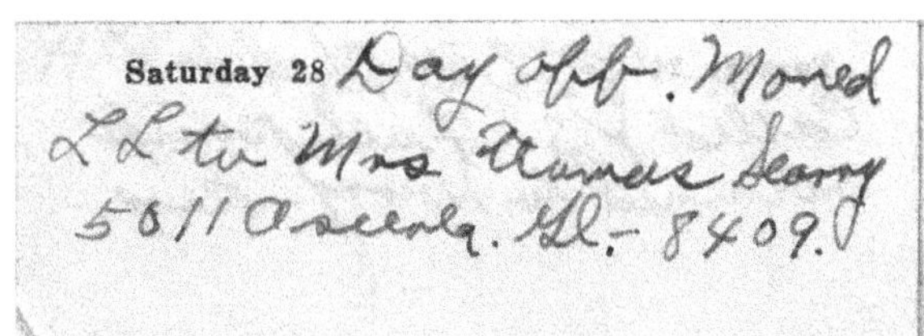

Saturday 28 Day off. Moved
LL to Mrs Thomas Scarry
5011 Osceola. Gl.-8409.

Figure 21.3 Steve's Journal noting Linda Lee's sixth move: September 28, 1947.

29 Had it out with Douglas E. and Yvonne. Shirley called.

October 1947

1 Cr 10 J. Power's 4 Pm - 12 Mid HSX

2 HS Left for Nebr 4 AM (10-3-47) Mrs. Johnson, Shirley and Grandma and Grandpa Johnsons over to see LL. HSX

3 Saw LL. 45.00 to Mrs Scarry for LL. Inc. 10-29-47.
4 YS came over. had a long talk with Doug E. YS has been taking him to and from work each day.
6 Out to ranch.
8 In Capt's office 5 Pm to 11 Pm Saw L.L. 20.00 to clark for Model A ford. HS called me from NEBR.
9 Furnace oiled and (1) filter installed. Shirley was over to see LL.
10 Out to ranch with LL. YS came over. YSX
11 5.00 to Clark for Model "A"
12 Day Off - Sutherland, Nebr. HSX
13 Sutherland, Nebr. HSX
14 Sutherland, Nebr. HSXS
15 Cr 10 J. Powers Saw LL. HSX
17 worked Shrine parade Out to ranch with HS YS called me twice. HSX
18 Parade "Shrine" 12 to 5 Pm Lunch downtown with YS HSX
22 YSX
24 Shirley called me.
25 HSX
27 Jazz - Harmonica Concert at Auditorium with HS.
28 HSX
29 Obtained Webster wire recorder from M W.

November 1947

1 Police Court 9AM HSX
2 Acting Capt. Hdqts. 7 Am to 3 Pm Blond Francis P. - lives 1200 Blk on Clarkson friend of Chris's and ed Karmigiasis.
3 Boggio a friend of Chuck Smith, radio man, lives at 1325 Corona St. HSX
4 Cr 10 J. Power's saw and talked to Milt Heisner not very friendly
5 Yvonne admitted she was out to a dance with DE the night of 11-1-47. she had said she was not talking to him at all. Told YS - I was "all through".
6 Told YS to have my things sent over.
7 Capts-Sgt's meeting 11:00 AM Mayor Newton and chief O'Donnell spoke. HSX
8 YSX
9 Acting Capt. Hdqts HSX
10 HS mad about YS Stayed home all evening.
11 HS still mad - have not heard from her YSX
12 saw YS getting out of DE car 12:15 AM. said she was visiting her sick father.
13 visited MILT HEISNER - said he has not seen YS. Ate dinner at HS house.
14 HS going on date tonight - was very mad at me. Don Bowman called me at work about Shirley taking LL.
15 Talked to HS - she still is very mad. talk to my lawyer C. Mills.
16 Acting Capt - Hdqts. No word from HS - she's still mad at me.

17 called HS - She wont see me at all. She went skiing yesterday. Talked to Shirley today about LL.

18 Called HS - she's still mad. said she may see me tomorrow.

19 Saw HS at her house 8 Pm - had a very long talk. She was hurt mentally very much. I was awfully sorrow.

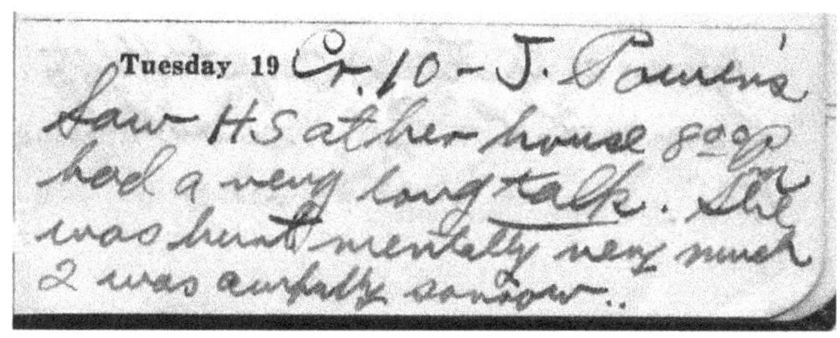

Tuesday 19 Cr. 10 - J. Powers'
Saw HS at her house 8 PM
had a very long talk. She
was hurt mentally very much
I was awfully sorrow..

Figure 21.4 Steve's Journal: November 19, 1947.

20 Did not go out at all. did not see HS

21 Called HS twice - she is going to a Bingo party tonight.

22 H.S. still mad - wont see me

23 Acting Capt Hdqts Saw LL No word from HS

24 Called HS twice - not to encouraging. Called Butterfild about LL's cold.

25 Saw LL. saw Dr. Butterfield - talked about HS. went out to ranch. Shirley bought LL (2) pairs shoes.

26 Called HS - talked good to me, for about 25 mins. saw Joe Dunn - St. Lukes Hosp.

27 Day Off - to Sutherland Nebr., alone. stayed at Archie Lew's place.

28 Sutherland, Nebr. Had nice talk with Auntie Bertha and Mother Briggs

29 Came back to Denver with Aunt Bertha - played "wire record" for "Her".

30 Acting Capt. Hdqts. saw LL.

December 1947

1 Cr 10 J. Power's 12 Mid to 8 AM aunt Bertha and I visited LL.

2 Aunt Bertha and I visited LL. again, no change with HS

3 saw LL.

4 Auntie Bertha left for Sutherland 4:30 Pm. Obtained diamond ring.

5 Called HS twice - she would not answer

6 Not a word from HS feel very sick. Met Rose Cavarra.

7 Acting Capt. Hdqts

8 Day Off - Ranch with LL no word from HS

9 No word from HS. Tried to call HS, she hung up on me twice.

10 Started to work D.D.G. received letter from Auntie Bertha.

12 Worked D.D.G. No word from HS.

13 Worked D.D.G. Letter from Auntie Bertha. No word from HS

14 Acting Capt. Hdqts. No word from HS.

15 Day Off - Out to ranch with LL dinner at Scarry's. No word from HS DNX

16 Worked D D G - 9 hr's No word from HS

17 worked D.D.G. Still no word from H.S. Talked to Helen Garrett - not so good. DNXX

18 Worked D.D.G Letter from Auntie Bertha. No word from HS

19 worked D.D.G. DNX

20 Worked D.D. Goods - 65.93 Still no word from HS rec (2) letter's from Auntie Bertha.

21 Jo McFadden. saw LL

22 worked D.D.G. Sent (2) Doz roses to Mother Briggs.

24 Worked at D.D.G. - 37.68

25 Cr. 10. J. Power's

26 Worked D.D. Goods Letter from Auntie bertha. Outlook not so hot. DNX

27 Worked D D Goods 27.49 DNX

28 Up to Butterfield's with LL and Jo McFadden.

29 Worked D.D.G. Received letter from Auntie Bertha.

30 Worked D.D.G. Changed badges from 25 to 14. DNX

31 worked D.D.G. Rec. letter's from Mother Briggs and Auntie Bertha.

In the back of the journal, there are three sections:

MEMORANDA

5-22-47 No. Prospect. J.P. SMITH for H.S. while in Colo. Springs, Colo.

4-21-47 Paint for ranch McDougal White outside paint. 1 or 2 qts of thinnier with each gallon of white paint. On second coat use 1 qt. of thinner to a gallon of either white or red paint.

6-29-47 See Mrs Warren Francis 9915 W 21st St. Lakewood for Shirts.

8-18-47 See Denny Harris for flower's at Elitches florial store.

ADDRESSES

4-26-47 Mrs. KAWAMATO - alias "Mamma" Asia Cafe.

Ruby Wright 321 Republic Hotel TA-5361

SPECIAL DATA

Hot Jazz

Art Tatum trio

The Man I love

Dark Eyes

Body and Soul

I know that you know
Flying Home
On the Sunny Side of the Street

This chapter could have been entitled "How Steve Cooks His Own Goose."

For two years he's been seeing Yvonne and Helen. Juggling the two, with a few others mixed in, might be a better way of describing it. But now as the year ends, he realizes, finally, that it's *Helen* he truly loves. But! By then, he's lost her - because of his philandering ways.

In May he had supposedly broken up with Yvonne, because she "ditched me for Doug E." Is this the same Doug Erickson that Shirley briefly dated in 1945? He begins to spend a lot more time then with Helen. But, he continues to see Yvonne. Besides talking, visiting, having dinner and having sex with her, he also spies on her, interrogates her new boyfriend and interviews her friends and neighbors.

He's still obsessed with Yvonne.

Meanwhile, he leads a double life with Helen. Although they had been infrequent lovers since August of 1945, now they begin to see each other almost every day. They visit Steve's dad at the farm on several occasions, spend several days in Hot Sulfur Springs together, take her son to the circus and even visit her family in Nebraska. Linda Lee celebrates her third birthday with a party at Helen's house in July.

On September 15 he reports that he's once again "Broke off completely with YS." But he just can't do it. By October he's seeing Yvonne again. In November, when he realizes that Yvonne is still seeing Doug, he breaks up with her, yet again, telling her he's "all through". The next day he tells her to "have my things sent over."

Four days later, *somehow* Helen finds out about Yvonne and Steve's affair! She's "mad", and refuses to see him for several days. When they finally do talk, she tells him that "She was hurt mentally very much".

He in turn, "was awfully sorrow".

Yes, *now* he realizes, too late, that it's Helen he truly loves. He tries desperately to win back her trust and love but things are never the same between them again. She's had it with Steve Allison.

The "H. Smith" photo-developing envelope held numerous snapshots of Helen and of her son, Jackie. In one, she wears a tailored summer dress and heels and Jackie wears a buttoned shirt tucked into trousers that show an obvious crease. He looks to be about eight or nine years old, and is blond. She has her arms draped lovingly around his shoulders. In another, Jackie, wearing a striped tee shirt and jeans, stands next to a horse.

With these pictures was a special one of Helen - one that Steve had obviously carried in his wallet for some time. On the back of it he wrote, "My Darling 1947" (see image at the beginning of this Chapter).

It, and several others that Steve saved, show us what appears to be a confident woman, probably in her early thirties, with a genuine and unaffected smile. Her thick dark hair is parted in the middle, pulled up and back from her face and tied up somehow in back. Her forehead in uncluttered by bangs of any kind. She's dressed in jeans, a work shirt and boots. It was probably taken at the farm or in the mountains – perhaps in Rollinsville or Hot Sulfur Springs.

In three other photos, Helen's holding an infant - and on the back of one is written, "Loren Briggs Rees, all of these 4 weeks old, taken at Briggs" (see Figure 23.4).

When Steve is trying to win her back, he goes to Sutherland Nebraska to enlist the help of Mother *Briggs* and Auntie Bertha. Auntie Bertha actually comes back to Denver with Steve, perhaps to help him try to convince Helen of his love and contrition.

I think Mother Briggs is Helen's mom, and Auntie Bertha's her aunt.

Do you remember the picture frame with two photos that I thought might be of Yvonne and of Steve's mother and her husband? Well, I now know that the pictures are of *Helen* and *her parents.* On the back of the framed picture, Steve wrote "October 1947", and we know Steve and Helen went to Nebraska in October of 1947. In her photo, Helen is standing beside a narrow river, holding her sweater tightly closed against the wind. Because of the wind, her hair is loosened and in disarray, but she's laughing.

Figure 21.5 Helen Smith and (?)her parents.

It's too bad that Steve messed up this relationship. Helen never gave him a chance to give her the diamond ring that he bought on December 4, 1947. Too little, too late, Steve. Shame on you.

The last photo in this North Pharmacy film-developing envelope indicates that Steve did not suffer alone for too long. It's of another woman and Linda Lee. On the back Steve's written, "OCT - 1948". Perhaps this is D.N. who makes her appearance as early as December 1947. Or could this be Yvonne!? Perhaps Steve's 1948 journal will identify her.

Steve's been a patrolman for many years by now. Was it very boring - driving around for eight hours a day, five days a week? I'd think so. He changes patrol partners many times throughout the year. He also changes his badge "from 25 to 14" on December 30. What does that mean? About once or twice a month he gets to be acting captain at police headquarters. That assignment was probably more interesting and carried with it a bit more prestige.

At Christmas time, he moonlights as a security guard at The Denver Dry Goods, a downtown department store. He did this seasonal work for many years - and was seriously injured while so employed one holiday season. A shoplifter whom he was attempting to apprehend had jumped onto a moving streetcar. When Steve tried to jump on, he was knocked to the street. He suffered a bad head injury and was hospitalized for some time. Thereafter, as a result, he often experienced what we nowadays call anxiety attacks - especially when he was in a large group of people. He shared this information with me in 1962, by way of explaining why he wouldn't be coming to my high school graduation.

He continues to be a dutiful son, making several trips to the farm to visit his father. Often Linda Lee and/or Helen accompany him. His cousin Chris and Chris's mother come with him to visit John in May. He brings his dad to town four times - to have teeth extracted. Grampa had a long and painful time with his teeth. I remember him suffering greatly with his dentures in the 1960's.

Uncle Gus and Aunt Micki enjoy several trips with Steve to Hot Sulfur Springs, where they all "take the baths". And on July 20th, the day before her third birthday, they have a party for Linda Lee at their apartment. That was so nice of them.

"I'm feeling <u>very</u> blue." Steve writes the next day.

In addition to his problems with Yvonne, perhaps he's sad that he's still trying to raise his child alone - after two and a half years. And probably Mrs. Forte has already told him that her eighteen-month stint of childcare for L.L. is soon coming to an end.

In August he visits "1170 Jersey St. a possible place for L L.". Whoever lives there offers to care for his daughter for $60.00 a month. That's too much. He looks elsewhere. What a continual worry.

Also in August, "L.L. fell from Chrysler". When I was an adult he told me about the shock and fear he felt during this traumatic event. Leaning on the door handle, Linda Lee accidentally opened the car door and tumbled out into the alley behind the house on Grove Street. He rushed her to the hospital, where they assured him that she was fine - there had been a lot of blood but no serious injuries. But, added to his worries about finding someone to care for L.L., this must have seemed like close to the final straw. Poor Steve.

Sure enough, in September, after sharing the Allison home for nine months, the Forte family moves out - without L.L.

Eight days later, on the day after his 37th birthday, Steve moves "L L to Mrs. Thomas Scarry, 5011 Osceola".

Who is this woman, and how did Steve find her? She only charges him $45.00 a month, which sure seems like a bargain to me. Could this be the woman I remember - the woman who lived in the house of the silent kitchen, where I sat for hours, looking out at the trees?

Nope, it's not her. On December 15, Steve has "dinner at Scarry's" - implying there's more than one Scarry. I lived *alone* with the woman I'm remembering. Hmm. Perhaps the quiet woman and her quiet house and her tall refrigerator perched on its thin legs will show up in 1948.

He notes that Cousin Steve was married in New York on September 18th. I thought this son of Frank had never married - but I guess I was wrong.

In October, Steve buys a "wine recorder" from Montgomery Wards. I was completely puzzled as to what that might be. But then, when Aunt Bertha comes to town in November, he plays the "wine record" for her. After several readings of that, I decided it was a "wire recorder" - whatever *that* is! Remembering the thousands of phonograph records I found at the farm after his death, I guessed that perhaps it was a mechanism used to play phonograph records.

Considering how much he loved the popular music of the day, you'd think he'd have taken his wife, and later his girlfriends, out to hear and dance to live bands more often. Perhaps he should have. I know that Shirley would have enjoyed it. She cherishes her memories of dancing to the music of the big bands with her sweetheart, and then husband, Max. He was a very good dancer, and during the early days of their courtship and marriage, they often danced the night away at Elitch Gardens' Trocadero Ballroom.

Speaking of Shirley, she visits L.L. six times during 1947. In November her lawyer talks to Steve about "Shirley taking L L." I think the request must have entailed more than just visitation arrangements, because the next day Steve discusses the situation with *his* lawyer. Perhaps this was when Shirley and Max were discussing the possibility of Linda living with them. After that - it's never mentioned again.

As the year ends, Steve sends a dozen roses to Mother Briggs, spends the early morning hours of Christmas day in Car 10 with J. Powers and gets a letter from Auntie Bertha telling him that the "Outlook not so hot."

Her words, of course, refer to his relationship with Helen. But could this unsettling prophecy apply to more than that?

"My Darling 1947"

Helen Smith's photo - 1947.

CHAPTER 22

More Artifacts

Yesterday Ken and I cleaned out the storage shed in our backyard. What a job! Over the years we'd used it to store things we felt we "might use someday".

But we'd also crammed the last of the farm stuff - pulleys, springs, fishing pools, tackle, saws, beds, a Hoosier cabinet, hundreds of canning jars, milk bottles, crockery devices (we learned later that they were used to water and feed the chickens), pots, pans, keys, tokens, dozens of guns (hand, rifle and shot) and a piano bench, for example - in there, as we were hurrying to be off the property by the sale date.

With these farm relics I discovered yet another unexamined box of documents, photos and letters that are pertinent to the story of John and Steve! After putting this aside - to deal with later - we began the process of getting rid of the rest.

After dispensing what we could to Chris and Jay, we still had a huge pile of stuff left at the end of the day. Much of it we threw away - into the Dumpster in the alley.

But what to do with the remainder? We probably could have sold most of it by holding a garage sale *someday* - but how disheartening to load it all back into the shed until that nebulous day in the future. While we were contemplating this, we saw a pickup truck stop in the alley. A man got out and began to go through the things we'd thrown away in the Dumpster. We watched through the slats of the fence as he loaded it all into his truck! When he came back for a second load, Ken went out to talk to him. Although he could speak very little English we came to understand that he had heart trouble and couldn't work at a "regular job". He scavenged through dumpsters, retrieving what he thought he could fix up and resale. Upon hearing this, we invited him into the yard to carry away the huge garage sale pile. Was he happy! He returned for three truckloads – all of it. Were we happy!

The only things he didn't take were the breakables - the jars, bottles, sundae and banana split dishes from the candy store and the crockery. I took these to the antique store, arriving ten minutes before closing time. The owner gave me $60.00 for the works.

And that's it! Finally - I've sorted through and assigned resting-places for everything from the farm. It's taken seven years. What a relief! Emotionally, psychologically and last but not least, physically!

And so today I turn my attention to the box we found yesterday - which contains, *I hope*, the last of the "sources" relevant to this story.

Actually, it isn't really a box. It's a very large, very heavy, wooden crate from the Ghirardelli Chocolate Company of San Francisco. In it are photographs, letters and business records that are tied together with ancient string -

and several smaller boxes, that contain tiny artifacts such as streetcar tokens, religious medals and foreign coins.

I probably need not mention that everything in this crate is covered with at least fifty years worth of dust and grime. So today, for one last time, I'll don the work clothes (Steve's overalls and a bandana for my hair) that I use for this sorting through process and begin in earnest to study the contents of the Ghirardelli Box.

Well, that took several weeks. I found that most of the pertinent material from this crate concerned John's life or Steve's life prior to 1947. So, you know what *that* meant. Once again I had to return to those earlier Chapters and re-write them with the benefit of the additional sources. Here's a few of the items I used. See if you can remember where they fit into the story:

- A very large, framed photo of John's elderly mother. It's very dirty and grimy.
- A framed photo of a young boy in traditional Greek costume. He's very serious, or sickly, and stands by a table holding a book (see image at the beginning of this chapter).
- A turn of the century photo of several men, wearing long white aprons, standing in front of a store.
- A photo of the interior of a candy store, with the proprietor standing proudly amidst his merchandise. This photo was also taken early in the 1900's.
- Several letters, received by George Kruskos at 1077 Fifteenth St., sent from Greece between 1923 and 1928.
- A 1924 "Road and Recreation Map" of Oregon.
- Seven checks, dated 1924, payable to John, that were returned to him because of insufficient funds or closed accounts.
- A November 27, 1924 report to the stockholders of the Farmers' High Line Canal Reservoir Company.
- A 1925 photo of many men, dressed as soldiers, standing on a very large gun type thing.
- A spiral notebook of essays written by Steve during his sophomore and junior years, 1926-1928, in high school.
- Hundreds of receipts for the years 1926-1929, from the Post Office Pool Hall, 824 18th Street.
- John's bank statements and cancelled checks for the years 1926-1929.
- Several scratch cards, games of chance, from the pool hall.
- A letter from D.S. Gray written to John Allison in 1926. It's all about the Iota Hotel and Fishing Resort "Located thirteen miles West of Gunnison on the Gunnison River."

- A letter to John Allison from the Elkdale Resort in Tabernash, Colorado - "Where your vacation will have variety." It's from O.N. Moore, the "OWNER AND MGR". He writes, "We arrived O.K. 3 hr late Tell the boys Hello for me. we found Everything in fine shape and the weather is fine no snow little cool nights we are ready for business"
- Four letters dated 1927, from the National Pepsin Gum Co., asking for payment from The Post Office Pool Hall.
- Several small notebooks containing names and money amounts. One records a payment to John of $70.00 from Buxbaum Gym for "Damages by water".
- A letter to John Allison, postmarked 1927, from the Grolier Society. It concerns the possible purchase of a set of the BOOK OF KNOWLEDGE.
- John's small notebook of class notes and rough drafts of writing assignments.
- Five brochures distributed by the Ku Klux Klan.
- An April 6, 1927 "Sailing Schedule - Cunard and Anchor Lines".
- A letter about "Transmitting Treasury Savings Certificates, due for Payment in January 1928".
- A letter to John from his friend Chris Collins dated 1939. Enclosed with it is a newspaper article about Greek American soldiers.

The Ghirardelli Box also contained hundreds of photographs of my stepmother and of her family – large framed photographs, two photo albums and many loose snapshots. Since Steve hasn't married Steppy in *our* story yet, I didn't have to insert them into any previous Chapters. They'll make their appearance in 1955.

But now, let's find out what the year 1948 holds for Steve.

More artifacts

CHAPTER 23

Your Western Agent

who presented this Diary to you is a trained and qualified insurance advisor.

Whatever your insurance problems or requirements may be, call him. It will be to your interest to seek his counsel as you would that of your physician or attorney.

His friendly, prompt and courteous service is, of course, without obligation.

Depend upon this local agent. His first obligation is serving your needs — with dependable STOCK Company insurance.

"Dependable Insurance Since 1910"

The Western Casualty & Surety Company

The Western Fire Insurance Company

Writing practically every line of Casualty and Fire Insurance and Fidelity and Surety Bonds

Home Office: Fort Scott, Kansas

"TIME MAKE ALL THINGS CLEAR"

But wait! There's no journal for 1948! Nor for 1949!

The remaining journal in The Box is for 1950.

Well, now what!?!

What was the final outcome of the Helen, Steve, Yvonne love triangle? Did Steve convince Helen to give him another chance? And if not, did he convince Yvonne to leave Erik and return to him?

And who's the woman in the photo labeled "OCT. 1948"? She's also a brunette, although I'd say she's more "perky" than Helen - it's kind of like comparing Donna Reed and Ingrid Bergman. She's kneeling down, and has her arm around four year old Linda Lee, who's standing. It looks like they've been playing in the hose on a warm summer day. L.L. wears only her underpants and has a towel over her wet hair. The woman wears shorts and a halter-top. Her wet hair is tied up with a scarf. Water is spraying in the background. Is this Yvonne? DN?

Figure 23.1 Linda Lee in October 1948.

And what about L.L.? She'd been living with the Scarrys at 5011 Osceola Street for the last three months of 1947. What happened to her for the next two years? Who was the quiet woman in the quiet house?

Will we ever learn the answers to these questions? I don't know.

Inside the front cover of his 1950 journal, Steve printed in large block letters; "TIME MAKE ALL THINGS CLEAR". I hope so.

This journal is, once again, primarily a record of Steve's love life. In the interest of brevity and of maintaining interest, I'll not report each encounter individually. Instead I'll summarize them monthly. Here then, is a condensed version of Steve's notes for his fortieth year, 1950:

January 1950

<no entries>

MVX = 8

February 1950

23 Branch put own ticket on his car

MVX = 1

LNX = 2

PFX = 2

March 1950

15 Shoot day – 86

24 Called H. Don Smith jailed

25 Called "H" she just looking for infor. Very Hard.

27 B D MILLIES

28 Deputy Chief Williams notified me I would go to Dist. #1 the first. Branch to be moved; I would be blamed.

29 Branch doing everything to get back on downtown detail.

30 Branch still very mad. Capt Sloan says I'll be on detail (His) for April. After that he wouldn't bet money on it.

MVX = 10

LNX = 3

PFX = 3

April 1950

5 JOE CONZONI TRIAL BRANCH witness.

7 (2) men disquised as women at 18th Curtis St.

15 Branch down to see and talk to Capt Morton. He called Sloan also.

21 Deputy Chiefs office states Branch will be back the 1st of May Branch says they don't know what to do with the "Greek".

24 Talked to Chief Forsthe 1 HR. Woman stated scene to Chief.

26 Meeting Chiefs office 2:00 PM Present - Chief Forsythe, Chief Williams, Capts Sloan, Girard, Morton shook Hand's Branch

MVX = 18

MPX = 1

SSX = 1

May 1950

<no entries>

MVX = 18

PFX = 2

MPX = 1

FRX = 1

June 1950

6 Saw Shirley Radovitch driving 1-94438

10 Grand Lake - Jim Andos

11 Grand Lake Jim

23 Lakeside - Frankie Carle - (MV)

26 Deposited 100 Security Life Ins Co.

28 Hot Sulphur

29 Hot Sulphur - MV

30 Hot Sulphur

MVX = 10

PFX = 2

FRX = 1

RAX = 1

July 1950

1 Hot Sulphur with Gus, Micki - MV

3 Saw Mother Louise

12 M Amos, B. Harold 20, Fitz Hosp, under age served by Gladys Levine 29, 1639 Clarkson served (2) glasses beer

13 1862 Larimer 10:15 PM Salomans Arrom Richtol 66, of 1452 Xavier in Chg. L O M - BARDI - CITO - KANOS - ETC. SEC. 64 - DISMISSED.

14 King of Clubs 12:15 AM No one in Kitchen, no food, Ice box locked. knew nothing of cutting that happen in place.

15 Bowery 12:35 AM Janet Stillman – 36 of 2217 Larimer asleep in booth, very dk, Talked to Mike Gatscous - trip to Europe.

21 11:30 PM - PHIL POOL HALL - 7 ARREST Joe prop. Rather put out.

MVX = 12

FRX = 1

RAX = 2

August 1950

7 MV Seen Dr. Frangos

11 Left Denver 5:30 AM for Cleveland, OHIO.

12 ARRIVED CLEVELAND, OHIO. 7:30 PM

14 BASEBALL CLEVELAND VS DETROIT

15 BALL GAME CLEVELAND VS. DETROIT

20 CLEVELAND OHIO LEAVING FOR NY 1:30 PM

21 Arrived N. York 7:30 Pm. Visited Auntie Bertha at Trenton N. York.

22 New York N.Y.

23 Left N. York 1:00 Pm. Wash D.C. 7:30 PM

25 Arrived in Denver from Wash D.C. 11:30 Pm

MVX = 7

PFX = 2

FRX = 1

September 1950

<no entries>

MVX = 7

PFX = 2

MPX = 1

FRX = 1

October 1950

6 Hennings started on their vacation.

11 SIGNED CONTRACT FOR SALE OF HOUSE 4:30 Pm.

MVX = 9

FRX = 2

JAX = 1

November 1950

1 Moved to 333-E-16th Ave, Apt # 708.

8 M - LEFT J. Mc - BABY GIRL BORN

23 MARY HENNING called - said they arrived Evening of 11-22-50

24 Denver Dry Goods (started), 1-9 Pm

25 Den. Dry Goods 7 HRS talked to M. Henning supposed to move 11-27-50.

27 D. D. G. 12 HRS

28 Rec. 40.00 from Henning

29 D. D. G.
30 D. D. G. - 12 Day Off
MVX = 5
PFX = 1
FRX = 2

December 1950
10 RP - 'END'.
14 Hennings moved out of house.
MVX =- 2
PFX = 1
RPX = 7

The last pages of this journal contain the first, and only, record of Steve's gambling - wagers and winnings from August 31 to October 13, 1950. Gambling was always a big part of Uncle Gus's life and on a smaller scale, it was also a part of Steve's. He visited the dog track twelve times and the horse track ten times during these six weeks - winning a total of $107.50 *but* losing $1030.00! $922.50 is a lot of money to lose!

Dog racing continued to be an important part of Steve's life for many years. During the time I lived with them, 1955-1957, he and my stepmother went to the track every single summer night. After his death, we found at the farm hundreds of programs, racing forms and ticket stubs - for tracks in Denver, Phoenix and Florida. They were neatly boxed, by year, and filled one large closet.

There are 71 entries in the ADDRESSES section. All are interesting to me, because they offer a glimpse of the city of Denver as it was a half century ago. It's interesting to see what businesses were located where, for example, and who owned what. But I've included only a small number of them here. Some relate to Steve's everyday, workaday activities and some identify significant people, girlfriends mostly, from his personal life:

ADDRESSES
R. Allen De 9073

EUGENIA BREES
#62 LINCOLN RA0435
1653 CALIFONIA #434 TA2058

BARBARA COBB

E. ROCKWELL
DDG

BOB CONNORS
1726 MARKET
SLATTERY CO
PLUMBING - WHOLESALE

Fred De Bell
3728 - W. 49th
Repairs fishing poles.

JIM DIKEOU FR – 8916 DE – 9901

Eddie Edwards
Mr. Townsend
Whitneys Sporting Goods Co.

Y E
1132 IRONTON
AURORO - 1089J

DR. FRANGOS FR – 4004

PATRICIA FRICK
1849 GROVE APT-6
DENVER 4, COLO GR 8037

Jim Kappos
3844 Mayfield Rd.
Cleveland Sta. Ohio

OLGA KATHAS
1700 Allison St. NE
Wash D.C. Adams 3910

LILLIAN NEDLABEK AL-1596
1275 PEARL #9 OFFICE - GA 5211

ROSEMARY PAULSINO
3158 - Clyde Pl. Gl. 2666

MILLIE POPOLICH
    1315 CURTIS #316

Phil Rattner
    Dave Cook Sporting Goods
    10% off on Merchandise   AL.-3434

HOWARD W. REES
    1265 LANSING
    48 Buick Sedanette 1-23758
    B. GIRL 6-5-50

FRANCES RAMIREZ
    2331 ARAPAHOE   CH. 0923
ROSE RODRIQUES
    1247 GALAPAGO   CH - 4691
    ARGONAUT COFFEE SHOP
    CITO'S GIRL FRIEND

JEAN STONE - CITO'S WIFE

7-9-50
    Betty Robertson
    STAR ROUTE BX 3A
    LITTLETON, COLO.
    Littleton 0391J5

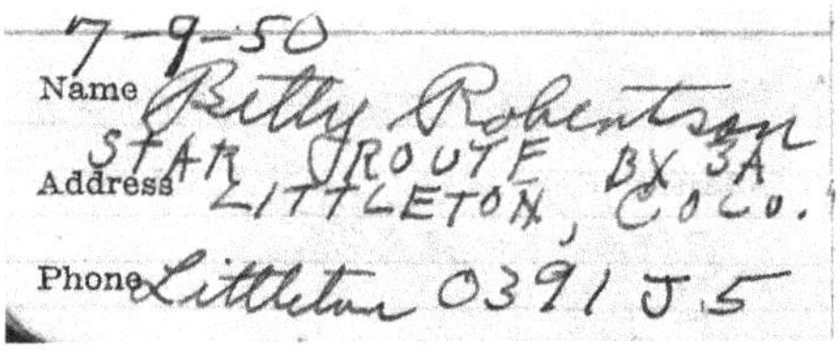

Figure 23.2 Steve's Journal with address for Betty Robertson.

SAM THREADGALE
    Work's at Winter Cigar Co. - NEGRO

Millie Valdez
    1850 Sherman   Ma. 0696

Among the "NOTES", are:

NOTES

HOUSE VAL	1941	3950	
	1942	3850	
	1943	3850	1944
4130			
	1945	4130	
	1946	4130	
	1947	4130	
	1948	4130	
	1949	4130	
	1950	4540	
Frank Stephen Allison	Born Aug. 23, 1949		

LOREN REES BRIGGS

BORN JULY 8, 1949

GIRL 6-5-50

48 Chev 1-c-9527

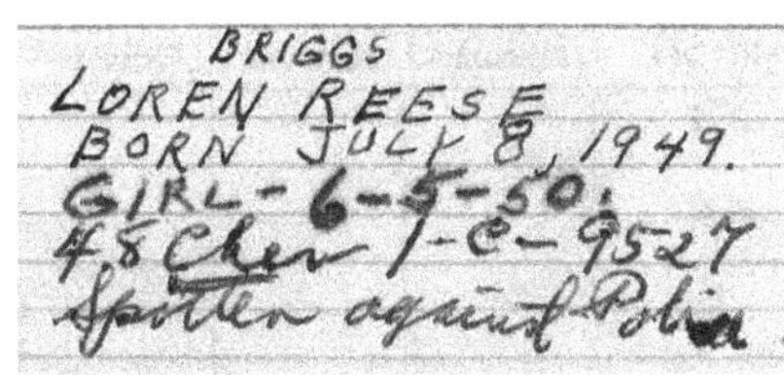
BRIGGS
LOREN REESE
BORN JULY 8, 1949.
GIRL - 6-5-50.
48 Chev 1-C-9527
Spotter against Police

Figure 23.3 Steve's Journal with address for Loren Reese.

TITSA BD. 11-25-22

KENNETH KUPKE ATTORNEY - "COMMIE" (?)

Sportcasters Monthly

Al Jeronimus

Uncle Henry

I'm still a little shocked at the number and variety of Steve's partners in intimacy – if, indeed, that's what the initials with upper case X represent. Maybe they just meant he had a date with that person? And I'm amused that he kept such a complete record of this aspect of his life. But I remind myself that I keep track of my running just as methodically and faithfully as Steve did his assignations. Perhaps it's just a strong need to keep track of the things that are important to us - a kind of recording gene or something.

It appears that he has very little emotional attachment with the women he dates. Only Millie Valdez, his main paramour, is ever mentioned in what could be considered a social context. And that was only once - when she went with Steve to Hot Sulfur Springs for a few days. He did make note that her birthday was March 27th and I'm hoping that he celebrated this day with her in some way. He also spends time with J.A., S.S., R. Allen, Patricia Frick, Lillian Nedlabek, Rosemary Paulsino, Millie Popolich, and Frances Ramirez. (I've changed the last names.)

But I don't think his heart is with any of these women. I think that, three years later, he's still in love with Helen Smith. He called her twice in March. Perhaps once was about the Don Smith who was jailed on the 24th. In a rare expression of emotion, he noted that it was being "Very hard".

In the address section under Howard W. Rees, 1265 Lansing, he notes the birth of a baby girl in June of 1950, and elsewhere in the NOTES section writes that "LOREN REESE BRIGGS" was "BORN JULY 8, 1949".

I think these are the children of Helen Smith, who had evidently married a man surnamed Rees. I went back to look at the photos of Helen holding an infant. On the back of one she had written "Loren Briggs Rees – all of these 4 weeks old taken at Briggs".

Figure 23.4 Helen Smith and baby.

I wonder why she sent these photos to Steve - long after they had broken up and she had married.

On the page noting the birth of the Rees children there's also a listing for Kenneth Kupke, attorney and "Commie". That's pretty interesting. Was Steve caught up in the "Red Scare" frenzy of the McCarthy era?

He describes other people with contemporary labels also. Sam Treadgale, of the Winter Cigar Co., is a "NEGRO". Evidently this company that did business with Grampa at the pool hall back in the 1920's - remember all the receipts? - was still in business. And we've seen that he adds the description "Mexican" to the names of certain people he deals with as a police officer. He must have felt it necessary to use such identifying adjectives - on the job especially.

Although I think he loves Helen still, he also keeps track of Yvonne - more than three years after *their* breakup. Y E lives at 1132 Ironton in Aurora, and now has a different last initial. She must have married D E, the man she was dating when last we encountered her in November of 1947.

Speaking of 1947 and of births, Steve records that a baby girl was born to J. Mc. in November of 1950. I think this might be the Jo McFadden that he dated briefly in December 1947. He also marks the birth of Cousin Chris's son, Frank Stephen on August 23, 1950.

I actually have memories of Rosemary Paulsino - very fond memories. Steve lists her address as 3158 West Clyde Place, which is only a few blocks from his home in north Denver. She lived there with her parents. She and Steve began dating in December 1950 and I can recall being at her home on several occasions.

Sometimes she and her mother would let me help them make pasta. The memory is crystal clear and involves smell and touch as well as sight...

> *The table and counters are covered with flour and dough. We use a knife to cut some kinds of pasta and a wire apparatus to cut others. We hang the pasta to dry on what resembles clothes drying racks. These racks are placed throughout the house because there's no room for them in the kitchen. I don't remember eating the pasta, only making it.*

Rosemary and her family were very nice to me. And Rosemary was as pretty as she was nice. She was a vibrant Italian woman, with dark hair and red lips. Steve was very happy when they were together.

Steve's journal for 1950 would lead one to believe that he had never a thought for his daughter the entire year. He never mentions her.

But I'm remembering differently. Jogged by my memories of being with Rosemary and Steve, I'm also just now remembering spending time with him at his apartment at 333 E. 16 Ave. - where he moved after selling the house on

Grove Street. I liked it there. It smelled of leather, pipe tobacco and books - the walls were lined with books.

That's good - he did see Linda Lee occasionally. He just didn't write about it.

And the address section lists the name of Betty Robertson! I went to live with Betty and her family sometime in 1949, when I was five years old. I was with them at their Denver home for a while before we moved to the country - according to the address notation - on July 9, 1950. Betty and Bill Robertson took me into their home and made me a part of their family. Betty changed my life - in fact, she probably saved my life.

Yes, it's all coming back to me now, as they say. I'm thinking that, even though Steve left very little information about the whereabouts of his daughter from 1948-1950, I'll be able to remember most of the chronology on my own.

And here's something else that will definitely help. I've rediscovered L.L.'s baby book. When it first surfaced at the farm, I put it up to look at later when things were calmer - and then forgot about it. A few weeks ago while looking for Chris's and Jay's baby books, I found it with theirs. *Another artifact surfaces.* We'll look through it soon. It'll help fill in those parts of the story left untold by Steve.

But first, a quick review of his 1950 journal highlights:

- Problems arise on the job during the first part of the year. On February 23 Steve reports that, "Branch put own ticket on his car." I'm not sure what this refers to, but it portends big trouble for the near future.

Since Steve never mentions patrol car assignments, I'm assuming that he's once again *walking* the beat in lower downtown Denver these days. Was that a demotion? Did he have a partner? And if so, was that Branch?

On March 28 he writes, "Deputy Chief Williams notified me I would go to Dist. #1 the first. Branch to be moved. <u>I would be blamed."</u>

Two days later, "Branch Still very mad. Capt. Sloan says I'll be on detail (His) for April. After that he wouldn't bet money on it."

The problem is still unresolved in April. On the 15th, "Branch down to see and talk to Capt. Morton."

On the 21st he learns that "Branch will be back the 1st of MAY" and that "Branch says they don't know what to do with the 'Greek'".

On the 24th Steve "Talked to Chief Forsthe 1 HR Woman stated scene to Chief."

Things come to a head on April 26 when there is a "Meeting Chiefs office 2:00 PM. Present Chief Forsythe - Chief Williams, Capts Sloan, Girard, Morton. Shook Hands Branch"

- In another job related happening, also in April, "(2) men disguised as women at 18 Curtis St." What's that all about? Police decoys? Con men? Transvestites?
- Shirley "Radovitch" is spotted driving "1-94938" in June. My brothers Dave and Marty had joined her and Max by this date - and Sister Kate was on the way.
- In July, "LOMBARDI - CITO - KANOS - ETC. SEC. 64 - DISMISSED."

These must have been police officers. One is listed in the address section of Steve's journal, along with the names and telephone numbers of his wife *and* his girlfriend. Another busy policeman.

- In July Steve mentions a possible trip to Europe. Nothing ever came of these plans. He never left the United States, as far as I know.
- Before leaving for a long road trip in August, Steve makes note of Millie V.'s visit to Dr. Frangos.
- He spends three days in Cleveland. Titsa told me that she, her brother and my dad drove "back east" to attend a Greek convention at about this time; and that they stopped en route so Steve could "meet" his mother. But, Titsa recalled, his mother "wouldn't see him." Maybe this was that trip - although he sure doesn't mention traveling companions, a convention or anything about his mother. But perhaps this was the time of which Titsa speaks. In The Box, along with the other items Steve placed there for me to find, was a photo of a group of people "at our picnic grounds and lakes" as is noted on back. Also on back is a diagram of the people and their positions in the photo. The woman seated second from left in the front row is identified as "your mother". I think this must be Steve's mother (Minnie, Margaret, Louise?) at about this time. Did a compassionate relative send this to him after his mother had chosen not to see him? We'll never know.

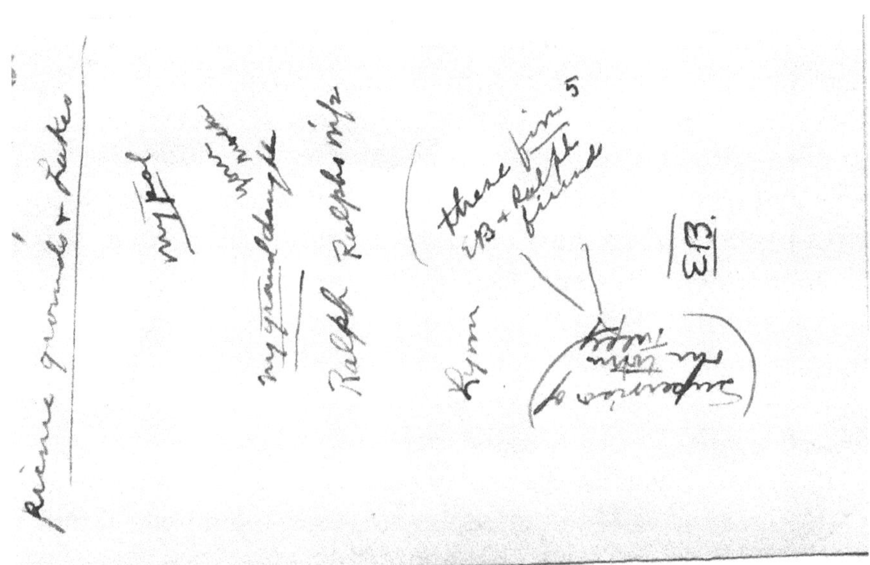

Figure 23.5 Family gathering in Ohio.

He does mention the baseball games he attended in Cleveland. In fact, he brings his dad back a souvenir program from one of the games. Remember that? John saved it, along with the postcard that his son sent him from Cleveland at this time.

Later in the trip, Steve visits Auntie Bertha in Trenton, New York. Is this the same Aunt Bertha he had visited in Sutherland, Kansas a few years ago - the one related to Helen Smith?

- And then, in the fall, shortly after his fortieth birthday, Steve sells the Grove Street house. According to his notes, it was valued at $4540.00. I wonder if he was forced to sell it because of gambling debts? It's during this period of time that he lost approximately 1/4 of this amount at the dog and horse races.

Good-bye to the house that his father and uncle had purchased more than twenty years before. Good-bye to the house that Shirley had tried so valiantly to keep clean and "straightened" in her days of playing married to Steve Allison. And good-bye to the house where *he'd* tried, in vain, to make a home for himself and his baby daughter. On November 1st he moves to 333 E. 16th Ave., Apt. 708.

- He moonlights as a security person at the Denver Dry Goods Co. for the after Thanksgiving shopping rush but not during the Christmas season.

At first I thought the final entry of this year's journal, was a Christmas cards received list. But on closer inspection of "XMAS 1950", I wonder if it records something else. No family or friends are listed, only the businesses on his police beat. Perhaps he was keeping track of another type of Christmas greeting. Longtime Denverites will recognize many of these businesses:

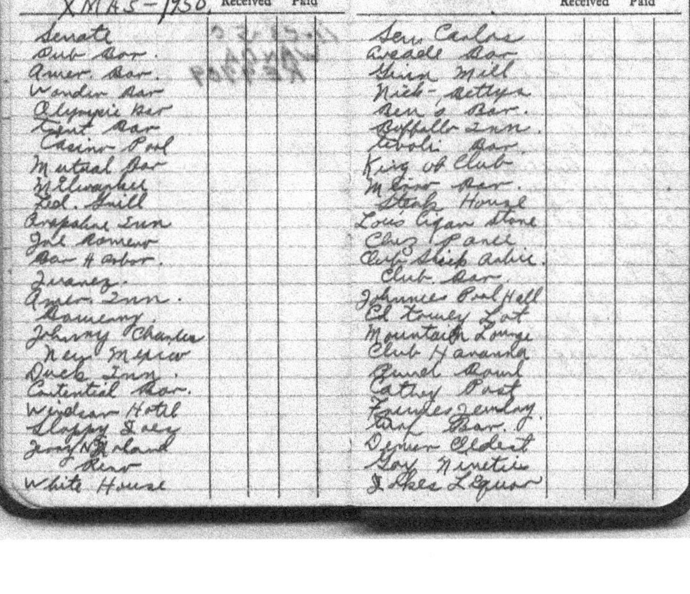

Figure 23.6 Final entry in Steve's 1950 Journal.

Senate*
Sub Bar
Amer Bar
Wonder Bar
Olympic Bar
Tent Bar
Casino Pool
Mutual Bar
Milwaukee
Fed. Bar
Arapahoe Inn
Joe Romero
Bar Harbor
Quanez
Amer. Inn
Bomenny
Johnny Charles
New Mexico
Duck Inn
Contential Bar
Windsor Hotel
Sloppy Joes
Jerry Noland
Reno
White House
Sam Carlos
Meade Bar
Ginn Mill
Nick - Bettys
Ben's Bar
Buffallo Inn
Tivoli Bar
King of Club
Mirro Bar
Steak House
Lou's Cigar Store
Chez Ponce
Club Shiek Arbic
Club Bar
Johnnies Pool Hall
Ed Towey Lot
Mountain Lounge

Club Havanna

Punel Bowl

Cathey Post*

Frances Jenlay

Turf Bar

Denver Oldest

Gay Nineties

Jakes Liquor

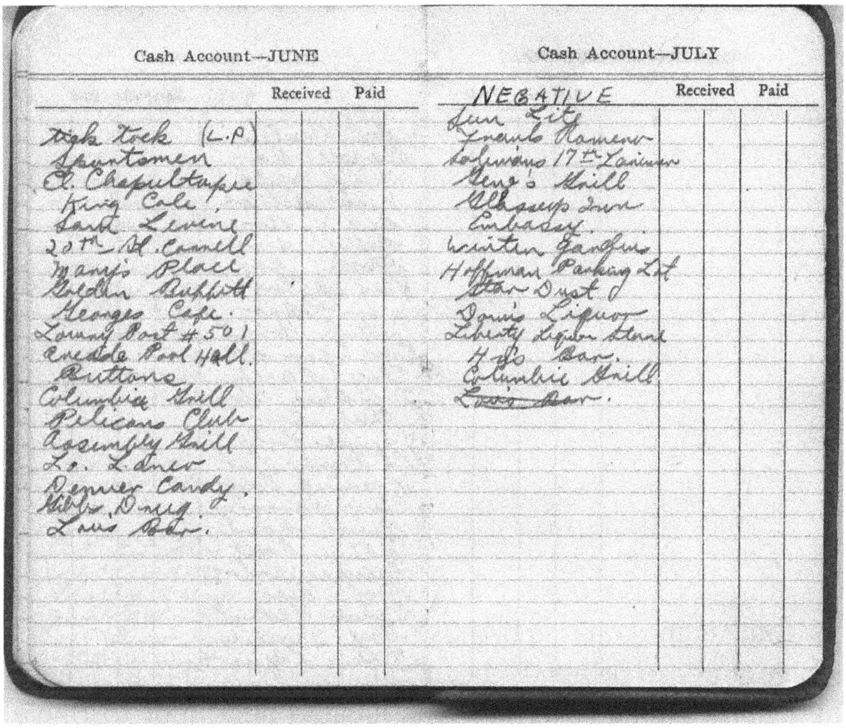

Figure 23.7 Final entry in Steve's 1950 Journal.

tick tock (L.P.)

Sportsmen

El. Chapultepec*

King Cole

Sam Levine

20th St. Connell

Mary's Place

Golden Buffet

Georges Cafe

Lowry Post # 501

Aveide Pool Hall
Buttons
Columbia Grill
Pelicans Club
Assembly Grill
Lo. Laveo*
Denver Candy
Gibbs Drug
Lou's Bar

NEGATIVE
Sun Lite
Frank Romero
Solimans 17th Larimer
Gene's Grill
Glassup Inn
Embassy
Winter Gardins
Hoffman Parking Lot
Star Dust
Davis Liquor
Liberty Liquor
Hy's Bar
Columbine Grill

*About some names on this list:

- Sophie Doronzo Bringoff - the infamous, soon to appear, Steppy - owned the *Senate* Lounge. Her bar was located next door to Uncle Frank's parking lot - which was across the street from his candy store. She'll become Steve's fourth wife in 1955.
- Sophie's aunt, *Lo. Laveo*, owned a bail bond company in the same area. Aunt Louise, also, will one day figure prominently in Linda Lee's life.
- *El Chapultapec*, which has long been a highly regarded gathering place for jazz enthusiasts, is still doing a great business; and I think *Cathey Post* is still serving up Chinese food.

And that's all he wrote.

Well, almost. Two pages, torn from a small notebook, are all that remain in The Box. They contain notations which we'll look at closer - later, written by Steve in 1958. Otherwise, this *is* the end of his self-documented history - the end of Steve's story as told by Steve.

By writing in his journals and by saving them for me in The Box, along with the other items found there, he made it possible for me to understand the logistics of those years of our lives. But even more importantly, these things let me come know the *person* of my father - something I never knew during his lifetime.

Time did, in fact, make many things clear.

Actually - except for the LL's baby book - this is the end of the story as revealed through artifacts found at the farm.

And so - to the baby book. Before relying on my own memories to bring the story to a close, a look through this childhood record will reveal, I think, a lot about the heart and soul of the baby's father.

We'll leave Steve then, as he looks forward to 1951 - and follow his daughter through her first six years, until *she too* arrives at New Year's Day 1951.

"TIME MAKE ALL THINGS CLEAR"

Steve's journal - 1950.

SECTION
- IV -

LINDA LEE ALLISON

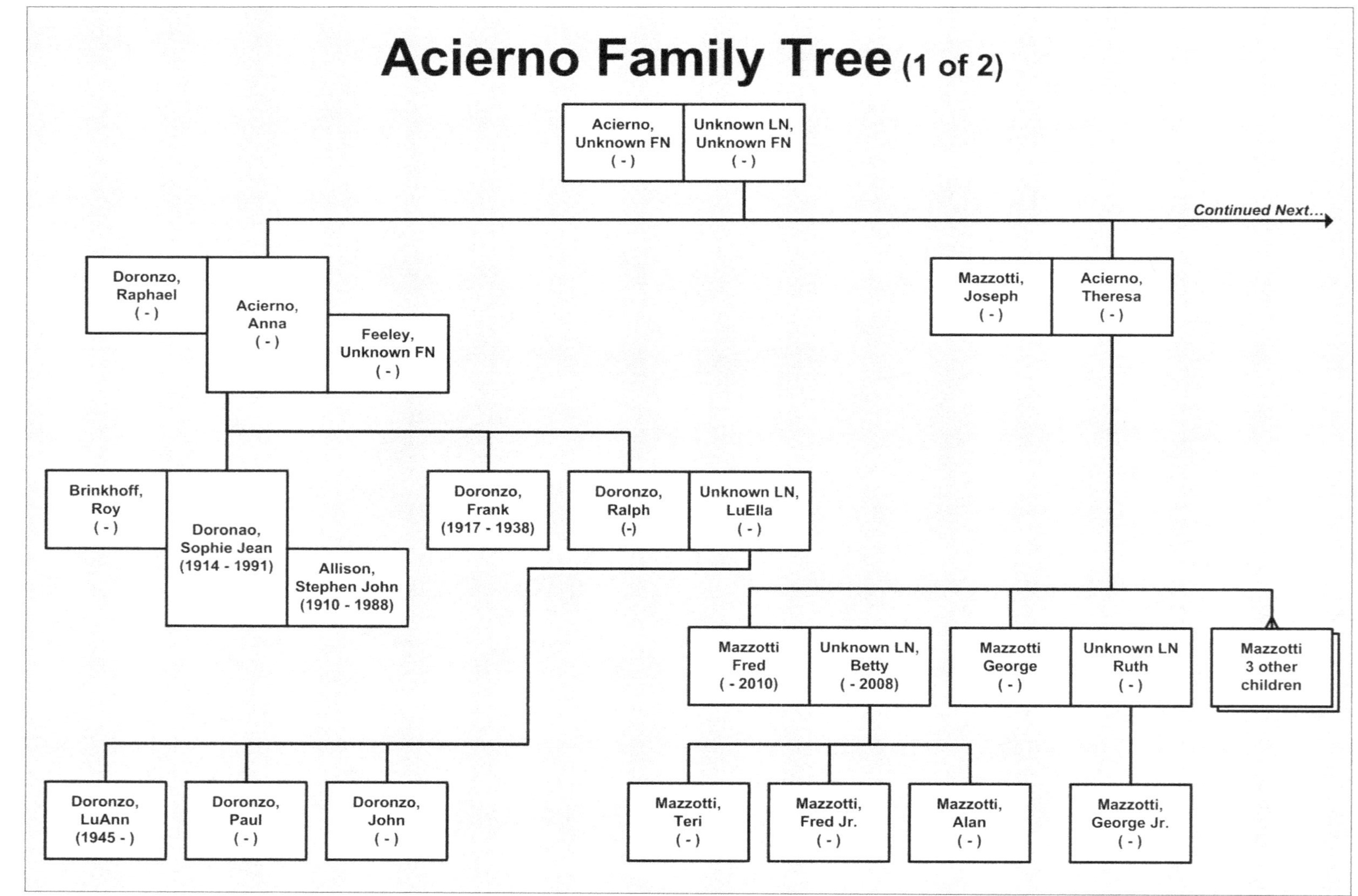
Acierno Family Tree (1 of 2)
Acierno, Unknown FN (-)
Unknown LN, Unknown FN (-)
Continued Next...
Doronzo, Raphael (-)
Acierno, Anna (-)
Feeley, Unknown FN (-)
Mazzotti, Joseph (-)
Acierno, Theresa (-)
Brinkhoff, Roy (-)
Doronao, Sophie Jean (1914 - 1991)
Allison, Stephen John (1910 - 1988)
Doronzo, Frank (1917 - 1938)
Doronzo, Ralph (-)
Unknown LN, LuElla (-)
Mazzotti Fred (- 2010)
Unknown LN, Betty (- 2008)
Mazzotti George (-)
Unknown LN Ruth (-)
Mazzotti 3 other children
Doronzo, LuAnn (1945 -)
Doronzo, Paul (-)
Doronzo, John (-)
Mazzotti, Teri (-)
Mazzotti, Fred Jr. (-)
Mazzotti, Alan (-)
Mazzotti, George Jr. (-)

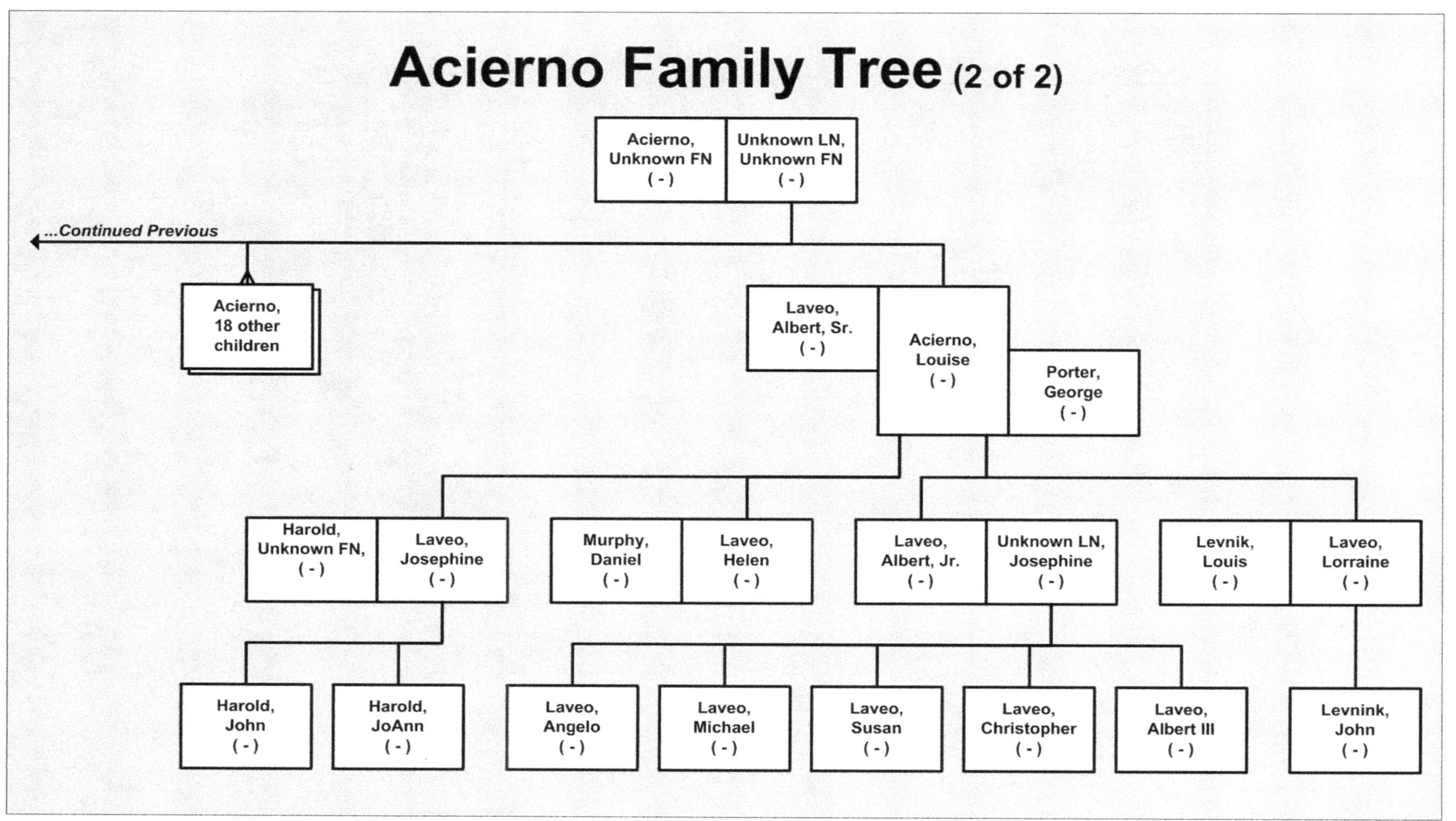

Acierno Family Tree (2 of 2)
Acierno, Unknown FN (-)
Unknown LN, Unknown FN (-)
...Continued Previous
Acierno, 18 other children
Laveo, Albert, Sr. (-)
Acierno, Louise (-)
Porter, George (-)
Harold, Unknown FN, (-)
Laveo, Josephine (-)
Murphy, Daniel (-)
Laveo, Helen (-)
Laveo, Albert, Jr. (-)
Unknown LN, Josephine (-)
Levnik, Louis (-)
Laveo, Lorraine (-)
Harold, John (-)
Harold, JoAnn (-)
Laveo, Angelo (-)
Laveo, Michael (-)
Laveo, Susan (-)
Laveo, Christopher (-)
Laveo, Albert III (-)
Levnink, John (-)

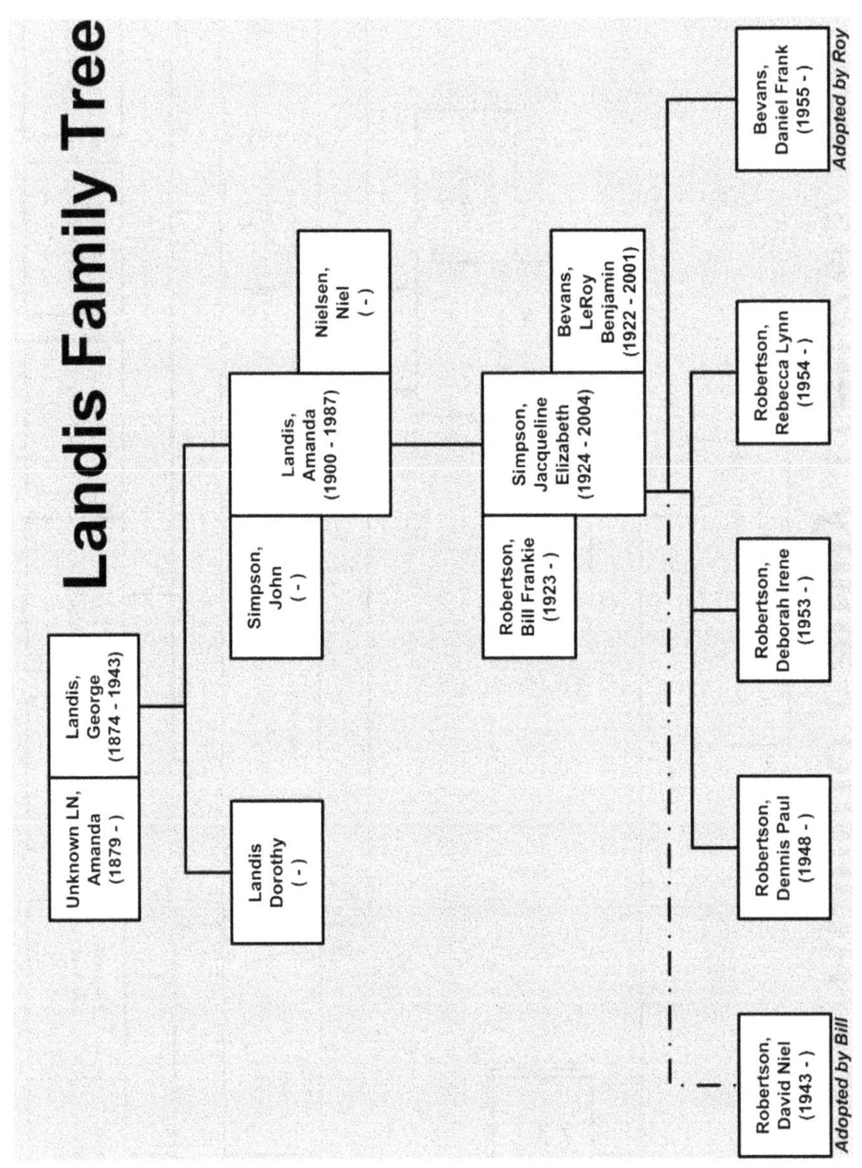
Landis Family Tree
Unknown LN, Amanda (1879 -)
Landis, George (1874 - 1943)
Landis Dorothy (-)
Simpson, John (-)
Landis, Amanda (1900 - 1987)
Nielsen, Niel (-)
Robertson, Bill Frankie (1923 -)
Simpson, Jacqueline Elizabeth (1924 - 2004)
Bevans, LeRoy Benjamin (1922 - 2001)
Robertson, David Niel (1943 -)
Adopted by Bill
Robertson, Dennis Paul (1948 -)
Robertson, Deborah Irene (1953 -)
Robertson, Rebecca Lynn (1954 -)
Bevans, Daniel Frank (1955 -)
Adopted by Roy

CHAPTER 24

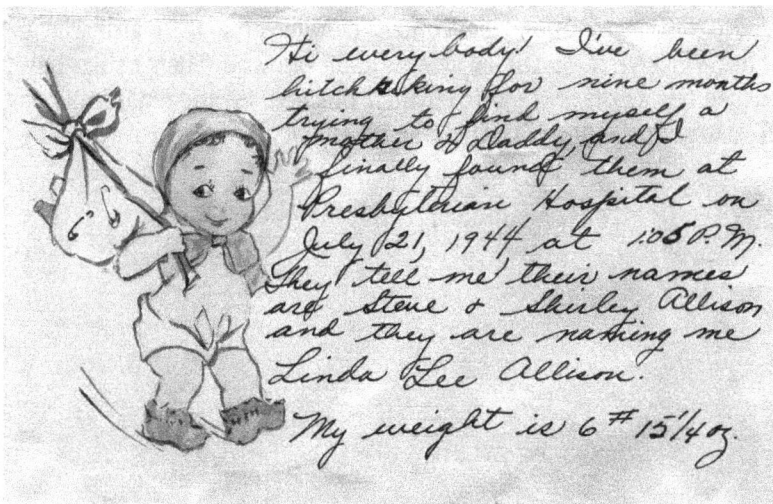

Hi everybody! I've been hitchhiking for nine months trying to find myself a Mother & Daddy, and I finally found them at Presbyterian Hospital on July 21, 1944 at 1:05 P.M. They tell me their names are Steve & Shirley Allison and they are naming me Linda Lee Allison.

My weight is 6# 15 1/4 oz.

"a good romp"

Our Baby's First Seven Years was published by the Mothers' Aid of the Chicago Lying-In Hospital in 1928, and was revised in 1941. It contains the story of my first two years, and is well traveled. Since I have no memories of these first few years, in this chapter I have decided to refer to myself in the third-person. Hopefully, this more accurately conveys my feelings of discovering the details of my early life. It makes my heart ache to realize that Steve made sure it accompanied his daughter as she made the rounds of caregivers. He tried so hard to bring some consistency and stability to her chaotic life.

And gosh, Shirley actually made a pretty good start at keeping this book. I didn't give her enough credit it seems. I had assumed that her postpartum depression, or whatever it was, had kicked in right away - dampening any interest she might have had in her daughter, even in the very beginning. But obviously not.

Here are some of the things that Shirley wrote, and some of the items that she saved, in this book:

- **SNAPSHOT**

  This snapshot is of three pregnant women, one of whom is Shirley.

  They're standing beneath a flowering tree, and Shirley has blossoms in her hair. They have their arms around each other. They look like little girls who are fat. Their dresses have little capped sleeves and - *waists*. Their bellies have simply pushed the waists way up under their breasts. Strange maternity clothes. Shirley's wearing loafers with anklets. It's an adorable picture.

Figure 24.1 Pregnant Shirley and friends.

➤ BABY'S BIRTH

Linda Lee Allison was born on Friday the 21st day of July, 1944 at 1:05 O'clock P.M. at Presbyterian Hospital City Denver County Denver State Colorado

Father - Stephen John Allison

Mother - Shirley Johnson Allison

Doctor - Jack Butterfield

Color of eyes - Brown (Were dark brown when born, instead of being blue and turning brown.)

Complexion - Fair. At six months Linda Lee's complexion was olive, like her Daddy's.

Shirley writes that the baby is "'tongue-tied, Dr. Butterfield cut it September 28th".

On August 4, 1944, the doctor writes that "L.L. is a very tiny baby".

➢ A BIRTH ANNOUNCEMENT

Shirley's neighbor, Flossie, made them - remember? A hitchhiking baby, carrying a knapsack on a stick, is drawn by hand on the front. The baby wears a pink bonnet - which Shirley must have colored in after the birth (see image at the beginning of this Chapter).

➢ CONGRATULATORY CARD AND LETTER

Enclosed with the congratulatory card was a letter from "Aunt Vista and Gloria". Seems they've moved, and now "have 5 rooms all on one floor and have no furnace to tend to. We have hot water heat, heated by gas and all I have to do is set the thermostat."

➢ NEWSPAPER CLIPPING

Shirley pasted this announcement:

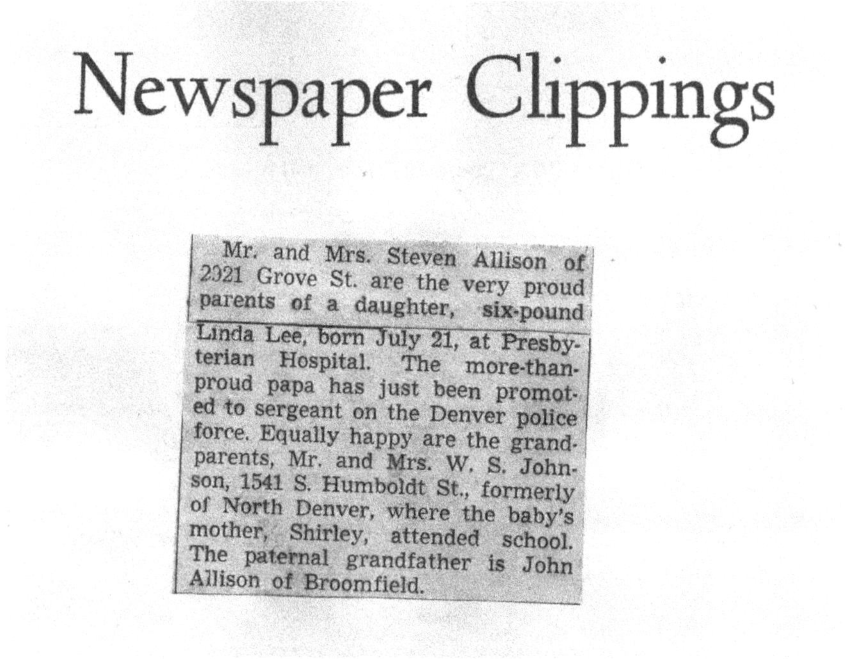

Newspaper Clippings

Mr. and Mrs. Steven Allison of 2321 Grove St. are the very proud parents of a daughter, six-pound Linda Lee, born July 21, at Presbyterian Hospital. The more-than-proud papa has just been promoted to sergeant on the Denver police force. Equally happy are the grandparents, Mr. and Mrs. W. S. Johnson, 1541 S. Humboldt St., formerly of North Denver, where the baby's mother, Shirley, attended school. The paternal grandfather is John Allison of Broomfield.

Figure 24.2 Newspaper clipping announcing Linda Lee's arrival.

➢ PETS

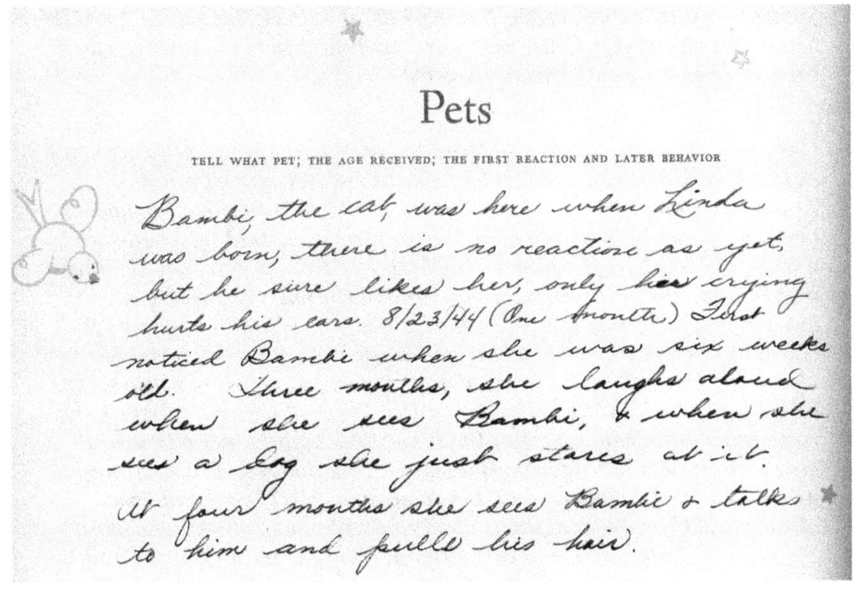

Pets

TELL WHAT PET; THE AGE RECEIVED; THE FIRST REACTION AND LATER BEHAVIOR

Bambi, the cat, was here when Linda was born, there is no reaction as yet, but he sure likes her, only her crying hurts his ears. 8/23/44 (One month) First noticed Bambi when she was six weeks old. Three months, she laughs aloud when she sees Bambi, & when she sees a dog she just stares at it. At four months she sees Bambi & talks to him and pulls his hair.

Figure 24.3 Information about pets.

Bambi, the cat, was here when Linda was born, there is not a reaction as yet, but he sure likes her, only her crying hurts his ears. - First noticed Bambi when she was six weeks old. - Three months, she laughs aloud when she sees Bambi, and when she sees a dog she just stares at it. - At four months she sees Bambi and talks to him and pulls his hair.

➢ TRIPS

Linda Lee is very good wherever and however you take her. Morrison, Colorado when three weeks old. Went to library and to 32nd Ave in buggy when one month old. Rode streetcar to Idella's at 5 weeks. Went down to depot to see Grandpa Johnson off when 5 1/2 weeks. Stayed one week at Butterfields' Oct. 22, till Oct. 29, 1944.

➢ HOLIDAYS

Spent her first Thanksgiving Day, November 23, `44 at Uncle Gus and Aunt Micki's house. Was very good girl. Also went over to see Hearld and Ruth Spiva and the boys. She was four months and two days old.

Christmas Eve, Grandma and Grandpa Johnson, and we Allison's went out to dinner and to a show, then came home and opened presents. Linda loved the Christmas tree that Doctor Jack Butterfield brought her. She got a big pink and blue elephant from her Daddy; a little lamb, a white snowsuit, a jumping swing and a new dress from her Mommy and Daddy. From Grandma and Grandpa she got a rag doll; pink sweater set; two pink and blue hangers made by Grandma, as was the rag doll; three pairs socks; a blue and white chenille robe. From Aunt Micki and Uncle Gus she received a pair of shoes; a pair of white socks, a blue bonnet with little gloves to match. From The Frank Allison's she recieved a blue kimona. From Uncle bob and Aunt Esther a beautiful blue blanket. From Professor Matsyama, Five dollars, From Grandpa Allison $2.50. Christmas day, Linda spent at Uncle Gus and Aunt Micki's and Christmas night at The Frank Allisons, where her cousin Steve called from San Francisco, after arriving from the South Pacific.

Now here's a weird thing. The page on Personal Habits says:

"Bowel control – Training began 2 months. Uses trainer almost always by three ½ months".

What the heck is a trainer, and why would anyone make a two-month old baby use it?

➢ SNAPSHOT

Tucked between the pages here is snapshot of Shirley with her arms around my dad's cousins, Georgia and Titsa. I'm not sure why Shirley placed it here, but it must have made sense to her.

Figure 24.4 Shirley (middle), Georgia (left) and Titsa (right).

➢ HOMES

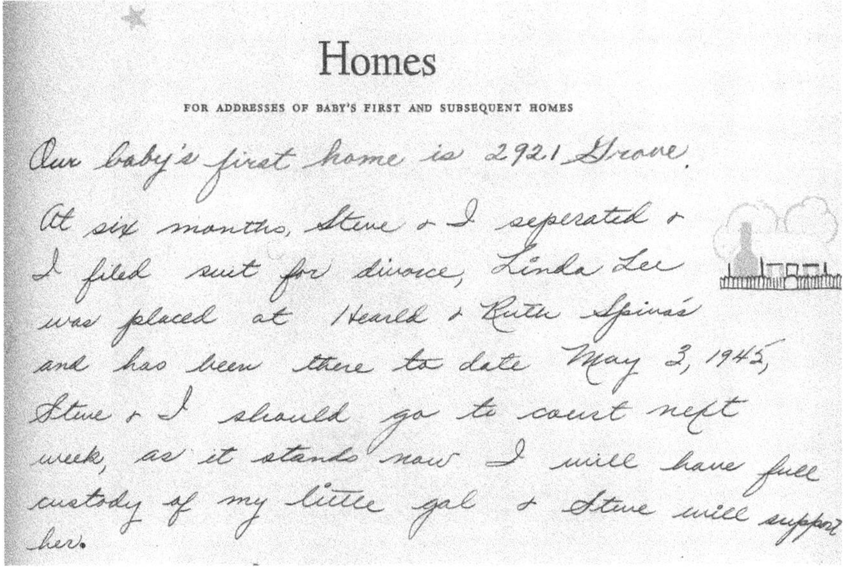

Homes

FOR ADDRESSES OF BABY'S FIRST AND SUBSEQUENT HOMES

Our baby's first home is 2921 Grove.

At six months, Steve & I seperated & I filed suit for divorce, Linda Lee was placed at Hearld & Ruth Spina's and has been there to date May 3, 1945, Steve & I should go to court next week, as it stands now I will have full custody of my little gal & Steve will support her.

Figure 24.5 Information about homes.

This first entry by Shirley will be followed by two other entries by subsequent caretakeres.

> *Our baby's first home is 2921 Grove.*
>
> *At six months, Steve & I seperated & I filed suit for divorce, Linda Lee was placed at Herald & Ruth Spiva's and has been there to date May 3, 1945, Steve & I should go to court next week, as it stands now I will have full custody of my little gal & Steve will support her.*

At six months, Linda Lee is now living with the Spiva family.. I found this photo of her, at about this age, with my father's things at the farm.

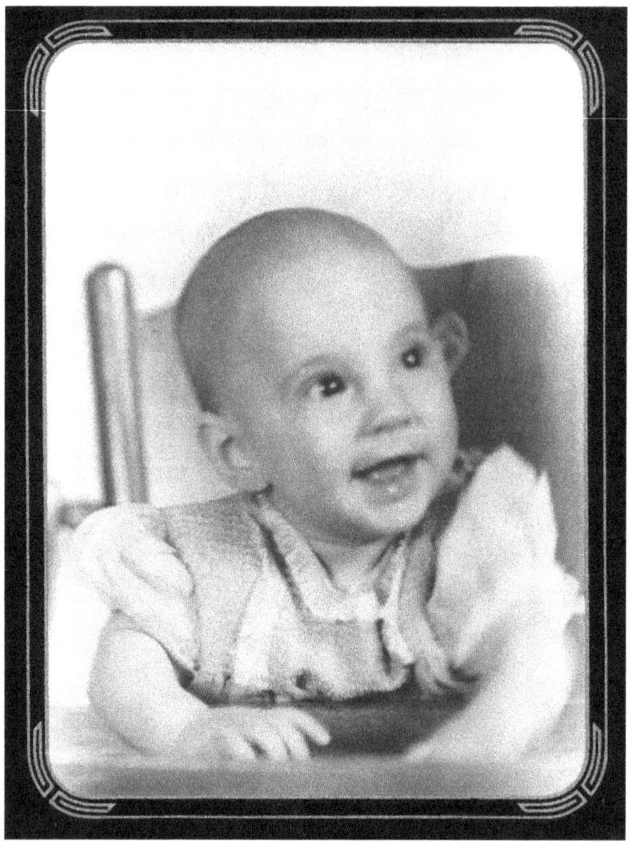

Figure 24.6 Linda at six months.

➢ PHYSICAL AND MENTAL DEVELOPMENT

Until her last entry, written on Linda's first birthday, Shirley wrote conscientiously and faithfully in this baby book. Again, I'm surprised. She must have paid close attention to her baby during these first months. All the sections - Record of Growth, New Foods, Physical and Mental Development,Talking, etc. are completed in great detail. For example, she writes that:

At one month Linda Lee "*Lifts head and turns it to either side then on her tummy*".

At two months she "*inspects own hand in play*".

At four months she "Puts rattle and every thing else in her mouth."

Even after Linda's gone to live with the Spivas, Shirley writes that:

At ten months she, "*Walks holding on to furniture. Says MaMa, DaDa. Imitates coughing and clearing throat. Waved bye bye on May 5, 1945.*"

"*Walked at 11 Months by her self*"

At a year "*says Bow-Wow, Kitty, Bye Bye*".

➢ A MOTHER'S DAY CARD

It is titled "To Daughter on Mother's Day" and is signed "Love, Mommy". Did Shirley bring this Mother's Day card on the May 5, 1945 visit? It was included in the baby book at this page. Linda Lee must have waved bye-bye when her mother left.

Figure 24.7 Mother's Day Card.

➢ FAMILY TREE

Shirley completed the Family Tree:

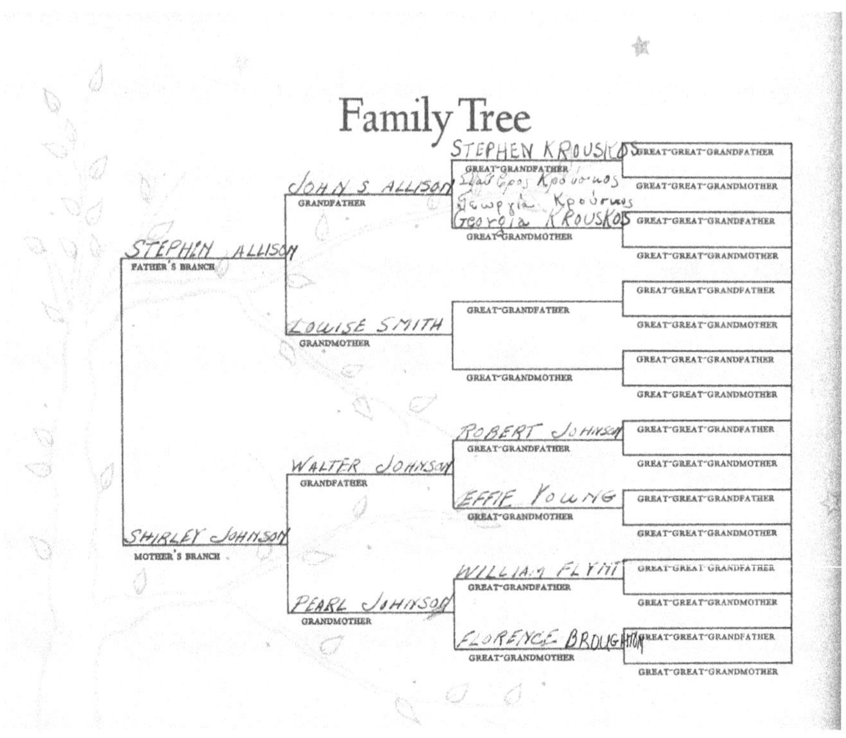

Figure 24.8 Linda Lee's Family Tree.

Who in the heck is Louise Smith? First, my stepmother told me that my paternal grandmother was named *Margaret.* Then, I found a marriage certificate for John and *Minnie.* And now this - *Louise* Smith! I'm remembering an entry in Steve's 1950 journal that now takes on new possibilities - "Saw Mother Louise". Was Steve's mother Minnie Novack or Louise Smith? And if she was Louise - did he see her in 1950?

The names of Georgia and Stephen Krouskos are written in both English and in Greek.

➢ PHOTO

With this family tree is a photo of Shirley's father as a young man.

Figure 24.9 Shirley's father, Walter Johnson.

- **BACK COVER**

The last writing by Shirley in this book is found inside the back cover. She wrote "Joe Danos".

Earlier this week, Shirley and I were at Common Grounds Coffeehouse at 32nd and Lowell. She and Steve used to walk to this corner from their house to buy ice cream, those many years ago. Hoping she could help me with some questions I had about the baby book, I'd brought it along.

Joe Danos, she said, was a friend of Idella's whom she'd dated after she and Steve separated. He was, she went on to say, a kind and thoughtful person who was particularly good to his mother - a woman with eight children, and many husbands.

While leafing through it, she came across the name of Professor Matsyama. He'd given Linda Lee $5.00 at Christmas in 1944, which was listed under **Gifts**. She told me an interesting story about this man and her father. It seems that Bud had strongly opposed the interment of Japanese Americans during World War II. By convincing the authorities that Professor Matsyama was indispensable in his position as a martial arts teacher at the Denver Police Department, Bud had negotiated his release. The professor then lived with Bud and Pearl for some years during the war years. Way to go, Bud.

Hoping to clear up some of the mystery surrounding Steve's mother, I asked her about Louise Smith. Although she'd written this name on the family tree, Shirley knew nothing about her. And she'd never even *heard* of Minnie Novack. So, no help there.

And, with that conversation, my mom's involvement with the baby book comes to an end. As always, we had a nice visit. She's an interesting, up-beat, fun person and I like spending time with her.

Linda lived with nine different familes in her first six years. I've numbered these homes as they occur throughout this Chapter.

Steve's journals tell much about the first three of these placements.

1. <u>The Allison Family – six months</u>

2. <u>The Spiva Family – three months</u>

3. <u>Mary Zinn at Steve's house – one month.</u>
   Neither Mrs. Spiva nor Mrs. Zinn recorded anything in the baby book.

4. <u>The Spalding family – seven months</u>

A few days before her first birthday, she went to live with the Spalding family, and stayed there for seven months. I don't know how Steve found them. I do know that, for baby Linda, it was a lucky placement. My heart is filled with gratitude to them. Mrs. Spalding added many comments to Linda's book. I've included only a few, but I think they make evident her kindness and loving ways:

- **HOMES**

At 11 months Linda Lee moved into the Spalding household at 1039 East 13th Ave. Seems quite happy in her new home with her two little playmates - Doug and Gary.

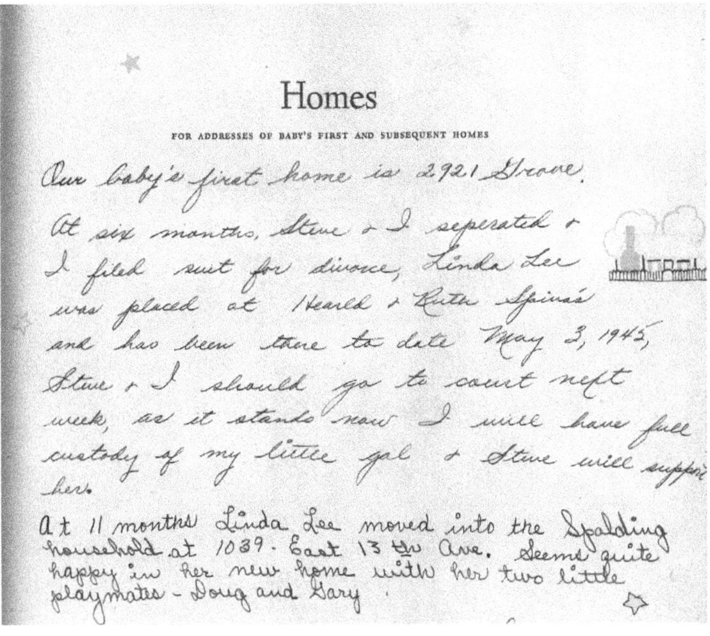

Homes

FOR ADDRESSES OF BABY'S FIRST AND SUBSEQUENT HOMES

Our baby's first home is 2921 Grove.

At six months, Steve & I seperated & I filed suit for divorce, Linda Lee was placed at Hearld & Ruth Spina's and has been there to date May 3, 1945, Steve & I should go to court next week, as it stands now I will have full custody of my little gal & Steve will supp her.

At 11 months Linda Lee moved into the Spalding household at 1039 - East 13 th Ave. Seems quite happy in her new home with her two little playmates - Doug and Gary.

Figure 24.10 Mrs. Spalding's information about homes.

With Steve's things at the farm, I found these photos of Doug and Gary Spalding and their new playmate Linda Lee:

Figure 24.11 Linda Lee with playmates Doug and Gary Spalding.

Figure 24.12 Linda Lee, Gary and Doug outside home on 13th Avenue.

➢ IDENTIFICATION MARKS

Has a small brown mole on the right side of her neck. Very definitely a beauty mark!

➢ BABY'S FIRST MEDICAL EXAMINATIONS

7/20/45 *One year - Dr. Butterfield*

Complete yearly check. Perfect health and weight.

Mrs. Spalding records that Linda Lee received inoculations on July 20, July 28 and August 10, 1945. I think it was probably she who encouraged Steve to have this done, since they began the day Linda came to live with her. According to a reminder letter from the health department found in the baby book at this page, these inoculations were already six months overdue.

➢ GROWTH OF VOCABULARY

'Oh My!' *July 22, 1945*

➢ ONE YEAR OLD

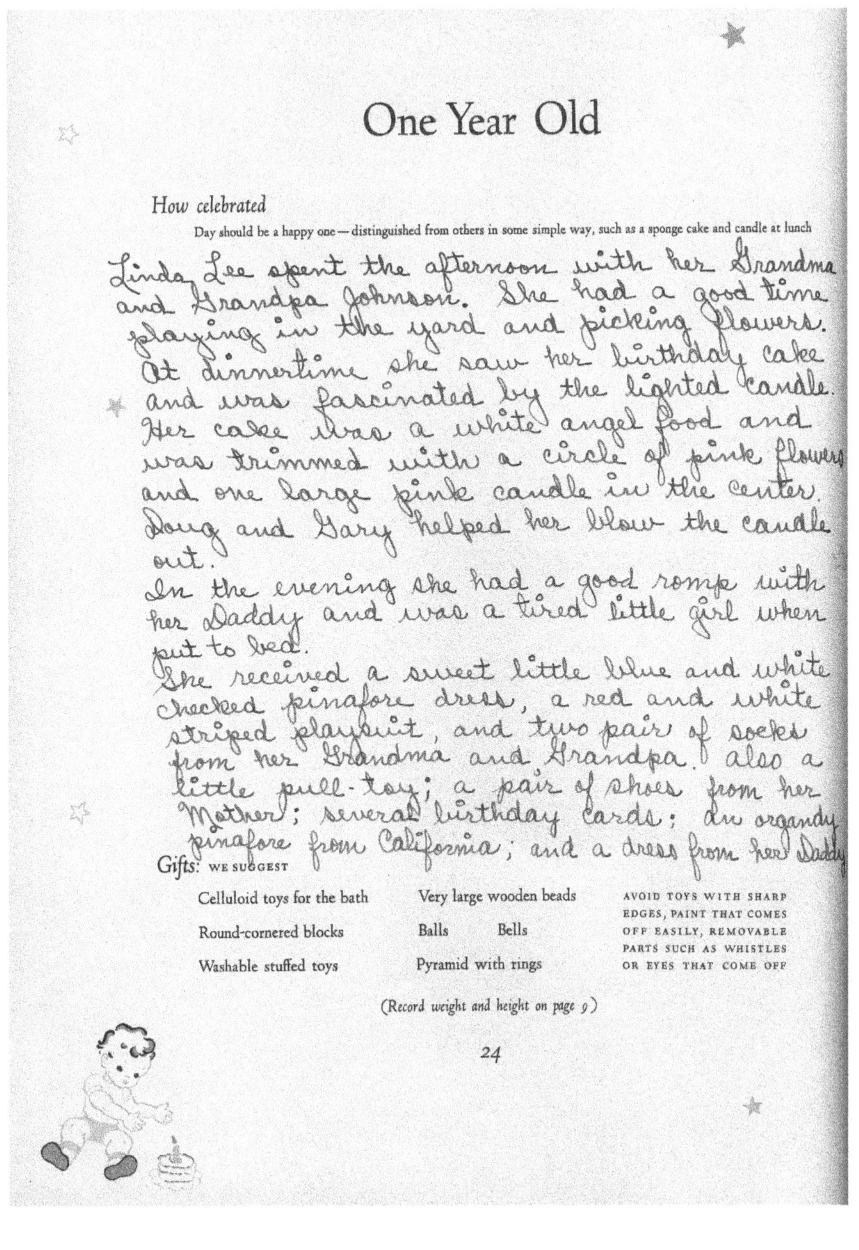

One Year Old

How celebrated

Day should be a happy one—distinguished from others in some simple way, such as a sponge cake and candle at lunch

Linda Lee spent the afternoon with her Grandma and Grandpa Johnson. She had a good time playing in the yard and picking flowers. At dinnertime she saw her birthday cake and was fascinated by the lighted candle. Her cake was a white angel food and was trimmed with a circle of pink flowers and one large pink candle in the center. Doug and Gary helped her blow the candle out.

In the evening she had a good romp with her Daddy and was a tired little girl when put to bed.

She received a sweet little blue and white checked pinafore dress, a red and white striped playsuit, and two pair of socks from her Grandma and Grandpa. also a little pull-toy; a pair of shoes from her Mother; several birthday cards; an organdy pinafore from California; and a dress from her Daddy

Gifts: WE SUGGEST

Celluloid toys for the bath	Very large wooden beads	AVOID TOYS WITH SHARP EDGES, PAINT THAT COMES OFF EASILY, REMOVABLE PARTS SUCH AS WHISTLES OR EYES THAT COME OFF
Round-cornered blocks	Balls Bells	
Washable stuffed toys	Pyramid with rings	

(*Record weight and height on page 9*)

24

Figure 24.13 Information about Linda Lee's 1st birthday.

Linda Lee spent the afternoon with her Grandma and Grandpa Johnson. She had a good time playing in the yard and picking flowers. At dinnertime she saw her birthday cake and was fascinated by the lighted candle. Her cake was a white angel food and was trimmed with a circle of pink flowers and one large pink candle in the center. Doug and Gary helped her blow the candle out.

In the evening she had a good romp with her Daddy and was a tired little girl when put to bed.

She received a sweet little blue and white checked pinafore dress, a red and white striped playsuit, and two pair of socks from her Grandma and Grandpa. Also a little pull-toy, a pair of shoes from her Mother; several birthday cards; an organdy pinafore from California; and a dress from her Daddy.

➢ PHYSICAL AND MENTAL DEVELOPMENT

Walks alone at a year - Very good balance.

➢ FAVORITE TOYS

Rag doll - 11 months. She can toss it around with no ill effects to the doll or herself.

This must have been the homemade rag doll Grandma and Grandpa Johnson gave Linda on her first Christmas.

➢ DEVELOPMENT OF SELF-HELP

Takes off stockings - one year.

➤ LIKES AND DISLIKES

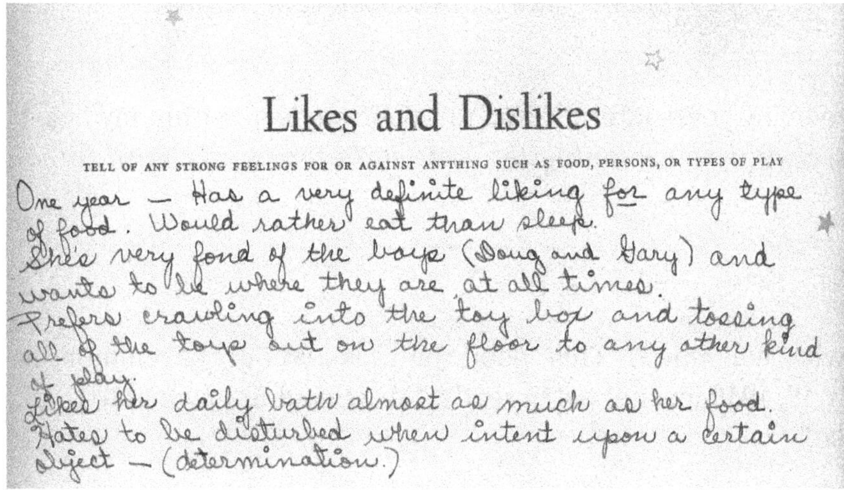

Likes and Dislikes

TELL OF ANY STRONG FEELINGS FOR OR AGAINST ANYTHING SUCH AS FOOD, PERSONS, OR TYPES OF PLAY

One year – Has a very definite liking for any type of food. Would rather eat than sleep.
She's very fond of the boys (Doug and Gary) and wants to be where they are at all times.
Prefers crawling into the toy box and tossing all of the toys out on the floor to any other kind of play.
Likes her daily bath almost as much as her food.
Hates to be disturbed when intent upon a certain object – (determination.)

Figure 24.14 Likes and Dislikes.

One year -Has a very definite liking for any type of food. Would rather eat than sleep.

She's very fond of the boys (Doug and Gary) and wants to be where they are at all times.

Prefers crawling into the toy box and tossing all of the toys out on the floor to any other kind of play.

Likes her daily bath almost as much as her food.

Hates to be disturbed when intent upon a certain object (determination).

➤ RHYTHM AND MUSIC

One year - Stands in her playpen and bounces up and down when radio is turned on. She thinks she's dancing.

➢ ATTITUDE TOWARD MEMBERS OF THE FAMILY

Very affectionate and likes to be held and cuddled.

These many years later, I'd like to say, from deep within my heart -"*Thank you Mrs. Spalding, for loving the little child that was placed in your care.*"

But what happened? This "good romp" lasted only seven months. Steve's February 18, 1946 journal entry reads, "Mrs Spaulding wants to put L.L. some place else."

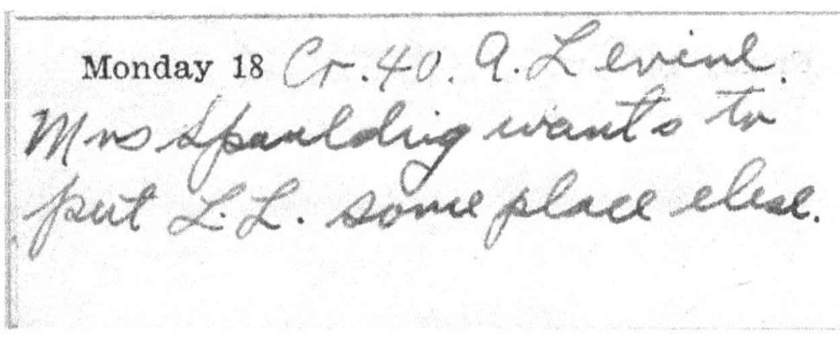

Monday 18 Cr. 40. 9. Levine.
Mrs Spaulding wants to
put L.L. some place else.

Figure 24.15 Steve's Journal, February 18, 1946.

5. <u>Mrs. Kartees – three weeks.</u>

On February 26, 1946, he notes that he's "Made arrangement to move L L 3-1-46 to 1366 Ogden St." and on March 1, 1946 that the move has taken place.

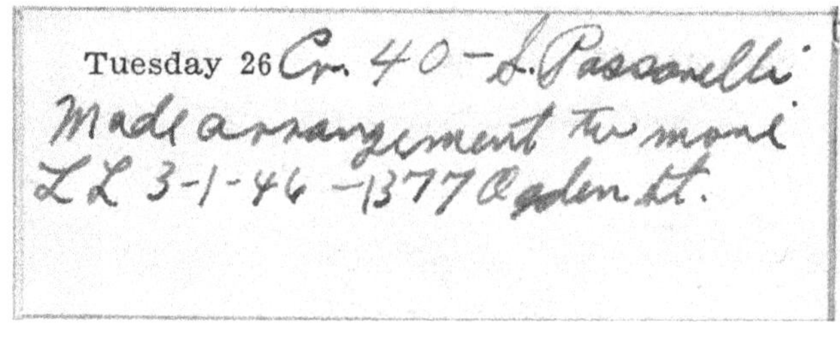

Tuesday 26 Cr. 40 – L. Pascarelli
Made arrangement to move
LL 3-1-46 – 1377 Ogden St.

Figure 24.16 Steve's Journal, February 26, 1946.

Mrs. Kartees, the new caregiver, is "nervous about L L." - and, there are other problems.

Officials from Denver General Hospital and officers from the juvenile court become involved.

Steve thinks L.L.'s grandparents are responsible for these investigations. He writes, "The Johnsons are making it tough on anyone I get to take care of LL. It seem's as though Mr's Johnson is a Mental Case." So, perhaps the Johnsons had something to do with Linda's departure from the Spalding home also?

The placement with Mrs. Kartees lasts only three weeks.

---

6. <u>The Forte family – eighteen months</u>

In the address section of Steve's 1946 journal is a notation for the "Children's Welfare Bureau of Denver General Hospital". The hospital must have directed him to a service provided by the Methodist Church - which in turn introduced him to Mrs. Forte and her daughters. The notation reads "Mrs. Forte, 2809 Perry. Gl. 8733 belongs to Methodist Church has (2) daughters". They become Linda Lee's next family.

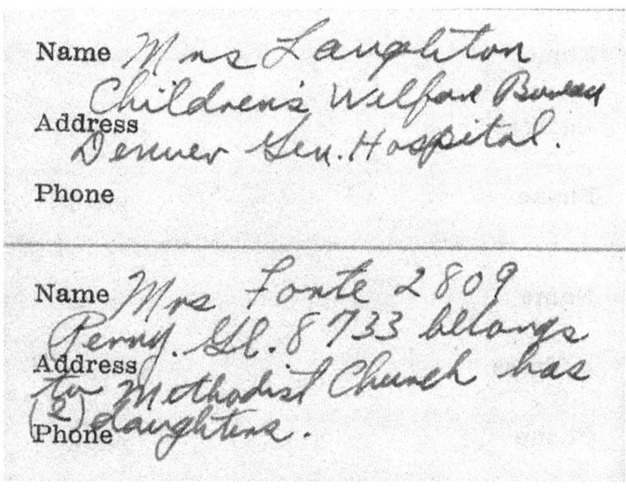
Name Mrs Laughton
Address Children's Welfare Bureau Denver Gen. Hospital.
Phone

Name Mrs Forte 2809
Address Perry. Gl. 8733 belongs to Methodist Church has (2) daughters.
Phone

Figure 24.17 Forte Family information from Steve's Journal.

➢ HOMES

On the Homes page of the baby book, Mrs. Forte writes, "At 20 months Linda Lee came to live with the Forte family - March 21, 1946. We sure love her, and she loves Mary Jo."

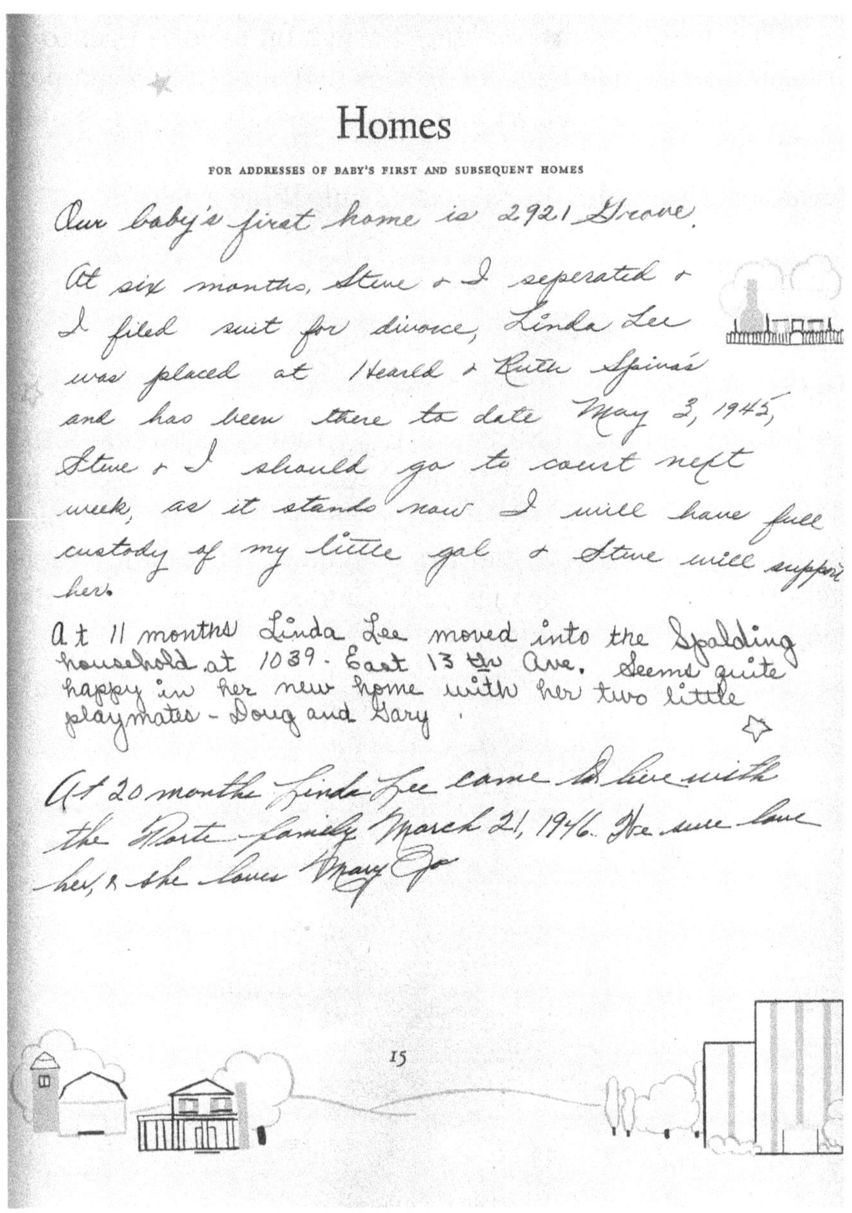

Homes

FOR ADDRESSES OF BABY'S FIRST AND SUBSEQUENT HOMES

Our baby's first home is 2921 Grove.

At six months, Steve & I seperated & I filed suit for divorce, Linda Lee was placed at Hearld & Ruth Spina's and has been there to date May 3, 1945, Steve & I should go to court next week, as it stands now I will have full custody of my little gal & Steve will support her.

At 11 months Linda Lee moved into the Spalding household at 1039 - East 13 th Ave. Seems quite happy in her new home with her two little playmates - Doug and Gary.

At 20 months Linda Lee came to live with the Forte family March 21, 1946. We sure love her, & she loves Mary Jo

15

Figure 24.18 Mrs. Forte's entry from the Homes section of the baby book.

Early on, someone, Steve assumes it's the Johnsons, notifies the health department that Mrs. Forte might have tuberculosis. But she's tested and her test "stood". L.L. gets to stay.

But, in Steve's opinion, the Johnsons continue to cause problems and Shirley's visits continue to upset Linda. He says that Shirley "caused a scene" at the Forte home on L.L.'s second birthday.

➢ **BIRTHDAY CARDS**

Although she never wrote in the book after her initial Homes entry, Mrs. Forte did save three cards from that 2nd birthday celebration. All have been man-handled (babyhandled?). L.L. must have really enjoyed them before they were put away in the Two Years Old section. The first is signed "Love Sherry". The second reads, to "Our darling Linda Lee", and is signed, "Lovingly, Grandma and Grandpa Johnson 1946". The last is signed "Love Mommy".

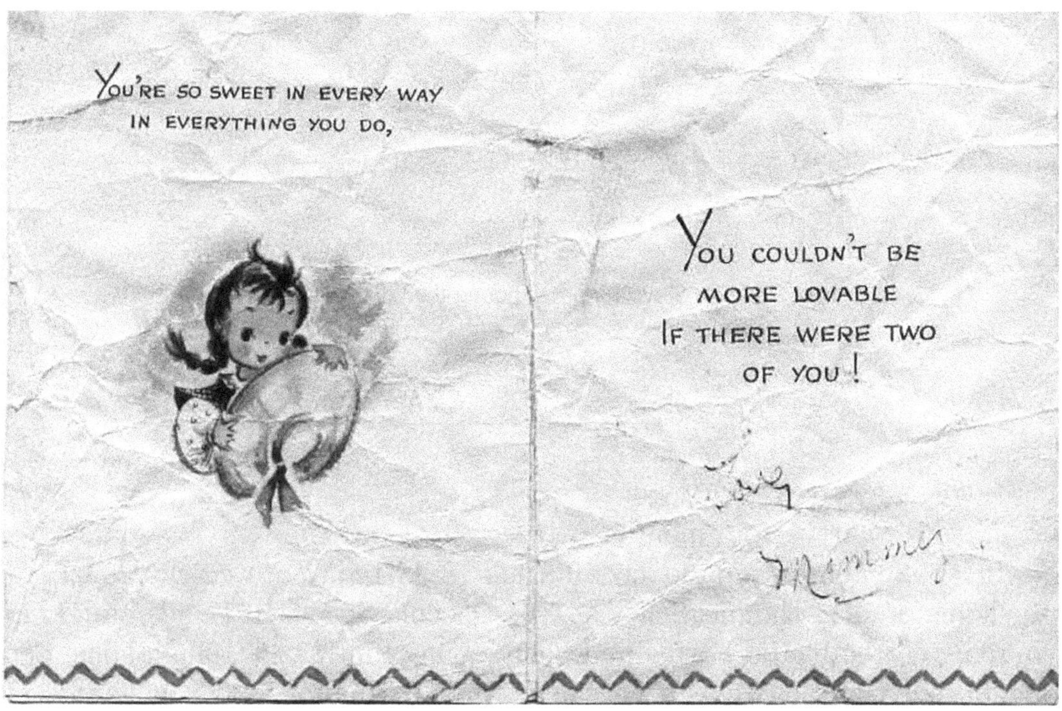

Figure 24.19 Birthday Card from Shirley.

And that's the last that we'll learn about Linda Lee from the baby book. I'm grateful to the two women who kept it up so faithfully - Shirley Mae and Mrs. Spalding. From them, I've learned much about my whereabouts during this time. Things I never knew.

Returning once again to Steve's journals as the source of information, we see that L.L. lived with the Fortes at their home until December of 1946. Steve visits two or three times a week and Shirley about once a month. And then, in December, the Forte family, including Linda, moves into the upstairs of Steve's Grove Street house.

And time goes by. L.L. celebrates her third birthday with parties at Uncle Gus and Aunt Mickie's *and* at Helen's. On September 10, 1947, eighteen months after L.L. first came to live with them, the Forte family moves out. L.L. doesn't go with them. They'd been her family for half her life. How she must have missed them.

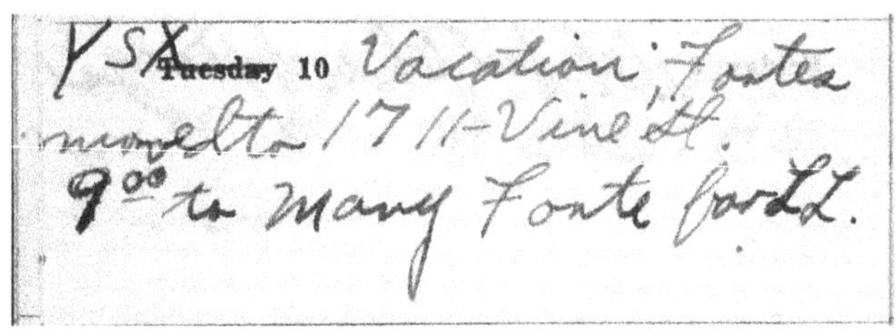

YSX Tuesday 10 Vacation; Fortes moved to 1711-Vine St.
9.00 to Mary Forte for L.L.

Figure 24.20 Steve's Journal, noting the Forte Family move.

---

7. Mrs. Scarry – four months.

In late September, on the day after his 37th birthday, Steve delivers L.L. to the home of Mrs. Thomas Scary at 5011 Osceola Street. If I understand his journals correctly, the Fortes had been paying him $42.50, plus phone, per month to live at the Grove Street house while caring for L.L. Now he makes arrangements to pay Mrs. Scary $45.00 per month to care for his daughter. His expenses have definitely gone up with this latest arrangement!

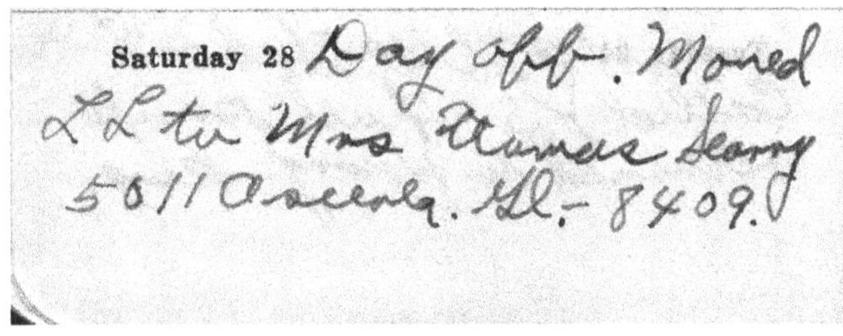
Saturday 28 Day off. Moved L L to Mrs Thomas Scarry 5011 Osceola. Gl.- 8409.

Figure 24.21 Linda Lee's move to the Scarry's as noted in Steve's Journal.

And that's the end of the written record of L.L.'s whereabouts. The Box contained no journals from the years 1948 and 1949 and the one from 1950 is silent on the subject - except for the listing for Betty Robertson in the address section.

But! This is where *my* memories begin.

So even though the story is uninterrupted, I'll begin writing from a first person present perspective.

In the autumn of my third year I enter what I *now know for certain* is the "quiet house" of my constant memory.

Mrs. Scarry must have lived in a small apartment on the second floor of an old house - why else would the kitchen be upstairs? As always, I can feel myself returning to that quiet kitchen...

> *Sitting perfectly still, I look out the window for hours. Watching the trees bend and twist in the wind, their leafy branches brushing the window.*
>
> *Sitting alone at the kitchen table eating soda crackers. I can hear the refrigerator humming, smell the oilcloth that covers the table and taste the salt on the crackers.*
>
> *I'm very lonely. I'm very sad.*

Evidently I was with Mrs. Scarry for less than a year, because the second thing I remember clearly from my early life is my fourth birthday party at my new home. I learned much later in my research, as you'll see in Chapter 31, that I left Mrs. Scarry in January 1948.

---

8. <u>The Lillian family – 18 months</u>

Friendly and good-hearted Alberta and Jerry and their daughter, who's a few years older than me, live on 11th Street in Brighton, Colorado. Today, my new family has given me a lovely birthday party. Several children have been invited to help me celebrate and it's a great party. We play Mother May I, Red Rover and Crack the Whip. We eat cake. And Shirley's here. She's very beautiful in a summer dress and very high heels.

A May Company photograph I found at the farm testifies to the fact that Shirley was indeed as beautiful as I remember her on that day. It's of her and me and was taken perhaps a month before the birthday party. She wears an elegant black velvet maternity dress - Brother Dave was born on August 9, 1948. Her light brown hair shines and her teeth sparkle - like the single strand of pearls she wears. She's lovely. I finally have some hair, which someone has attempted to curl, and I wear a blue cotton dress with white eyelet trim.

Figure 24.22 Linda Lee, with Shirley, 1948.

The birthday party glimmers in my memory, but I must have forgotten some things about it that weren't so happy. Although I remember only her beauty, Shirley told me recently that *it was on this day* that she decided her visits were too traumatic for her daughter. She stopped seeing me after that. Our next encounter was nineteen years later, in 1967.

Alberta and Jerry are very good to me, and their daughter and I are good friends. We share a bedroom and talk and laugh after her parents have turned out the lights at bedtime. Often, we lean on the windowsill, side by side, looking out at the starry nights.

Sometimes, on Saturdays, Alberta and Jerry take me to the train station and see me aboard for a trip to Denver to visit my dad. I'm so happy to see him when he meets the train. He's very handsome and his smile is beautiful. When he hugs me, his clothes - a buttoned shirt with a sports jacket and trousers - are nice to feel and smell. We spend the day together. His house smells like him - like aftershave, tobacco and books. In the afternoon, he drives me back to Brighton.

This whole arrangement seems fine to me, so it's unclear why, sometime after my fifth birthday, it's time for me to move once again. The people at an "agency" have arranged for me to live with a "foster family" - a family screened and selected by the agency.

---

9. <u>The Robertson family – six years</u>

Betty and Bill Robertson live at 210 South Kalamath Street. Upon my arrival, I'm immediately impressed - because they live in the same building as a grocery store! They're young, in their twenties, and have two sons - six year old David, and one year old Dennis.

Very soon after my arrival, in my self-important little way, I inform Betty that I can't have any foods with tomatoes in them, nor eat ice cream, nor chew bubble gum. Nor can I be around any dust or feathers. During the preceding year, I'd had several tests to determine the extent and severity of some allergic reactions I'd been having. I remember them clearly - hundreds of tiny pins in my back. Betty is standing at the ironing board as I reel off the list of forbiddens. As she listens, I can tell that she's very interested and concerned. But then! She calmly tells me that I won't have allergies any more - now that I live here. And I don't! Just like that. No kidding.

David and I go to Alameda Elementary School. He's in first grade. I'm in kindergarten - graham crackers and milk and naps on individual rugs. Once on the way to school, David and I decide to climb up on the huge billboards beside the railroad tracks. It's amazing. I can fit inside a mouth! We're very late for school and get into a lot of trouble. But I'm so glad we did it. It's my first real adventure.

Bill's a meat cutter at the local supermarket. After he and Betty have saved enough money, they buy a house on twenty acres about thirty-five miles southwest of Denver, in Jefferson County. Grampa Allison's farm was also in Jefferson County, but it was about twenty-five miles *northwest* of Denver.

This has been a story of discovery—getting to know my grandfather and father through what they left behind at the farm. With that in mind, my plan was to follow Linda Lee through her first six years until 1950 - when Steve's journals ended.

But I've changed my mind somewhat. I'd like to continue further with Linda's story for two reasons. First, it's so easy. I can relate it as I remember it. No need to interpret artifacts from the farm. And secondly, I want to tell of a kind and loving family that gave me love, shelter and safety for the next five years.

Our new home's on Coal Mine Road, between Wadsworth and Kipling - and it's a dream come true place for me.

"a good romp"

Linda' s baby book - July 21, 1945.

CHAPTER 25

"Betty Robertson LITTLETON, COLO."

An entry in the address section of Steve's last complete journal pinpoints the time and place of our move to the country:

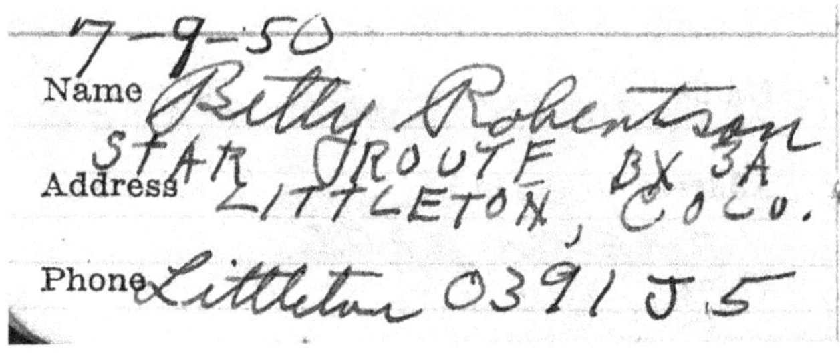
7-9-50
Name Betty Robertson
Address STAR ROUTE BX 3A
LITTLETON, COLO.
Phone Littleton 0391 J 5

Figure 25.1 Entry in Steve's Journal for Betty Robertson.

7-9-50
Betty Robertson
STAR ROUTE BX 3A
LITTLETON, COLO.

If I could, I'd put that name and that place "in lights".

Betty becomes, and will always be, the person I think of as - "mother". She pretty much saved my life. She also, by word and deed, pretty much shaped my character and made me the person that I am. I love her unfailingly and forever. And our farm, five miles west of Littleton, Colorado, is the place of my dearest childhood memories.

During these early years with Betty and Bill, Steve still brought me into town on some weekends, to spend time with him and Rosemary, his girlfriend. Sometimes I stay at her parents' house. Occasionally I stay with him at his apartment downtown. On one such visit he and I had our photograph taken (Figure 25.2). At the farm, after he died, I found three large, beautifully framed photos that had been taken at this time. In them, forty year old Steve seems happy and healthy, as does six year old Linda Lee. Perhaps that's because they'd found for her a stable, loving home with the Robertsons. And this happy arrangement will last for *six years*!

Figure 25.2 Linda Lee, with Steve, 1950.

Steve's visits, however, become fewer and fewer. He becomes an outsider to his daughter and her new family. They give very little thought to him between his visits. Although I'm sure this hurt Steve, I think that he must have found comfort in knowing that L.L. was well cared for and loved. Hopefully, he was then able to more fully enjoy *his* life, free of the worry he'd known since her birth. With his peace of mind somewhat assured, at least for a few years, we'll return to the doings of his young daughter.

> *Momma and Daddy Bill bought our farm from Mr. Jacobs, a man who came here from New York. He's very old and sick and now lives at the Silver Saddle Motel on South Sante Fe Drive. He adores my mom you can tell and she, in turn, treats him like a dear relative. She takes him food at the motel and helps him out in all kinds of ways.*

Our house is white and has two stories. David and I each have upstairs bedrooms. His faces the back of the house and all the farm buildings. In a year or so Dennis will join him in this bedroom, but for now he's downstairs with my parents. My bedroom faces the front of the house, overlooking the yard and a long driveway, which is lined with tall evergreen trees and leads to the road. Fields of alfalfa lie on three sides of the house.

What a perfect place to live.

While writing this book in the 1990s, my mom gave me some photos that capture a moment in the lives of her other children during these early years of the 1950s. Of course during my childhood, I had no idea that I had brothers and a sister elsewhere who were living their own special and unique lives.

Travis Taylor (Michael) is growing up as an only child of doting parents in Lufkin, Texas.

Figure 25.3 Travis Taylor, circa 1950.

Meanwhile, Max and Shirley Radovich and their children Dave, Marty, Kathy and Paul live in the Denver area.

Figure 25.4 The Radovich Family, circa 1952; Shirley (holding Paul), Dave, Kathy, Marty and Max.

David and I go to school at Bear Creek Elementary. My school years there, the next five, are filled with happiness. Mrs. Cooper, Mrs. Humboldt, Mrs. Appenseller and Mrs. Bingham are each, in turn, my favorite teachers. ***(I've forgotten the name of my second grade teacher. My apologies to her.)*** *I love to read. I love recess.*

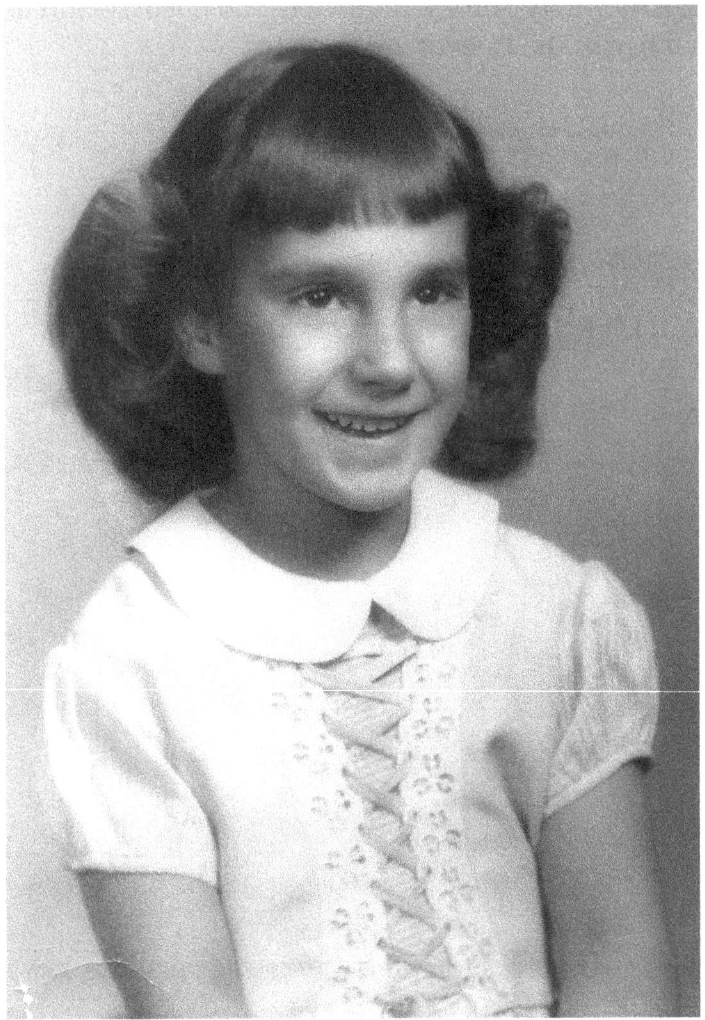

Figure 25.5 Me, age 7.

And I love the bus ride! We yell and sing and tell funny jokes and stories. On the way home each night our bus driver stops at the little store about half a mile from school and lets us buy candy and pop. (Once, when I was drinking pop, someone bumped the bottle and chipped my front tooth. That hurt for the longest time.) Sometimes I buy the little wax containers that hold some kind of sugary liquid. But mostly I buy Black Cows. They last all the way home, and then some.

By the time I get to fifth grade, our school is overcrowded. It's decided that the two fifth grade classes will meet for the year in the CCC Camp about five miles up the road. Each day we ride another bus to and from this site. What an adventure! The entire school year is like a fantasy. In nice weather we eat lunch next door at Red Rocks, the natural amphitheater made of gigantic up-thrusting slabs of red rock. During the Depression, CCC workers added the seating and amenities to this outdoor theater. That's why their camp was built here.

After lunch, and on recesses, we tear around the deserted buildings and discover all kinds of treasures left by those men who lived here some twenty years ago. Early in the fall we accidentally learn how to enter one of these buildings and then often, secretly, spend our recesses and lunchtimes there. Our teachers never find out - all year! It's a deserted building, but not an empty one. A huge stuffed buffalo head hangs on the wall and tables and cupboards hold all kinds of interesting things. Some of the boys and girls kiss in there. Not me. I'm not one bit interested. In fact, I hate it when we have to dance during PE. It's in another cavernous building, which is so cold in the dead of winter. I have sweaty hands and the boys tease me. But mostly it's fun - day after day after day.

After school, David and I change into our work clothes and do our chores. Our faithful and very loving pit bull, Tuffy, keeps us company. David has a round earnest face, glasses, and a gentle heart. His sand colored hair is slicked back with water as we leave for school each morning, but sticks out in all directions by the time we start our afternoon chores. Then he troubles it even more in cold weather by wearing his hat with earflaps that snap under his chin. He is a very good brother and I love him very much. We never fight or argue. Although I did throw a fit once when he picked the hand with the nickel and I picked the hand with the penny. Let me explain. My mom found the coins while cleaning house. She put one in each hand and let us choose. She took a picture of me in the middle of the tantrum and showed it to me later. She wanted me to see how ridiculous such behavior looks. It worked.

I feed the chickens and gather eggs and sometimes feed the baby calves with a nipple bucket. But I don't work very hard. Not compared to my mother, father and brother. Mostly I take care of my other brother, Dennis. But that's not work. I love him hugely and unconditionally. Even though he's two, then three, then four, five and six years old - he'll always be my baby.

His nickname is Dennis the Menace though - and for good cause. But he's always sincerely surprised when his actions land him in trouble - which they do, a lot. One day, when he was four, he took my dad's pay envelope out into the field and cut up the five twenty dollar bills it contained - throwing the pieces to the wind. Once, he wanted to see if his kiddy scissors could cut skin. He took out a big chunk out of my arm. I could see the small veins running through the hunk of flesh as it lay there on the paper dolls. **(I still have the scar.)** *Our dad has to spank him a lot because he* *gets into so much trouble. It breaks my heart each time. Afterwards, I hold and rock him while he sobs in my arms.*

(I learned many years later, in the 1970's, that Bill wasn't David's natural father. Betty had been married before. Considering this, you'd think that perhaps David would have been the one to receive the harsher treatment from Bill, but as I remember it, it was always Dennis who was in trouble with our dad. It was probably just a personality thing. Dennis was "mischievous" almost from birth it seemed, and David was a very earnest boy who always tried to do the right thing.)

David's seven when we move to the farm and from the beginning he works side by side with our dad (and very often our mom) running it. It's hard and continuous work. Bill still works eight hours a day cutting meat at Miller's in town, so late into night, after returning from that job, he and David milk the cows and tend to the calves and pigs. Then, early the next morning they do the same again. On his way to the store each morning Bill delivers the milk to Sterns Dairy. In season, they plant, irrigate and harvest the hay. Plus, some piece of farm machinery is always broken down and in need of repair. And it's all done before and after Bill's store job or on weekends!

Sometimes it's so cold that David cries. Although he wears his leather pilot's cap with the earflaps and a heavy wool coat, still his face is often red and chapped from the cold. His coat, as well of most of our outdoor clothing and our blankets come from the Minnesota Woolen Mills. Once a year a salesman from that company comes to our house for our order. That's always a fun day, as are the visits from the Raleigh man and the Fuller Brush man, who come in their big brown trucks filled with spices, pots, pans and all kinds of household products for farm wives. Our most frequent visitor though, is the Holsome Bread man. He comes about once a week.

For me in winter, life is mostly school, feeding the chickens, collecting their eggs, entertaining Dennis and trying to keep warm - inside the house as well as outside. We have a coal furnace and a coal stove. We take turns sitting in front of the stove or close to the floor heat registers. Once when Dennis was just a toddler, he fell down on the big one in the living room and burned his legs really bad. He screamed and screamed - then sobbed and moaned for hours. He wore a crisscross pattern of raw sores for many, many days. It broke my heart.

It soon becomes apparent that we need more money. Daddy Bill makes $100.00 a week cutting meat at the store and Daddy Steve gives us some money each month - but there's never enough.

So my mother goes to work at Gate's Rubber Company, on the fan belt assembly line, from 11 P.M. to 7 A.M.

Now she's always tired. David and I take turns rubbing her swollen feet. The cement floor at Gates makes them ache and her pregnancies make them swell. Still she found time and energy to clean us up and take us to Easter services at our Presbyterian church (see image at beginning of this Chapter). A few weeks later, in April 1953, our baby sister, Deborah, is born. Our other baby sister, Rebecca, is born the following spring. Daddy Bill lets David, Dennis and I play in the small park across the street from the hospital (St. Luke's, in Denver) while he visits our mom in the days after each birth.

I love these babies and love taking care of them. But the person who really helps Momma take care of them is Gramma Landis, her maternal grandmother. During the time of the babies, she often comes to stay with us for months at a time. This lean and spunky little Irish woman cooks and cleans and sings Irish lullabies to the babies. She can also cuss a blue streak - in Spanish! Sometimes she lets a stink and is embarrassed. But, she says, her body has a mind of its own these days. We kids love Gramma Landis. Her visits always mean lots of fun!

When she's not with us, she lives alone in a tiny house in the town of Walsenburg, which is about 140 miles south of Denver. Her neighbors there speak mostly Spanish. She sweeps the floor with a handmade broom and has chickens in her yard - and sometimes in her house. She's all around great!

Her daughter, Betty's mom, is altogether different. Gramma and Grampa Neilson live about 20 miles from Walsenberg on a 650-acre ranch, which originally belonged to Gramma Landis. Gramma Neilson was a schoolteacher - in fact, she was the superintendent of her school district. She's very strict and puts up with no nonsense from us kids when we visit her once or twice a year.

She actually has a "parlor", with furniture that's stiff and hard. Formal portraits and landscape paintings hang by wires in oval frames. We sleep in feather beds and use a hand pump to get the water in the kitchen. Grampa Neilson is a quiet, soft-spoken man. He's not our mom's "real" dad (her last name was Simpson), but she loves him very much. In fact, David's middle name is Neil, in his honor. He often takes David and I with him as he and the hired hands see to the many duties of ranching.

In the summer, at home, David and I get our paybacks for working hard in the winter. Those long, sun-filled days without school are a joy. Sometimes we play with the Renzelman twins, Roger and Rodney, from across the road. Sometimes we go to the

Gurlett's house. They live in a big house that holds lots of children. They have a lake just out their back door. We ice skate there in the winter - David with his old black hand-me-down skates, and me with my beautiful new white skates that Daddy Steve gave me one Christmas.

Figure 25.6 Momma (Betty), Grandma, Great-Grandma and David.

There's an older boy, a teenager, Daniel Banks, who spends some time at our house. He's very respectful to my parents and really nice to us kids. He lives a few miles up the road, in a shack by the dump, with his mother who's "strange". She rides her white horse to town, Littleton, and back every single day, but never speaks, except to herself.

Figure 25.7 Me and Trooper.

We hardly ever ride our horse, Trooper. (Figure 25.7). David and I prefer our bikes, I guess. In summer, we pretty much live on them. As soon as our chores are finished in the morning, we head out and are gone from home for many hours at a time. We ride for miles on the dirt roads, exploring and just being free.

During my ninth summer, and David's tenth, however, we encounter two new experiences. First, we start attending 4-H meetings, where he learns about farming and livestock and I learn about sewing. I'm not much of a success at sewing. Sweaty hands make for sweaty thread and sweaty material. The needle has a hard time penetrating the cloth. I try to pull it through with my teeth, but then the needle breaks. Somehow I finish my first and only project, an apron. Whew! Since David's experience isn't much better, thankfully, our mom lets us quit. And, we get our first television! While the deliverymen "set it up" that bright summer morning, we eagerly anticipate our first entertainment. But when we sit down to watch, there's nothing on, except a sewing program! Sewing – my favorite. You can bet I'm thrilled. Nevertheless, Momma, David and I watch the entire program.

All in all, my life is great.

Figure 25.8 Me... Life is great!

But it's not all laughter and happiness for everyone though. Daddy Bill works hard at the store all day and far into each night with the cows, pigs and chickens. Momma works hard all day at home and then all night at Gates. They're both very tired. Plus, he's often unhappy with her. When they argue, sometimes us kids hide on the stairs trying not to hear them, while at the same time trying to hear them. It's a scary thing - yet intriguing.

Also, money is always short. Daddy Steve pays the Robertsons monthly, through the Community Chest. ***(For real, that's what it was called - The Community Chest.)*** *Although this amount is supposed to cover all my expenses, it just doesn't. Betty is always hesitant to ask him for any additional money and he's always hesitant to give it. She usually just buys what extras I need out of her own pocket.*

But every once in awhile, he gives her money for something special - and then what fun we have!

He's just come through with an extra $20.00 and we're in high spirits as we drive into Littleton to shop for a new winter coat. After lunch at Woolworth's, our usual, hot beef sandwiches, we head over to Penny's. David and I love to come to this store because of the "tubes". When you pay, the salesperson puts your money into a container and the container into a transparent tube that whisks it away! We watch as it flies to a glass room that sits just under the ceiling. There, someone takes the money, and sends the container with the change, flying back down the tube. It's like science fiction! The stuff of the future.

Well anyway, we pick out a beautiful brown coat with embroidered trim. I'm thrilled! But when Betty takes out her wallet to pay for it, the twenty-dollar bill is gone! We're in shock. We don't know what to do. There's no way to admit to Daddy Steve that the money has been lost. Finally, Betty puts the coat in layaway. She pays it off a few dollars a week for two months. It's the middle of winter when we finally get the coat. But I treasure it even more because of her kindness and good heart. She always puts her children before herself, and shows her love for us in a thousand ways. We laugh the days away, and in the evening we rub her feet before she heads off to work.

And then, a small cloud that's been hovering on the horizon grows dark and overtakes us.

Figure 25.9 Daddy Steve comes to visit.

On those Sunday afternoons when my Daddy Steve comes to visit - about once a month - I dread seeing his Hudson Hornet turn down our long driveway. His visits are always sad and uncomfortable. He wears shiny loafers and pressed trousers and we wear muddy farm boots and jeans. His car is clean and new and ours is old and dirty. He smells of cologne and always has a fresh shave and haircut. We are rather unkempt. I don't want to be a part of him or his world and I'm sure he knows this.

Documents that I found at the farm 30 years later indicate that Steve had recently been promoted to Lieutenant under the supervision of Shirley's father, Bud Johnson, who made Police Chief the following year.

The newly created position of lieutenant was made on the Denver Police Department in September 1953. ernard F. Maloy, third from right, acting manager of safety, hands lieutenant certificates to six sergeants ho won competitive examinations for the new-created positions. Deputy Chief Grant B. Girard, second from ight, and Division Chief Walter F. "Bud" Johnson, right, look on. The new lieutenants from left to right re James F. Jordan, Stephen J. Allison, Royal M. Tangye, James F. Shumate, Leo Wery and Glen L. rcher.

Figure 25.10 Steve is promoted to Lieutenant.

1954

Johnson Named New Police Chief

Walter F. (Bud) Johnson, Denver's new chief of police, Monday points with chagrin at his cast-covered leg. Appointed chief to succeed Herbert A. Forsyth, Johnson limped into the chambers of District Judge William A. Black to take his oath of office. The new chief broke a bone in his left ankle when he stepped out of a police car Friday night.

See story on Page 12.

—*Rocky Mountain News Photo by Dick Davis.*

A New Police Chief

WALTER F. (BUD) JOHNSON brings to his new job as Denver's police chief an unusually wide range of experience.

He steps into this vitally important municipal position with apparently solid support and high respect from his superiors in the City Administration and from the men on the force alike.

Chief Johnson is one of those educated policemen, in that he has studied police administration at Northwestern University, has attended law classes and has taken other courses in law enforcement.

He is also one of those practical policemen, in that he has served in virtually every division of the department.

He has walked a beat on Larimer st. and he has been in charge of traffic enforcement. He has ridden a motorcycle and he has been in command of North Denver substation.

He has been a detective and he has been a sergeant in the uniform division downtown. Since the reorganization of the Police Department last year, he has been chief of the uniformed division.

In 20 years on the department, Chief Johnson has had the fullest opportunity to learn law enforcement from the theoretical and the practical side alike.

In the past, there has been criticism that Denver's Police Department was allowing paper work and records to take precedence over practical patrol duty and investigative activity.

Under Chief Johnson, there should be no room for such criticism.

Denver has always been proud of its record as a clean city. Chief Johnson has pledged that that record will be maintained during his administration.

The job of police chief is no easy one. It has many problems and many difficulties.

We wish Chief Johnson well. And we urge for him the fullest co-operation and support of every citizen who is interested [in] a clean and crime-free city.

Figure 25.11 Bud Johnson appointed Police Chief.

Daddy Steve sometimes has girlfriends with him who are coifed and classy. My Momma is a bit overweight and often tired. He and his girlfriends try to ignore the slop buckets that sit in our kitchen, collecting garbage for the pigs. They try to step over and around the chicken poop in the yard. But they're uncomfortable and so are we. He tries to stay close to me, but I withdraw and give him nothing back. I know it hurts him and I'm sad for that.

In a futile attempt at bridging this gap between us, Steve makes arrangements to take me out to dinner for my tenth birthday. He and his girlfriend "Jean" **(real name Sophie - later known as Steppy)***, take me to a very fancy restaurant, the Top of the Park. He wants it to be so special - but it's a disaster. Jean is disgusted with my* *clothes and manners. Plus, I can't stop itching! Daddy Steve gently asks me over and over to please stop scratching and squirming. I try, but I can't!*

The next morning I wake up - covered with chicken pox! And so it goes.

It was probably at about this point that he decided he'd better retrieve me or lose me forever - and began considering marriage to Steppy as a first step toward this reunion.

We continue to endure Steve and Sophie's visits. Sophie has pitch-black hair, pitch-black eyebrows, that are drawn on, and a very red mouth. She dresses exquisitely. She actually lifts her nose with distaste during their visits. She gingerly steps with her high heeled shoes over and around real and imagined pieces of manure while walking to the house. In the house, she actually wipes the chair with a tissue from her purse before sitting down! She keeps her handkerchief close to her nose and mouth. Momma and I are embarrassed and somewhat intimidated by her - while she's here. But we think she's hysterically funny when she's gone, and laugh uproariously when one of us imitates "her highness".

But the ax is about to fall. The small cloud will soon create an eclipse of the sun. My happy life is soon to end - and I'll not emerge from the coming disaster for many years.

In February 1955, forty-four year old Steve marries forty-year-old Sophie. They inform us that I'll be coming to live with them as soon as possible. We're in shock! Betty contacts the Community Chest people to see if there's any way that she can keep me. They say no. She asks Steve if she and Bill can adopt me. He says no. He's always told me that he loves me, that I'm his daughter and that someday I'll live with him. Well, that someday is now. There's no way out.

Except, we do get a half-year reprieve. Momma convinces him to wait until school is out in June. Each day is full of sorrow as our time together dwindles. Now Steve and Sophie's visits generate no jokes - only anxiety and dread. Our stress is so great that Betty's afraid she'll have a miscarriage. Consequently, social services and Daddy Steve postpone my departure again - until her July due date. Betty's water breaks while we're sitting in the yard on a fine summer afternoon. (This birthing process isn't shocking or distasteful to me at all - it's just incredibly amazing.) Once again we pack her bag for another trip to St. Luke's. That night, our baby brother Daniel is born. He's named for another Daniel - Betty and Bill's beloved baby who died, shortly before Dennis was born.

A few weeks later, I have to leave - for real. My mom and I have cried for days and we cling together as Steve makes his last approach up the long driveway. She hangs on to me. She won't let me go. Apologizing, he tries to separate us and finally does.

My heart is broken.

"Betty Robertson, LITTLETON, COLO."

Steve's journal - 1950.

CHAPTER 26

6-10-58 - L.R. slapped, blood on floor at 2256 So. Osceola

"blood on floor at 2256 So. Osceola"

With the best of intentions, Steve heads home with his daughter; my tenth family arrangement. He has the highest hopes for their happiness - with Sophie, they'll finally be a family.

10. Allison Family – 21 Months

But his dream of a happy family soon dies.

And becomes instead - a nightmare. When I first contemplated telling Steve's story, I had a nightmare about my son Chris going to live with Steppy - remember? In anticipating telling my father's story, I'd remembered my time with him and Sophie. I'd felt anew the fear/trepidation/panic of those days. I think the nightmare about Chris was my subconscious also revisiting that time and those feelings.

> *The house at 2256 South Osceola is like a tomb compared to our house on the farm. It hasn't an ounce of life. The furniture is elegant but untouchable. Plastic runners cover much of the carpet. The heavy, perfectly pleated drapes are never opened. It's dark and sterile.*
>
> *My stepmother's disgust and anger surfaces immediately. The day after my arrival, while Steve's out, she tells me that I'm "crawling with chicken shit and infested with lice"* (of course, I'm not) *and that I've contaminated her house. She tells me to carry the all boxes containing my belongings out to incinerator in the backyard. She burns everything, except what I'm wearing. Everything! Next I'm ordered into the laundry tub in the basement and told to scrub myself with a bar of Fels Naphtha soap. Then we begin to "disinfect everything you've touched" with Lysol. It takes several hours.*
>
> *Steve gives her money to buy new clothes for me, which she does the next day. He's decided that I'll have no contact with Betty or my family, since he thinks I'll accept my new home easier that way. I miss them every minute. Sophie informs me that I'm to call her Mom. So I do. But in my heart, she's already become Steppy to me. The weeks go by in a blur of loneliness.*
>
> *And fear. Although I sometimes hear Steve, I begin to see him less and less.* ***(I think he must have already known we were heading towards disaster.)*** *By the time I start to school in September, I'm lucky if I see him once a week. He's in bed when I leave for school in the morning and has left for work when I come home from school in the afternoon. And I guess he goes to the farm on weekends - I don't know. It becomes clear that his presence had been my protection.*
>
> *Each afternoon I clean the bathroom and the basement. But I never do these chores right. After I've cleaned the bathroom, for example, Steppy might find a fingerprint*

on the faucet of the tub. She explodes. She crashes my head into the tub to "show" me the print. Or perhaps I've neglected to return the shower curtain to its proper "setting". She explodes. And hits me. It's the same with all my other chores. I just can't seem to clean "right". It's so hard to know what she'll find wrong.

Then I sweep the sidewalks. Betty and I would have had a good laugh over this! Sweeping the sidewalks! Once, in the beginning, a neighbor woman spoke to me while I was sweeping. When I came in the house, Steppy took me to the basement and beat me with the belt for "looking pitiful" while talking to the lady. Now I keep my head down and acknowledge no one.

At supper, she and I sit alone at the table, but only I eat. She folds and refolds a paper napkin, pressing the creases with her long red fingernails. Or she stares at me while pointing her fingers at me in a strange sign. ***(I learn much later in my life that it's the sign to "ward off" the evil eye.)*** *Then I wash the dishes and clean the kitchen. But, again, something's always wrong - especially with the cookware. The pots and pans are black, so I truly can't see the stains she points out after I've washed them. Grabbing my hair, she smashes my face into the pan, hoping I'll see it better. If I scream too loudly, she takes me to the basement for a beating with the belt.*

I'm in my bedroom for the night by 7 PM. The hours are endless. I know how the hairs lay on my arms and every design and hidden picture in the wood grain of the furniture.

Saturdays, we clean the rest of the house. With Lysol, we scrub the woodwork, the walls, and the floors of every room. We also dry everything - so there'll be no water spots or marks left from the rag! Can you imagine? We polish every piece of furniture, most of which has not been touched since we polished it the week before. Steve keeps his police revolver under the sofa cushions in the living room. Therefore he walks into this room twice a day. But that's the only time anyone goes there. Nevertheless we clean it from top to bottom each Saturday. We finish by sweeping and scrubbing the garage floor. If I could only tell Betty, she and I would laugh so hard! Scrub the garage floor! I cry in my bed at night when I think of Betty and my brothers and sisters. They seem like a world I must have dreamed.

One winter's day during this first year at 2256 South Osceola, I discover that I'm bleeding. Fortunately, we've seen a film in school by the Kimberly Clark Company about menstruation and so I understand the cause. But I'm panicked nevertheless - not because I'm bleeding, but because it's obvious that right now I must use more toilet paper than I'm allotted for each visit. What should I do? I need to use more. Plus I need something to wear. I'm petrified to tell Steppy, but I must.

Actually, she's pretty nice about it. She gives me two old bath towels and tells me to cut them into fourths to use as pads. I pin these to my underpants and wash them out each morning and each evening on the washboard in the basement. After a few washings with the ever-popular Fels Naptha soap bar, they're very, very stiff and they make me very, very sore. And after a few months, the safety pins are rusted and bent out of shape, making it difficult to even pin the darn things on. I hate this time of every month.

You might ask why I don't try to escape from this situation, or at least tell someone - like Steve - who might help me. I'm too afraid. She's convinced me that she has supernatural powers. Sometimes she stands very still, points her fingers at me, makes strange signs and repeats strange words under her breath. And, she's convinced me that she knows my every move. Without saying a word, she's let me know that my life would be in danger if I ever spoke to anyone about anything that happens in our house.

She demonstrated these "powers" to me early on:

School had, for a short time at least, offered a sweet escape. I really liked my teacher, Mr. Peacock, and my days as a sixth grader at Gust Elementary were filled with lovely, normal things. But then, somehow she infiltrated this sanctuary also...

Someone from school suggests that I need glasses. Steve (in person!) takes me to an eye doctor and purchases the glasses. He spends a great deal of time explaining to me how expensive they are, how delicate they are and how careful I must be with them. For some reason, Steppy is irate about the whole situation with the glasses. Can't he feel it?

At school I put them - oh so carefully - into their case, and put the case in my cigar box, before going to lunch or recess. I have them only three days, when, returning from recess, I find them completely destroyed - glass crushed and frames twisted unmercifully! How could that have happened?! I think I know.

Steve buys me another pair. Each night I wrap them in Kleenex, put them in their case, and put the case in the dresser drawer. Not a week later, I unwrap them one morning and feel glass shards falling to the floor. Cold fingers of fear run through my body. Trembling, then shaking, I drop to my knees in horror. Could I have done this? Yes. But I didn't! She did.

My father is so disappointed. He puts me over his knee and gives me a gentle "spanking". With his open hand! I don't even feel it. But it breaks my heart that I've hurt him. It's the only time he's ever disciplined me. The glasses are never replaced.

After that, in so many ways, Steppy reinforces my belief that she can see me when I'm away from her, and even do things to me when I'm away from her. It's so scary - and so tiring.

But two things save my sanity, if not my very life. The Catholic Church finds me and I find books. They become, by turns, my comfort and my joy.

One day, our next-door neighbor asks if I can accompany her three daughters to church!

(Looking back, I'm sure she was concerned about my welfare. Doubtlessly, she and her family were continuously subjected to Steppy's screams of anger and my screams of pain.)

Her girls are about my age. They go to a Catholic school across town, but go to confession and mass on weekends at All Saints, a church about two miles from our houses. Since Steppy was raised a Catholic, perhaps her conscience lifts its faint little voice and speaks up on my behalf. And, because she also believes in some kind of weird religious/magic thing I think she's a little afraid to refuse. She says yes! It's the beginning of a magnificent escape.

Soon I'm going every Sunday! At some point during my early childhood, I remember attending a Methodist church - but when and with whom, I don't know. Betty had all of her children baptized at the Bear Creek Presbyterian Church and we often attended Sunday School and Vacation Bible School there. I'd liked the biblical stories and illustrations, but that was about the extent of my religious involvement. But now, I've fallen in love with the Catholic Church - with its customs, traditions and pageantry. It's so old. It's so rich. It's so comforting. I love the colors, the smells and the drama of the mass. And besides - going to church, being in church and coming home with the Skeen girls is so much fun! That glorious morning goes a long way toward making up for the misery of the other six days a week.

Although I know in my heart that it's the history and the feel of the church more than its theology that attracts me, I ask to be baptized. Steve buys me a beautiful dress and Steppy actually lets me wear it. Her bother Ralph and his wife Luella are my godparents.

As winter becomes spring, my life continues to improve. Now I'm allowed to play with the girls for a few hours after mass. Such happiness! Their house reminds me so much of Betty and Bill's. It's rumpled, messy and full of good will and noisy kids.

They, too, have a baby - a boy whom everybody spoils. We play jacks by the hour, cook up weird experiments and talk and joke with their mom.

And, at about this time, a lovely thing happens at school also. Larry comes into my life. He has black hair, black sparkling eyes and long black eyelashes. His jeans are always pressed and his loafers shined. One rainy day, during indoor recess, he gently places in my hand a tiny boat he's carved for me from balsa wood. And that's the beginning of our young love. He writes notes to me. Sometimes we hold hands during outdoor recess. It feels good to be touched - gently.

As summer arrives, the Skeen girls and I move our play outside, and are joined by all the other neighborhood children. It seems that they too, are all Catholics and they soon begin to accompany us to church. What a group - Janice and Gary who live next door to the south, beautiful Lillian from up the street, Kathy P. from around the corner and five or so other kids so typical of a suburban neighborhood in the 1950's. I run wild with joy for these few hours each Sunday!

Life is now definitely bearable - although anxiety and dread still descend upon me when it's time to go home. There, Steppy still rages and beats on me most every day and I see Steve even less - Maybe twice a month. He works days now, but he and Steppy go to the dog races every night in the summer. To ensure that I stay in my bedroom while they're gone, she "paper locks" my door by placing a piece of paper between the door and the wall on the outside of my room. If I open the door, it'll fall to the floor and there's no way to replace it from inside my room. All the drapes in our house are permanently closed because the sun will "bleach" the furniture, but to ensure that I don't look out my windows during their absence, she plants "hair traps" on the drapes. Afraid to disturb the hidden hair, I never go near them, although I'm dying to peek out at my friends as they run through the long summer nights, shrieking and yelling with glee.

But it's okay, because locked in my bedroom night after night, I've discovered something precious - a treasure that's right at my fingertips and has been all along. It's The Book of Knowledge! Since it's copyright is 1944, I think Steve must have purchased this set of encyclopedias when I was very young, back when he still had visions of providing a happy home for us. I read each volume cover to cover, at least once. I love these books more than anything in my life. They are my loving parents, my true companions, my faithful friends and my way out of this room, this house and this life.

It's July 1956. In a few days I'll turn twelve. And shock! Steppy's decided to give me a party. She's actually trying to be nice? Will I suffer later for this? Probably. She and her sister-in-law plan a party to be held at Washington Park. Luella's kids, the neighborhood friends, and some of my schoolmates are invited. Luella drives us all to the park in the back of her pickup truck.

But it's just too weird. Steppy keeps talking about my "boyfriend", Larry, and encouraging us to kiss! We'd never dreamed of kissing before, and have no desire to do so. We're both just very embarrassed. I'm in a daze trying to figure out her motivation and the possible consequences I might suffer later for this fiasco.

(In hindsight, I think she really had been trying to do something nice for me with this birthday party, but it was a disaster nevertheless.)

And then, I get a wonderful reprieve. I spend the month of August with Steppy's Aunt Theresa and her family. She, Uncle Joe and two of their sons and daughters-in-law own and operate a large produce farm northeast of Denver and my job is to care for George and Ruth's three-year-old son during the harvest. What a relief! Besides being blessedly normal, all the Mazzottis are loving, decent people (see Figure 27.1). Betty, Fred's wife, is especially kind to me and I'm grateful for her attention and friendship. At least once a day, all of us gather around Aunt Theresa's large wooden table - to eat tomatoes, onions and cucumbers in vinegar and olive oil (sent by relatives in Italy) and always - pasta. I wish I could live here forever. But it lasts only a month, and shortly after Labor Day I'm headed home with a very heavy heart.

Which becomes even heavier, because during my absence, something drastic has changed with Steppy. She was a mean and frustrated person always, but now she's gone completely crazy. It must be something involving Steve. Their arguments have grown louder and more violent. She tells me that he's broken her eardrum. Before I left in early August, my life had been precariously balanced, but bearable. Now, in early September, it completely unravels - as her hysteria grows.

It's the beginning of a descent into a hell that will last for the next two years.

My Sundays of playing with the neighborhood children end, no questions asked. But that's meaningless, now that I'm fighting for my life. The beatings have become life threatening. I know that I might die. She hits me with whatever is at hand and bruises cover my body. My legs and arms are always covered with welts from the belt.

She pulls my hair - out. She curses me and puts curses on me. Her hatred is like a fire burning. I can feel the heat whenever she comes near.

Suddenly I'm a 7th grade student at St. Francis de Sales Catholic school. How, and why, did that happen? It's all a blur to me. I take the city bus to and from school, since it's several miles from our house. For some reason, I'm allowed to wear only one set of clothes now - the same red and green plaid dress everyday. Each night I wash it, along with my socks and underwear, on the washboard in the basement. Steppy often tears the skin from my knuckles, "showing" me how to do it right.

One afternoon, after an autumn snowfall melts by noon, I forget my boots at school. They're boy's black galoshes, the ones with the clasps up the front, and an embarrassment to begin with - but now, to punish me for my forgetfulness, Steppy decides that I'll wear them to school every day.

Early on, I try taking them off after I get on the bus in the morning and then putting them on just before getting off the bus in the afternoon. But, believe it or not, somehow she knows that I've not worn them into and out of school. She's waiting for me with the belt as I trudge up the walk from the bus. I get a beating for not wearing them the whole time and another for "dragging up the street, hoping people will feel sorry" for me.

She knows EVERYTHING.

And so, I wear the galoshes everyday, even on the sunniest, driest days, into class in the morning and out of class each afternoon.

My humiliation is complete and constant. The same dress every day. If only I went to a school that required uniforms. It's just my luck that I attend one of the catholic schools in the city that doesn't. The welts, black eyes and bruises. The ever-present galoshes. My classmates don't know what to make of me. For the most part, they're simply puzzled. Most just try to avoid me, although some of the boys tease me. But the embarrassment is secondary. I'm mostly just trying to stay alive. Although the will is there, I begin to fear that I won't be able to save myself. And some days I find that, instead of being angry at Steppy and wishing her dead like I used to, I pray only that I'll die soon.

But, once again, the church and books sustain me. The church of St. Francis is not more than twenty steps from the school of St. Francis and I go there every day at lunch. It's comforting to me to contemplate the life and times of Jesus. Over and over, through the Stations of the Cross, I trace his last journey. I feel a bond through our sufferings.

And the lifelike statues and exquisite stained glass windows lead me to an ethereal time and place far removed from my daily existence. Later, in the school library, I read about the events portrayed in those kaleidoscopic windows and about the saints whose statues stand in the darkened church. They're as colorful, vibrant and outrageous as my imagined stories! It's a great escape.

I begin checking out religious books and magazines, which I read while locked in my room each afternoon and evening. On one such gray and dreary winter afternoon, while reading about Mother Cabrini, an intriguing thought slips quietly into my mind - I could escape from this house, and from this life, by becoming a nun. And then I realize - IT'S THE ANSWER!

Steppy is very happy to hear that I've received a vocation. She encourages me to write the religious orders advertised in the magazines I've checked out from the library. Within a few months I've been invited to join the Sisters of St. Ursula, and, I can report to their motherhouse in Illinois when I'm thirteen years old! At this point, Steve actually makes an appearance to ask if this is what I really want to do. Does he have no idea of the danger I'm in, if I stay here? I guess not. I assure him that I want very much to become a nun. He consents.

I'll be thirteen in July, in about four months. I'll have survived!

It's a mild afternoon in May and I'm counting the days until I leave for Illinois. But it's not to be. Enraged because I've not cleaned a skillet properly, Steppy hits me in the head with it. It's very heavy - cast iron. Steve comes home at that moment - and finds me unconscious.

That night, in their bedroom, he and Steppy have a very long and a very loud argument. The next day he takes me to the home of Steppy's mother, Anne. She tells me that - because of me - her daughter's had "a nervous breakdown" and that I'll be staying with her until they "figure out what to do" with me…

My nightmare with Steppy had come to an end. Well, almost - except for one week, one year later, I never lived with her or with Steve again. His journal entry of June 10, 1958 explains why that homecoming was *short, if not sweet*:

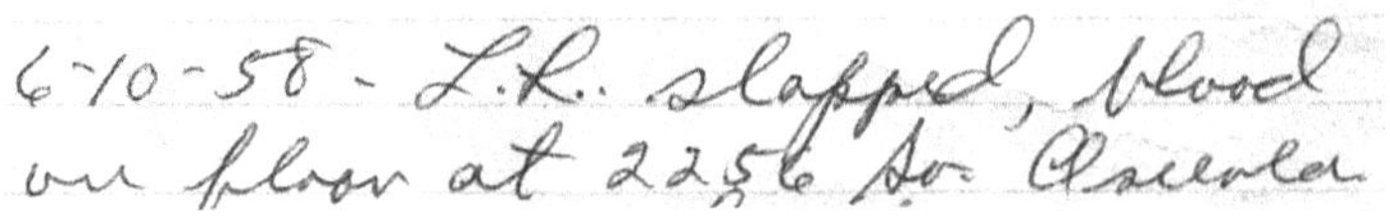

6-10-58 - L.L. slapped, blood on floor at 2256 So. Osceola

Figure 26.1 Steve's Journal entry noting Linda being abused.

"L.L. slapped, blood on floor at 2256 So. Osceola."

Those words could pretty much describe my two years at that address.

Poor Steve. That certainly wasn't what he'd had in mind - when he married Sophie and brought me to live with them. Our attempts at being a family had failed completely. Plus, we'd *all* been badly damaged in the process.

"blood on floor at 2256 So. Osceola"

Steve's journal - June 10, 1958.

CHAPTER 27

Neighbors next door to 379 So. H. Complaining about people being beat up in neighbor-hood.

"people being beat up in neighborhood."

Making a bad pun, you could say that Linda now went "from the frying pan into the fire."

11. Anna Feeley – 14 Months

Whereas Sophie had *some* redeeming qualities - sometimes she was actually funny, sometimes she at least *tried* to do the right thing - in my opinion, her mother had none. To me, she was a diabolical, alcoholic sadist. Steppy had learned from a master - or perhaps, *monster.*

She was born Anna Acierno, to Italian immigrant parents - and I don't know why she was so downright mean. I would come to know many of her *twenty-one* siblings - Theresa Mazzotti whom we met earlier at her farm, was a sister, as was Louise Laveo, the bondwoman Steve listed on his Christmas list in his journal - and they definitely weren't that way.

Anna married Raphael Doronzo and they raised three children, Frank, Sophie and Ralph, before divorcing. I often went with Steppy to visit her father in the Italian neighborhood of old north Denver. Many of the Acierno twenty-one still lived there too. It was a great place. I lived a sociology and history lesson with each visit.

Frank was killed when he was nineteen years old - as a result of a love triangle, or so I've heard. They say that Anne's hair turned completely white within two weeks of his death. Steppy and I often visited Frank's grave at Mt. Olivet Cemetery, and after her dad died, we'd visit his grave there also. We spent a lot of time at the cemetery. I liked it there though - *more* interesting stories of the family and it's history.

Many years later Anne married and divorced Mike Feeley. Sophie had no children. Ralph and his wife had three - LuAnn, Paul and John.

When he retrieved her things from the farm after Steve's death, Ralph overlooked a box of photos and papers belonging to my stepmother. I've included descriptions and/or photos of some of these items below. Some are presesnted simply because they are historically interesting but others pertain to people we've met before.

- **PHOTO OF ITALIAN SOLDIER.**

  An old photo of an Italian solider, in a regal uniform complete with a plumed tri-cornered hat. "FOTO-BASURTO Riproduzione Ingrandimenti RACALE" is printed on the back. Handwritten in Italian is "Leppino".

- **FUNERAL CARD.**

  For Pasquale Garramone who died September 9, 1936.

"people being beat up in neighborhood."

- **LOUISE ACIERNO LAVEO PORTRAIT.**

  With a baby (see Figure 28.2).

- **MAZZOTTI WEDDING PARTY PORTRIAT.**

  An 8"-10" portrait of the Freddie, Aunt Theresa's second son, and Betty Mazzotti wedding party. We're talking a big Italian wedding here. The newlyweds are standing second and third from left followed by Steppy, Ruth (?) and George Mazzotti.

Figure 27.1 Mazzotti Wedding.

- **A PHOTO OF GEORGIE.**

  Aunt Theresa's third son, Georgie, and Ruthie Mazzotti at their wedding.

- **PHOTO OF GEORGIE MAZZOTTI.**

  In his navy uniform.

➢ PHOTOS OF ANNE.

Before she had white hair!

Figure 27.2 Anne Doronzo.

➢ PHOTOS OF FRANK DORONZO.

Tall, dark and handsome.

Figure 27.3 Frank Doronzo (right).

"people being beat up in neighborhood."

- **FUNERAL CARD.**

  For Frank Doronzo who died on December 23, 1936.

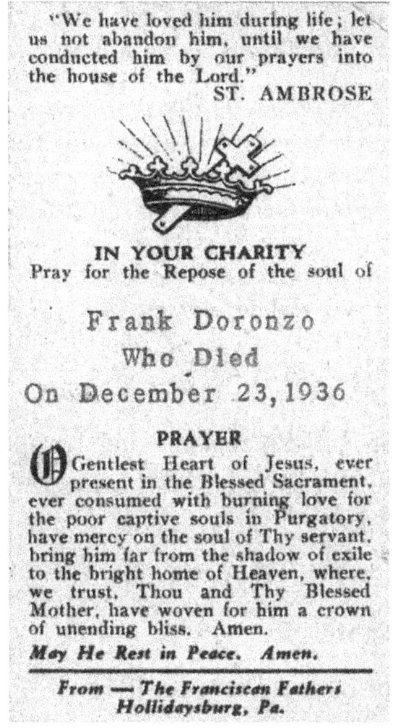

"We have loved him during life; let us not abandon him, until we have conducted him by our prayers into the house of the Lord."
ST. AMBROSE

IN YOUR CHARITY
Pray for the Repose of the soul of

Frank Doronzo
Who Died
On December 23, 1936

PRAYER

O Gentlest Heart of Jesus, ever present in the Blessed Sacrament, ever consumed with burning love for the poor captive souls in Purgatory, have mercy on the soul of Thy servant, bring him far from the shadow of exile to the bright home of Heaven, where, we trust, Thou and Thy Blessed Mother, have woven for him a crown of unending bliss. Amen.

May He Rest in Peace. Amen.

From — The Franciscan Fathers
Hollidaysburg, Pa.

Figure 27.4 Frank Doronzo Funeral Card.

- **RALPH DORONZO PHOTO.**

  In his navy uniform with his wife Luella.

Figure 27.5 Ralph and Luella Doronzo.

➢ UNDATED NEWSPAPER CLIPPING

DENVER MAN SEES SERVICE IN THREE CAMPAIGNS

Ralph Doronzo on Leave After 21 Months in Pacific.

Ralph A. Doronzo, 22, electrician's mate second class, is in Denver on leave after twenty-one months of duty in the Pacific. He has served in three campaigns, Solomons, New Guinea and the Admiralties. His naval construction battalion received a Presidential Citation for its part in the last-named action. Doronzo was graduated from West high school in 1941. His wife, Luella, lives at 1317 Marion street.

Anne must have worried constantly about her second, surviving son. And - didn't Steve inquire about childcare for his daughter with someone who lived in the 1300 block of Marion St.?

➢ BIRTH ANNOUNCEMENT

A birth announcement for LuAnn Doronzo, 1947.

➢ PHOTOS OF CIVILIAN RALPH

Scores of photos of civilian Ralph, Luella and their children.

➢ STUDIO PORTRIAT OF SOPHIE

Taken when she was 29 years old, in 1943.

"people being beat up in neighborhood."

Figure 27.6 Sophie in 1943.

➢ **ANOTHER PORTRIAT OF SOPHIE**

Another huge photo of Sophie, this time with her first husband, Roy Bringoff. It's undated, but Roy looks a lot older than his ravishing young wife. On the back of the photo is written, "ACCEPTED FOR EXHIBIT AT THE LAMME SCHOOL OF PHOTOGRAPHY, DENVER, COLORADO". It was mailed to Mr. and Mrs. Bringoff at 5600 West Colfax.

Although brief, hopefully the above introduction has provided a feel for the background and setting of Linda's next home.

...Steve leaves, and I'm face to face Anna Acierno Doronzo Feeley, a woman I barely know. We've met maybe four times in the years I've lived with Sophie. But it's hate at first sight - at least on "Gramma's" part.

"You've ruined my daughter's life! And now your father thinks he can unload you on me!" she hisses.

Figure 27.7 Anna and her daughter in-law Luella.

Anne is a large matronly woman with striking snow-white hair. Like Steppy, you could describe her as regal. But she's not regal at night when she unleashes herself from her corset - and drinks. She drinks a lot - several cases of beer a week. She begins to beat me soon after my arrival. No - not beat me. Steppy did that. Anne beats me up. She's like a street brawler - scratching, punching, kicking and stomping.

Our apartment's part of a court arrangement - five units around a central courtyard. It's at the corner of Mississippi Ave. and Lincoln Street in Denver. She screams at and fights with our neighbors three doors down to the south. This couple drinks as much as she does, and the encounters are often loud and vicious.

Our immediate neighbor to the north is a lovely young woman from Germany. Helen's a single working mother. Briefly, before my arrival, Anna had cared for her three-year-old son during the day. But I think Helen must have soon realized that her son wasn't safe with Anne. Now, when she hears the commotion from our apartment, she tries tactfully to intervene - asking Anne if I can watch her son, Ralphie, while she does her schoolwork, or chores or whatever. Then I'm safe for a few hours. She gives me clothes to replace the rags I've come with from Steppy's. Sometimes Gramma lets me wear them, but sometimes they enrage her so, that she rips them to shreds. Thank God for Helen. She is so kind and so beautiful, and I find a haven in her home.

When summer arrives, Gramma and I work during the day at the Anchor Hotel on South Broadway. She sometimes runs the office, but mostly we clean the rooms.

But evidently the money we get from this job, Anna's social security checks and my father's payments aren't enough. We are constantly in debt - badly in debt! Bill collectors haunt us. They call, they send letters, and they show up on our doorstep daily. It's my job to lie to them - on the phone or in person, while Anna hides in the basement.

Speaking of the basement, that's where I sleep. It's an unfinished basement and my bed sits on the concrete floor next to the furnace and the laundry facilities. One day after she's vented her frustration and rage on me for something, I find myself downstairs, curled up in a ball on my bed. As I rock back and forth in pain and misery, a small miracle happens. In my stomach, a warm and comforting feeling blooms like a flower. Then it envelops me. It feels like love - perhaps my body's love for its battered self.

If you think things couldn't get worse - they do. Anna moves downstairs with me! She's decided to rent her bedroom upstairs to an elderly couple whom she will "care" for, in return for their social security check.

My heart breaks for them. These frail, quiet, gentle people have found themselves in hell. She verbally abuses them from day one. They are completely intimidated. Mrs. Sanger cries, and Mr. Sanger tries to comfort her. One day while I'm preparing their breakfast in the kitchen, I hear Mrs. Sanger scream. Has Anna hit her?! She turns the radio up full blast to drown out the old woman's sobbing. But I can still hear weeping while "A White Sport Coat and Pink Carnation" blares from the radio. Even Mr. Sanger's crying.

Summer ends. I've not seen Steve or Sophie since May. I guess I'm here for awhile.

School starts. I take a different city bus now, the Broadway #3. I don't go to the church at lunch any more. I don't have much interest in the color or the stories these days - and the idea of a caring God has lost its meaning.

(Looking back, I find it interesting that the nuns felt no concern about a student who was covered continually with open wounds and contusions. But nothing was ever mentioned.)

The students in my eighth grade class are now young men and women. Most still avoid me. I'm just too weird. But then a ray of sunshine enters my life in the form of Rita - a quiet, shy girl in my class. We become good friends. We spend our time at school together. And since one thing I don't have to worry about with Anne, is her having supernatural powers and knowing what I do when I'm away from her - I sometimes go home with Rita for lunch. She lives with her mother and grandmother by Washington Park. We have a fun time on these outings, because although her mom's at work, her grandmother's very good to us. Sometimes we just mess around in the park instead of going to her house for lunch.

And then, deliverance comes for the Sangers. We have to move to a smaller apartment and the old people won't be coming with us. They'll live to see a happier day!

(We'd probably been evicted.)

Anna and I move to 1278 South Sherman Street. She drinks more and more. I can always tell when all hell is going to break loose. First strings of saliva spew from her mouth during angry tirades. Then she pushes and shoves. Then the full attack begins. She hits with her fists. She claws and tears at my face. She kicks me when I'm down. If I vomit while she beats me, that really makes her mad. She rubs by face and hair in it until I can't see. Many times I'm knocked senseless.

(Many years ago, a college professor told us that abused children were usually under the age of three. At that age, he said, they're helpless and can't protect themselves nor change their circumstances. That night in class I asked myself how it was that, between the ages of 11 and 14, I was constantly beaten - yet never once attempted to get myself out of the situation. I couldn't come up with a real answer, but now, in remembering those times, I realize that I had no place to escape to and knew of no one who might have helped me. I felt 100% trapped - totally alone and incapable of changing the situation. I lived with a fear so great, all of the time, that I can now hardly believe that it could exist in such intensity. But it did. I was always and completely afraid.)

A month after our move, two at most, we have to move again. Now we live in a house at 379 South Humboldt, and Anne is going to support herself by providing day care! Licensed, if you please! Soon we're caring for four children - a one year old baby girl with brown curls and a lovely smile, a two and three year old brother and sister - and Joey. Joey's a wild but loveable red headed four-year-old. Anna gets very angry with him and spanks him way too hard. His mother, who also has a beautiful head of red hair, is "down on her luck". Before I know it, she and Joey have moved in with us. It's great for Anna because she needs the added income desperately. It's a great for me because I don't get beat when Joey's mom's home. But of course it's not good for Joey and his mom. Anna makes her cry one night, and the next day they move out. Once again, it's my time to cry.

I walk to and from school now. It's about two miles and takes about a half-hour each way. To her credit, Anne doesn't continue Sophie's practice of making me wear only one set of clothes to school, and - she washes my clothes in the washing machine with the rest of the laundry. That's one small improvement in my life. She also lets me wear sanitary napkins. So much more pleasant! I miss a lot of school though. More and more, she has me stay home to help her with the children.

(I'd said before that I was puzzled at the nuns' lack of concern about an abused student. I'm further puzzled by their lack of interest as to why that student was absent so much - about half the time.)

I never mention anything about school to Anne; for fear that she'll show up there. But somehow, she gets hold of a letter asking for parents to chaperon an eighth grade dance! She decides she'll do it - and of course I'll go too! Oh my God! Please don't make me go. But the more I beg not to go, the madder she gets. We begin to dress - she in her giant corset and imposing purple dress, and I in a lovely dress and crinoline slip that Helen, our neighbor on Lincoln Street, had given me.

As we dress, she gets drunker and drunker.

She demands that I wear some of her bright red lipstick. I've never worn lipstick, and for sure don't want to start tonight. The "good" girls at school, whom I admire so much, would never wear it until they're in high school. I try to talk her out of it, but soon the melee is on. She smears it all over my face and hair - and arms, as I try to fight her off. My beautiful dress is ripped off and ripped up. Soon blood's flying everywhere.

Enraged, she drags me into the bathroom. The blood looks bright and almost beautiful against the white tiles of the floor. She raises me by the hair and slams my head into the bathtub. There's still water there from one of our baths. She's screaming that she'll clean me up, but I think she's going to drown me. As the water turns red, I find the plug and pull it. Again she bangs my head against the porcelain and I fall to the floor unconscious. At least now we don't have to go to the dance.

And spring comes around once again. I've seen Steve and Sophie perhaps four times since leaving their house a year ago. I never think about them.

But what *have* they been up to? Two pages ripped from a small spiral notebook hold the last of Steve's self-documented history. They're also all that remains in The Box. These offer only an intriguing glimpse into Steve and Sophie's life during that past year.

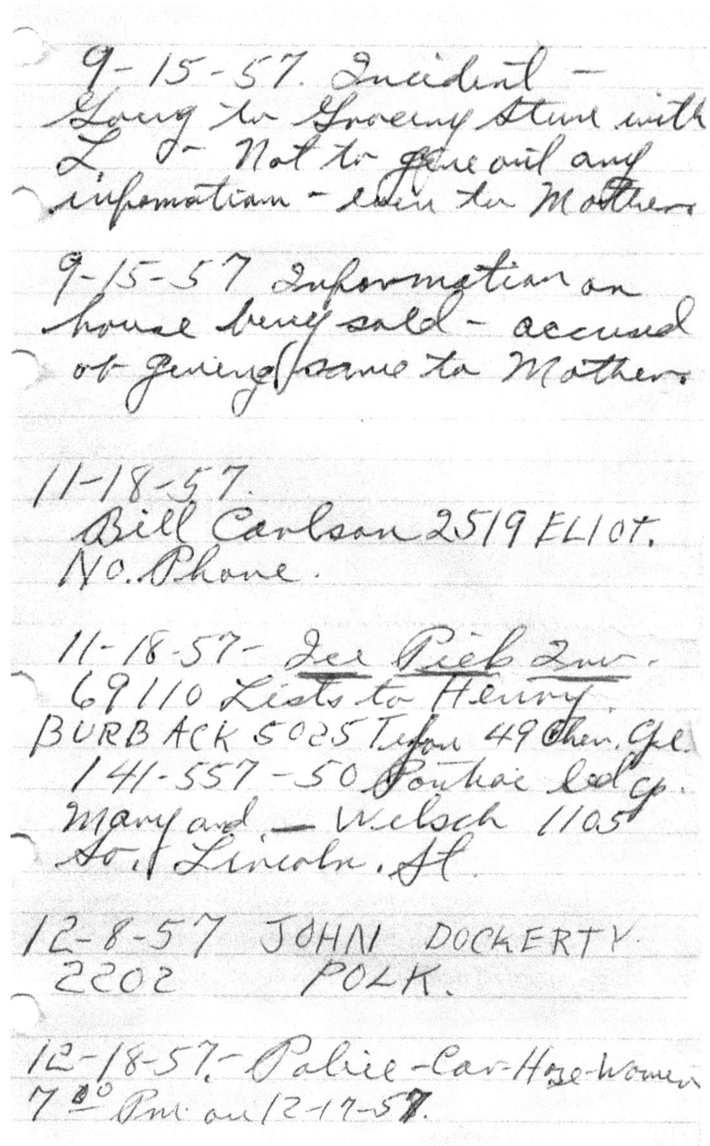

9-15-57. Incident -
Going to Grocery Store with
L. - Not to give out any
information - even to Mother

9-15-57 Information on
house being sold - accused
of giving same to Mother.

11-18-57.
Bill Carlson 2519 ELIOT.
No. Phone.

11-18-57 - [illegible]
69110 Lists to Henry.
BURBACK 5025 [illegible] 49 Chev. Cpe.
141-557-50 Pontiac [illegible]
Mary and - Welsch 1105
So. Lincoln. St.

12-8-57 JOHN DOCKERTY.
2202 POLK.

12-18-57 - Police - Car - Hose - Women
7:00 Pm. on 12-17-57.

Figure 27.8 Steve's Journal entries in fall of 1957.

9-15-57

Incident - Going to Grocery Store with L.

Not to give out any information - even to Mother.

Information on house being sold - accused of giving same to Mother.

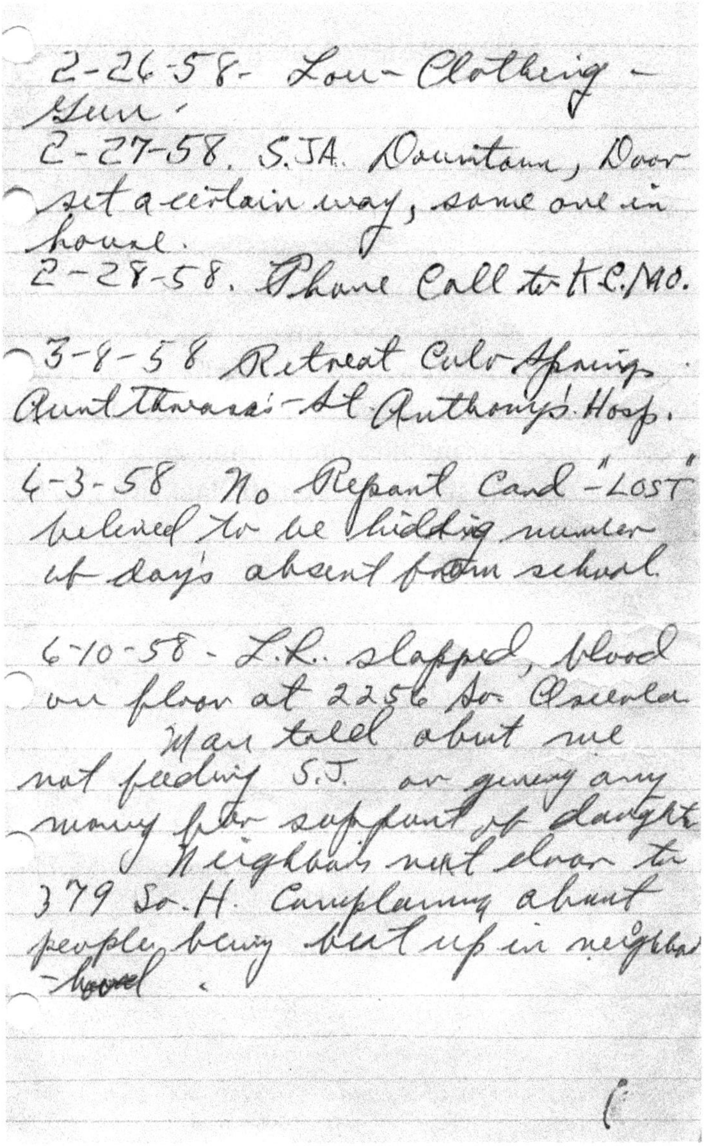

"people being beat up in neighborhood."

2-26-58- Lou- Clothing -
Gun.
2-27-58. S.JA. Downtown, Door
set a certain way, same one in
house.
2-28-58. Phone Call to K.C.MO.

3-8-58 Retreat Colo Springs.
Aunt Theresa's - St. Anthony's Hosp.

4-3-58 No Report Card "LOST"
believed to be hiding number
of day's absent from school.

6-10-58 - L.R. slapped, blood
on floor at 2256 So. Osceola
Man told about me
not feeding S.J. or giving any
money for support of daughter
Neighbors next door to
379 So. H. Complaining about
people being beat up in neighbor
-hood.

Figure 27.9 Steve's Journal entries in 1958.

2-27-58

S.J.A. Downtown, Door set a certain way, someone in house.

2-28-58

Phone Call to K.C. MO.

3-8-58

Retreat Colo Springs. Aunt Theresa's - St. Anthony's Hosp.

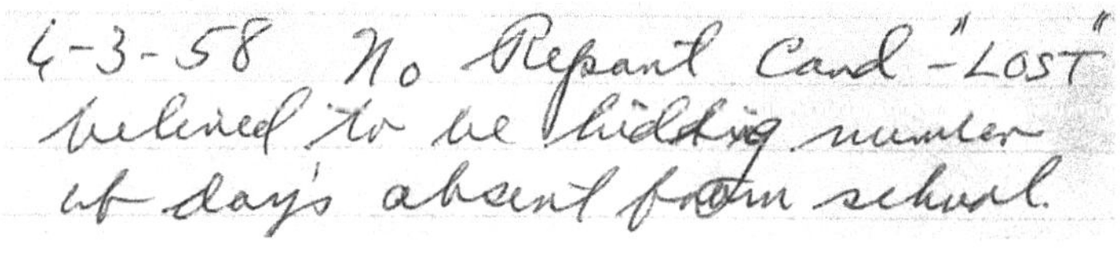

6-3-58

No Report Card - "LOST" believed to be hiding number of day's absent from school.

6-10-58

L.L. slapped, blood on floor at 2256 So. Osceola Man told about me not feeding S.J. or giving any money for support of daughter. Neighbors next door to 379 So. H. complaining about people being beat up in neighborhood.

Your guess is as good as mine about most of these entries. In September something happened involving Linda and going to the grocery store. And it seems that Steve was trying to sell the house on Osceola. It also seems that he was spying on Steppy - noting her phone calls and visitors as well as her whereabouts. I can, however, tell you about the last two entries.

6-3-58 No Repart Card "LOST" belived to be hidding numer of days absent from school.

Figure 27.10 Steve's Journal noting lost report card.

My end of the year report card shows that I've missed many, many days of school and on one of his infrequent visits Steve asks to see my report card. Because she doesn't want him to see the absences, Anna lies and says it's lost. And then, for some reason, after years of intimidation and fear - I DECIDE TO FIGHT BACK!

"It's not lost." I tell him. "I'll get it."

I'm about to come out of my room with it, when I realize that Anna has followed me and is blocking the door. Silently, savagely, she tears my glasses from my face. She twists them until they break. (What was it with these women and my glasses?) She grabs my shirt at the collar and begins to choke me. But - it's a miracle! Steve has followed her in, and has witnessed the whole scene. He's shaking as he pulls me from her grip. He carries me out of the house and puts me in his car. He wraps his jacket around me before going back in the house to get Steppy.

My god, it's over.

But, you guessed it. There's no place to take me except back to Steppy at 2256 South Osceola. You can imagine her enthusiasm about this turn of events. A week later Steve finds blood on the floor. He knows it's not safe to leave me there. He also knows that it's unsafe to return me to Anne's. His journal entry of June 10th notes that her neighbors have complained about "people being beaten up" there (see image at the beginning of this Chapter).

Poor Steve. Once again, he must find a place for his daughter. He turns to an old acquaintance, Louise Laveo Porter, the bondwoman, and asks if Linda can stay with her temporarily - until he can find a permanent place. She agrees and this is my eleventh move. But! Louise is Anna's sister and Steppy's aunt - not a good recommendation...

Don't worry, things could only get better.

There's nothing else in The Box. It's empty. Nor is there anything left from the farm that would further our knowledge and understanding of my father and of his father. The artifacts describing the lives and times of John Stephen and Stephen John have been discovered and interpreted. And so, in effect, this story is ended. We've accomplished what we set out to do.

My father had hoped that I'd find The Box and thus understand him better. In time, I did - and I did. We've each played our parts - done our jobs. His journals, and Shirley's, have given me a "clearer" understanding of our lives together those many years ago:

Steve was the parent of my childhood.

I know now that he tried desperately, especially in the early years of my childhood, to be a responsible single parent. I'm forever grateful for his wisdom and grace, during the middle years of my childhood, in placing me and leaving me with Betty. And even though, in the last years of my childhood, he seemed to have looked the other way while I suffered, I'm grateful that he saw me through to adulthood.

It was no easy job. I'll love him always and completely for the hardships we endured together in the beginning. I understand that he was only human when he pretty much threw in the parenting towel, so to speak, toward the end.

And Shirley's been the parent of my adulthood.

I know now that she was too young, too naïve, too gullible, too impressionable and too immature when she married my father. She was emotionally starving and he wasn't able to provide the sustenance she craved. He only made her want to run away. She made decisions in her youth that we all paid dearly for, down through the years. But she too, was only human, and since the day we were reunited, when I was 22 years old, she's been a completely loving and giving mother.

He was the better parent in the beginning. She was the better parent in the end. For each, I'm thankful. In 1950 Steve wrote in his journal "Time make(s) all things clear." For the most part, it has. Things are clear - and good.

However.

For two reasons, I want to add a few pages more. First, I don't want to leave Linda Lee in such a disheartening state. Let's see her through a few more years. And secondly, I want to tell a little about Steve's remaining years. But it'll be a brief telling. Although my father lived another thirty years from that day he carried me out of Anne's house, my knowledge of his life during those years is very limited.

And so, a few pages more.

"people being beat up in neighborhood."

Steve's journal - June 10, 1958.

CHAPTER 28

ST. FRANCIS DE SALES
GRADUATION CLASS 1962

"After a hundred spills and a hundred sores"

12. <u>The Laveo/Porter Family – Four Years</u>

So. Here I am with another of the Acierno sisters, Louise Acierno Laveo Porter. And - shouts of joy - she's not a psychopath, nor does she drink! Living with her and her husband here, at 30 Colorado Boulevard, are several relatives and a dog. Looking good. I'm hoping I can stay here for awhile.

And I can! By the time I start ninth grade in the fall of 1958, it's somehow been decided that I'll be staying here - at least for awhile! It's especially nice of Louise, since she, unlike Anne, really doesn't need the money that Steve pays for my keep. I'm so relieved! And so grateful! Thank you, thank you, thank you Louise.

Remember the essay that Steve wrote as a freshman in high school - about ice-skating at City Park? In it, he told of starting to improve "after a hundred spills and a hundred sores"? Well, Linda Lee, after fourteen years, and "a hundred spills and a hundred sores" - has survived. And hallelujah! From the moment of this decision, to let her stay with Louise, from this date forward - her life just kept getting better and better.

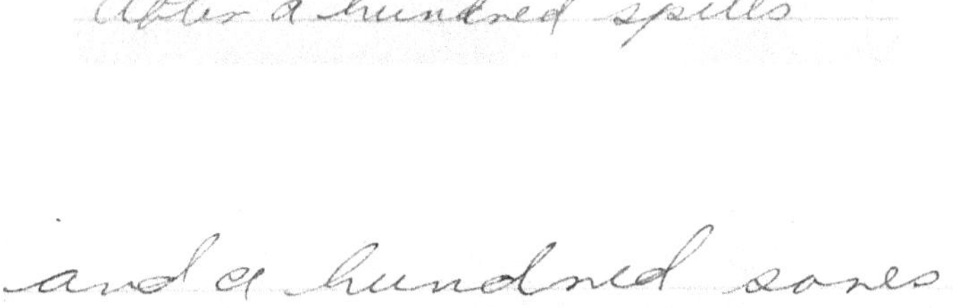
After a hundred spills
and a hundred sores

Figure 28.1 Essay from Steve in High School proving to be applicable later in life for his daughter.

Everyone is very kind to me. I can't describe my happiness at once again being part of a loving family.

Louise was first married to a man named Laveo, who came to their marriage with two daughters, Josephine and Helen. Together, they had another daughter, Lorraine, and a son, Albert. This beloved husband died at a very young age from kidney disease. Some years later, Louise married kind, soft-spoken George Porter. Besides me, they currently share their home with Helen and her husband, Danny Murphy, with Lorraine's sixteen-year-old son, Johnny. Henry, a medium sized, good-natured, mixed breed (mostly terrier) dog, also lives with us.

Since she was the baby of the 21 Acierno children, Louise was pretty much raised by her brothers and sisters. I think they did a good job. She's as thin and wiry as Anna was stout and boxy. She smokes a lot, as do Helen, Danny and George, and drinks a lot of coffee. We all do. Aunt Helen makes a huge pot each morning and we drink from it all day long.

Figure 28.2 A young Louise and an unknown baby.

Helen was first married to Danny's brother, but he was killed in a railway accident. Danny has heart trouble and a bit of a drinking problem, which is probably why they live with Louise. Johnny's here because his father also has a drinking problem.

Louise's only son, Albert, married another Josephine and they had five children. Shortly after their youngest child was born, Albert died as a result of the kidney disorder he'd inherited from his father. I think that Louise pretty much supports Albert's widow and her children – Angelo-16, Michael-15, Susan-13, Christopher-10 and Albert Jr.-four years old.

Christopher would die in a skiing accident in his early twenties. And the same disease that had claimed his father and grandfather would also take Angelo, a young husband and father of three daughters. Very sad.

One, some, or all of them are at our house daily. With his red hair and slight build, Angelo most resembles his mother. He's very mature, since he's the man of their family. He smokes, drinks coffee and discusses family affairs with his mom and grandma for hours. He's a good son, brother, nephew and grandson. For example, he often takes Aunt Helen out for a night at her favorite place - the dog track. His elegant girlfriend, Gisela, has a most intriguing German accent. They're very much in love. I love him too. From the beginning. But only in my heart.

It's a full household - a busy, active place - with lots of eating, talking and laughing. But the house itself is very large and we're not crowded.

The customs and traditions of this family, as well as their day to day interactions and subtle nuances, were classic Italian-American. They and the extended Acierno family as a whole, *except* for Steppy and her mother, were much like the quintessential Italian family as it's often portrayed in films and on television. For the most part, they were delightful people, whose strong personalities and rich culture greatly influenced my life.

Sometimes Gramma (Louise) catches Aunt Helen and I trying to slip Uncle Danny into the house after he's had a few drinks on his way home from work. She runs a very tight ship, and at such times there can be a bit of a confrontation and commotion. She's very strict about my comings and goings also - but after life with the maniacs, she seems pretty benign to me.

And Aunt Helen's the absolute greatest person. She's a little/big woman - about 4'9" tall and about 225 pounds. But she's all heart. Although her job is to cook, do laundry and keep the house clean, she finds time to help me learn how to be a normal teenager. We watch American Bandstand together, to see what's hot and what's not - like in clothes and hairstyles. Then we make or buy clothes that are in style and experiment with my hair. How much fun! She also introduces me to deodorant and shaving. How lovely I must have been before.

Dear gentle Aunt Helen, I love her so. And with her help, I'm now pretty much a normal, at least normal looking, teenager as I step into the world of high school.

St. Francis is a K-12 school, so I've just changed buildings. But inside that new building, it's a whole different, wonderful world. To me, learning from six or seven different teachers a day, instead of one or two, is much more efficient, effective and fun. The nuns and lay teachers are excellent and dedicated, and my mind joyfully opens to receive their knowledge.

Figure 28.3 Sister Agnes Marie, standing in center.

My history teacher, Sister Agnes Marie in particular, is intelligent, cultured and wise. Her classes are the highlight of my day. She studies in Rome during my senior year and writes to me from there.

JMJ

Via Marcantonio Colonna 52
Rome, Italy
October 9, 1961

Dear Linda,

Greetings from the Eternal City! A city of new and old--a city of extremes.

Linda, I have thought of you so many times--and you have been in my poor prayers, too. I am wondering how you are getting along this year. I am sure that you realize that the year is going so very fast, for you. Make the mst of it, you will be a senior only once, remember.

Our classes have not started as yet. They will began next Monday, the 16th of October and then, we shall go to school until the end of June. You will have had a whole month's vacation by that time. Even the grade and high schools did not begin here in Rome until last Monday. They do not go as long as we go, however.

We have seen much since we arrived here. First of all, we docked at Naples and then took the "Rapido"--fast train to Rome, after going thro gh customs at Naples. We were anxious to see Rome and all that it had to offer. Our first trip once we had arrived was to St. Peter's naturally. Since the convent where we stay is only twenty-minute walk from there, we have gone back and forth many times.

We went yesterday at noon to say the Angelus with Our Holy Father and to receive his blessing. What a thrill it was to see him. He is such a short man that not too much of him was visible from the high window, but he has a powerful voice. For a man his age, it is amazing. Of course, they do use a loud speaker, nevertheless, you can perceive the strength of his voice. We hope to get tickets for an audience this Wednesday. This should be wonderful too.

We have visited all of the major basilicas save one--St. John Lateran. The ones we have seen are St. Peter's, St. Mary Major and St. Paul-outside-the Walls. These are beautiful churches, in fact, all the churches of Rome are beautiful even the simple little parish churches. They all contain many rich mosaics and frescoes. It is amazing. They are not as clean as American churches however.

We have visited the Roman Forum, the Palatine Hill and the Colosseum, too; however, we shall return to these spots again, since the archaeology class take tours of these places as part of their course. This should prove very interesting. There is much to see, naturally, on every street car or bus trip that one takes, inspite of one's destination. You just have to keep peering out of the window, so that you don't miss anything.

Needless to say, we are picking up some Italian, too; I guess that I should out of self-defense. It is always nice to know what people are saying to you. We found this out the day that we went to customs for our trunks. We used all ten words that we knew and then, we had to have recourse to sign language. This all proved very interesting.

Well, Linda, as I said before, we are in my prayers. May God less you always, and have anice year.

Sincerely yours,

Sister Agnes Marie

Figure 28.4 Letter from Sister Agnes Marie.

Johnny, Angelo and Michael (and soon Susan) also go to St. Francis. Aunt Helen often talks Johnny or Angelo, who drive, into taking me with them to extracurricular school activities, since I'm not allowed to attend without a family member. Once there, though, they're happy to have me disappear, and I'm happy to do so. I can mess around with my friends without any interference.

Figure 28.5 John Levnik, Michael Laveo and Susan Laveo.

Yes, friends! I can have friends now - is this great or what? During the next four years I enjoy the friendship of many unique and wonderful girls and young women. They're many, and because they've come to this high school from many different grade schools throughout the Denver metropolitan area, they're varied.

My bus friends went to school together at St. Vincent's, and are known as "preppies." I just think they're fun. Johnny takes me to school in the mornings, but since he has to go to football practice or to his job after school, I take the city bus home each afternoon. Sherry, Tootsie and Mary Pat and I have so much fun on these bus rides home! We hang out in Walgreens, Wally Green's to us, at Broadway and Colfax while waiting to transfer from the #3 to the #4 bus. We laugh till our jaws ache. Sherry's the queen and Tootsie's her senior attendant at Homecoming. Mary Pat's such a dear friend and the funniest person I've ever met.

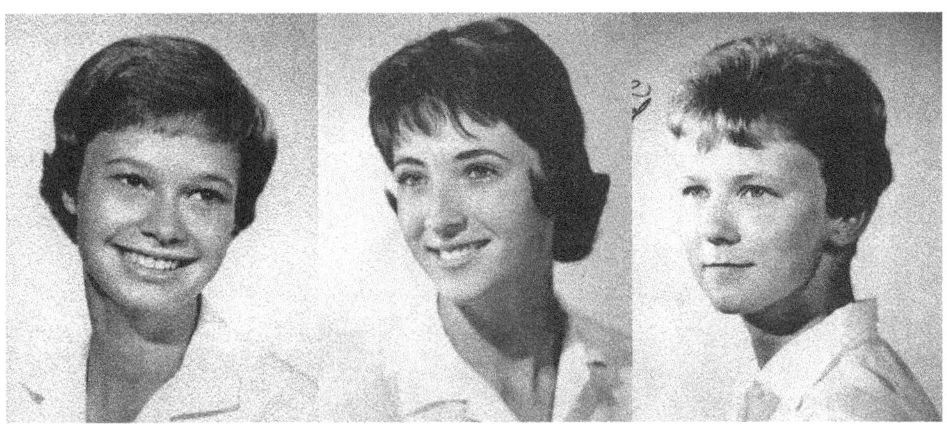

Figure 28.6 Sherry, Tootsie and Mary Pat.

Kathy B. is much more serious than my bus friends. She and I went to school together in 7th and 8th grades, although I hardly knew her then. (I think that Rita, my dear companion from eighth grade, must have moved. Or perhaps she went to a public high school.) Kathy's a good student, a good citizen and everyone's favorite "good girl". She is voted Senior Attendant at Senior Prom and and because of her piety, she also reigns as our May Queen.

Figure 28.7 Kathy B., May Queen.

Mary Kay was also with us in the 7th and 8th grades. And like Kathy, she's of a more serious nature - but in a completely different way. She lives with her mother and loving grandmother, like Rita did, but right next door to our high school. And like I did with Rita, I often go home with her for lunch. She's always been mature for her age, and she's always been a bit of a rebel. She often dates older boys - boys who don't even attend Catholic school! By the time we're juniors and seniors, she's dating men who are out of school!

Susan is sophisticated and cultured. She and her family, mother, father and eight brothers and sisters, live in Brighton. Each day, her very successful father drops her and some of her sisters, at school on his way to the business he owns downtown. Academically they're superior to most of us. Sometimes Gramma lets me spend the weekend at their house. What an eye opener. Perhaps we might go to "the club", Denver Athletic Club, or host a lovely lawn party. What's great is that these are really nice people - not pretentious at all. They're a down to earth, fun-loving, generous family. I'm sad when she leaves St. Francis after our freshman year to attend the more elite St. Mary's Acadamy.

Figure 28.8 Me, as Sophomore Attendant.

My sophomore classmates decide that I'll represent them at the annual Peb Club Dance as an attendant. The shocking thing is, Steve has bought me a dress to wear and Steppy and I actually shopped for it together.

Figure 28.9 Pep Club royalty.

By the time we're juniors, several of my friends can drive. I can't. It was never a consideration. Since Johnny's graduated, Gramma lets me ride to and from school with three of them. Mary Alice, Cheryl and Kathy K. have been friends with each other since grade school. They attended a Catholic school in their City Park neighborhood. They take turns driving each week. They make me laugh as much as my bus buddies, but they're a whole lot worldlier. Mary Alice is very beautiful and very popular and is Prom Queen when we're seniors. They're able to maintain excellent grades even though some of them may have tried - smoking, drinking and occasionally ditching school!

Figure 28.10 Mary Alice, Cheryl, Kathy K.

Not me though. I don't smoke, drink or ditch - well just once, I did ditch. I'm not about to mess up a good thing. And I know not to cross Gramma. She's only hit me once. Through a miscommunication, Johnny left me at school when I thought he was bringing me home. I walked, since I had no bus money, and arrived home several hours late! (It must have been at least five miles.) She wanted to hear no excuses and sent me reeling with an open-handed slap when I started offering one. I know not to cause her any grief. I don't want her to "send me packing". I try never to do anything wrong.

About once a month I take the bus to visit my grampa. These visits to the nursing homes or private homes where he's cared for are not fun, nor are they easy. Each visit finds him more helpless, more neglected and more pitiful. But they're always worth it. He's always so happy to see his "Linna Lee". Sometimes he cries with happiness – and with sadness.

Steve and Steppy no longer live at 2256 South Osceola. They've moved to an apartment in North Denver at 38th and Grove Street. I see them only a few times a year – usually in the summer, when they take me with them to the farm for the day. Steve always has a lot of work to do there; trying to keep up with the buildings, grounds and crops. Steppy and I sunbathe while he cuts, cleans, weeds, welds, rakes etc. She is, on these occasions, actually friendly, kind of fun and somewhat endearing. I guess now that she knows I'll never live with her again, she can relax.

A serious police scandal rocks the city of Denver in 1959/60. We hear rumors that perhaps Steve, who's now a lieutenant, is being investigated. If he is, nothing is proven. He retires from the Denver Police Department in 1961, after twenty years on the force.

Bud Johnson, who had made Police Chief in 1954, also retires. Although he certainly wasn't untouched by the scandal, he was completely untarnished by it. Bud, his wife and their other five grandchildren, of course, are unknown to Linda at this time. Travis Arthur Taylor, in Lufkin Texas, is a fifteen year old teenager by now. And in Denver, Dave Brian turns thirteen, Martin turns twelve, Kathy Irene turns eleven and Paul Walter turns ten in 1961.

In the summer of my sixteenth year, my life changes dramatically. Steve arranges for me to interview for a position in the Data Processing Department of Mountain Bell. I get the job! It's a momentous happening! It's the first step toward a time when only I will control what happens to me! And I know it from the start. From the first day I report to work, I begin to distance myself, not only from Louise and her family, but also from all of my past. It's truly the beginning of my own life. Every paycheck goes to Steve, to help pay Louise for my room and board. It feels very good to be able to contribute some towards my keep.

Like Shirley, my first real job was at the Telephone Company. Times had definitely changed however, in the fifteen years between our employments. She'd operated an elevator; I operated a computer. But she too, at this time of my life, was an unknown to me - I didn't even know her name. Steve was my only parent - and helping me get this job was one of the last, but also one of the best, things he ever did for me.

Many of us in this department are high school students, and mostly we attend Catholic schools. My friends Kathy B. and Kathy K. both work here, as do several others from St. Francis. Some are students at Cathedral High School. Judy and Bob, who're going steady, go to Holy Family.

Our computers are large with panels full of wires and metal. We enter data into punch cards, collate the cards and then transfer the information onto large reels of tape.

During my junior and senior school years I work from 4:30 to 8:30 each evening. During that first year, I take the bus to work and Johnny picks me up in the evenings. I work full time in the summers of 1960, 1961 and 1962.

Bob and I work next to each other. He makes me laugh - a lot. He has a great sense of humor. And besides, it's easy to laugh - because life is good.

After he and Judy break up, Bob and I become even better friends. He starts coming over to my house. This is a very definite first - no boy has ever visited me at home. Gramma seems to like him though, and by the end of our junior year, she's agreed to let him bring me home from work in the evenings. It's quite a trip for him, since we live on opposite sides of town - he lives in Wheatridge, west of Denver, our work is in the center of Denver and I live in east Denver. But I don't think he minds. He loves "cruisin" around in his spotless, white '58 Ford convertible.

Soon, we're going together. My friend is now my boyfriend.

His parents are a bit reserved at first. I don't think they like that I'm from across town - and have no visible parents. His sister Marilyn and the family chihuahua, however, are at once warm and welcoming. As are his friends - and we have many teenage adventures with his North Denver friends.

Borrowing Kathy B.'s Prom dress, I attend Holy Family's senior prom with Bob. I liked this dress so much better than the one Steve and Steppy bought me two years ealier. I hope I didn't hurt their feelings.

Figure 28.11 Bob and me at Holy Family's Prom.

Sometimes, after work during the summers, we drive to the Highline Canal. A wonderful tire swing hangs from a giant tree at the water's edge there. Bob pushes me on it and I soar out over the water and far into the night. I love our times there. And I know by now, too, that I love Bob.

We married three years after leaving high school - and with our sons, Christopher John and Jason, became the DeAndrea family.

Our homeroom teacher announces, one morning during my senior year, that we can soon sign up to take the ACT. What? I'm completely at a loss. Sister explains that it's necessary to take this test if one wants to go to college. College. Hmmm ... I've never even thought of college. In fact, I've never made any plan, in my whole life. I've always just gone where I'm taken. But this sounds like a great idea. I'd be on my own and I could study history for four more years! That evening I phone Steve to see if he'll help me go to college. He's happy with my plans and agrees to help me financially.

On a cold gray Saturday morning I open the test to page one. I'm asked to name the college or university that I plan to attend. Once again, I've no clue… Since I don't know the name of a single college, I ask the girl sitting in front of me what college she's applying to. She slides over so I can see her paper - Colorado State University in Ft. Collins, Colorado. Sounds good to me!

Shortly before graduation we gather for our senior class photo (see image at beginning of this Chapter.) I'm fifth from the left in the front row. It's time to say goodbye to some very dear friends and classmates.

Because of his anxiety in crowds, from his streetcar accident many years ago, Steve doesn't come to my graduation in May of 1962. In fact, no one does. It doesn't matter.

In September 1962, I say goodbye to Louise and her family.

(I couldn't know it at the time, but this was the last time I would ever see them.)

And I'm off to CSU! It'll be my first time there. My happiness is somewhat tempered however. I learn, too late, that by making arrangements to ride to Ft. Collins with Bob, I've hurt Steve - badly. It seems he and Steppy had planned to take me. I didn't know. Therefore, this eagerly anticipated beginning to my new life is tinged with sadness. I've hurt my oft-hurt father yet again.

After we meet Steve and Steppy at my dorm, Bob leaves. He knows his presence is unappreciated and unwanted. Now I feel badly for him. This is not being easy. Steve very kindly sets me up with a bedspread, lamp and rug - from the bookstore - that's so odd to me. He explains that my freshman tuition and room and board have been paid and that he'll be sending me $20.00 per month for books, supplies and personal expenses. Sounds great! Thanks Steve.

And *that* was the last of the best things Steve did for Linda Lee.

- He'd touchingly tried to care for her when she was an infant.
- By luck and hard work, he'd found a loving, nurturing home for her when she was a young child.
- As her childhood ended, he'd removed her from danger after his attempts at making a family had utterly failed.
- When she was a young adolescent he'd placed her with a boisterous, vibrant family who'd made her a part of their adventure.
- He'd helped her gain her first meaningful employment, later in her adolescence.
- And lastly, he now sent her into a confident and competent adulthood by giving her two years of college - the magnificent gift of knowledge with all its attendant joys of learning.

They leave. Standing alone as night falls, my heart knows that I'm going to love it here.

And I do.

Thanks to on-campus jobs, by my junior year Steve no longer needs to contribute to my personal or college expenses. I'm an adult - a self-supporting adult. Now I, only I, control my destiny. It's the best feeling ever.

I'M ON MY OWN!

Figure 28.12 Colorado State University, 1962.

"After a hundred spills and a hundred sores"
Steve's high school essay - 1925

SECTION

- V -

Westminster

CITY Edition

APRIL/MAY 2005

An Informational Newspaper for Residents of Westminster

City Designates Semper Farm as Historic Landmark

THE WESTMINSTER CITY COUNCIL RECENTLY designated the Charles and Julia Semper Farm as a local historic landmark. The Semper Farm, located at the northwest corner of 92nd Avenue and Pierce Street, is one of the last remaining reminders of the pioneer heritage of the northwest part of Westminster.

Charles Semper, a native of Great Britain, immigrated to Denver and was employed as the first printer of the Rocky Mountain News. Semper and four other printers staged Denver's first labor strike in 1860 and organized Denver's first labor union. When the Civil War started, Semper joined the Confederate Army. He was captured by the Federals and spent time in a camp in Mississippi. After the war, he travele[d] to New York to pursue his education. There he met and married his Irish-born wife, Julia, and they moved to Denver, where Semper continued to work as a printer. They owned several properties in the Auraria area and were well-known socially in Denver.

In 188[illegible], they homesteaded 160 acres north of the present-

Please see **HISTORIC** on page 3

VOLUNTEER VALUE

Learn more about ho[w] you can help in your community

Page 3

CLEANUP COMING

The city's annual large item cleanup dates are fast approaching

Page 6

HISTORIC

BACK TO THE FARM

CHAPTER 29

"STEPHEN JOHN ALLISON, 77, of Arvada"

After parting at CSU that September evening in 1962, Steve never called nor visited me again. I think he was immensely relieved that I was grown and safe - and that his responsibilities had ended.

Over the next twenty-five years I saw him, *at most*, perhaps ten times. Two were accidental meetings - the others were initiated by me.

What little I know about the last third of his life, I learned from Steppy. Much of what follows, she told me. We danced a weird dance together, her and I, during these last years. She always kept in contact with me, and as time went on, I think she actually came to think of me as a daughter. I think, too, that she felt more than a little remorse for the person she had been.

In the early 1960's, at about the time Steve retired from the police department, the downtown Allison properties - the candy store and the parking lot where Bob's dad had worked for Brother Frank - were sold. They, and all the other buildings on the block of Curtis between 15th and 16th Streets, including Steppy's old bar, were razed. A high rise condominium complex, Brook's Towers, was then built on this valuable piece of real estate. John and Frank must have split the money from this sale. (I seem to remember hearing a six million dollar figure.) But, because they were very old by now, the profits probably went straight to their children. I don't recall Gus having any investment in this property. In any event, he had no children. Georgia, Titsa, Little Steve, Chris and Big Steve reaped the benefit of their fathers' many years of hard work and perseverance.

My father, who was 50 years old, never worked at a regular job, again. He spent his days managing his finances and managing the farm. Two or three days a week, he'd dress up - as smartly as ever - and spend the day downtown with his accountant, broker, lawyer and whatnot. And two or three days a week, he'd don his overalls and spend the day attacking weeds, cleaning beehives, or whatever, at the farm.

At CSU, I attended classes year round. I never saw Steve and Steppy. I'd never seen them much before college, why should things have changed? Nevertheless, our "non-relationship" was amiable.

But then, unintentionally and unknowingly, I did two things that estranged me from my father for the rest of his life. Years later, Steppy told me about his distress. In 1965, while still in college, I became pregnant and got married. This was a great disappointment to him - but he never told me so himself. He didn't attend the ceremony nor did he ever acknowledge my marriage. *And then*, in 1966, I researched Shirley's whereabouts and re-established contact with her. This was the beginning of my small family's happy inclusion in the large extended Radovich family.

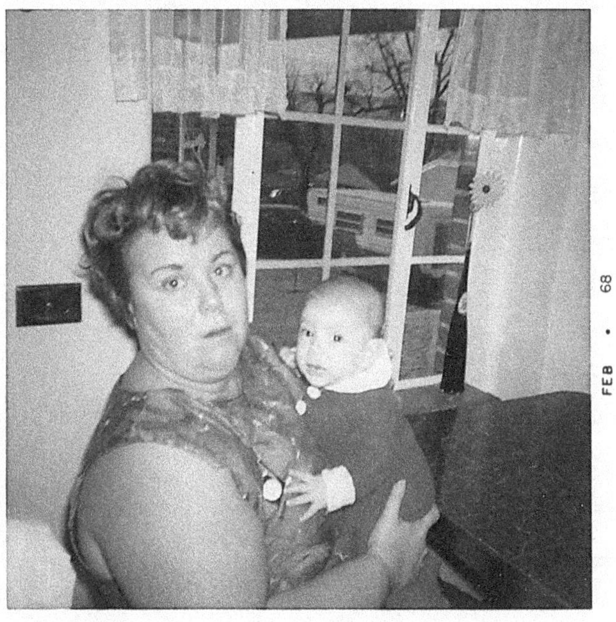

Figure 29.1 Shirley and 3 month old Jay.

Again, many years after the fact -in the late 1970's, when I was trying to discover why Steve wanted no contact with me, or my family - my stepmother told me that he'd felt *"completely betrayed"* by this mother/daughter reunion. I didn't understand why it had hurt him so - *until*, after his death, when I read his journals. There I discovered a frantic father - trying his best, alone, to care for his daughter. *Only then* did I understand why he'd been so hurt when I invited Shirley back into my life. In that regard, time *did* make "all things clear".

When Chris and Jay were very young, I tried to introduce them to their grandfather. Since he never answered the phone, either at home or at the farm - and *if* Steppy ever gave him my messages, he never responded - one day Bob and I took the boys to the farm, hoping to find him there. And we did. He was a bit uncomfortable, but cordial and welcoming. He was loving and gentle with Chris and Jay and told them stories about the animals that lived with him at the farm. I loved him so that day.

He gave us a parting gift - two farm kittens. We named them North and South. Perhaps they were distant ancestors of Molly, whom we brought home from the farm some twenty years later. Because of my ignorance and negligence, South died within the year, but North lived with us for many years.

Figure 29.2 Linda, Chris, and Jay 1973.

In 1972 Bob and I separated. My serious failures as a wife had shattered our young family. A few years later, in 1974, I ran into Steve and Steppy at the grocery store. By this time, Bob and I were in the midst of our divorce and the strain probably showed. Steve seemed genuinely worried about my appearance and health. About an hour later he and Steppy rang the doorbell at our house! I was so surprised! They'd brought a very thoughtful gift - Arby's sandwiches for all. He seemed to enjoy visiting for about an hour with his grandsons, but when they left after a very short visit, as usual, no one mentioned getting together again. So, I must amend my statement - he *did* visit me, if only once, after that day he left me at Green Hall back in 1962.

Ken and I met at Metropolitan State College in 1975. We fell in love and have been together ever since. When we were first dating, he and I and the boys visited Steve at the farm.

Figure 29.3 Ken with Duke in 1984.

I was very surprised to find, upon our arrival, that he'd sold *more than half* the farm. Houses covered the fields where wheat used to grow!

I wanted him to meet Ken and I still hoped that I could initiate some type of family relationship between my sons and their grandfather. Chris and Jay were older by then and loved to play baseball and football. I thought he'd love that. Although we had a nice visit and he told the boys some stories of *his* football and baseball days, nothing further came from that attempt either.

Almost a decade later, Ken and I made our final visit to see Steve at the farm in 1984. We asked if we might buy some of his land to build a house. He thought not.

By then, he'd sold the rest of the land – everything except for the five acres surrounding the house. This land sat vacant for many years, but in 1996 U.S. Homes began to build houses there. In the fall of that year, Chris and Jay each bought a house in this development. Things had come full circle. Their houses sit on land first purchased by their great-grandfather eighty years before. They now live on the northeast corner of "the farm".

Figure 29.4 The DeAndreas. Jay holding Claire, Phil and Chris. 1987.

By this time Bob had remarried and added two more children to his family. Chris was 15 years old and Jay 13, when their new brother Phil was born. Claire joined her brothers three years later.

My last encounters with Steve were at St. Anthony Hospital. In the early 1980's he had a heart attack and triple by-pass surgery. A few years later he had a follow-up operation to patch up the earlier repairs. *Then* he fell about 20 feet, breaking four ribs, while trimming trees at the farm! He had always taken great pride in keeping the trees trimmed and healthy. (The image at the beginning of this Chapter was taken about two decades earlier in the 1960s.) Each time, he spent several days at St. Anthony's. When I visited him there he was as gracious as ever, but our conversations there were, as always, purely surface.

In 1986, Steppy was hospitalized at St. Anthony's with Guion Beret Syndrome. On one of my visits to see her, I literally *ran into* Steve in the hallway.

Right then and right there we had the conversation for which I'd waited a lifetime.

Figure 29.5 Steve and Sophie (Steppy) 1975.

He spoke of things that were in his heart. He spoke of things he loved - working outside, nature, animals and especially sports. He told me he had season tickets for both the CU Buffaloes and the Denver Broncos - "his" football teams. And he spoke of his two great loses - his mother and his daughter.

I wanted to ask him about our early years together. I wanted to ask him why he'd been so distant from me all my adult life - but I didn't ask and he didn't tell.

Maybe it was after this meeting that he put together the things in The Box - things that *did* reveal to me, after his death, answers to the questions I'd wanted to ask him in that hospital hallway.

I'm grateful that we talked. It was the last time I saw him alive.

My father and stepmother loved and hated each other until the day he died. They never traveled, never had friends and, in my opinion, never did one fun thing - *except* go to the dog races, which I assumed they enjoyed. They just stayed together and made each other miserable.

My father never knew much happiness in his life. He tried hard to be pleasant and to do the right thing, at least in regards to his daughter and his father. But he was, down deep, a very sad and disappointed man. On June 21, 1988 he got up, ate breakfast and prepared to go to the farm. He bent over to tie his shoelaces, had a heart attack and died. He was 78 years old.

I felt like I'd barely known him. My three mothers, whom I knew well, lived on. But I'd lost my one and only father.

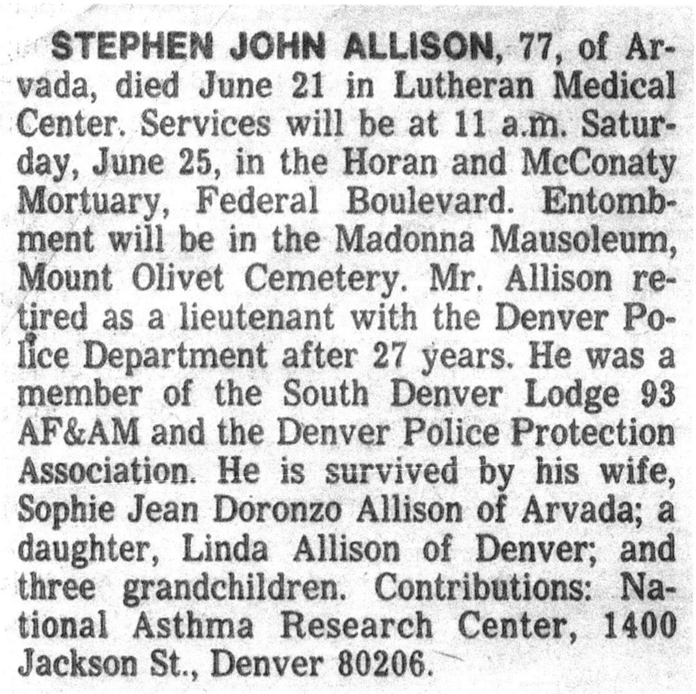

STEPHEN JOHN ALLISON, 77, of Arvada, died June 21 in Lutheran Medical Center. Services will be at 11 a.m. Saturday, June 25, in the Horan and McConaty Mortuary, Federal Boulevard. Entombment will be in the Madonna Mausoleum, Mount Olivet Cemetery. Mr. Allison retired as a lieutenant with the Denver Police Department after 27 years. He was a member of the South Denver Lodge 93 AF&AM and the Denver Police Protection Association. He is survived by his wife, Sophie Jean Doronzo Allison of Arvada; a daughter, Linda Allison of Denver; and three grandchildren. Contributions: National Asthma Research Center, 1400 Jackson St., Denver 80206.

Figure 29.6 Obituary in local paper.

I must not have read the obituary notice very carefully at the time I cut it out of the newspaper. Rereading it now I realize that it says Steve has *three* grandchildren! Misprint? *Or*, do I have a niece or nephew out there somewhere that I know nothing about? Not to mention another half brother or half sister! Chris and Jay, the two real-life grandsons Steve had hardly known, had by now graduated from high school and were in college, the day they dutifully carried out their pall bearer responsibilities at Steve's funeral.

The "three grandchildren" part was probably just a miscommunication between Steppy and her brother Ralph. He took charge, at Steppy's request, of the funeral arrangements and was therefore responsible for the information supplied to the newspaper. That's why, I suppose, the Asthma Research Center was chosen to receive contributions – Ralph suffers from asthma, as did his son. Ralph was also named, again at Steppy's request, executor of Steve's estate.

And what are the odds of this happening? On the same page as this obituary is an article about the annual Greek Festival - "Market's Greek to them, and they like it". Also on the same page are two articles about police departments - "Aurora police snub city's contract offer" and "Search on for police chief". What a coincidence.

Steppy lived alone and miserable until she died two years later. Her crypt and Steve's are side by side. I guess that's only right, since she did share his life for close to forty years. So when I visit my dad, I visit her also. Which is fine, because it was her after all, who instilled in me so long ago, the habit of visiting the final resting places of dead people. How many times, in my youth, she dragged me to the cemetery. And how often, as an adult, she coerced me into taking her there.

Many others, who played parts both large and small in this story, also passed on while it was being written. Among them:

- **SHIRLEY'S FRIEND, IN YOUTH AND OLD AGE, IDELLA.**

- **MY LONG AGO FRIEND FROM HIGH SCHOOL, KATHY B.**

- **STEVE'S COUSIN, TITSA.**

  I'll always be grateful to Titsa - for her time and her thoughtfulness. She provided so much of the information contained in the early chapters of this book. I attended her funeral service at the new Greek Orthodox Church. Sitting, an unknown stranger, in that elegant Byzantine structure, my mind returned to the old Greek Orthodox Church where she had been married. That church, where I'd been her six-year-old flower girl, had reminded me of a majestic stone box - filled with dazzling jewels. Both ceremonies, the wedding and the funeral, were almost dreamlike to me. Priests sang and smoke from incense filled the air - against a backdrop of brilliant murals and beloved icons. Her obituary read:

> TITSA DIAMANTIS, 76, of Denver died oct.2 [1999]. Services will be at 2 p.m. Thursday, oct. 7, at Assumption Greek Orthodox Church, with burial at fairmount cemetary. Mrs. Diamantis was born in Denver on Nov. 25, 1922. She married George Diamantis. She worked for her father's candy store until 1962. Survivors include son Theodore of Denver; brother Christopher Allison of Denver; sister Georgia Allison of Denver.

- **STEVE'S COUSIN, GEORGIA.**

  She died less than one month after her sister, Titsa. They were close in life *and* in death it seems.

- **MY STEPFATHER, MAX.**

  He was, for so many years, a kind stepfather to me and a loving grandfather to Chris and Jay. He left when he was ready.

Figure 29.7 From top: Shirley, Max, sister Kate and niece Melissa, 1988.

Figure 29.8 Radovich Family, 1995. From left Marty, Dave, Paulie, Max (seated), Travis, Shirley, Katy, Linda.

- **MY BROTHER PAULIE.**

  He died in 1997 of a heart attack at age 45, leaving a beloved wife, daughter and stepson. He was *always the true sunshine* of our family.

Figure 29.9 Paulie celebrates with Shirley on her 70th birthday, 1994.

Shirley will always be my best and only "adult mom" - the parent of my adult years. She's a good friend, a good mother and a wonderful grandmother to my children. In a way completely different from how I feel about Steve, I love her very much. I love her eternal optimism, always choosing to look on the bright side. I love her company - she's gifted at making any time, a good time. I love her for welcoming me with open arms into her large, diverse, fascinating, close-knit family. I love her for giving me my brothers and my dear "Sister". They mean the world to me. To us, and to all her *very extended* family, she is the undisputed, but ever-gracious, matriarch.

I visit Steve at the cemetery each year on his birthday - September 27th. Without fail, the weather's always *perfect.* The sparkling blue sky is dotted with clouds. The trees, still green, are beginning to show just a hint of color. Swans, geese and ducks glide across still waters that echo the sky. The flowers, in their muted autumnal hues, warm the hillsides. The day is bathed in golden sunlight.

In the warmth of the sun and the quiet of the surroundings I think of my father and of his life. I try to imagine that day, in the fall of 1910, when he was born. I think about his mother. I think about his father. I think about his childhood. I think about his life as an athlete and as a police officer. I think about his loves and his lost loves. I think about him as a parent.

I thank him for all he did - *and for all he tried to do* - for me. I tell him that I love him.

"STEPHEN JOHN ALLISON, 77, of Arvada"

Steve's obituary - June 1988

CHAPTER 30

"the Allison property at 92nd Avenue and Pierce Street"

And time went by.

In 1989, the city of Westminster purchased the remaining five acres of "the farm". They promised to keep it as an open space area. Christopher and Jay graduated from college. Separately and/or together our family experienced wonderful travels throughout the world. Jay met his lifetime love, Melissa.

Figure 30.1 Sister Kate and Jay help Chris celebrate as he graduates from Colorado School of Mines,1988.

Figure 30.2 Jay and Bob at Jay's MBA Graduation, 1992.

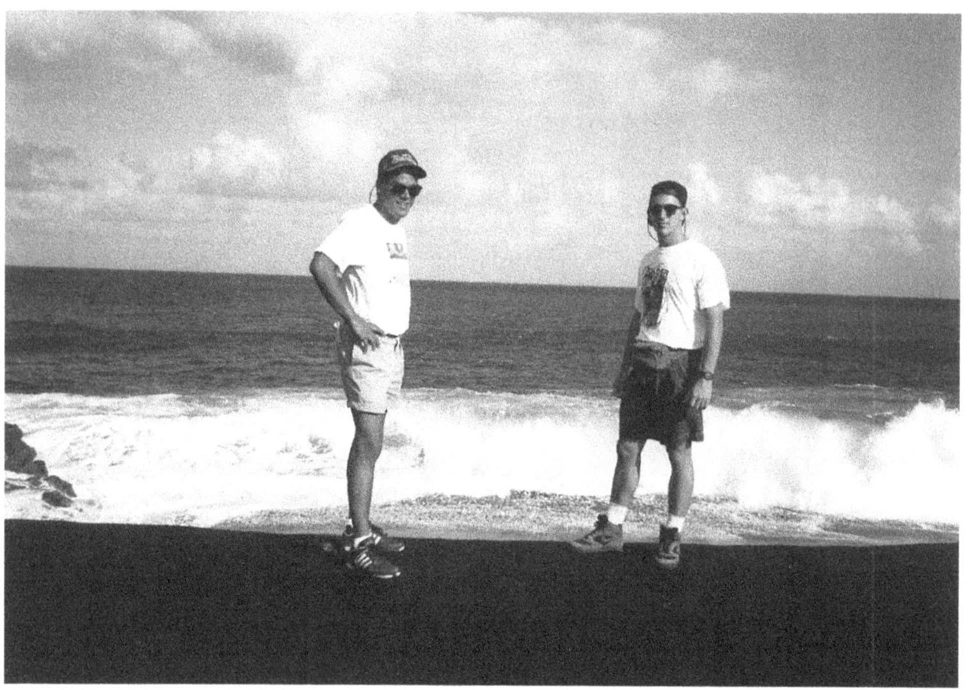

Figure 30.3 Cousin Carl and Jay in Hawaii, 1992.

Figure 30.4 Ken and guide, visiting the gorillas in what was then Zaire, 1993.

Figure 30.5 Ken and Linda in Greece, 1994.

Figure 30.6 CJ (Chris) at the World Trade Center, 1995.

Figure 30.7 CJ in Greenwich Village, 1995.

Figure 30.8 CJ and our friend Jane in Milan, 1998.

Figure 30.9 Jay and Melissa at cousin Carl's wedding, 2000.

We drive by "the farm" every time we go to Chris and/or Jay's house.

Keeping their promise, officials from the city of Westminster have preserved the land as open space. They'd kept the house and out buildings as well - hoping eventually to restore them - as examples of an early 20th century farm setting.

But they had to change their minds about a few of the buildings.

Increasingly, the neighbors complained of noise and disturbances coming from the property. Plus, recently the caretakers discovered a lock, other than the city's, on the door to one of the buildings. When they opened it, they found bales of hay someone was storing there. It was decided that it would be easier to manage if three of the more dilapidated structures were removed. The house, the old garage, and the newer garage were spared.

When a friend called to tell me about the "demolition" notice in the newspaper, I hoped that some of our family could be there - to pay our final respects to the buildings - and their occupants throughout the years. And we *were* able to be there - all of us that is, except Ken. We were having our kitchen remodeled at the time and he had to stay home to work with the contractor that day. But the rest of us went. Ten years after we'd packed up Molly and left - we returned. Once more, back to the farm.

> Demolition volunteers needed
> WESTMINSTER — Volunteers are needed for two demolition projects on Westminster Open Space property.
> Ten volunteers will be needed to disassemble several old sheds on the Allison property at 92nd Avenue and Pierce Street on Saturday. Participants should register by Thursday.
> Both projects will be from 8:30 a.m. to 11:30 a.m. Volunteers should bring heavy-duty gloves and water bottles.To register call (303) 430-2400. The Rocky Mountain News February 1, 2000

Chris, with his half-brother Phil, was there as the Westminster staff and the volunteers began to demolish the buildings. Jay and his girlfriend, Melissa, worked all morning helping to tear down the chicken coop and barn. I brought doughnuts - and watched (see image at beginning of Chapter 30).

The representatives of Westminster were very thoughtful - and glad we'd come. The people from the horticulture department told me that we were standing next to the oldest and biggest apple tree in the state! They often bring colleagues to see it, they said - and, they'd served pies from its apples at their national convention.

I also spoke, briefly, to a very young newspaper reporter. Her shoes were not very appropriate for the terrain - so she moved little, and left quickly.

Everyone was excited when they found a wooden barrel with George Allison's name on the side. It had been delivered to the candy store, full of sugar. They thought I might want to take it home! No thanks! If they had *any idea* how many years I'd struggled to find homes for all that I'd *already* taken home! We watched as it was loaded into the dump truck.

But it did my heart good to see that much of the wreckage *was* recycled. The Horse Rescue group took all the doors and big pieces of lumber. Many of the smaller pieces were salvaged by a man who makes picture frames. An apparatus for chickens to roost on was taken as a planter for someone's yard. And the city people took a large watering trough that was made from huge wooden planks. They said they'd have a plaque put on it, something about the

Allison Farm, and use it as a planter in the gardens surrounding the Westminster Municipal Building. That's great.

And, I was thrilled to hear of their plan for a part of the farm. It's to be a *Community Garden*! Grampa would have loved that! *He so loved his garden!*

"the Allison property at 92nd Avenue and Pierce Street"

The Rocky Mountain News - February 1, 2000

CHAPTER 31

"to work and wish - a patient man"

John returned home from Puerto Rico and received his army discharge papers in February 1899 - and the documented part of this story began.

One hundred and one years later, in February 2000, the notice in the newspaper about the demolition projects at the farm appeared. With that news article and with Chapter 30, I thought this story was at its end.

But it wasn't. Not quite.

One last (I promise - <u>*the*</u> last) "surfacing" has occurred.

We'd finished one phase of our house-remodeling project in early March 2000 and I was reorganizing on a grand scale. I'd always kept John and Steve's papers and photos in a very stout wooden crate, circa 1920's, from Ghirardelli Chocolates of San Francisco. It was heavy and cumbersome and during this reorganization I decided to transfer the contents to a new lightweight Rubbermaid container. In doing so, I discovered four last vestiges of my father's life.

From the very bottom of the Ghirardelli box - out tumbled a very used looking bicycle bell and an ancient wooden top! (See image at beginning of this Chapter.)

The toys were such a poignant reminder to me of Steve's early years - the years he and John spent without benefit of a woman's gentle touch. I think John must have saved them, don't you? Especially the adorable wooden top - it could make you weep! This battered toy had obviously provided many hours, days and perhaps even years of enjoyment. It has a strong metal tip that it twirled upon and a notch to catch the string that set it in motion. But it's nicked and scarred from its hard life - bounced from pillar to post. It symbolizes perfectly, I think, my father's *childhood.*

And, lo and behold, the Ghirardelli box held two additional journals!

These previously "missing" journals are final testaments from Steve's *adulthood.*

<u>He works.</u>

A 1946 record of his police activities is quite detailed and provides a good picture of his professional life at that time. Steppy's bar, the Senate, is mentioned in this regard. Unfortunately, these writings indicate that Steve exhibited some subtle, *or not so subtle,* prejudices in the process of carrying out his duties.

<u>And he wishes.</u>

In January 1948 he takes the captain's exam but doesn't get the promotion. His wait for professional advancement is long and frustrating - but this wish to become a captain is never fullfilled.

He wishes on the home front also. His hopes of finding a loving wife and providing a lasting home for his daughter come to naught.

Members of the Allison extended family and several friends make brief appearances. On these pages:

- L L turns four years old.
- Shirley gives L L a permanent and then they see each other again at L L's fourth birthday party in July. They'll next meet again nineteen years later, in 1967.
- Shirley's father, Bud, offers Steve some advice.
- Steve makes many trips to visit L L at 617 Bridge St. in Brighton, or brings her to visit him in Denver.
- He also makes numerous visits "out to Dad's ranch". During one of these visits, Steve takes some photos. In one, Steve holds his little daughter and in another, John holds his little granddaughter. All three people are laughing happily. These photos hung on my grandfather's kitchen wall until I took them down, 41 years later.

Figure 31.1 Linda and John at the farm and Steve and Linda at the farm.

- Uncle Gus and cousin Steve get in a fight at a picnic.
- And of course there are the girlfriends. He sends candy to Helen on Valentine's Day. A week later she tells him everything's over. With ring in hand, asks Yvonne to marry him in June. Yvonne refuses. All while he continues seeing DN. Steve continues to wish - hoping to *someday* find love and happiness in a marriage.

Why hadn't he placed these journals in The Box along with the others? Perhaps he'd misplaced them. And I wonder - is there a 1949 journal, still missing somewhere? And, the more pressing question of the moment - what should I do with them *now*?

Of course - I'll include them. (Small portions of them actually.) But it seems way too difficult, at this late date, to go back, yet again, and insert them where they belong chronologically...

So, forgive me, but, I'm leaving them *here* - a brief "return visit" to thirty-something Steve.

And perhaps it's also more fitting - that Steve should have the last word.

February 1946

2-23-46

Beverley Garden's located at 927 Newton Street and owned by one Elih Saunders (N) of 2300 blk. Downing St. was checked by Officer R. Brown, B Hammonds, W. Stromp and myself. We observed violations such as

drunks

empty bottles inside and outside of buildings

a minor, Robert Grant, age 14 of 2500 blk. Emerson was admitted to the dance hall without being questioned as to his age.

A negro girl was supposed to have been raped this same night at this place.

Saunders did not keep a register for juveniles.

beer on Sunday after 8 pm.

All parties concerned were ordered into Capt. J. O'Donnell's Office for 2-26-46, 2:00 Pm where E. Saunders was warned about (3) specific violations.

3:30 AM 800 Blk on Platte St., Arrested JOE MARQUES, 21, of 1800 blk. Platte St. and MAX MARQUES, 25, 2500 blk. Curtis St., supposed to be JOE'S uncle.

Florine Kichniloff KE 7131

Officer L. Thompson called said he was asked the question yesterday in the oral examination about what he would do if asked the question weather he beat up Fennirity or would tell who beat up Fennirity. Thompson answered by saying he did not see a thing.

March 1946

3-23-46

Tejon Bar and Café, Anthony Smaldone runs the place - Ralph Smaldone, 24, 3400 blk. Osage was party making strange phone calls to Tejon Bar and Café.

April 1946

4-4-46

1 automatic pistol 666557 recovered from Larry Ruggles, age 9, by Officer Joseph Kearney on 1-24-46, was taken from this boy at Smedley School, 43rd Shoeshone, principal Vittermeyer. I received this gun from H. Conner without the clip

May 1946

5-5-46

Milwaukee Tavern 1004 19th, Owners Fred Cliner and sister Frieda.
Chez Paree, 236 16th St. owner Veto and Romelo. I met Tony - bartender.
American Inn 2046 Larimer, Roy Bailes - Prop.
Arrest Verle L. Brookshaw, 2:25 PM. Dk - 18th Larimer.
Oriental Garden's, Sam Apple.
King of Clubs, Al Saunders - Bros
Arapahoe Grill 2163 Arapahoe, Owner Ben Trinidad - crippled Dk., Sanchez sent home from this place.
Canioca, 21st Champa, Owned by Ang, Geo Strafface.
Jewlery Store, 1600 Blk. Welton in Masonic Bldg. See Mr. Pedderson, a watch repair man.

5-10-46

Senate T - 1445 Curtis Owner Jim Cappuaplo
Boston Bar 16th Curtis, Owner Bill Angelos
New Yorker, Curtis, Mr. Raeder
Quincy's Bar, Henry Miltstein and Nate Natetheson

5-25-46

A radio call from Capt. Trimier to go to Windsor Hotel. Labor trouble. Mr. Joe Gonsales and Harry Quinlan Chairman of R.R. brother's Union.

5-31-46

2:55 Pm. I was acting capt. Mr. Jesse Mara, 4312 Umatilla, made a complaint against officer Morton Gottschalk for stopping traffic at 10th Grant.

August 1946

8-8-46

Frederick Petronni arrested for death of man in Whitehouse Buffett.

November 1946

11-25-46

To accept good advice is but to increase one's ability.

Understand your antagonist before you answer him.

Books are a finer world within a world.

The best teachers of humanity are the lives of great men.

The true university of these days is a collection of books.

Difficulties strengthen the mind, as labor does the body.

The greatest remedy for anger is delay.

Opportunity, sooner or later, comes to all who work and wish.

To be proud of learning is the greatest ignorance.

None but a fool is always right.

Beware of the fury of a patient man.

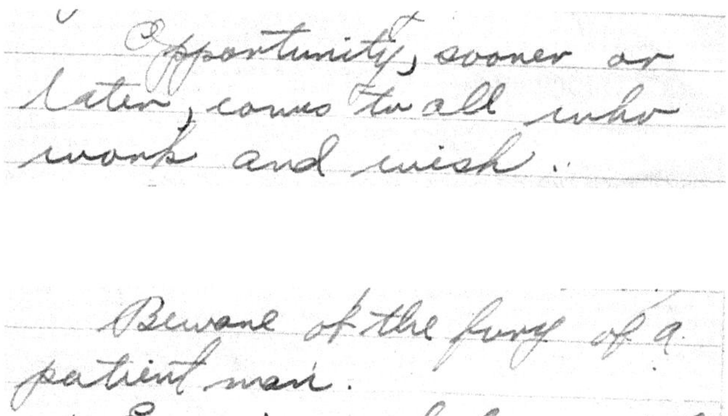

Figure 31.2 Steve's Journal: November 25, 1946.

Examine what is said, not him who speaks.

Enjoy present pleasures in such a way as not to injure future ones.

Getting into debt is getting into a tanglesome net.

Education is the best provision for old age.

Brevity is the soul of wit.

The secret of success is constancy to purpose.

Cunning is the dwarf of wisdom.

Better be three hours too soon than one minute too late.

The result proves the wisdom of the act.

Refrain from covetousness and thy estate shall prosper.

Courage in danger is half the battle.

Philosphy is the art of living.

Oh my goodness! –Here it is!

Here is Steve's record of my time in Brighton. 1948. He's confirmed all my vivid memories of that time! Alberta, the train rides, visits to his city apartment, my birthday party...

I was so surprised to see my Brighton beginnings right off the bat in the newly discovered 1948 journal.

January 1948

1-25-48 Day Off - To Brighton to see Mrs Lillian about taking care of LL - went with J. Mc.

1-27-48 Cr. 10 J. Riggs. 21 degrees below zero. Airmail spec. from Auntie Bertha. Results of Capts. Exam - my grade 84.53 - 7th place.

1-28-48 Cr.10, J. Riggs. LL to 617 Bridge St., Brighton, 12:00 Noon - Mrs A. Lillian. DNX

1-31-48 Cr. #10, J. Riggs. LL came down from Brighton. 20.00 to Lillian. YSX

February 1948

2-8-48 Day off. Saw LL at Brighton. DNX

2-11-48 Cr. 10, J. Powers. Sent box candy to HS for Valentines day.

2-15-48 Day Off. LL was brought down from Brighton, Colo.

2-19-48 Cr. 10, J. Powers. Talk to Ada (very short). Went to Brighton to see LL with BC.

2-22-48 Day Off. Out to Dad's ranch.

2-26-48 Cr. 10, J. Powers. Called HS - talked to her 45 min. - everything over. DNX

2-29-48 Day Off. LL came in from Brighton - 35.00 to Lillian

March 1948

3-7-48 Cr. 10, J. Powers. Went to Brighton - saw LL, she is in good health.

3-14-48 Acting Capt. Hdqts. LL came in from Brighton.

3-18-48 Acting Capt Hdqt. Call HS by Phone - talked 1 hr - 20 mins.

3-28-48 Acting Capt. Hdqts. LL in from Brighton - 35.00 to Mrs Lillian for LL. out to Ranch with BC

April 1948

4-4-48 Acting Capt – Hdqts. Went out to Brighton to see LL with BC

4-5-48 Cr. 10, J. Powers. Shirley saw and gave LL permanent.

4-10-48 Cr. 10, Maddock. Brought dad in from Ranch. YSX

4-11-48 Acting Capt. Hdaqt. LL came in from Brighton, Colo. Rec. Letter from Aunt Ameil. DNX

4-13-48 Cr. 10, J. Powers. Lowen plumber put in plumbing for Automatic washer. DNX
4-18-48 Day off. Brought LL in from Brighton, she stayed all night.
4-30-48 Cr. 10, J. Powers. Greek Parade. then worked 4 Pm till 2 Am with officer Riggs

May 1948

5-2-48 Acting Capt. Hdqts. Communist incident, 2501 Welton. Visited LL at Brighton with BC.
5-14-48 Day Off. Out to Ranch. Dinner at Country Kitchen with YS (E and FB).
5-16-48 Acting capt. Hdqts. Up to Brighton with the kids and YS.

June 1948

6-1-48 Cr. 10, P. Duffy - 3:30 Am to 11:30 Am. DNX
6-4-48 Day off. to Monarch Lake - fishing with officers P. Duffy, L. Foster - had bath at Hot Sulphur.
6-6-48 Acting Capt. Hdqts. LL was in from Brighton. Gus and Steve in fight at picnic. DNX
6-8-48 Cr. 10, J. Powers. Up to Turkey Creek with YS and kids, picnic.
6-12-48 Cr. #10, J. Powers. Priesten came over and helped me wash. Dinner at DN house.
6-13-48 Acting Capt. Hdqts. Dinner at BC House. to Brighton with BC to see LL.
6-18-48 Cr. 10, J. Powers. A. Priesten came over and help me with house cleaning.
6-19-48 Cr. 10, J. Powers. Al Priesten came over, we painted. YSX
6-25-48 Day Off. 50.00 Loan pd. Back to Gus. Talked with YS and decided to break up with her.
6-26-48 Day Off. Offered YS ring - refused. DNX
6-30-48 Day Off. Painted. Dinner at DN house. YS was over with the kids.

July 1948

7-4-48 Day Off. Dinner with LL at BC house. YS to DU Stadium.
7-11-48 Day off. To Brighton with BC to see LL. DNX
7-21-48 LL Birthday. To Brighton with YS and kids. DNX
7-25-48 Acting Capt. Hdqts. To Brighton with Chris and Betty to see LL. 35.00 to Mrs Lillian for LL.

August 1948

8-6-48 Visited LL. 35.00 to Mrs Lillian for LL.

So! After spending only four months with Mrs. Scarry, September 1947 – January 1948, once again things weren't working out with Linda Lee's placement.

On a cold day - Steve notes that the temperature the day before was "20 degrees below zero" - that late January she went to live at the home of "A. Lillian , 617 Bridge St., Brighton Colorado".

And I'm amazed! While juggling two, if not three or four, girlfriends and proposing, this time to Yvonne - Steve spends more time with his daughter than at any time of her life.

I did "come down" from Brighton to visit him in Denver sixteen times during the next six months. No wonder I can still so clearly remember the sway of the train, the sight of him on the platform, the smell (leather and tobacco and aftershave) of his apartment and the feel of his cheek against mine. I can actually hear him singing "You are My Sunshine" and "I Wonder" as we walk along.

And – he visited LL in Brighton fourteen times during these months! I love the entry on March 07th. "Went to Brighton - saw LL, she is in good health." In all, that's about once a week that we were together! The four-year-old in me thanks you,Steve, for these treasured memories. Thank you for being a loving and responsible father to your young daughter. *You tried so hard to do your best for her.*

For that, I will always love you.

And so, with these journal entries, I say good-bye, with love, to my father.

"to work and wish - a patient man."'

Steve's journal - November 25, 1946

CHAPTER 32

"Be true to your memories."

Although this has been the story of my grandfather and my father, it opened with thoughts of two of my mothers. And it seems it will end the same way.

For Mother's Day 2000, I sent Betty a copy of her chapter of this book. I wanted it to be a gift of my love on this special day.

Immediately after mailing it, however, I had big-time second thoughts. I stayed up all night, worrying. Instead of finding it complimentary, which of course I'd meant it to be, perhaps she'd be hurt or insulted!

Fortunately, she read and accepted it in the spirit in which I'd sent it. She also then asked for, and read, all the chapters – as did her oldest son David. In the course of our conversation that followed, however, we decided that perhaps I should print a short "disclaimer" at the end of the book.

This was because she said she'd noticed one small "discrepancy" in my record of those years with her.

Betty said that Great-gramma Landis never had chickens - not outside, and certainly not inside, her house in Walsenburg. She took great pride in her clean house and would not have considered such a thing. Outside the house, she had very beautiful flower gardens - only.

Betty went on to relate a short story that illustrated just how much her Gramma had valued her image as a good housekeeper.

She said that in those days there were very few opportunities for women to gain recognition and reinforce their self-esteem. But one such opportunity presented itself each week. When doing laundry, sparkling whites were much admired. As a young married woman living in the mining camps of Colorado, Gramma Landis came up with her own unique solution to the problem of presenting a bright, white wash.

Each week she'd wet two, never used, white sheets that she kept for this purpose. Then she'd hang them on the line - with her other regular white items in between!

I'm not sure where I came up with the "chickens in the house" story. Perhaps I saw chickens at her neighbor's house, I don't know.

Betty feels that such minor discrepancies are unimportant in the overall picture, however. In her opinion, when writing about the past, it's best to, "be true to your memories."

I have, I think, been true to my memories. But I've also seen that my memory is not perfect. I feel the need, therefore, to say that - regarding the parts of this book that were *written from my memory* - I've done my best to describe the people and the events accurately.

I’ve written things - as I honestly remember them.

And now, hoping that she’ll come to understand my true intentions (and hoping also to reassure her of my love and affection), I’m going to read this story to Shirley - page by page.

I hope, in the end, that she’ll be glad we told it.

“Be true to your memories.”

Betty’s phone conversation, May 2000

SECTION

- VI -

EPILOGUE

CHAPTER 33

May 2006

May 2006

I "put the pen down" for the last time and finished writing this family history six years ago this month.

I did share it with my mom on First Mondays over the next three months.

When my mom lost her sight some years before, we'd arranged to spend the first Monday of each month together. We'd do her shopping, write her letters, visit doctors, clean up paperwork, etc. Now we added two hours of reading aloud from this manuscript. Her neighbor Josie, and Josie's sister Rose, would also come over for "story time". Over coffee and pastries, I shared these pages with Mom and her long-time friends. We spent a lovely summer together and I think they *all* enjoyed our time together as much as I did.

And then, life got more complicated and I put these pages away for the next six years.

In the spring of 2001, Ken and I and his sister and her husband opened a restaurant in our neighborhood. We all – especially Ken and Sharon - put in many, many hours there over the next five years. Our lease ended and we served our last panini this past February.

We were at Poggio's that fall morning of 2001 when a customer ran in at 7:15 AM telling us to turn on the television because a plane had flown into the World Trade Center. We, and our customers, watched in horror throughout the rest of the day. But life reassembles itself somehow, and our great sadness is made bearable by the good that continues in the world.

Our son Jay married his sweetheart, Melissa Martin, in October 2001. Their mountain wedding was a joyful happening. She brings a whole new realm of beauty and love to our family.

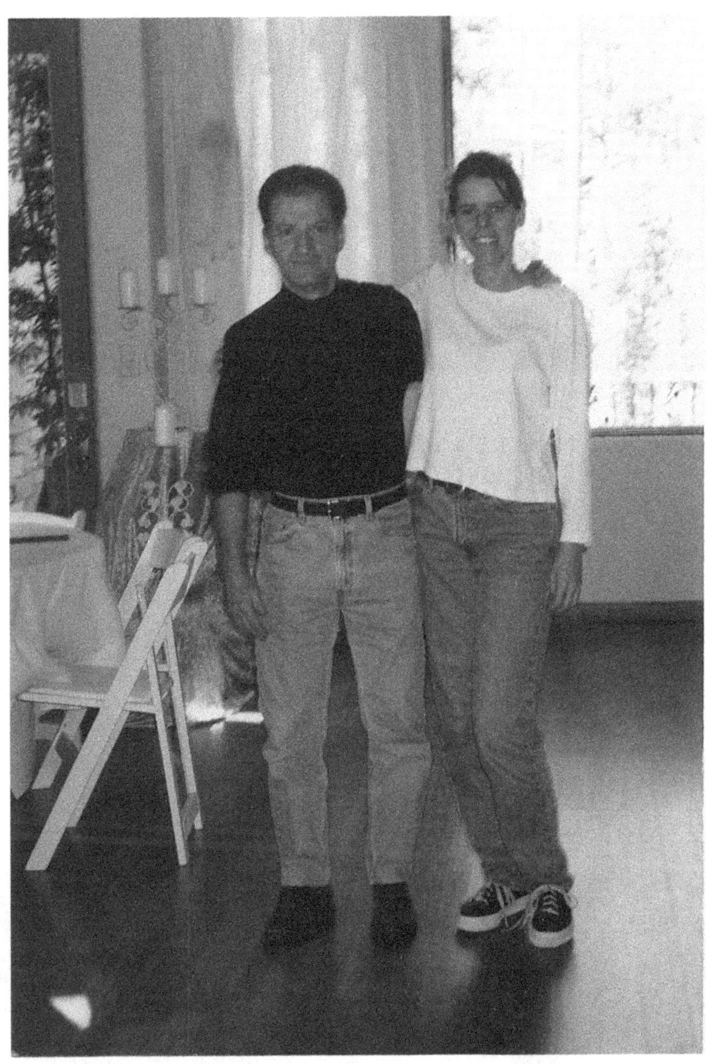

Figure 33.1 Ken & Melissa prepare for the DeAndrea wedding, 2001.

Figure 33.2 Melissa, Shirley and Jay at the DeAndrea wedding, 2001.

Figure 33.3 Shirley at the DeAndrea wedding surounded by some of her loving family. L-R Melissa, Jay, sister Kate, Tracy, Chris, Carl, Linda and Ken.

My joy and happiness were immeasurable when, on May 17, 2005, Melissa and Jay became parents! Twins Jackson Tyler and Brooks Christopher were full term and healthy (see image at the beginning of this Chapter). CJ became an uncle and Ken and I became grandparents, as did Bob. Life doesn't get much better!! I am overwhelmed with love and gratitude. They joined their second cousins, Dani, Kylie, Destinee, James Henry, and Reese to become Shirley Mae's sixth and seventh great grandchildren.

Figure 33.4 Brooks and Jackson DeAndrea, 2006.

Our family also knew great sadness in 2005. Ida, our beloved sister-in-law died of cancer in October and Shirley Mae left us in November.

My mother was an optimistic, loving, fun-loving, good-hearted person until the day she died. She'd suffered a stroke earlier that year in May and had spent her last months in a nursing home. True to form, within weeks of her admittance, she'd learned the names and life stories of most of her caregivers. She was sincerely interested in them and cared about them. She never complained and did all she could to make their jobs easier. She needed much and could have asked for much, but she asked for very little. As had happened all of her life, her giving spirit won over every one she met – even as she was dying.

She died in the loving arms of her very large and very extended family and a multitude of friends.

Betty, my other mother, left this life the year before, in 2004. She, too, had been a role model for graceful dying. Even as cancer gradually claimed her, she remained always cheerful, funny (with her great sense of humor), interested, involved, loving and accepting. She, too, died within the loving arms of a large extended family and a multitude of friends. (*See image at beginning of Chapter 32. This photo was taken 3 months before Betty died. She is surrounded by her children, L-R: Linda, Deborah, Dave, Paul, Rebecca, and Daniel.*)

I was blessed to have these two women as my mothers.

Lastly, there's good news about "The Farm". It's now officially a Historical Landmark (*see images at the beginning of Sections 5 and 6*).

Semper gets grant for orchard restoration

Plans for Semper Farm received a boost with a $3,000 grant from the Westminster Legacy Foundation. The funds will go toward restoration of the historic apple orchard at the farm, located at the northwest corner of 92nd Avenue and Pierce Street. Other work on the property continues, with an access drive, parking area and water supply now in place along with a community garden. Crusher-fines path construction and interpretive signage highlighting points of interest will be completed in the next two years with volunteer labor, donations and grant funding. For more information, contact community development at 303-430-2400, ext. 2111.

Figure 33.5 Newspaper article about the farm, 2006.

This designation is in large measure due to the efforts of Vicky Bunsen, an official with the City of Westminster, - a person who first loved the farm and then found herself in a position to help save it. Strangely, Vicky was told by the researchers hired to do background that there were "no living Allison heirs". Thankfully, my friend Jane Darling and Linda Graybeal (who is a neighbor of the farm and loves it as much as I do), brought me to Vicky's attention. And now the Allison family is part of the ongoing restoration and preservation of the house, the remaining outbuildings and the grounds. To aid in this effort, in 2007 Vicky applied for and received a grant of $3,000 for rehabilitation of the apple orchard and $50,000 (!) for building restoration.

And the Allison Community Gardens are also now a reality.

Semper Farm Community Garden Organizational Meeting

A PLANNING MEETING WILL BE HOSTED AT 6 P.M. Monday, March 6 (snow date is March 13) by Denver Urban Gardens for a proposed community garden at the historic Charles and Julia Semper Farm, located north of West 92nd Avenue and the Farmers' High Line Canal trail on the west side of Pierce Street. The meeting will be onsite. Carpooling and walking are suggested, as parking is limited along Pierce Street. All persons interested in community gardening in this neighborhood should attend to indicate their support and share ideas about design and organization of the garden. The Semper Farm is a City of Westminster open space property. Denver Urban Gardens (http://dug.org) operates and assists with the creation and management of more than 60 gardens in the metropolitan area serving more than 25,000 gardeners. The first community garden established in Westminster is located north of West 72nd Avenue and Raleigh Street. **For more information, contact Community Development Programs Coordinator Vicky Bunsen, 303-430-2400, ext. 2111, or vbunsen@ci.westminster.co.us.**

Figure 33.6 Newspaper article about the Community Gardens, 2006.

Christopher and I attended many of the planning meetings for this effort. During one such meeting, he drew a quick sketch of a future Allison Community Gardens.

Figure 33.7 Chris envisions Allison Community Gardens, 2006.

Here are the actual gardens as they look in the winter months.

Figure 33.8 Linda at the Allison Community Gardens, 2007.

What a great thing!

My Grandpa John would be so happy. He always had a large, beautiful garden and the apple orchard was his pride and joy. My dad would smile too. He protected and nourished all that grows on that land for decades. Now, neighbors who love gardening tend the soil and the city protects and nourishes the trees.

All's right on the farm.

"May 2006."

CHAPTER 34

2011

Once again, life went on, and this book sat waiting.

Two great-grandchildren were added to Max and Shirley's family tree. Sister Kate's third grandchild, Chase Paul was born in 2007 and Brother Travis' third grandchild, Joy Marie in 2008. Their other great-grandchildren contnued to grow and thrive.

A small part of this extended family posed for the above photo in 2010. Marilyn (holding Scooter), Beau and Dave Radovich are in front. Behind them are Travis Taylor, Linda Allison, Ken Griffin, Chris DeAndrea, Kate Radovich, Melissa and Jay DeAndrea. Jackson and Brooks DeAndrea are held aloft in the rear.

Our country elected its first African American president. The global economy "recessed" and the global landscape shifted with the uprisings that came to be known as The Arab Spring. And the earth continued to get warmer. But the grass was still green, the sky was still blue and the birds still sang. We were, and are, so grateful.

The days were full and the years flew by. In 2009, fifteen years after I'd first begun to tell this story, I decided it was time to figure out how to go about getting it into print. But first, I asked our son, Jay, if he could insert a few scanned photos into the narrative I'd written. He convinced me that we should include, not only the fifteen photos I'd chosen, but also many (hundreds!) additional photos, documents, news articles, letters and other items. It's taken us two years to do this. Since I'm technologically inept, it was up to him to do the work. And since he has a family and a job, months often went by between work on these inclusions. But we're finished at last!

A note of apology, however, is in order. Since I wrote the narrative before realizing that we would include pictures – I'd often described in detail objects and people that are now easily seen by the reader. Sorry for these instances of describing the obvious.

We hope that the inclusion of these visuals will more intimately convey the feeling of the times and the emotions of the people involved. We hope that the words, now joined with the images, come close to fulfilling Steve's wishes that "time" would indeed "make all things clear".

One hundred years after Steve's birth in the fall of 1910, his great-grandsons, Brooks and Jackson, started kindergarten in the fall of 2010. A few weeks later, their mom gave me a photo of them dressed for a special day at school (see Figure 34.1). Of course I loved it, and the thought quickly followed that it would be perfect as the last picture on the closing page of this book. They represent, after all, John's and Steve's continuing story – the future. The boys' photo also brought to mind, perhaps it was the caps, a photo/postcard that Ken and I had purchased in Greece (see Figure 34.1) We liked it so much that we had it framed, and it hangs on the wall at our home. The two men in it remind me so much of my grandfather when he was young and of the country he left so long ago, to come to America. My heart tells me that these two photos belong together as this book, finally, comes to an end. The past and the future – both are beautiful.

Figure 34.1 Past and Present.

"2011"

www.ingramcontent.com/pod-product-compliance
Lightning Source LLC
Chambersburg PA
CBHW081142270326
41930CB00014B/3011

* 9 7 8 0 6 1 5 5 8 4 7 8 2 *